CHRISTIAN-JEWISH
DIALOGUE

A READER

CHRISTIAN-JEWISH DIALOGUE

A READER

Helen P. Fry

With a Foreword by Dr Jonathan Sacks, the Chief Rabbi of the
United Hebrew Congregations of the Commonwealth

UNIVERSITY
of
EXETER
PRESS

First published in 1996 by
University of Exeter Press
Reed Hall, Streatham Drive
Exeter, Devon EX4 4QR
UK

British Library Cataloguing in Publication Data
A catalogue record of this book is available
from the British Library

Paperback ISBN 0 85989 501 7
Hardback ISBN 0 85989 502 5

Typeset in 11.5/13pt Bembo
by GreenShires Icon, Exeter

Printed and bound in Great Britain
by Short Run Press Ltd, Exeter

'If I am not for myself, who will be for me?
But if I care only for myself, what am I?'

Hillel

In memory of my friend David Hill
1959–1995

For his wife Cath, and their children Antonia, Jessica and Reuben that
they may understand their roots

Contents

Publisher's note on using this book

To help the reader, several useful reference sections are included in the book. A Glossary explaining terms that may be unfamiliar to the general reader can be found on pages xv–xvii, immediately following the Foreword by Dr Jonathan Sacks. Within the main text, all Chapters begin with a comprehensive contents list of the topics they cover. Finally, in addition to the Index, a list of authors and sources quoted throughout the book, and their locations by Chapter, can be found on pages 315–319.

Acknowledgements

Little did I know when I first embarked on the *Reader* that during its preparation I would lose a very close friend and dialogue-partner. This book is dedicated to that friend, David Hill. David shared some of my own religious questioning and searching. We were drawn by two interests: theology, and the desire to improve Christian–Jewish co-operation and understanding. We shared a great deal, not just in theological discussions but in the struggles during his illness and death. It is a marvellous tribute to him that his challenging approach to life has left its mark in more ways than one—not least on the Jews and Christians who worked with him in the local branch of the Council of Christians and Jews. He gave so much. And he would have enjoyed wrestling with the contents of this book!

Special thanks to Dr Jonathan Sacks, Chief Rabbi of the United Hebrew Congregations of the Commonwealth for writing the Foreword. It is a fine and inspiring introduction to the book. I am indebted to Dr Ian Markham for meticulously working through the editorial content of the book. His constructive comments have enhanced the quality of the *Reader*.

Three other people deserve a special mention for the time and effort that they have given in the production of this *Reader*: Sandra Doney for the hours spent proof-reading the extracts; Lucy Coleman for compiling the Index and typing the Bibliography, and the copyright acknowledgements; and Jane Nethsingha for advising on its use for teachers. Any mistakes or errors which may remain in the text are entirely my responsibility.

My thanks to Simon Baker and Genevieve Davey of the University of Exeter Press for their enthusiastic interest in this book and the work that they have done in its production.

I could not have got this far without the high standard of theological training from the Theology Department at the University of Exeter. Thanks to Professor David Catchpole, Dr Ian Markham, Mr Donald Murray, Revd Dr Alistair Logan, and Dr Esther Reed. My thanks to them for their support and encouragement.

It is not possible to thank everyone who has influenced me in the dialogue; however, I would like to mention the following: Frank Gent, Jane Nethsingha, Jonathan Gorsky, Margaret Shepherd, Daniel Rossing, Avraham Zvi Schwartz, and Sandy Martin. Last in this list, but not least, my thanks to Revd David Julian Friend for introducing me to the Christian–Jewish dialogue!

Without whom... My final thanks are to my husband Martin for his continuous support and dedication to those things close to my heart. He has not only supported my research and the production of this book, but has taken an enthusiastic interest in the issues raised in the Christian–Jewish dialogue. It has been a privilege to spend many hours reflecting and wrestling with ideas together. He has shared in, and contributed to, my own religious quest. Thank you for all your love and support.

Foreword

Friendship or fratricide: these are the alternatives which the twentieth century has set before religions, and they have rarely been more stark. Today we meet and talk together because we must; because we have considered the alternative and seen where it ends and we are shocked to the core by what we have seen. If a voice from heaven can be heard, however faintly, in human history, then it has been calling us these past fifty years to meet at the troubled border between faiths and learn to live together, which means understanding one another, discovering what we have in common and where our differences lie and seeing in both the creations of our shared God. Such, at least, has been the conclusion reached by many Jews and Christians as they have meditated, separately and together, on the history of our times.

That history began with a specific hope, albeit a secular one. The modern nation state was born in 1789 with the French National Assembly's Declaration on the Rights of Man. It was intended to usher in a new age of tolerance. A state which separated religion from politics would surely end the centuries of prejudice and conflict. Citizens would have rights regardless of their faith. They would be respected as human beings whatever their religious confession. Political change would be sufficient to end the wars and persecutions inflicted by one group on another. Today, fifty years after the Holocaust, we are wiser but also sadder.

Ninety years after the French Revolution, a new word entered the vocabulary of Europe. Coined by the German journalist Wilhelm Marr, it gave a name to a phenomenon that was emerging precisely in those countries which had been at the forefront of the Enlightenment. The word was *anti-Semitism*. What it signalled, ominously, was that prejudice had not died, it had merely changed form. Religious hostility was reborn as racial animosity. By 1895, a Jewish journalist, Theodor

Herzl, having witnessed the Dreyfus trial in Paris, came to the conclusion that a century of 'liberty, equality and fraternity' had not ended—if anything it had intensified—anti-Jewish prejudice. A half-century later, two-thirds of the Jews of Europe had been murdered, and even those like myself, born after the Holocaust, still mourn.

If the twentieth century has taught us one thing it is that change, the kind of change that makes a difference, that endows our lives with grace and brings the Divine presence into our midst, must take place in the human heart. Political structures alone do not create tolerance and mutual respect. That requires the direct face-to-face encounter with one-who-is-not-like-us, a genuine conversation with otherness. It means that people of different faiths must meet and talk and come to know one another. It is a conversation that often begins with trepidation, but if carried through it brings with it a great discovery, that one who is not in our image is nevertheless in God's image, and that God speaks to us in many languages, traditions and faiths.

The conversation between Jews and Christians, begun in earnest only after the Second World War, is one of the most important developments in the long history of our two faiths. Rabbi Hayyim of Sens once told the story of a man who had been lost in a forest. For several days he had wandered, unable to find the way out. Eventually he heard a sound, looked up and saw someone coming toward him. At last, he thought, I will be shown the way. But the stranger said to him, 'Do not think that I know the way, for I too am lost. But this I can tell you: do not take the path I have come from, for it too leads back into the forest. And now let us search for a new way together.' That, for me, is what Jews and Christians have tried to do for the last fifty years. We do not know the route in advance, but we have searched for a new way together.

Helen Fry's new anthology brings together some of the results of that search. In it we hear the voices of Jews and Christians as they reflect on some of their deepest beliefs: God and His presence in the world, redemption or salvation, the sacred texts of our traditions and how they are to be interpreted, and our respective roles in acting as witnesses to God. Together they consider the implications of anti-Semitism and the Holocaust, and such contemporary dilemmas as the role of women in the life of faith, and whether Jews and Christians are called upon to act separately or together in a secular world.

Listening to the conversation we become aware of the many different voices within Christianity and Judaism themselves. There is not one theology here or even two but an immense variety. What unites them and gives them their particular resonance is that they are testimonies to a profound internal struggle, one that recalls with great vividness the wrestling match between Jacob and his unnamed adversary at the river Jabbok at the dead of night. Few biblical passages are more tantalizing. We do not know with whom Jacob was struggling: was it with 'the other' or with himself, or in some mysterious sense with both? But we do know that Jacob had to undergo this struggle before he could become himself, Israel, a 'prince of God'.

This, for me, is the significance of the dialogue. It may begin in fear—fear of having our certainties challenged, overcome by the still greater fear of what may happen if we do not talk and learn to live at peace. But it ends in self-knowledge. We come to understand what, within our own heritage, makes us unique, and what makes us like others, human beings created in the image of God. If we had nothing in common, we could not converse. If we had everything in common, we would have no need to converse. Between the two lies the unpredictability of human life and its overarching religious challenge: can those who live differently live together? Can the bonds which unite us with God unite us with one another instead of setting us against one another at the cost, ultimately, of God's most precious creation, human life itself?

What would I, as a Jew, hope that we would take with us as we search for a new way together? Three insights seem to me the most important, and they are set out in the book of Genesis, the book which means 'beginning' and to which those within the biblical tradition must always turn as they seek to begin anew.

The first is that creation precedes revelation. Long before Abraham begins his journey, even longer before the Israelites hear the word of God at Mount Sinai, the Bible teaches us that we are made by, and in the image of, God. The dignity of the individual and the sanctity of human life come before all else. Only when the foundations of our common humanity are secure can we pursue our distinct if related paths to heaven.

The second is that through coming to know the other we come to know ourselves. The Hebrew Bible expresses this in a most beautiful way, but one that is often lost in translation. When the first woman was created, the first man said: 'She shall be called woman [*ishah*], because she was taken from man [*ish*].' We sometimes fail to notice that this verse is the first time that man is called *ish*, meaning a person, a distinct human individuality. Until then he has been called *haadam*, a purely biological description meaning 'that which was taken from the ground' or man as part of nature, the talking primate. Man had to pronounce the name of woman before he became conscious of himself as man. He had to know otherness before he could know himself; he had to discover that he was not alone before he could realize what, uniquely, he was. We do not lose our identity when we come to know those who are different from us. In a profound sense we find it in a new way.

The third insight is that there is hope. Genesis already foreshadows the human condition in its narrative of the first human children, Cain and Abel. Each brings an offering to God. Abel's finds favour, Cain's does not, and the result is murder—the first journey from faith to fratricide. As the twentieth century draws to a close, we cannot read this passage without fear and trembling, knowing as we do how often and tragically it has been re-enacted. The book which begins with one act of violence almost ends in another—the brothers' attempt to kill Joseph. But unexpectedly, like the appearance of a brilliant sunset at the end of an overclouded day, it concludes on a note of reconciliation. Joseph seeks no revenge for the harm that has been inflicted on him. He says—and how powerfully his words remind us that peace is the deepest instinct of faith—'You may have intended harm, but God intended it for good, to bring about the survival of many people.' If the tragedies of the past lead us to find a new way to friendship, that verse may yet stand as the verdict of faith on an age that at times has come so close to despair.

In a world still scarred by ethnic and religious conflict, at the close of the bloodiest century since human life began, the path to reconciliation still awaits us if we can find it, and the only way to do so is to search for it together. In South Africa, Northern Ireland and Israel, old antagonisms are being challenged by a new determination to establish peace. And when it comes to the pursuit of peace, great change comes about through small beginnings, through a willingness to talk across the boundaries of faith. Helen Fry's anthology is a step towards this path, and we need to listen to the voices it contains.

Rabbi Dr Jonathan Sacks
Chief Rabbi of the United Hebrew Congregations of the Commonwealth

Glossary of terms

Aggadah	Legends and myths.
Aliyah	Meaning 'ascent'. It refers to a person being called up to read the Torah in the synagogue. It can also refer to Jewish emigration to Israel under the Law of Return.
Apocalyptic	Particular ideas or scriptural books, such as the Book of Daniel or the Book of Revelation, which reveal the mysteries of the transcendent, heavenly world.
Ashkenazim	Jews from Germany and Eastern Europe.
BCE	Before the Common Era. It is equivalent to BC.
CE	The Common Era. It is equivalent to AD.
Challah	A mitzvot requiring that the dough for baking should be separated.
Christology	The doctrine of the person of Christ.
Diaspora	Meaning 'dispersed'. It refers to Jews living outside the land of Israel.
Ecclesiology	The doctrine of the Church.
Encyclical	A Papal letter sent to all the Catholic bishops.
Epistemology	The theory of knowledge.
Eschaton	The End Times.
Evangelical	An expression of Christian faith which can transcend denominational boundaries. There is usually an emphasis on personal conversion, the infallibility of scripture, and salvation from

sin through the conscious acceptance of Christ as saviour.

Exegesis — Interpretation.

Haggada — The narrative recited for the Passover festival.

Halakhah — The legal part of Jewish literature.

Kaddish — The mourner's prayer.

Kashrut — Jewish dietary laws.

Kiddush Ha-Shem — Sanctification of the Divine Name.

Midrash — Jewish interpretation. Finding new meanings from scriptural texts.

Mishnah — Codification of Oral Law which forms part of the Talmud consisting of Rabbinic Laws. It is divided into six sections.

Mitzvot — Commandments or good deeds.

Monotheism — Belief in one God.

Nerot — The lighting of candles for the Sabbath and holidays.

Niddah — The commandments concerning ritual purity for a woman during her menstrual period.

Ontological — Refers to the essence or 'being' of something.

Parousia — The Second Coming. The term is usually used with reference to the return of Christ to judge the earth.

Pauline — Pertaining to the apostle Paul.

Pentateuch — The five books of Moses.

Rabbinic — Pertaining to the Rabbis.

Rabbinic Literature — The codification of Jewish law by the Rabbis after the destruction of the Temple in 70 CE.

Reconstructionism — A form of Judaism founded by Mordecai Kaplan in America in the 1930s.

Sephardim — Jews who originated from Spain, North Africa, Palestine, Egypt, and the Turkish Empire.

Shabbat/Shabbos — The Sabbath.

Shiva — The first seven days of mourning.

Shoah	The Hebrew term for the Holocaust.
Soteriology	The doctrine of salvation.
Summa Theologica	A complete systematic theology
Supersessional	Overriding or replacing something.
Talmud	The name given to two great compilations of academic discussions on Jewish law called the Babylonian Talmud and the Jerusalem Talmud.
Theodicy	A defence of God's justice even though there is evil in the world.
Yom Ha-Shoah	Holocaust Memorial Day
Yom Kippur	The Day of Atonement

CHAPTER ONE

INTRODUCTION

CHAPTER ONE

INTRODUCTION

The purpose of this *Reader* is to provide an introduction to the key themes and trends in the Christian–Jewish dialogue over the last fifty years. The book brings together, in a unique way, influential texts from both Jewish and Christian writers from across the theological spectrum. It incorporates Orthodox, Reform, and Liberal perspectives from each faith. Organized thematically, it covers a wide range of significant topics within the dialogue. The material in each chapter offers an invaluable resource for academics and lay people seeking an accessible overview of the major issues and trends in the Christian–Jewish dialogue.

The extracts cover the major writings and official documents from the last fifty years of the dialogue. They are therefore from the period after the Holocaust. Whilst the Holocaust did not initiate the dialogue—there was some, even if limited, dialogue before then as well as the founding of the Council of Christians and Jews in Britain in 1942—the Holocaust was the main impetus for the wide-ranging changes in Christian attitudes to Judaism. It is for this reason that I have limited the material to the last fifty years. Furthermore, it is not practical to cover two thousand years of Christian–Jewish relations in this one volume. I have not included primary scriptural texts in this *Reader* except in Chapter 7 where the study of scriptural texts is part of the dialogue. It is important to clarify that the extracts are reprinted as they appear in their original source (except for their footnotes). I have maintained the spellings as found in the original text. This means that there are often variations between the American and English spelling of particular words.

The criteria for selecting the extracts have been twofold: first, that they provide a clear picture of the issues which Jews and Christians express in the contemporary dialogue; and second, that they are self-contained and self-explanatory. The extracts are taken from those who are participating, or have participated, in the dialogue. The views expressed reflect the diversity of both Christianity and Judaism: neither of these traditions is monolithic.

By way of introduction to the material, I will briefly comment on the content of each chapter before moving to an overview of the history of Christian–Jewish relations. First then, a look at the content of chapters.

The first collection of material constitutes Chapter 2 of the *Reader*. It explores the possible link between centuries of anti-Jewish teaching by the Church and the emergence of secular anti-Semitism. It also examines the link between that teaching and the events of the Holocaust. The majority of Christians and Jews in the dialogue would recognize that the policies of Hitler could not have succeeded had the groundwork not been laid by centuries of Christian polemic and persecution of Jews. As this chapter shows, the changes in official Church teaching in this century are significant. In 1965 the Catholic Church renounced the charge of deicide; i.e. that in killing Jesus the Jews had killed God. The rejection of deicide also appears in statements made by the World Council of Churches, the Anglican Church, and some non-conformist traditions. The relevant statements are reprinted in this chapter.

Having discussed the possible links between Church teaching and the Holocaust, Chapter 3 examines the theological impact of the Holocaust. No dialogue can remain unaffected by what has been described as the 'Tremendum of our Age'. Its impact has been far-reaching. Jews and Christians have tried to make sense of this horrific suffering. For many, it has raised the issue of how to speak of God. Why did God not intervene? The views expressed in this chapter range from the radical 'death of God' theology to a defence of traditional concepts of God as all-powerful and all-loving. But perhaps more poignantly, as two writers ask, 'where was humanity?'

Chapter 4 examines the difficult issue of mission. One of the biggest stumbling blocks in the dialogue has, and sometimes continues to be, the Jewish fear of Christian missionary activity. That apprehension is often in the background of any dialogue. This is not surprising given the nature of Christian mission to Jews throughout the centuries. Through the encounter many Jews and an increasing number of Christians feel that any attempts to convert 'the other' undermine the relationship of trust and place the dialogue in jeopardy. This chapter explores how Jews and Christians understand their respective mission and witness to the world. Extracts include perspectives from evangelicals involved in the dialogue who are still committed to the evangelization of all people. Jewish responses to Christian mission are also included here. Some of the changing attitudes expressed in official Church documents are reprinted.

Like the topic of the previous chapter, Israel is an emotive subject. Chapter 5 looks at Jewish and Christian understandings of the Land. It soon becomes apparent that they have very different ways of viewing it. For Jews, the attachment is part of their identity and essential for survival in a post-Holocaust world. It is a more this-worldly and practical approach. On the other hand, the Christian approach tends to be more theological and to focus on the celestial—particularly the future heavenly Jerusalem. Whilst the impact of politics and history in shaping the current situation is not being ignored, the extracts focus on the religious significance of Israel. The chapter includes writings from indigenous Jews and Christians.

In Chapter 6 Jews and Christians share their respective views on Jesus the Jew. To be dialoguing on the key figure that separates the two faiths—given the long history of persecution in the name of that figure—is a remarkable achievement. In this chapter Jews and Christians rediscover the essential Jewishness of Jesus. It includes a dialogue script between an Orthodox Jew, Pinchas Lapide, and the New Testament scholar Ulrich Luz. It will become clear that in spite of the emerging consensus on the historical Jesus, there remains a huge question about the Christ of faith. Was Jesus more than a prophet? What is his significance, if any, for Jews and Christians? Jews can accept the Jesus of history but not the Christ of faith. As some extracts will show, there are Christians who seek to incorporate this Jewish 'no' to Jesus into their theology.

Chapter 7 explores the insights and benefits of studying the scriptures together. Often this involves acknowledging that Jews and Christians have different approaches to the text. The dialogue has brought a deeper understanding of the differences and yet the opportunity to study together. The chapter includes, for example, a Jewish reading of the Lord's Prayer; a Christian writing on the significance of the Letter of James; a Christian and Jewish understanding of Jacob at the Jabbok; and a joint textual study on 'the Greatest Commandment' by a rabbi and a Dominican priest.

In Chapter 8 Jews and Christians offer their respective views on personal salvation and the redemption of the world. It is a theme common to both faiths. For Jews, the righteous of all nations have a share in the world to come. For Christians, traditionally, the figure of Jesus has been the mediator of salvation. Some of the texts express the diverse Christian approaches to salvation.

Chapter 9 explores a relatively new and undeveloped area of the Christian–Jewish dialogue; namely the distinctive contribution of women. The extracts touch on two main areas: the position of women in their respective traditions; and the anti-Judaism which is inherent in much Christian feminist theology. The final extract offers a perspective on the two biblical figures of Rachel and Mary; providing a practical example of how biblical characters can express women's experiences.

In contrast to the previous chapters, Chapter 10 focuses on the practical rather than the theological aspect of the dialogue. It examines issues of social responsibility, the joint witness of the two faiths, liberation theology, and the search for a global ethic. The final article, commissioned for the book, highlights some of the main achievements of the dialogue over the last few decades.

The final chapter offers my own perspectives on the future of the Christian–Jewish dialogue. It outlines some of the unresolved challenges for the contemporary dialogue and suggests new directions for the future. This chapter is structured around the topics already covered in the *Reader*.

USING THIS READER

For many Jews and Christians, this *Reader* will be a quick and easy way of accessing a range of positions that the dialogue is generating. It will challenge one's faith. Different texts pose different questions: 'is the Judeo–Christian tradition oppressive to women?' or 'in the light of the Shoah, surely it is wrong for Christians to continue their efforts to convert Jews?' What sense can faith make of a God who did not act to save the Jews from the gas chambers? The range of writings will stimulate and challenge Jews and Christians to think about their faith.

In addition, it is hoped that the *Reader* will enhance the dialogue. Jewish and Christian groups may wish to organize study groups based on particular chapters. Take a chapter a week, read and reflect in dialogue together on the different positions that are expressed. Rabbis and clergy may wish to incorporate some of the challenges into their sermons or study groups.

Teachers and lecturers of courses in Judaism or Christian–Jewish relations will find the *Reader* a useful textbook. It will be particularly valuable for teaching scripture and courses which seek to address a theodicy for the twentieth century. The extracts provide a window into the dynamics of the contemporary Jewish and Christian communities—their religious struggles and questions. The *Reader* offers a collection of source material for the background preparation of lessons and lectures. A study of the issues raised in the texts can enable students to confront their inherited prejudices. Teachers and lecturers are well aware of the issues and will be grateful to have the main texts in one volume.

CHRISTIAN–JEWISH RELATIONS: AN HISTORICAL OVERVIEW

This is a brief thematic overview of the history of Christian–Jewish relations. Until the middle of the twentieth century the history of the Jewish encounter with Christianity was a painful one, often marked by severe persecution and oppression. There were periods of calm and co-existence between the two faiths, particularly in Spain in the medieval period, but on the whole the history was characterized by a negative portrayal and treatment of Jews by the dominant Christian culture. There were many strands to the Church's teaching on Judaism over the centuries. The main areas were anti-Jewish legislation, forced baptisms and conversions, limited tolerance, and the myths of deicide and Blood Libel. Many, although not all, of the Church Fathers were responsible for developing certain myths about Jews and Judaism.

What about the relationship between Jews and Christians in the first century CE and in particular the period immediately after Jesus' death? Chapter 6 of this *Reader* focuses on the Jewishness of Jesus and the fact that during his lifetime his renewal movement did not step outside the boundaries of Judaism. It was only after his resurrection that some of his followers began to move away from Judaism. During the first century there were many different and diverse expressions of Judaism and Christianity. Partly through disagreements over identity and the incorporation of Gentile converts, and partly due to the developing affirmations about Jesus' divinity, Judaism and Christianity went their distinctively separate ways. The relationship in the first century was characterized by a general hostility. On both sides the parting of the ways happened over several decades and occurred at different stages for different strands of Christianity and Judaism; but the final break had occurred by the end of the first century.

The decisive change in the relationship came with the conversion of Constantine to Christianity in 312. Although anti-Jewish teachings were emerging in the homilies of the Church Fathers before then, the conversion of Constantine marked the beginning of anti-Jewish legislation.

ANTI-JEWISH LEGISLATION

Constantine's conversion endorsed Christianity as the official religion of the Empire. He implemented various measures designed to restrict the influence of Jews in society. Jews were forbidden to convert Christians to Judaism—it was a criminal offence punishable by death. They were forbidden to have Christian slaves or to marry a Christian; they could not serve in any military capacity or take up civil positions where they could judge Christians; and their privileges were severely restricted. The aim of these policies was to separate Jews and Christians from any social life or worship together. Since the Church and State were inseparable at that time the political policies of the State often became official Church teaching.

In 438 the Theodosian Code did offer a limited degree of protection for Jews in that they were protected from mob attacks on their homes and synagogues. However it did legislate that all converts to Judaism lost their rights of inheritance. Synagogues could no longer be considered places of legal asylum. Missionary activity was legal for Christians but illegal for Jews. During the sixth century the Justinian Code abolished more than half of the statutes of the Theodosian Code. Under the Justinian Code, Judaism had no legal existence or protection and property rights were severely narrowed. Those who publicly denied the resurrection and the Last Judgement could face excommunication or the death penalty.

It was at the Church's Fourth Lateran Council in 1215 that Jews were required by law to wear distinctive dress. It was legislated that they should wear a yellow badge to distinguish them from non-Jews. In 1239 Pope Gregory IX declared the Talmud to be heretical and copies of it were burned all over Europe. A widespread persecution of Jews followed from these measures. A number of anti-Jewish laws were passed in the thirteenth century: at the Council of Oxford in 1222 there was a ban on the building of synagogues; at the Synod of Breslau in 1267 Jews could only live in Jewish quarters of a city; and during the fifteenth century at the Council of Basel (1434) it was legislated that Jews could not acquire academic degrees. And so the repressive measures went on. The Jew was allowed no legal status in Europe. Throughout the subsequent centuries anti-Semitic riots and wide-spread massacres of Jewish communities became the dominant picture throughout Europe.

FORCED CONVERSION AND BAPTISM

Periods of forced conversion and baptism of Jews followed logically from the Church's anti-Jewish legislation. The Jews had not converted to Christianity as expected and so they were given a choice: to convert or face certain death. The Justinian Code in particular had devastating consequences resulting in the forced baptism of Jews and the total outlawing of Judaism in North Africa. Christianity was now so tied up with the State that any practice of Judaism was seen as a crime against the State. However, this policy of forced conversions did not go unchallenged. Some Church leaders condemned it as counter-productive, for example Pope St Gregory I (c.540–604) in a letter to the Bishops of Arles and Marseilles. And later, in 787, the Second Council of Nicaea decreed that Jews who had converted to Christianity but who still practised their Judaism should not be considered Christians but should be permitted to practise their Judaism openly. In spite of these tolerant measures there were those who were determined to enforce religious and cultural unity on Christendom.

The medieval period was a particularly brutal period for Christian missionizing. There were waves of persecution and forced baptisms for both Jews and pagans. Jews were forced to accept immediate baptism, compulsory attendance at Church services, and were not allowed to distinguish between meats. Jewish children over the age of seven were taken out of their homes and brought up in Christian families. During the sixteenth century they were still subject to forced conversion or expulsion from their land. Forced conversion was not just a political motif but was actively encouraged by the Church. This marked Christian mission at its worst.

LIMITED TOLERANCE

By the fourth century the Church had considered the practice of Judaism a heresy; but Christian theology did allow a limited tolerance towards Judaism. An ambiguity emerged in the Church's teaching on Judaism. On the one hand it developed a theology of contempt and required the conversion of all Jews, and on the other it had a deep respect for the tradition that was the root of Christianity. The Church wanted to preserve the identity of the Jewish people for two reasons: firstly the belief that the Jews were the recipients of God's providential care as his chosen people, and secondly, their role in the final redemption of all humanity. This raised a tension on the mission field between the belief that the conversion of Jews was an essential element of Christian mission and the belief that if the Christian mission was successful before the full number of Gentiles had come into the Kingdom (cf. Rom. 9–11), then the Church might have stalled God's plan of salvation. This tension was never adequately addressed by the Church.

Nevertheless, there was a further reason for developing a degree of tolerance for Judaism, advocated by Augustine in the fifth century. He developed the myth of the wandering Jew. This myth allowed for a limited degree of tolerance. Augustine argued that although the Jews should have suffered death for the killing of Christ, they were allowed to survive as a witness to the truth of Christianity. They survived as a testament to the world of the consequences of rejecting Christ and incurring the wrath of God. As a result of killing Christ the Jews were destined to wander the earth, never to be settled in one place for very long. They bore the mark of Cain who was destined to wander the earth for killing his brother, Abel. Jewish survival was necessary but Jews were not to enjoy a high standard of living. They were always to be a subservient people. As Moses Mendelssohn has written: 'but for this lovely brainwave we would have been exterminated long ago.'

Luther (1483–1546), an Augustinian monk, also advocated a tolerance towards Jews. But even this limited tolerance soon faded when his hopes that the Jews would convert to Christianity did not materialize. He had preached a more limited tolerance than Augustine—just enough tolerance to allow Jews to convert. But even that limited tolerance came to an end just before his death in his statement: 'if they (the Jews) turn from their blasphemies we must gladly forgive them; but if not, we must not suffer them to remain'. What was to follow from this teaching was to have devastating consequences for European Jewry in the twentieth century, culminating in Hitler's use of Luther's teaching to justify the extermination of European Jewry.

The limited tolerance argued for by Augustine and Luther was clearly not adequate as a theology of Judaism but it did ensure a limited degree of protection during certain periods of history. However, many have argued that it proved inadequate when confronted with Hitler's Final Solution. It was only after the foundation of the State of Israel in 1948 that the Church finally renounced the teaching that God had rejected the Jews and had destined them to wander the earth for all times.

THE CHARGE OF DEICIDE AND THE MYTHS OF JEWISH DEPRAVITY

Three myths characterized the stereotypical picture of the Jew throughout the centuries: the charge of deicide; the medieval myth of blood libel and the Jew as the incarnation of the Devil; and the image of the Jew as conspirator.

The charge that the Jews killed Christ appears very early in the New Testament writings (Matt. 27:25; Acts 2:36; 1 Thess. 2:15–16). The first recorded charge of deicide, that in killing Christ the Jews had killed God, did not occur until the second century with Melito the Bishop of Sardis. The belief that the Jews were responsible for the death of Christ and hence the death of God is found repeatedly in writings of the Church Fathers. They had been influenced by Melito's theology. The charge appears in the homilies and writings of John Chrysostom, Augustine, and Luther. The Jews were seen as inherently evil and the murderers of the prophets and finally the murderers of Christ. They were destined to suffer as a result.

The medieval period saw the rise of the Crusades and the widespread massacre of Jews across Europe. A few Christian leaders did speak out against this treatment of Jews but with little effect. During the medieval period new myths about Jewish depravity emerged. Jews were portrayed as the incarnation of the Devil in league with all the forces of evil. They were linked to superstitious practices and witchcraft. It was suggested that they could perform magic against the Christian community as the earthly agents of Satan. It was from this

11

demonic picture that the charge of ritual murder and defamation of the Host was added. These charges were taken seriously by the ordinary people. They believed that the Jews were responsible for killing Christian children and using their blood in the Passover meal. The charge of ritual murder was initially made in 1144 and 1147. The charge provoked mob riots and attacks on Jewish homes. Many Jews lost their lives during this period. The charge of ritual murder was investigated by Pope Innocent IV leading to the issue of a Papal Bull in 1247 declaring the allegations to be groundless, but this had little impact on local people. The Jews were blamed for the outbreak of the Black Death and once again suffered the consequences. Many were forced to live in ghettos for fear of their Christian neighbours.

This medieval legacy was taken up by Luther during the Reformation period. He drew on the centuries of anti-Jewish teaching in the Church and the medieval myths of Jewish depravity. In 1543 he wrote 'On the Jews and Their Lies' in which he called for the burning of synagogues and Jewish homes and the end of safe-conduct passes for Jews. He argued that they were parasites on society, harder to convert than the Devil, and destined for hell. He tried unsuccessfully to pursuade the German prince to expel all Jews from Germany.

During the nineteenth century a different myth emerged: the Jew as conspirator. It was widely believed that the Jews were organizing a conspiracy to take over the world. This partly arose because they were involved in the management of finance and business. They were blamed for the Boer War and the Russian Revolution. When World War I broke out in 1914, many people felt that the Jews had too much influence in society. After the First World War Hitler used the image of the Jew as conspirator to blame all Jews for the Allied Powers' demands for war reparation. His propaganda literature portrayed the Jews as conspiring to undermine German independence and sovereignty; they alone were responsible for German misfortunes during the war; they were parasites on society and the physical incarnation of the Devil. He argued that the country had to be purged of their influence and their presence. When he came to power in 1933 he reversed the laws which had enabled emancipation to be a reality for European Jewry. Once again the Jews experienced the burning of their homes, synagogues, and businesses; their legal right of existence was taken away, intermarriage was forbidden and employment was restricted to non-civic office. Hitler's 'Final Solution' to the 'Jewish Problem' was formulated, resulting in the virtual destruction of European Jewry. To the present day the conspiracy theory still circulates, but in a different guise. Revisionists such as Richard Verrall and David Irving deny that the Holocaust ever took place. They argue, in spite of the evidence, that the Holocaust is just another Jewish conspiracy theory.

The Holocaust, although not necessarily the sole impetus for the new Christian–Jewish relationship, did mark the beginning of widespread changes in Christian attitudes to Judaism. There were individuals, such as James Parkes and Bill Simpson, who brought an awareness of the consequences of anti-Semitism, to the fore in the 1930s and 1940s but such work was rare. The Council of Christians and Jews in Britain was also founded in 1942.

It was the Holocaust which highlighted for many Christians the urgency of a reappraisal in Christian teaching *vis-à-vis* Judaism. The extracts in the following chapters of this *Reader* speak for themselves in just how far the Churches and individual Christians have come. However, the progress is not just one-sided. The Jewish community has travelled a long way in accepting Christians as partners in the dialogue. A significant number of Jews, some Orthodox, are prepared to dialogue on a wide range of difficult topics which separate the two faiths. This is done on the presupposition that they are equal partners and the dialogue will not have a hidden missionary agenda on the part of the Christians. A new relationship of trust and co-operation is emerging between Jews and Christians—a remarkable achievement given the history of Christian–Jewish relations and the continued attempts by some Christians to convert Jews. It is a relationship that deserves widespread, serious reflection. The following chapters offer a valuable insight into the dynamics of that dialogical relationship.

FURTHER SUGGESTED READING

Braybrooke, Marcus. *Children of One God: A History of the Council of Christians and Jews*, SCM Press, 1991.

Daz-Mías, Paloma. *Sephardim: The Jews From Spain*, The University of Chicago Press, 1992.

Dunn, James. *The Partings of the Ways Between Christianity and Judaism and their Significance for the Character of Christianity*, SCM Press, 1991.

Fisher, Eugene (ed.). *Interwoven Destinies: Jews and Christians Through the Ages*, Paulist Press, 1993.

Flannery, Edward. *The Anguish of the Jews*, Paulist Press, 1985.

Hood, John. *Aquinas and the Jews*, University of Pennsylvania Press, 1995.

Maclennan, Robert. *Early Christian Texts on Jews and Judaism*, Atlanta, 1990.

Oberman, Heiko. *The Roots of Antisemitism in the Age of Renaissance and Reformation*, Fortress, 1984.

Oesterreicher, John. *The New Encounter Between Christians and Jews*, Philosophical Library, 1986.

Parkes, James. *The Foundations of Judaism and Christianity*, Vallentine Mitchell, 1960.

Rousmaniere, John. *A Bridge to Dialogue: The Story of Jewish–Christian Relations*, Paulist Press, 1991.

Segal, Alan. *Rebecca's Children: Judaism and Christianity in the Roman World*, Harvard University Press, 1986.

Simpson, William. *Jews and Christians Today*, Epworth Press, 1940.

Trachtenberg, Joshua. *The Devil and the Jews: The Medieval Conception of the Jew and its Relation to Modern Anti-Semitism*, The Jewish Publication Society of America, 1961.

Wigoder, Geoffrey. *Jewish–Christian Relations since the Second World War*, Manchester University Press, 1988.

Wilken, Robert. *John Chrysostom and the Jews*, University of California Press, 1983.

CHAPTER TWO

———

ANTI-SEMITISM

CHAPTER TWO

ANTI-SEMITISM

Many Jews believe the dialogue to be important because they hope that it will provide a way of combating anti-Semitism. Although historically there have been periods of calm, there have also been significant periods of persecution, forced conversions, and anti-Jewish legislation in which the Church was actively involved. Even during periods of calm, anti-Jewish preaching dominated the pulpit. It seems that Christian hatred of Jews and Judaism was rooted at the heart of the Church's teaching and preaching. A crucial turning point in Christian–Jewish relations came with the annihilation of six million Jews in the Shoah. Although a few Christians did try to improve relations prior to the Shoah, their work was rare. The major changes in the Church's attitude and teaching of Jews and Judaism came after the Shoah. Given the history of Christian–Jewish relations these changes were long overdue.

Until this century the charge of deicide was often made against the Jews. It laid the blame for the death of Jesus not only on the Jews of Jesus' day but on all subsequent generations. Melito of Sardis, living in the second century CE was the first Christian Bishop to accuse the Jews of deicide—namely that in killing Christ the Jews were guilty of killing God. This charge of deicide was endorsed by many theologians —from Augustine to Luther. It was only in 1965, with *Nostra Aetate*, that the Catholic Church explicitly renounced the charge of deicide. Other churches have now followed suit.

H.P.F.

THE TEACHING OF CONTEMPT AND THE SHOAH

Many theologians, both Jewish and Christian, argue that there is a direct link between the centuries of anti-Jewish teaching by the Church and Hitler's Final Solution. Although it is true that the Church never officially ordered the genocide of the Jews, it seems that Hitler was only putting into practice what the Church had tried to do spiritually for centuries—to wipe out Jews as Jews, and to wipe out the Jewish faith. When Hitler came to power in 1933 he reversed the laws which had led to the emancipation of European Jewry. He ordered the burning of synagogues, Jewish businesses and homes; and legislated that Jews could not hold civic office. **Marcus Braybrooke**, *an Anglican theologian, clearly believes that two thousand years of the Church's anti-Jewish preaching laid the foundations for Hitler's Final Solution and led to a society undisturbed by his intentions:*

On the night of November 9th, 1938, the Nazis launched a vicious attack on Jews in Germany. Hundreds of synagogues and Jewish shops were destroyed. Many Jews were beaten or murdered. The night is known as Kristallnacht or the Night of Broken Glass, because so many windows were smashed.

Hardly any Christians protested. Archbishop Robert Runcie asked, 'Why this blindess? Because for centuries, Christians have held Jews collectively responsible for the death of Jesus. On Good Friday, Jews have, in time past, cowered behind locked doors for fear of Christian mobs seeking "revenge" for deicide'.

Jews were quickly blamed for the death of Jesus, 'their Messiah', whom they rejected. In punishment, Christians claimed that God had banished them from the land of Israel. In the Middles Ages, other accusations were added. They were called 'children of the devil'. Jews, in the 'Blood Libel', were falsely accused of killing Christian children and of stealing and mutilating the host or consecrated wafer. During the crusades, Jews were often the victims of attack and their wealth plundered to finance these same crusades.

Once the Roman Empire became Christian, the Jews' privileges were withdrawn. Conversion to Judaism and mixed marriages were forbidden on pain of death. Throughout the centuries, Jews have been expelled from countries where they seemed secure, such as Spain from where they were banished five hundred years ago in 1492. They have been the victims of prejudice and persecution. Antisemitism still lurks in our society today and is reappearing in Eastern Europe.

The causes of antisemitism are very complex. Clearly one factor has been anti-Jewish teaching by the churches. Some of this has been blatant, such as blaming the Jews for the death of Jesus. Other prejudice is more subtle. For example, Christians tend to read the Hebrew Bible 'typologically', merely as pointing forward to the coming of Christ. Sometimes 'the fierce God of the Old Testament' has been contrasted with 'the God of love of the New Testament'. Yet the psalms constantly speak of God's loving kindness and the New Testament is not without its note of warning. One God of mercy and judgement speaks through the whole bible.

Centuries of anti-Jewish teaching prepared the ground for Nazism. Although some Christians risked their lives to save Jews, too few Christians opposed the Nazis. The overwhelming evidence is of the silence of the churches.

Today, Christians need to enter into the painful horror of the Shoah (the Hebrew term for the Holocaust) and readily confess their penitence for the churches' shameful record. Further, if they believe that God's promises to Israel are eternal and unfailing, then they will recognise that the Jews are still a people of God.

[Marcus Braybrooke, *Christian–Jewish Relations: A New Look*, The Council of Christians and Jews, 1992, pp. 8–10]

In a similar vein **Norman Solomon**, *an Orthodox Rabbi and Fellow of Modern Jewish Thought at the Centre for Hebrew and Jewish Studies in Oxford in England, argues that Hitler used the rhetoric and policies of medieval Church teaching and legislation. Solomon then goes on to explain the pain that has been caused to Jews by the siting of a Carmelite convent at Auschwitz. Auschwitz is a symbol of Jewish persecution and annihilation not of Christian suffering. The reason for this, he explains, is that Jews see the Shoah as the culmination of centuries of Christian persecution of Jews:*

a) The Link—The Teaching of Contempt

Neither the reticence of the churches in opposing the destruction of the Jews nor the readiness of ordinary Christians to implement the *Shoah* was accidental.

Hitler's core message about the Jews was Christian; only his methods were not. (There were of course other differences, but from the victim's point of view they were not very important. For instance, the inquisitor had tortured and killed out of Christian love, for the benefit of his victim's immortal soul; Hitler did not preach a religion of love.)

In his early writings and speeches Hitler, seeking the support of the masses, spoke overtly Christian language. 'Hence I believe that I am acting in accordance with the will of the Almighty Creator: *by defending myself against the Jew, I am fighting for the word of the Lord.*' His attacks on Jews and Judaism were consciously expressed in the language of traditional Christian antisemitism and the infamous laws of Nuremberg consciously modelled on the legislation of the medieval church. It *was* the church that had instigated trade restrictions against the Jew (a direct model for the Nazi boycott of April 1, 1933), and the ghetto and the yellow badge; it *was* Christians who first utilised the blood libel as an excuse to murder Jews. It *was* the church that sewed into the fabric of western culture the images and stereotypes of the Jew that allowed so many of its faithful sons to accept without demur the alienation and vilification of the Jew preached by Hitler. For it was the church whose gospel concerning the Jews was, as Jules Isaac called it, *l'enseignement du mépris*, the teaching of contempt. Hitler's *Judenhaß* was not significantly greater than that of Luther—and it has taken all the courage of the post-holocaust Lutheran Church to repudiate that aspect of the 'great reformer's' teaching.

b) Appropriation

In reality there is an inherent ambiguity in the Christian situation in the Holocaust. It is beyond any shadow of doubt that the ultimate aim of the Nazis was totally to destroy Christianity—though not Christian people who, unlike Jews, could be Aryans and thus 'save' themselves by abjuring Christianity.

The Roman Catholic Church at the present time seems intent on creating the image of itself as victim of the Holocaust, if not to the same extent as Jews. The beatifications of Maximilian Kolbe and Edith Stein belong to the church's search for its own Holocaust martyrs. In Poland the process is a natural enough one. Auschwitz has become, to Poles, a national symbol of suffering under the Nazis, and Polish Catholics now come there to pray and to seek atonement and reconciliation. After all, Auschwitz was set up as a concentration camp for (non-Jewish) Poles, and hundreds of thousands of them perished there.

One asks, therefore, why Jews reacted so strongly to the siting of a Carmelite convent in the 'Old Theatre' on the perimeter of the

Auschwitz site. Why did they see the Catholic presence at Auschwitz as the appropriation of a uniquely Jewish symbol—worse, as the oppressor donning the garb of the victim? Why do Jews find it so hard to recognise Christians in general (they are very ready to note the exception) as their brothers and sisters in suffering?

The fact is that Jews tend to view the Shoah as the culmination of their degradation and persecution at the hand of Christians. They see Christians by and large as persecutors, with a relatively small number as victims and an even smaller number showing the least concern for Jewish victims. Since the Holocaust, Jews have ceased to take the moral credibility of the church seriously.

Yet a recent consultation of Jews and Catholics in Poland was remarkable for the way in which both Jews and Catholics began to share the sense of brotherhood in suffering, even though—perhaps because—it was recognised that the church had made errors of both omission and commission. To stand at Auschwitz, as I did, with the archbishop of Cracow and the assembled company of Jews and Catholics, and to recite *kaddish* together, was an act of joint sorrow and reconciliation, not a sweeping aside of the past nor a false appropriation. It was a sign that a new understanding and constructive relationship is possible.

c) The Jewish Response

On the basis of the foregoing it is evident that Jews see the Holocaust as the culmination of the centuries of Christian 'teaching of contempt'; the response is the culmination of Jewish rejection of Christian moral credibility. That is, no Christian, simply in virtue of being a Christian believer, is accorded moral credibility, let alone superiority. The individual Christian rather may earn such credibility through the conduct of his own personal life. Those who helped Jews during the Holocaust are given special honour, as in the Memorial to the Righteous Gentiles at *Yad Vashem*; they are seen to have triumphed as individuals, not as Christians.

Such a view is harsh toward Christians. While it contains too much truth to be ignored, the way forward lies in recognising that Christianity is a complex cultural construct, diverse in its manifestations, and though Christendom has indeed nurtured the 'teaching of contempt' in its bosom, there have been and certainly are today many other Christian approaches to Jews. Even though the New Testament and the fathers lend themselves readily to an anti-Jewish interpretation —sometimes, particularly with the fathers, inescapably so—resources are available from within Christianity to develop a constructive relationship with Jews and Judaism.

[Norman Solomon, 'Themes in Christian—Jewish Relations' in *Toward A Theological Encounter: Jewish Understandings of Christianity*, edited by Rabbi Leon Klenicki, Paulist Press, 1991, pp. 27–30]

THE SILENCE OF THE CHURCH

*The Shoah destroyed two-thirds of European Jewry. The great cultural centres of Jewish learning were no more. As if this was not pain enough, Jews had to come to terms with the failure of the majority of Christians to voice any protest. They did not find an ally in the Christian Church. The silence of Church leaders and politicians has sent shock waves through the Jewish community. **Mary Athans**, a contributor to Catholic—Jewish dialogue in the States, believes too that this passive silence on the part of Christians was due to the history of anti-Jewish preaching:*

The key question remains: 'If the Christians had really been *Christian* over the centuries, would the holocaust have occurred?' Was the holocaust the result primarily of racial antisemitism, or were there religious roots as well? Jewish and Christian scholars, interfaith activists, and church and synagogue dialogue groups have analysed and agonised over this matter both with depth and in pain. The results strongly suggest that the culmination of years of simplistic biblical interpretation, anti-Judaic pronouncements, legislation by the churches, and the behaviour of Christians as noted above laid the groundwork for the events of the Nazi era. While it is true that the basic orientation of Nazi ideology was atheistic, the Christian writings and proclamations of the centuries provided a fertile soil in which the hatred of Jews could grow. The abiding contempt for Jews which had been inculcated in Christians over the centuries served Hitler's purposes well. Ultimately this contributed to an environment in which some irrational leaders attempted a 'final solution' and the majority of Christians responded passively in silence.

[Mary Christine Athans, 'Antisemitism or Anti-Judaism?' in *Introduction to Jewish—Christian Relations*, edited by Michael Shermis and Arthur E. Zannoni, Paulist Press, 1991, pp. 135–136.]

ANTI-JUDAISM—THE LEFT HAND OF CHRISTOLOGY

The Shoah has raised serious questions for Christianity and Judaism—calling into question the nature of a God who could permit such evil in the world. These particular theological problems will be explored in Chapter 3. For Christianity there is a further fundamental challenge. The Shoah has highlighted the urgent necessity for a revised Christian theology of Judaism. For **Rosemary Radford Ruether***, a Christian theologian, the fratricidal side of Christianity can only be overcome through a genuine dialogue between the two faiths. In her book* Faith and Fratricide *she shocked the Christian world by claiming that the shadow side of Christology was anti-Semitism. To deal with anti-Judaism the Church has to reappraise its Christology. In the following extract from her book* To Change the World *she argues that, in the light of Auschwitz, a profound reassessment of Christian teaching is required:*

The anti-Semitic heritage of Christian civilization is neither an accidental nor a peripheral element. It cannot be dismissed as a legacy from 'paganism', or as a product of purely sociological conflicts between the church and the synagogue. Anti-Semitism in Western civilization springs, at its root, from Christian theological anti-Judaism. It was Christian theology that developed the thesis of the reprobate status of the Jew in history and laid the foundations for the demonic view of the Jew that fanned the flames of popular hatred. This hatred was not only inculcated by Christian preaching and exegesis. It became incorporated into the structure of canon law and also the civil law formed under the Christian Roman emperors, such as the Codes of Theodosius (AD 428) and of Justinian (sixth century). These anti-Judaic laws of the church and the Christian empire laid the basis for the debasement of the civic and personal status of the Jew in Christian society that lasted until the emancipation in the nineteenth century. These laws were, in part, revived in the Nazi Nuremberg Laws of 1933.

The understanding of Christology is, I believe, at the heart of the problem. Theologically, anti-Judaism developed as the left hand of Christology. Anti-Judaism was the negative side of the Christian affirmation that Jesus was the Christ. Christianity claimed that the Jewish tradition of Messianic hope was fulfilled in Jesus. But since the Jewish religious teachers rejected this claim, the church developed a polemic against the Jews and Judaism to explain how the church would claim to be the fulfillment of a Jewish religious tradition when the Jewish religious teachers themselves denied this.

At the root of this dispute lies a fundamentally different understanding of the Messianic idea that developed in Christianity, in contrast to the Hebrew Scriptures and the Jewish teaching tradition. Judaism looked to the Messianic coming as a public, world-historical event which unequivocally overthrew the forces of evil in the world and established the reign of God. Originally Christianity also understood Jesus' Messianic role in terms of an imminent occurrence of this coming reign of God. But when this event failed to materialise, Christianity pushed it off into an indefinite future, that is, the Second Coming, and reinterpreted Jesus' Messianic role in inward and personal ways that had little resemblance to what the Jewish tradition meant by the coming of the Messiah. An impasse developed between Christianity and Judaism, rooted in Christian claims to Messianic fulfillment and supersession of Judaism, that were not only unacceptable but incomprehensible in the Jewish tradition. The real difference between these two views has never actually been discussed between Christians and Jews in any genuine fashion because, at an early stage of development, these growing differences of understanding of the Messianic advent were covered over with communal alienation and mutual polemic.

Christian teachers sought to vindicate their belief in Jesus as the Christ by reinterpreting Hebrew prophecy to accord with the Christian view of Christ. This Christian exegesis also denied the ability of the Jewish teachers to interpret their own Scriptures. The Jews, Christians said, had always been apostate from God and their teachers spiritually blind and hard of heart. In effect, Christian theology set out to demonstrate the rejected status of the Jewish people and the spiritual blindness of its exegesis and piety in order to vindicate the correctness of its own exegesis and its claim to be the rightful heir of Israel's election.

According to Christian teaching, it is the church which is the true heir to the promises to Abraham. It is the spiritual and universal Israel, foretold by the prophets, while the Jews are the heirs of an evil history of perfidy, apostasy, and murder. As a result the Jewish people have been cut off from their divine election. Divine wrath has been poured down on them in the destruction of the temple and the national capital city of Jerusalem. They have been driven into exile and will be under a divine curse as wanderers and reprobates until the end of history, when Jesus returns as the Christ and the Jews finally have to acknowledge their error.

In effect, the church set up its polemic against the Jews as a historical task of Christians to maintain perpetually the despised status of the Jews as a proof of their divine reprobation. At the same time, the church taught that the Jews must be preserved to the end of history as "witness" to the ultimate triumph of the church. This theological stance was expressed in the official policy of the church toward the Jews through the centuries, combining social denigration with pressure for conversion. It also unleashed waves of hatred and violence that were seldom controllable within the official church policy of minimal protection of Jewish survival. In Nazism the Christian demonization of the Jew's spiritual condition was converted into a demonization of their biological condition. Hence the Nazi final solution to the Jewish question was not religious conversion but physical extermination, to make way for the millenium of the Third Reich.

For us, who live after the Holocaust, after the collapse of Christian eschatology into Nazi genocidal destruction, profound reassessment of this whole heritage becomes necessary. Although Nazis hated Christians as well as Jews, the church nevertheless must take responsibility for the perpetuation of the demonic myth of the Jew that allowed the Nazis to make them the scapegoat of their project of racial purity. This Christian tradition also promoted an antipathy in Christians, who too often felt little need to respond to the disappearance of their Jewish neighbors. We have to examine the roots of the theological patterns that fed this demonic myth of the Jew and its perpetuation, even in liberal theologies, today.

[Rosemary Radford Ruether, *To Change the World*, SCM Press, 1981, pp. 31–33]

A JEWISH RESPONSE TO ROSEMARY RADFORD RUETHER

Yosef Yerushalmi, former Professor of Hebrew and Jewish History at Harvard University in the United States, provides an interesting Jewish response to Radford Ruether's argument. He does not deny the impact of medieval anti-Semitism on contemporary anti-Semitism but he does question whether modern anti-Semitism is 'merely a metamorphosed medieval Christian anti-Semitism'. Although the anti-Jewish teaching of Christianity did influence secular anti-Semitism, he points out that the Church never advocated genocide. For him the Shoah was the result of 'a thoroughly modern, neopagan state':

Coming to modern times, Rosemary Ruether states that 'modern anti-Semitism is both a continuation and a transformation of the medieval theological and economic scapegoating of the Jews.' Few, I think, would deny that medieval anti-Semitism survives into the modern age both in its original and in certain secularised forms, and that there is a continuum between the two. The crucial word is 'transformation', and it is this which raises more complex questions.

Is modern anti-Semitism *merely* a metamorphosed medieval Christian anti-Semitism? Through what conduits and channels did the transformation occur? If, as has been proposed by some, it was through the French Enlightenment, then one must obviously take into account its non-Christian sources as well. But this is not the time to discuss such purely historical matters. More important, what is the nature of the transformation itself, and what are the consequences thereof? What happens along the way in the shift from religious to secular, theological to racial, anti-Semitism? Here, it seems to me, Ruether's formulation explains little and glosses over much.

The issue is physical extermination. Not reprobation, discrimination, or any variety of opprobrium, but—*genocide*. From Rosemary Ruether we gather that genocide against the Jews was an inexorable consequence of Christian theological teaching. I do not think that is quite the case. If it were, genocide should have come upon the Jews in the Middle Ages. By this I do not in any way intend to exonerate the church of its real and palpable guilt. There is no question but that Christian anti-Semitism through the ages helped create the climate and mentality in which genocide, once conceived, could be achieved with little or no opposition. But even if we grant that Christian teaching was a necessary cause leading to the Holocaust, it was surely not a sufficient one. The crucial problem in the shift from medieval to modern anti-Semitism is that while the Christian tradition of 'reprobation' continued into the modern era, the Christian tradition of 'preservation' fell by the wayside and was no longer operative. To state only that modern anti-Semitism is a 'transformed' medieval anti-Semitism is to skirt this central issue. Surely there must be some significance in the fact that the Holocaust took place in our secular century, and *not* in the Middle Ages. Moreover, medieval anti-Jewish massacres were the work of the mob and the rabble. State-inspired pogroms of the type that took place in Czarist Russia, state-instigated genocide of the Nazi type—these are entirely modern phenomena. The climactic anti-Jewish measure of which the medieval Christian state was capable was always expulsion and, on rare occasions, forced conversion. The Holocaust was the work of a thoroughly modern, neopagan state.

[Yosef Hayim Yerushalmi, 'The History of Christian Theology and the Demonisation of the Jews', in *Auschwitz: Beginning of a New Era?* edited by Eva Fleischner, Ktav, 1977, pp. 102–103]

TOWARDS A CHRISTIAN THEOLOGY OF JUDAISM

*Continuing this discussion with Ruether's work, this next extract comes from a previously unpublished paper that I delivered at a Conference at the University of Bristol, England in 1994. I acknowledge that **Radford Ruether's** work was crucial for opening up the issue of the root cause of anti-Judaism, but in contrast to her I suggest that soteriology not Christology is the problem. Any new Christian theology of Judaism must re-examine traditional exclusive understandings of salvation:*

In her book *Faith and Fratricide* Ruether disturbed the Christian world by claiming that the shadow side of Christology is anti-Semitism. I suggest that it is soteriology (salvation), and not absolutist Christology, which has led to anti-Judaism in Christian theology. Ruether has argued in the preceeding excerpt and her book *Faith and Fratricide* that the disagreement between Jews and Christians over the Messiahship of Jesus led to the denigration of Judaism. Christians believed that Jews had wilfully rejected and killed their Messiah, which meant all the promises made to them in the Scriptures were forfeited. Christians in accepting the Messiahship of Jesus had become the true heirs. Ruether then argues that Christian anti-Semitism forthwith was always focused on the Jewish rejection of Jesus, and it was from this disagreement that the Church developed various myths of deicide, Jewish blindness and depravity, the mark of Cain, and ritual murder. Christology and anti-Judaism had become so intertwined that now 'it may seem impossible to pull up the weed without uprooting the seed of Christian faith as well' (Ruether 1974 p.226). There are two problems with Ruether's linking of Christology and anti-Judaism; first, many who do hold an ontological, absolutist Christology are trying not to denigrate the status of Judaism. There were, and still are, other options available to the Church; namely two-covenant theology, inclusivism, and pluralism. Second, it seems odd to say that a simple disagreement over the status of Jesus is denigrating. Why should the fact of disagreeing with a different tradition be viewed as so insulting? The fact that I disagree with a person does not mean that I am denigrating her. Take Islam for example, we have a prime example of a faith which disagrees with Christianity over the status of Jesus, but one has not denigrated the other. Disagreements in themselves between different religious traditions should not be construed as denigration.

I suggest that the difficulty lies not with a disagreement over Jesus but with traditional understandings of salvation. Theoretically, the Church has for centuries defended the idea that there can be no salvation apart from conscious knowledge of Christ. An ultimate disagreement arose between Jews and Christians over the nature of salvation. According to certain strands of the Christian tradition, Judaism had forfeited its right to be the people of God by rejecting Christ and no longer had the power of salvation. All the promises in the Scriptures had been transferred to the Church in effect making Judaism worthless and therefore dispensable. This disagreement over salvation led to the denigration of the Jews because the very idea of *saving the other* means that *the other* has no separate validity and is deemed to be inferior. Given this theological outlook it was difficult for the Church to appreciate Judaism.

The denigration of Judaism was not in the early days focused on an absolutist Christology. It was later that Christology became blurred with soteriology. The Church Fathers developed a fulfilment Christology which fully expected the Jews to convert to Christianity. This exclusivist position necessarily led to an active mission to convert Jews. In making Christianity a viable option on the mission field it was necessary to view Judaism as sinful and to ultimately demonize and satanize it. Christian hostility often intensified when Jews refused to convert and the Jewish faith itself was still attracting considerable numbers of Gentiles. Historically, this linking of mission and soteriology had severe consequences for Judaism: leading directly to periods of forced conversions, forced baptisms, legislation against Jews, the development of certain myths about Jewish depravity, and an overall denigration and persecution.

This link between salvation and denigration was particularly evident in the life of Luther who initially appeared to understand why the Jews had not previously converted to Christianity, i.e. because of

Papal interpretations of the Gospel. The younger Luther had high hopes that once the Christian message was stripped of the misleading Roman Catholic influence then the Jews would see the truth of Protestantism and convert to the true faith. But this very attitude contained within itself the seeds of his later disappointment. For he was to spend his life expounding justification by faith in Christ, only to discover that the Jews still did not convert. Within twenty years his attitude towards them had turned violently hostile and bitter. In his work *On the Jews and their Lies* he accused them of being wilfully blind, renewed the charge of deicide, and accused them of ritual murder. It was his defence of an exclusivist concept of salvation which drove him to the ultimate demonization and denigration of Jews. This led to his suggestion to the secular authorities that they should burn Jewish homes and synagogues; Jewish travelling privileges should be taken away; and all Jews should be expelled from Germany. Luther provides just one example of the consequences for Judaism of a Christian theology which is based on an exclusivist soteriology.

It might be objected that if disagreement over christology is not necessarily denigration, then why does a disagreement over soteriology lead to denigration? Why can't a Hindu explain that the problems of karma are best dealt with by meditation? I have argued that soteriological disagreement necessarily implies the other is either satanic, sinful, or both. This is clearly denigration of *the other* and therefore any tradition which believes itself to be the universal path of salvation tends towards denigration. A further objection might be that in fact if the Christian narrative is true then it is not denigration to inform others. So for example, if a person is drowning it does seem odd to say that saving them is denigration. However, this analogy makes my point clear. The soteriological claim implies that another religious tradition, in its entirety, leaves its faithful adherents drowning (or in effect without salvation). It is just like a person who is standing on one island and tells the occupants of the other islands that they are drowning and ought to join her on her island. It would be implying that they need 'saving from' the faith of their culture. This is denigration and cannot be true primarily because, as Hick has pointed out in his books *Unanswered Questions and Interpretation of Religion*, if the Christian soteriological claim is true then we would expect it to be significantly better at producing saints than other faiths. There is in fact no evidence to suggest that Christianity is more advanced than other traditions.

So against the rather simplistic link of Christology and denigration I suggest that the main problem is found in exclusivist concepts of salvation. This remains within much of the Christian approach to the Jew today, which I fear could again provoke the ultimate denigration and demonization of the Jew. I suggest that if Christianity wishes to combat anti-Judaism then it must re-examine its soteriology.

[Helen Fry, 'Towards A Christian Theology of Judaism', paper delivered to the Second Annual Postgraduate Conference on Religious Pluralism, 1 March, 1994, Dept of Theology and Religious Studies, University of Bristol.]

HAVE CHRISTIANS TAKEN ON BOARD THE LESSONS OF THE SHOAH?

The Protestant theologian **Franklin Littel**, *for years the main Christian exponent of the view that Christian anti-Judaism led directly to the Shoah, questions whether the lessons have been taken on board by the Church. He outlines the practical results of the reassessment so far but issues a number of challenges for the Church—not least the suggestion that the Church should incorporate the meaning of the Holocaust into its confession of faith:*

This is precisely the problem in the ecumenical councils today: the lessons of the Holocaust and even the Church Struggle have not been mastered in most churches; the terrible guilt of Christendom and its centuries of false teaching about the Jews has only been admitted by those who learned of Nazi ideology and practice at first hand, and the tiny Christian ghettos in the Muslim world are primarily controlled by political considerations. With the rise of the 'Third World' myth, the ecumenical movement and its chief organs are even less inclined to make the ruthless self-assessment and take the corrective measures necessary to reestablish Christian credibility. In America, where the delusions of nineteenth-century culture-religion are still regnant, only the impact of the preliminary stage of a new church struggle has served to move some churchmen to reflection and reappraisal.

The most significant practical results of a beginning reassessment in America have so far been threefold: (1) the release of a 'Statement to Our Fellow Christians' by a working party of Roman Catholic, Protestant, and Orthodox theologians; (2) the founding of 'Christians Concerned for Israel', a voluntary fellowship with an occasional newsletter; (3) an Annual Scholars' Conference on the Church

Struggle and the Holocaust. But the crucial long-range question is how the Christians are to reestablish their credibility vis-à-vis humanity, signalised in the concrete historical situation by the way they rework their relationship to the Jewish people. The Holocaust was the consummation of centuries of false teaching and practice, and until the churches come clean on this 'model' situation, very little they have to say about the plight of other victimised and helpless persons or groups will carry authority. There is a symbolic line from Auschwitz to Mylai, but what the churches have to say about Mylai will not be heard until their voice is clear on Auschwitz. The tune must be played backward, the ball of scattered twine must be rolled up through the difficult and mysterious byways of the maze, before we come again into a blessed day-light of faith.

Finally, the meaning of the Holocaust for Christians must be built into the confessions of faith and remembered in the hymns and prayers. That was the turn in the road that most of the churches missed, and many of them are still plodding down a dead-end trail that leads away from the Kingdom of God. We Christians must go back to the turn of the road and reject the signs and signals which, expressing a spiritual and intellectual teaching which was false though familiar, turned us toward Auschwitz.

Nor is it enough to take the right turn for the sake of the church. Karl Barth was quite right in criticising the Confessing Church in 1936 for having shown no sympathy for the millions suffering injustice, for speaking out always on her own behalf. The theologian who condemned the church's seeking to gain her own soul also sensed and defined, though not as strongly as he later wished, the fatal error: 'The question of the Jews is the question of Christ.' 'Anti-Semitism is sin against the Holy Ghost.' Right! For Christians, Antisemitism is not just a peculiar nasty form of race prejudice, Antisemitism is blasphemy—a much more serious matter!

When the Christians denied their obligations to the Jews, the way to boasting and triumphalism was opened wide, and most churchmen are still marching cheerfully through it. Even the Confessing Church, though it came closer to the issue than most, spoke no clear word for the Jews at the Barmen Synod (1934) and never mentioned the Holocaust in the Stuttgart Declaration of Guilt (1945)!

The Christians must draw the knife on their own Antisemitism for the sake of the truth, not to save the church but for the love of Jesus of Nazareth and his people. There remains far too much of cunning and calculation, even among Christians well disposed toward the Jews. For example, a fine churchman has recently called on Christians and Jews to unite against the 'secularism' which reduces all religious mysteries: 'Believing Christians and believing Jews, living on their isolated islands, have been battered by a sea of unbelievers. We must build a bridge between those islands.' This is not good enough: (1) It is calculating, whereas brotherhood-love is spontaneous and unbounded. (2) It presupposes a parity of guilt and goodwill between the 'islands'. As a matter of fact, the relationship of Christendom to the Jewish people has been so wretched for so long that a number of outspoken Jewish leaders say frankly that they expect nothing and desire nothing from the Christians except that they keep their distance. We must earn our way back to the right to build a bridge, and that requires a flood of fraternal and loving actions of which we have so far proven quite incapable. (3) Finally, we need each other to be sure, but we Christians need Jewry first. The Jewish people can define itself in history without Christianity: Christians cannot establish a self-identity except in relationship to the Jewish people—past and present, and whenever the Christians have attempted to do so, they have fallen into grievous heresy and sin.

[Franklin Littell, *The Crucifixion of the Jews*, Mercer University Press, 1986, pp. 64–66]

AN ORTHODOX PERSPECTIVE

Perhaps one of the greatest advances in the future of Christian–Jewish relations will be the increased dialogue between Orthodox Christians and Orthodox Jews. Dialogues and meetings have already taken place but are still in their early stages. **Yves Dubois**' *article, as yet unpublished elsewhere, provides an honest and open assessment of Orthodox Christian–Jewish relations. He writes from the perspective of an Orthodox priest working in a parish in Bath, England. He is deeply committed to the dialogue. He acknowledges the anti-Jewish heritage which is still evident in Orthodox liturgy. He comes to the dialogue aware of the positive and negative elements of Orthodox theology:*

Every Sunday or feast of the Orthodox Church has two main services. The liturgical day begins in the evening. The first service is therefore the Vigal service which is celebrated at night. It contains most of the theological elaborations on Biblical themes, and therefore the teaching of the feast. The next morning there is a Eucharistic Liturgy or escha-tological communion with the Kingdom of God. The Vigal service, not only by its length, but also by its contents, is probably the Christian service most in continuity with Synagogue services. Indeed the love of services understood as 'leitourgia', (the Greek translation of the Hebrew 'avodah') a work and an essential responsibility towards God and the creation, and numerous shared attitudes and symbols, should lead to Jewish–Orthodox Christian dialogue and friendship. Today I am painfully aware of the difficulties ahead. To illustrate this, I would like to read just one paragraph from our service for the feast of the Meeting of the Lord:

> The Ancient of days, who in times past gave Moses the Law on Sinai, appears this day as a babe. As Maker of the Law He fulfils the Law, and according to the Law He is brought into the Temple and given to the elder. Simeon the righteous receives Him, and beholding the fulfil-ment of the divine ordinance now brought to pass, rejoicing he cries aloud: 'Mine eyes have seen the mystery hidden from the ages, made manifest in these latter days, the Light that disperses the dark folly of the Gentiles without faith and the glory of the newly-chosen Israel. Therefore let Thy servant depart from the bonds of this flesh to the life filled with wonder that knows neither age nor end, O Thou who grantest the world great mercy.'

In this short text we find all the elements, positive and negative, of the Orthodox Church's present relationship with Judaism. There is a great reverence for Moses, for the Torah, for Sinai, for the Jerusalem Temple. There is a deep sense that Gentile paganism must be replaced by the light of Biblical revelation. The Syrian origin of our liturgical tradition guarantees its Semitic culture and approach. Here we have a human and religious sensitivity which is better placed than most other Christian cultures to appreciate Judaism.

Secondly, the Orthodox Church is conscious of being a living Tradition, open to new insights but thoroughly committed to faithful continuity in beliefs and life. Therefore we come to our dialogue with Jewish people and we make our attempts at reconciliation with Judaism as Trinitarian Christians, believers in the divine as well as the human nature of Jesus. We cannot achieve complete harmony with the Jewish community just by condemning the past verbal violence against Judaism, and the past physical violence against Jewish people. The very nature of our beliefs establishes an inevitable tension with

Judaism and the Jewish community. We must learn to be faithful to our Tradition, while learning to refrain from using it as an argument against Judaism or the Jewish community.

Nowadays, the Orthodox Church, like other religious bodies, is beginning to make efforts not to show contempt or aggressiveness towards people whose beliefs differ from ours. Not everybody in our Church realises that it is an essential moral duty to refrain from aggressiveness towards Judaism. Fortunately, there are people in both communities who are convinced that deep respect and friendship could develop between us as we trust that God's mysterious ways allow for both ways of believing, worshipping and living, the Jewish and Christian.

There is however a third aspect of the liturgical text just quoted which presents a more insurmountable problem: the twisting of Scriptural texts to make them mean that God has made Judaism and the Jewish community redundant, substituting the Gentile Church for Israel. Here, the words of the Nunc Dimittis 'a light for the Gentiles and the glory of thy people Israel' have been replaced by 'the light that disperses the dark folly of the Gentiles without faith and the glory of thy *newly-chosen* Israel'. The idea of the Church as the New Israel, the true inheritor of all God's promises through the Prophets, is today almost as generally accepted and unquestioned among Orthodox Christians as it was among all Christians twenty-five or thirty years ago.

The idea that God made promises to Israel, then substituted the Gentile Christian Church for the people of Israel, is morally and theologically untenable. It is morally untenable because it questions God's truthfulness and faithfulness. This doctrine, nowadays referred to as 'supersessionism', because it sees Israel as superseded by the Church, is theologically untenable because it questions God's consistency. It also contradicts some Gospel texts, like the Song of Zechariah in Luke 1:68–75: 'Blessed be the Lord God of Israel, for he has visited and redeemed his people, and has raised up a horn of salvation for us in the house of his servant David, as he spoke by the mouth of his holy prophets from of old, that we should be saved from our enemies, and from the hand of all who hate us; to perform the mercy promised to our fathers, and to remember his holy covenant, the oath which he swore to our father Abraham to grant us, that we, being delivered from the hand of our enemies, might serve him without fear, in holiness and righteousness before him all the days of our life.' Surely this text makes it abundantly clear that we Christians, if we wish to be faithful to our own Gospel, must on no account work at the dismantling of either the Jewish community or Jewish faith.

Serious questions need to be raised within the Orthodox Church on this point. It is not sufficient that occasional parishes and monasteries both in the West and in Eastern Europe should edit supersessionist or anti-Judaic liturgical texts when they use them in their own communities, while the printed liturgical books remain unchanged. The whole supersessionist approach must be questioned and eliminated from the life of the Orthodox Church. It has begun to be questioned and eliminated by the Roman Catholic, Anglican and Protestant Churches in recent years. In the Roman Catholic Church, for instance, in spite of the ambiguity of the Vatican II document *Nostra Aetate*, the liturgical texts have abandoned the more strident anti-Jewish and supersessionist expressions. Some Orthodox Christians hope to see a similar liturgical development in the Orthodox Church, but there are few signs that it is about to take place. The urgency of a break away from anti-Judaism in the liturgical texts of the Orthodox Church is increased by the presence of anti-Semitism in our Church.

[Father Yves Dubois, 'Recent Developments in the Liturgical Life of the Orthodox Church', unpublished paper]

SOME OFFICIAL CHURCH STATEMENTS

The following section provides a survey of various official Church statements that confront the problem of anti-Jewishness in the light of the Holocaust.

Anglican

Christians and Jews share a passionate belief in a God of loving kindness who has called us into relationship with himself. God is faithful and he does not abandon those he calls. We firmly reject any view of *Judaism* which sees it as a living fossil, simply superseded by Christianity. When Paul reflects on the mystery of the continued existence of the Jewish people (Rom. 9–11) a full half of his message is the unequivocal proclamation of God's abiding love for those whom he first called. Thus he wrote:

God's choice stands and they are his friends for the sake of the patriarchs. For the gracious gifts of God and his calling are irrevocable. (Rom. 11:28–29, NEB)

God continues to fulfil his purposes among the Jewish people.

However, with some honourable exceptions their relationship has too often been marked by antagonism. Discrimination and persecution of the *Jews* led to the teaching of contempt; the systematic dissemination of anti-Jewish propaganda by Church leaders, teachers and preachers. Through catechism, teaching of school children, and Christian preaching, the Jewish people have been misrepresented and caricatured. Even the Gospels have, at times, been used to malign and denigrate the Jewish people.

Anti-Jewish prejudice promulgated by leader of both Church and State has led to persecution, pogrom, and, finally, provided the soil in which the evil weed of Nazism was able to take root and spread its poison. The Nazis were driven by a pagan philosophy, which had its ultimate aim at the destruction of Christianity itself. But how did it take hold? The systematic extermination of six million Jews and the wiping out of a whole culture must bring about in Christianity a profound and painful re-examination of its relationship with Judaism. In order to combat centuries of anti-Jewish teaching and practice, Christians must develop programmes of teaching, preaching, and common social action which eradicate prejudice and promote dialogue.

['Jews, Christians, and Muslims: The Way of Dialogue', from the Lambeth Conference, 1988]

The World Council of Churches

Hatred and persecution of Jews—a continuing concern:

3.1: Christians cannot enter into dialogue with Jews without the awareness that hatred and persecution of Jews has a long persistent history, especially in countries where Jews constitute a minority among Christians. The tragic history of the persecution of Jews includes massacres in Europe and the Middle East by the Crusaders, the Inquisition, pogroms, and the Holocaust. The World Council of Churches Assembly at its first meeting in Amsterdam, 1948, declared: 'We call upon the churches we represent to denounce antisemitism, no matter what its origin, as absolutely irreconcilable with the profession and practice of the Christian faith. Antisemitism is a sin against God and man.' This appeal has been reiterated many times. Those who live where there is a record of acts of hatred against Jews can serve the whole Church by unmasking the ever-present danger they have come to recognize.

3.2: Teachings of contempt for Jews and Judaism in certain Christian traditions proved a spawning ground for the evil of the Nazi Holocaust. The Church must learn so to preach and teach the Gospel as to make sure that it cannot be used towards contempt for Judaism and against the Jewish people. A further response to the Holocaust by Christians, and one which is shared by their Jewish partners, is a resolve that it will never happen again to the Jews or to any other people.

['Ecumenical Considerations on Jewish–Christian Dialogue' in *The Theology of the Churches and the Jewish People*, World Council of Churches Publication, 1988, pp. 40–41]

The Catholic Church

Even though the Jewish authorities and those who followed their lead pressed for the death of Christ (cf. John 19:6), neither all Jews indiscriminately at that time, nor Jews today, can be charged with the crimes committed during his passion. It is true that the Church is the new people of God, yet the Jews should not be spoken of as rejected or accursed as if this followed from holy Scripture. Consequently, all must take care, lest in catechising or in preaching the Word of God, they teach anything which is not in accord with the truth of the Gospel message or the spirit of Christ.

Indeed, the Church reproves every form of persecution against whomsoever it may be directed. Remembering then, her common heritage with the Jews and moved not by any political consideration, but solely by the religious motivation of Christian charity, she deplores all hatreds, persecutions, displays of antisemitism levelled at any time or from any source against the Jews.

['Declaration on the Relation of the Church to Non-Christian Religions', *Nostra Aetate*, 28 October 1965]

IN GRAVE PERIL FOR OUR LIFE

Finally this chapter concludes with an extract from **Yosef Yerushalmi**, *part of which appeared earlier in this chapter. He issues a warning to Christians—Jews cannot wait for Christians to reformulate their theology. 'My people are in grave* *peril of its life', he writes. Although written in 1974 this extract remains relevant to Christians as they approach the end of the second millennium—facing once again the rising tide of anti-Semitism and ethnic cleansing in many European countries. This generation will be judged not by the failures of its ancestors but by its own response or silence:*

Theology? In 1974, after all that has happened, do we still have to await a reformulation of Christian theology before the voice of the Jewish blood can be heard crying from the earth? Is our common humanity not sufficient? In any case, Christian theology is an internal affair for Christians alone. Perhaps my trouble is that I am more oriented toward history than toward theology, more to what Unamuno called 'the man of flesh and bone' than to the theologian in him. My fundamental problem has not been resolved, and perhaps is insoluble. I want to know why Rosemary Ruether is my friend, and one of the *hasiday 'umot ha-'olam*, the righteous among the nations. Her theology alone does not explain it, for there are others who share all her theological concerns and reformist causes, but who do not speak for the Jews as she does.

To Christians generally I should like to say: I hope that the condition for our dialogue is not our mutual secularization (though at times it certainly seems so). You do not have to repudiate everything in the Christian past concerning Jews. Much of the record is dark. There were also patches of light. There was 'reprobation' and there was 'preservation', and each has to be understood in its historical context. It is up to you to choose that with which you will identify. If it is important to you, integrate and reinterpret what you cull from the past into your theology, as you will. Be it known to you, however, that not by your ancestors, but by your actions, will you be judged. For my people, now as in the past, is in grave peril of its life. And it simply cannot wait until you have completed a new *Summa Theologica*.

[Yosef Hayim Yerushalmi, 'The History of Christian Theology and the Demonization of the Jews' in *Auschwitz: Beginning of a New Era?* edited by Eva Fleischner, Ktav, 1977, pp.106–107]

FURTHER READING

Charlesworth, James. *Jews and Christians: Exploring the Past, Present and Future*, Crossroad, 1990.

Cohn-Sherbok, Dan. *The Crucified Jew*, Harper Collins, 1992.

Evans, Craig & Hagner, Donald. *Anti-Semitism and Early Christianity*, Fortress, 1993.

Flannery, Edward. *The Anguish of the Jews*, Paulist Press, 1985.

Gager, John. *The Origins of Anti-Semitism*, Oxford University Press, 1983.

Klein, Charlotte. *Anti-Judaism in Christian Theology*, SPCK, 1978.

Parkes, James. *The Conflict of the Church and Synagogue*, Atheneum, 1969.

Ruether, Rosemary Radford. *Faith and Fratricide*, Seabury, 1979.

Saperstein, Marc. *Moments of Crisis in Jewish–Christian Relations*, SCM Press, 1989.

Wistrich, Robert. *Anti-Semitism: The Longest Hatred*, Thames Methuen, 1991.

CHAPTER THREE

THE HOLOCAUST

CHAPTER THREE

THE HOLOCAUST

One cannot overstate the impact of the Holocaust on world Jewry. The impact of the annihilation of six million European Jews devastated numerous families and communities. In just six years, two-thirds of European Jewry and ninety per cent of its rabbis were annihilated by Hitler's Final Solution. The most learned and culturally-rich centres of Jewish learning were wiped out. Numerically and psychologically they are still recovering. Theologically, questions continue to be raised about the non-intervention of both God and the rest of the world in the face of such horrific suffering and death. Why the silence of God? How could an all-loving, omnipotent God not intervene to prevent it? What does that say about the nature and power of God? How can one speak of God after Auschwitz? And why did the Gentile world let it happen?

Many tentative responses have been suggested by Jewish and Christian thinkers. It has to be said, though, that the Holocaust has had less impact on the churches. If one enters a Christian bookshop one will be hard pushed to find a Christian author writing on the Holocaust; and likewise if one listens to sermons throughout the year rarely, if ever, are the issues of the shoah raised by the preacher. In contrast, if one enters a Jewish bookshop one is immediately aware that nearly two-thirds of the books are addressing issues directly related to the Holocaust. This in itself speaks of the impact on the Jewish world. The Christian world has yet to fully comprehend it. It will be no surprise that the majority of texts in this chapter are from Jewish thinkers. Although the issue of Christian silence has provoked some discussion, this chapter concentrates on the theological problem. How do we make sense of the silence of God? How do we respond to what Arthur Cohen has described as 'The Tremendum of our Age'?

H.P.F.

RENEWING THE COVENANT

*In the first extract **Jonathan Sacks**, Chief Rabbi of the United Hebrew Congregations of the Commonwealth from September 1991, highlights what will shortly become apparent in this chapter, that there is no uniform Jewish response to the Holocaust. There is a multiplicity of interpretations. For him, the Jewish people do not have a common language to reflect on its fate; nevertheless the Holocaust has revealed that they share a common destiny. In the face of their total destruction, the Jewish people have renewed their covenant commitment to survive as the people of God:*

An analysis of contemporary Jewry and Judaism must begin with the Holocaust because in it, the covenantal people came face to face with the possibility of its own extinction. It took several decades before theologians felt able freely to articulate their thoughts about it. In some circles, silence is still felt to be the best, perhaps the only, response.

The Holocaust reveals to the full the problematic nature of the religious interpretation of history. It has not yielded a single meaning but a vast multiplicity, of which only a narrow range has been touched on here. In the absence of prophecy there are no such things as events which carry with them their own interpretation. And yet Judaism must continue to wrestle with the problem. For one of its primary expressions is narrative: telling the story of the covenantal people through time. Judaism is not simply a faith. It is a faith embodied in a particular people, the way of life it lives and the path it takes through the complex map of history.

Reflection on the *Shoah* reveals two significant facts about contemporary Jewish existence. The first is the absence of a shared set of Jewish meanings which alone might have allowed the Holocaust to be incorporated into Jewish memory. For the religious believer, the Holocaust confirms his faith; for the unbeliever it confirms his lack of faith. For the radical it creates a *novum* in history; for the traditionalist it recalls earlier catastrophes. For the pietist it testifies to God's suffering presence in the world; for the secularist it proves His absence. These variant readings have shown no tendency to converge over time.

The fundamental divide is between those who see the Holocaust as an unprecedented event which shatters our previous understanding of the covenant, and those who insist that the covenant survives intact even in the valley of the shadow of death. Those who take the first view see *Yom ha-Shoah*, Holocaust Memorial Day, as a seminal addition to the Jewish calendar, a turning-point in history. Those who take the second see the Holocaust as a new dimension in an ancient grief, such as that expressed on the ninth of Av, the day of mourning for the destruction of the Temples.

It is important to understand that the ambiguity of the Holocaust is not a feature of the event itself. It is a feature of the pre-understandings that different thinkers bring to it. For many centuries, from the destruction of the second Temple to the threshold of European emancipation, Jews shared a broad framework of belief that allowed them to understand their present situation, why it had come about and to what it eventually would lead. They were in exile because of their sins, and one day they would return to their land. That shared framework, which experienced stresses from the Spanish expulsion onwards, finally collapsed in the nineteenth century. Those who held to traditional beliefs were now not Jews *tout court*, but a subsection of the community known to their critics as 'Orthodox' Jews. The multiplicity of responses to the Holocaust testifies to the still fragmented nature of Jewish consciousness, which lacks a common language through which a people might reflect on its fate. This preceded the Holocaust itself and has persisted since.

But the second fact is in sharp contradistinction to the first. For the *Shoah* confronted Jews with an inescapable reminder that though they might not share a common language, they shared a common fate. The Final Solution made no distinctions between Jews. The assimilated half- or quarter-Jew from Vienna or Berlin was cast into the same camp with the pious talmudist from Vilna and the bearded mystic from Berditchev. Jews had different self-definitions. But they were subject to the same other-definition. They might not see themselves, but they were seen by others, as members of the same people.

That fact has significantly shaped post-Holocaust Jewish awareness. The sense of being a people apart and alone, held together in a collective destiny and exercising collective responsibility, has grown. Its focus is the land and state of Israel, symbol and reality of the Jewish determination never again to be homeless, powerless victims. Israel, the land and state, has brought in its wake intractable problems, political, military and ethical; and over these, too, Jews have been divided. But this does not detract from its centrality in Jewish life world-wide. Nor is this a political proposition only. It is in its own right a theological proposition, albeit a controversial one. For the Bible and all subsequent Jewish thought has seen in the return of the Jews to their land a new chapter—perhaps the ultimate one—in the covenantal story.

Jewish responses to the Holocaust, then, reveal not only the divisions that still exist in Jewish thought but also a new impetus towards unity: towards a clear and collective sense of peoplehood. For what is striking is that Jews of all kinds, religious and secular, have responded to their threatened destruction with a fierce determination to survive. 'I will not die, but I will live', says the Psalm, and that has been the Jewish response to the journey through the valley of the shadow of death. There may be no common understanding of the Jewish destiny, but there is a common conviction that it must be continued. Faced with its eclipse, the Jewish people has reaffirmed its covenant with history. The story of contemporary Jewry begins with what in retrospect is a not unremarkable fact: that the people of Israel lives and bears witness to the living God.

[Jonathan Sacks, *Crisis and Covenant*, Manchester University Press, 1992, pp. 48–51]

THE 614TH COMMANDMENT

Emil Fackenheim, *Jewish theologian and a Holocaust survivor now living in Israel, shares with Sacks the importance of surviving as the people of God. His famous phrase resounds throughout Jewry: the Jewish people must not grant Hitler a posthumous victory. Traditionally there were 613 commandments in Judaism; now there are 614 commandments: the 614th is the imperative to survive. Belief in the God of Israel must continue however hard that belief may be. One must not despair—for despair would grant Hitler a posthumous victory:*

Can we confront the Holocaust, and yet not despair? Not accidentally has it taken twenty years for us to face this question, and it is not certain that we can face it yet. The contradiction is too staggering, and every authentic escape is barred. *For we are forbidden to turn present and future life into death, as the price of remembering death at Auschwitz. And we are equally forbidden to affirm present and future life, at the price of forgetting Auschwitz.*

We have lived in this contradiction for twenty years without being able to face it. Unless I am mistaken, we are now beginning to face it,

46

however fragmentarily and inconclusively. And from this beginning confrontation there emerges what I will boldly term a 614th commandment: *the authentic Jew of today is forbidden to hand Hitler yet another posthumous victory.* (This formulation is terribly inadequate, yet I am forced to use it until one more adequate is found. First, although no anti-Orthodox implication is intended, as though the 613 commandments stood necessarily in need of change, we must face the fact that something radically new has happened. Second, although the commandment should be positive rather than negative, we must face the fact that Hitler did win at least one victory—the murder of six million Jews. Third, although the very name of Hitler should be erased rather than remembered, we cannot disguise the uniqueness of his evil under a comfortable generality, such as persecution-in-general, tyranny-in-general, or even the demonic in general.)

I think the authentic Jew of today is beginning to hear the 614th commandment. And he hears it whether, as agnostic, he hears no more, or whether as believer, he hears the voice of the *metzaveh* (the commander) in the *mitzvah* (the commandment). Moreover, it may well be the case that the authentic Jewish agnostic and the authentic Jewish believer are closer today than at any previous time.

To be sure, the agnostic hears no more the *mitzvah*. Yet if he is Jewishly authentic, he cannot but face the fragmentariness of his hearing. He cannot, like agnostics and atheists all around him, regard this *mitzvah* as the product of self-sufficient human reason, realizing itself in an ever-advancing history of autonomous human enlighten-ment. The 614th commandment must be, to him, an abrupt and absolute *given*, revealed in the midst of total catastrophe.

On the other hand, the believer, who hears the voice of the *metza-veh* in the *mitzvah*, can hardly hear anything more than the *mitzvah*. The reasons that made Martin Buber speak of an eclipse of God are still compelling. And if, nevertheless, a bond between Israel and the God of Israel can be experienced in the abyss, this can hardly be more than the *mitzvah* itself.

The implications of even so slender a bond are momentous. If the 614th commandment is binding upon the authentic Jew, then we are, first, commanded to survive as Jews, lest the Jewish people perish. We are commanded, second, to remember in our very guts and bones the martyrs of the Holocaust, lest their memory perish. We are forbidden, thirdly, to deny or despair of God, however much we may have to contend with him or belief in him, lest Judaism perish. We are forbidden, finally, to despair of the world as the place which is to become the Kingdom of God, lest we help make it a meaningless place in which God is dead or irrelevant and everything is permitted. To abandon any of these imperatives, in response to Hitler's victory at Auschwitz, would be to hand him yet another posthumous victory.

How can we possibly obey these imperatives? To do so requires the endurance of intolerable contradictions. Such endurance cannot but bespeak an as yet unutterable faith. If we are capable of this endurance, then the faith implicit in it may well be of historic consequence. At least twice before—at the time of the destruction of the First and of the Second Temples—Jewish endurance in the midst of catastrophe helped transform the world. We cannot know the future, if only because the present is without precedent. But this ignorance on our part can have no effect on our present action. The uncertainty of what will be may not shake our certainty of what we must do.

[Emil Fackenheim, *The Jewish Return into History*, Schocken Books, 1978, pp. 22–24]

WRESTLING WITH GOD

Many Jews find the Hebrew Bible a rich resource of material. An undoubted theme of the Bible is the suffering of the people of Israel and the biblical charac-ter Job is marvellous for grappling with the reality of innocent suffering. The main Jewish writer to use Job is **Eliezer Berkovits**, *a leading Jewish philoso-pher and Talmudic scholar. The identification with Job is one way of explaining why righteous people experience inexplicable suffering. Job's response to his suffering was to wrestle with God. For Eliezer Berkovits, the Jewish people today must wrestle with God and ask deep, searching questions. There is a reli-gious imperative to do so. However, Berkovits does recognize that there is a profound difference between Job's situation and the Shoah—God remained completely silent and inactive in the death camps:*

Undoubtedly, for our generation Auschwitz represents the supreme crisis of faith. It would be tantamount to a spiritual tragedy if it were otherwise. After the Holocaust Israel's first religious responsibility is to 'reason' with God and—if need be—to wrestle with Him.

The 'reasoning' with God is a need of faith; it issues from the very heart of faith. When in Elie Wiesel's *Night*, at the hanging of the little boy, someone asks: 'Where is God now?' it is the right question to be

48

asked. Not to ask it would have been blasphemy. Faith cannot pass by such horror in silence. Faith, because it is trust in God, demands justice of God. It cannot countenance that God be involved in injustice and cruelty. And yet, for faith God is involved in everything under the sun. What faith is searching for is, if not to understand fully, at least to gain a hint of the nature of God's involvement. This questioning of God with the very power of faith stands out as a guidepost at the earliest beginnings of the Jewish way in history. Abraham wrestled with God over the fate of Sodom and Gomorrah. We note how the man, who in the humility of his piety sees himself as mere 'dust and ashes' yet has the audacity to challenge God with the words: 'The judge of all the earth shall not do justice?!' There is no contradiction here. The man of faith questions God because of his faith. It is the faith of Abraham in God that cannot tolerate injustice on the part of God. This is also the essence of Job's dilemma. The sustained fire of his plaint is not derived from his personal plight, but from the passion of his faith. There is no weakening of faith here. On the contrary. It is the very power of the faith that lends force to the accusation. What has happened to Job is wrong; it is terribly wrong because it is judged by the ideal of justice that Job formed for himself on the strength of his faith in God. That Job did not accept the arguments of his friends in defense of divine providence is not a matter of stubborn self-righteousness, nor is it due to a sense of exaggerated self-importance. What the friends attempt to do is to defend a wrong as justice. By doing so, they—without being aware of it—degrade Job's idea of God. Because of his faith Job cannot accept a defense of God that implies an insult to the dignity of the God in whom he believes.

The questioning of God's providence in the death camps was taking place within the classical tradition of Judaism. Unfortunately, unlike the case of Job, God remained silent to the very end of the tragedy and the millions in the concentration camps were left alone to shift for themselves in the midst of infinite despair. To this day, theologians are arguing about the meaning of God's answer to Job. Be that as it may, one thing is certain: in the denouement God appears to Job; He makes himself known to him. Thus Job is able to find peace with God in the words: 'I had heard of Thee by the hearing of the ear;/But now mine eyes seeth Thee;/ Wherefore I abhor my words, and repent, /Seeing I am dust and ashes.' No such denouement to the drama of faith took place in the camps. To the very end God remained silent and hiding. Millions were looking for him—in vain. They had heard of Him by the hearing of the ear, but what was granted to their eyes to behold was 'dust and ashes,' into which they—and everything dear to them—were turned. There were really two Jobs at Auschwitz: the one who belatedly accepted the advice of Job's wife and turned his back on God, and the other who kept his faith to the end, who affirmed it at the very doors of the gas chambers, who was able to walk to his death defiantly singing his *'Ani Mamin—I Believe'*. If there were those whose faith was broken in the death camp, there were others who never wavered. If God was not present for many, He was not lost to many more. Those who rejected did so in authentic rebellion; those who affirmed and testified to the very end did so in authentic faith. Neither the authenticity of rebellion nor the authenticity of faith is available to those who are only Job's brother. The outsider, the brother of the martyrs, enters on a confusing heritage. He inherits both the rebellion and the witness of the martyrs: a rebellion not silenced by the witness; a witness not made void by the rebellion. In our generation, Job's brother, if he wishes to be true to his God-given heritage, "reasons" with God in believing rebellion and rebellious belief. What is it then he may hope for? He is not searching for an understanding, in terms of his faith, of what had befallen his people. He is not attempting to steal a glance at "the hand" of the Almighty in order to be able to appreciate what meaning the senseless destruction of European Israel might have in the divine scheme. To understand is to justify, to accept. That he will not do. He looks to his religious bearings. He desires to affirm, but not by behaving as if the Holocaust had never happened. He knows that this generation must live and believe in the shadow of the Holocaust. He must learn how this is to be done. If his faith is to remain meaningful, he must make room for the impenetrable darkness of the death camps within his faith. The darkness will remain, but in its "light" will he make his affirmations of faith, and it will accent his affirmations. The inexplicable will not be explained, yet it will become a positive influence in the formulation of that which is to be acknowledged. The sorrow will stay, but it will be blessed with the promise of another day for Israel to continue on its eternal course with a new dignity and a new self-assurance. Thus, perhaps in the awful misery of man will be revealed to us the awesome mystery of God. But when this happens, who can say that it will not be we who, seeking His consolation, in consoling Him shall find our comfort?

[Eliezer Berkovits, *Faith After the Holocaust*, Ktav, 1973, pp. 68–70]

THE AFTER-LIFE

In all of these attempts to wrestle with the significance of the Holocaust no mention has been made of the Hereafter. **Dan Cohn-Sherbok**, *lecturer at the University of Canterbury in England and visiting Professor at Middlesex University, seeks to bring this dimension of Jewish thinking back into focus. The horrific suffering and deaths in the Shoah necessitates for him the belief in an after-life. The righteous servants of God who suffer for the sanctification of the Divine Name will be vindicated in the Hereafter. There is therefore for Cohn-Sherbok, no necessity to give up belief in God, rather the focus should shift to the traditional affirmation of a life beyond death for righteous sufferers:*

One element is missing from all these justifications of Jewish suffering; there is no appeal to the Hereafter. Though the Bible only contains faint references to the realm of the dead, the doctrine of Life after Death came into prominence during the Maccabean period (2nd century BCE) when righteous individuals were dying for their faith. Subsequently the belief in the World to Come was regarded as one of the central tenets of the Jewish faith. According to rabbinic scholars, it was inconceivable that life would end at death: God's justice demanded that the righteous of Israel enter into a realm of eternal bliss where they would be compensated for their earthly travail. Because of this belief generations of Jews have been able to reconcile their belief in a benevolent and merciful God with the terrible tragedies they have endured. Through the centuries the conviction that the righteous would inherit eternal life has sustained generations of Jewish martyrs who suffered persecution and death. As Jews were slaughtered, they glorified God through dedication to the Jewish faith —such an act is referred to as *Kiddush ha-Shem* (Sanctification of the Divine Name). These heroic Jews who remained steadfast in their faith did not question the ways of God; rather their deaths testify to their firm belief in a providential Lord of history who would reserve a place for them in the Hereafter.

In Judaism this act of sanctification was a task for all Jews if tragic circumstances arose. Thus through centuries of oppression *Kiddush ha-Shem* gave meaning to the struggle of Jewish warriors, strength of endurance under cruel torture, and a way out of slavery and conversion, through suicide. In the Middle Ages repeated outbreaks of Christian persecution strengthened the Jewish determination to profess their faith.

Kiddush ha-Shem became a common way of confronting missionary coercion—if Jews were not permitted to live openly as Jews, they were determined not to live at all. When confronted by force, Jews attempted to defend themselves, but chose death if this proved impossible. Thousands of Jews in the Middle Ages lost their lives. Some fell in battle, but the majority committed suicide for their faith. In the chronicles of this slaughter *Kiddush ha-Shem* was the dominant motif; Jews endeavoured to fight their assailants, but when efforts failed they died as martyrs.

During the Medieval period Jews also suffered because of the accusation that they performed ritual murders of Christian children, defamed Christianity in the Talmud, desecrated the Host, and brought about the Black Death. As they endured trials and massacres, they were fortified by the belief that God would redeem them in the future life. Repeatedly they proclaimed their faith in God and witnessed to the tradition of their ancestors. In later centuries *Kiddush ha-Shem* also became part of the history of Spanish Jewry. Under the fire and torture of the Inquisition chambers and tribunals Jews remained committed to their faith. The principles of *Kiddush ha-Shem* supported multitudes of Jews as they faced calamity and death. The reality of their sacrifice and the image of their martyrdom became a dominant element in the Jewish consciousness. Due to the belief in divine reward, the Jewish community escaped disillusionment and despair in the face of tragedy: the courage of those who gave their lives to sanctify God's name became an inspiration to all those who faced similar circumstances. The history of the Jewish people thus bears eloquent testimony to the heroic martyrs who were convinced that reward in Heaven would be vouchsafed to them if they remained faithful to God in their life on earth.

In the concentration camps as well a number of religious Jews remained loyal to the tradition of *Kiddush ha-Shem*. Joining the ranks of generations of martyrs, they sanctified God with unshakeable faith. As they waited the final sentence, they drew strength from one another to witness to the God of Israel. In the camps many Jews faced death silently. When their last moments arrived they died without fear. They neither grovelled nor pleaded for mercy since they believed it was God's judgement to take their lives. With love and trust they awaited the death sentence. As they prepared to surrender themselves to God, they thought only of the purity of their souls. The martyrs of the concentration camps were convinced that their deaths would serve as a prelude to redemption. In Heaven they would receive their just reward.

[Dan Cohn-Sherbok, *Issues in Contemporary Judaism*, Macmillan, 1991, pp. 15–17]

THE DEATH OF GOD

*A different response from those above can be found in the work of **Richard Rubenstein**—Holocaust survivor and the Robert Lawton Distinguished Professor of Religion in the United States. It took some ten years before he could even begin to reflect on his experiences in the death camps. His reflections probably constitute the most radical theological response yet to the Shoah. For him, after Auschwitz it is no longer possible to believe in God. The God of traditional Judaism has died; however, he shares with Fackenheim and Sacks the stress on Jewish survival. However, for Rubenstein, it is survival in the face of the death of God:*

In the spring of 1965, I experienced something of a crisis upon reading William Hamilton's article, 'The Death of God Theologies Today', in the *Christian Scholar*. To my surprise, I learned that Hamilton regarded my writings as an example of death-of-God theology. My first reaction was one of acute embarrassment. *God simply doesn't die in Judaism.* The symbolism upon which the metaphor of the death of God rests is of obvious Christian origin. Although the divinity of the Christ is not supposed to have expired on the cross, the age-old, anti-Jewish deicide accusation bears witness to the fact that the crucifixion was often regarded as the occasion of the death of God. Of course, it has always been possible for Christians, in asserting the death of God, to look beyond death to a new epiphany of the divine. Although we live in the time of the death of God, the Christian death-of-God theologians do not rule out the possibility of a reappearance of the resurrected God.

Because of our alienation from the symbolism of the cross, it is impossible for Jews to use the words, 'God is dead'. Nevertheless, I believe we must use these words of alien origin and connotation. American Jews share the same cultural universe as contemporary Christian thinkers; we experience the radical secularity of our times as they do. We have been deeply influenced by Freud, Sartre, Hegel, Dostoevski, Melville, and Kierkegaard. Above all, we have been moved by Nietzsche.

If I were asked to cite the text *par excellence* from which I derive the verbal origins of the radical mood, I would unhesitatingly follow William Hamilton and point to the chapter in Nietzsche's *Gay Science* entitled 'The Madman'. In it the Madman proclaims his search for God, asserts that we have murdered Him, and becomes affrighted at the terrible event that has already happened but is yet too distant for us to comprehend. The Madman rhetorically asks the question, also crucial to Thomas Altizer's apocalyptic theology: 'Shall we not ourselves have to become gods merely to be worthy of it?' The Madman then enters a church, which he has declared to be a sepulchre of God and there sings his *Requiem aternam deo.* After Nietzsche, it is impossible to avoid using his language to express the total absence of God from our experience. Martin Buber felt deeply the profanity of our times. He attempted to soften its harshness by speaking of an 'eclipse of God'. Buber's formulation would, however, seem to be a compromise. No words are entirely adequate to characterize a historical epoch. Nevertheless, I believe the most adequate theological description of our times is to be found in the assertion that *we live in the time of the death of God.* The vitality of death-of-God theology is rooted in the fact that it has faced more openly than any other contemporary theological movement the truth of the divine–human encounter in our times. In truth, the divine–human encounter is totally non-existent. Those theologies that attempt to find the reality of God's presence in the contemporary world manifest a deep insensitivity to the art, literature, and technology of our times. Whatever may be its shortcomings, death-of-God theology is very much aware of the cultural universe of which it is a significant expression. Radical theology is no fad. It will not be replaced by some other theological novelty in the foreseeable future. Too many tendencies in classical theology, philosophy, and literature have intersected in this movement for it to disappear as rapidly as it gained attention.

Nevertheless, *I believe that radical theology errs in its assertion that God is dead.* Such an assertion exceeds human knowledge. The statement, 'God is dead', is only significant in what it reveals about those who make it. It imparts information concerning what the speaker believes about God; it reveals nothing about God. I should like to suggest that, since this information has strictly phenomenal import, *we ought to formulate it from the viewpoint of the observer.* It is more precise to assert that *we live in the time of the death of God* than to declare 'God is dead'. The death of God is a cultural fact. *We shall never know whether it is more than that.*

The ultimate relevance of theology is anthropological. Though theology purports to make statements about God, its significance rests on what it reveals about the theologians as well as the theologian's community and culture. All theologies have a subjective component. They are statements about the way the theologian experiences the world.

The theologian is really closer to the poet or the creative artist than to the physical scientist. The value of artistic creation lies in the fact that someone with a highly sensitive subjectivity is able to communicate something of a personal experience which others recognize as clarifying and enriching their own experience. Theologians, no matter how religiously committed they may seem to be, in reality communicate an inner world they believe others may share. The term "God" is very much like the unstructured inkblot used in the Rorschach test. Its very lack of concrete content invites us to express our own fears, aspirations, and yearnings concerning our origin, our destiny, and our end. From a technical point of view, theological statements would seem to be most precise when they are enunciated in a phenomenological context. There are some indications that Professors Altizer and Hamilton accept this methodological limitation on theological assertion. Nevertheless, it is not clear whether they speak of what they have experienced or whether they believe God has literally perished.

Although my first reaction to Professor Hamilton's identification of my writing as death of God theology was embarrassment, I am grateful to him for causing me to reconsider my theological moorings. I have concluded that, alien and non-Jewish as the terminology may be, Christian death-of-God theology is closer than any other movement in Christian theology to my own theological writing. We are at least agreed upon our analysis of the radical secularity of contemporary culture as a starting point for theological speculation. We concur that ours is the time of the death of God. We are, each in our own way, convinced that both the methods and the conclusions of contemporary theology will reflect the radical hiatus between our world and the traditional communities out of which we have come.

Nevertheless, *in the time of the death of God the Jewish radical theologian remains profoundly Jewish, as the Christian radical remains profoundly Christian.*

From the concluding section of his argument on page 306, Rubenstein suggests that even though we may live in the time of the death of God, God is both life and death. The God of traditional Judaism has died but we need not despair:

God is not death; He, so to speak is the source of both life and death, Death is the final price we pay for life and love, but death is not all there is. Life has its deep, abiding, and profound moments of joy and fulfilment. Were there no death of the individual, there would be no biological need for love in the order of things. Moreover, every act of love truly consummated is to some degree a joyful dying to the self. It is a distortion to see God solely as love, for love and death are inseparable. God creates, so to speak, out of his own substance; He nurtures, but He also sets a term to individual existence, which in its individuality is no less indivisible an epiphenomenal manifestation of the divine substance. The creative process is a totality. It is impossible to affirm the loving and the creative aspects of God's activity without also affirming that creation and destruction are part of an indivisible process. Each wave in the ocean of God's nothingness has its moment, but it must inevitably give way to other waves. We are not, like Job, destined to receive back everything twofold.

The world of the death of the biblical God need not be a place of gloom or despair. One need not live forever for life to be worth living. Creation, however impermanent, is full of promise. Those who affirm the inseparability of the creative and the destructive in the divine activity thereby affirm their understanding of the necessity to pay in full measure with their own return to the Holy Nothingness for the gift of life.

[Richard Rubenstein, *After Auschwitz*, Johns Hopkins University Press, 1992 edition, pp. 249–251, 306]

A NEW THEOLOGY?

In response to the radicalism of Rubenstein, **Norman Solomon** *believes that the Jewish tradition has the resources to engage with the Holocaust without dramatic changes. Solomon writes as an Orthodox Rabbi and Fellow in Modern Jewish Thought at the Centre for Hebrew and Jewish Studies in Oxford England. For him, the Holocaust does not demand a new theology. He blames certain unhelpful tendencies in post-Enlightenment philosophy for these demands. Solomon points out that suffering has been a constant feature of life and therefore the Holocaust itself should not challenge belief in God. It is still* *possible to believe in an omnipotent, all-loving God. The focus for Judaism should continue to be faithfulness to the* mitzvot, *the commandments of God as revealed in Torah:*

If the Shoah does not itself demand a new theology, and the demands for new theologies made by post-Shoah theologians do not result in anything really new, why have so many of them felt impelled to distance themselves from traditional Jewish theologies of suffering? There are two reasons.

First, the traditional theologies of suffering *never were satisfactory*. In the words of the second-century rabbi Yannai, 'It is not in our power to explain either the prosperity of the wicked or the affliction of the righteous.' Yannai's words did not stop rabbis in his own or later generations speculating on the problem of evil. Indeed, though none of the answers is satisfactory, they may all *contribute*, if only a little, to the upholding of faith in the face of evil.

Second, the reason why non-orthodox Holocaust theologians reject 'traditional' answers may be something quite other than the intrinsic inadequacy of those answers. In section 7.2.2 it was stressed that the traditional interpretations of suffering depend heavily for such cogency as they may have on the belief in life after death and/or the transmigration of souls. Equally, they depend upon a belief in the inerrancy of scripture and in the authenticity of its rabbinic interpretation. These beliefs have been under attack in modern times for reasons which have *nothing to do with* the Shoah. Jews, like Christians, have been challenged by, for instance, modern biblical studies, which tend to undermine the traditional type of scriptural belief and demand a new kind of attitude to the authority of the Bible. Likewise, modern intellectual developments, such as the radical questioning of Cartesian dualism, have placed new strains on the concept of life after death. These changes have so weakened the traditional arguments justifying the ways of God with humankind that the Shoah has provided the *coup de grâce* to lead the modernist wing of Judaism to abandon traditional theodicy altogether.

Thus it is not that the Shoah poses a new challenge to theology, but rather that the Shoah came at a time when theology was already in a greater ferment than ever before in its history, a ferment occasioned by the intellectual movements of the modern world. This explains why earlier tragedies, such as the expulsion from Spain, occasioned not the abandonment but the development of traditional modes of response to suffering.

It is dangerously misleading for Holocaust theologians to base their challenge to traditional beliefs on the fact of the Shoah. The serious intellectual issues of faith in the modern world thereby become submerged in a deep emotional trauma which prevents them from being directly faced. The agenda for Jewish theologians ought to comprise not only the broad social issues which confront theologians of all faiths in contemporary society, but also the intellectual problems that lie at the root of theistic, revelation-based faith. It would be superficial to ignore the Shoah in these contexts, but to centralise it distorts the very framework of the Jewish faith.

It is a remarkable fact that, not withstanding a long and continuous tradition, from the Bible onwards, of a theology of suffering, and notwithstanding a history of martyrdom second to none, suffering has not in the past been the focus of Jewish theology. In rabbinic Judaism, certainly, the focus has consistently been God and his commandments. I submit that there is no reason for this to change even after the Shoah.

Is it otherwise for the historian, or for the politician whose first concern is 'to work for the abolition of that matrix of values that support genocide'? Even for them it is salutary to remain aware of similarities as well as dissimilarities between the Shoah and other events, for to ignore the similarities would be to fail to encompass the Shoah in human terms at all, to remove it from history and transform it into a supernatural event.

We may likewise ask whether there is a new and radical challenge to Christianity arising from the Shoah. Of course, there is the same challenge, on the level of 'explanation of suffering', as arises in Judaism—and for the same reason: the radical change of perspective of modern thought. But what of the special challenge (see section 7.2.8A) posed to Christians in view of their complicity in the Shoah, whether by preparation of the anti-Jewish ideology or by actually doing the work of the Nazis? Here, likewise—and this, if properly understood, is a terrifying thought—there is not a *new* problem for the Christian theologian. Those elements in traditional Christology which lie at the heart of this particular Christian failure have been there since New Testament times. The implications of supersessionism were *always* there to be faced. The Shoah may have concentrated the mind, but that is all. Yet this is a 'problem' which *can* be solved by people, for people formulate creeds and liturgies. And—again for reasons which have less to do with the Shoah than with the ability for self-criticism achieved by the Church in modern times, and by the Roman Catholic Church notably since Vatican II—it has at last become possible for the Church to face up to this inglorious aspect of its heritage.

A church which has the courage to question its own past is one with which it is a privilege to engage in dialogue. But only time and consistency will alleviate the age-old fears and mistrust which culminated in the terrifying eruption of the Shoah into history.

[Norman Solomon, *Judaism and World Religion*, Macmillan, 1991, pp. 198–200].

GOD'S PAIN, OUR PAIN

In the next three extracts we move into Christian responses to the Holocaust. These responses tend to question the nature of God and move towards a rejection of an all-powerful Being. The first extract is significant because it is written from a German Christian perspective. In it **Dorothee Sölle**, *a German theologian, questions the traditional Christian formulation of God as an omnipotent, all-loving, and intelligent Being. She succinctly summarizes why each of these attributes cannot logically be combined in the Godhead. For her, ultimately God can be conceived of as all-loving, but not all-powerful. Belief in God after Auschwitz is credible only if God is on the side of the victims and experiences their pain. The only valid response is to see our pain as God's pain:*

In a relatively short period of the history of Western philosophy, the proponents of theodicy have attempted to reconcile three qualities of God: omnipotence, love, and intelligibility. The result of the debate can be summarized in that only two of these three theologumena are conceivable at any one time, while the remaining one must always be excluded.

The first position is that God is omnipotent and intelligible. God stands, metaphorically speaking, at the head of the universe as the great disposer, the organizer, the one who is really responsible; as the one who can step in and end the torment of humankind, assuming, of course, that God wishes to. In this context we often speak of the suffering of the innocent, of children, for example, who are tortured. But in a deeper sense all people are innocent. No one deserves to starve and of the six million gassed, not one of them ever, even a liar or thief, 'deserved' the suffering that was inflicted on them.

An omnipotent God, who imposes suffering, who benignly looks down on Auschwitz from above, must be a sadist. That kind of God stands on the side of the victors, and is, in the words of a black American theologian, 'a white racist'. This is the position of Satan in Wiesel's play: he always appears where murder is committed. He is the advocate of submission. His God is pure power. And a theology that conceives of such a supreme ruler, organizer, responsible provoker and creator, reflects the sadism of those who invented it.

The second position conceives of God indeed as omnipotent and all-loving, but at the same time as unintelligible God eludes us. Belief in God becomes absurd or, at best, a paradox. 'I lost my belief in God at Verdum' is a well-known expression of mass atheism. If God has become completely unintelligible, God can no longer be held fast to in the long term, even in paradoxical belief.

What does this tenet from the First World War mean for the things that happened after? I suspect that after Auschwitz, from the point of view of the Germans (for whom I alone can speak here), nothing like this was said, not only because God had long been forgotten, but also because the element of guilt, even if not confessed to, makes the innocence of the first tenet impossible. In view of the Holocaust I cannot talk simply of 'losing' God: chance participation compels one to other forms of speaking of God and must thus lead beyond the omnipotent all-loving God.

The third position conceives of a God of love, but not as omnipotent. Between the victors and the victims, God is credible only if God is on the side of the victims, if God is capable of suffering. This position is represented today by such different Jewish philosophers as Elie Wiesel, Abraham Heschel, and Hans Jonas, but also by a popular theologian such as Rabbi Kuschner. On the Christian side I can name, above all, Dietrich Bonhoeffer, who became increasingly close to the suffering God while in prison. I can also mention litigation theology, which articulates God's indigence and growth, and I can mention the theology of liberation, both in its Latin American and in its feminist forms.

In the following I wish to think of the suffering godhead, which is the only possible response to the question of the suffering of the innocent. I do not wish to respond to the question of theodicy, but to show it to be a false question. The religious question of suffering is no longer the one so often heard: How can God permit that?, but a more difficult one, which first has to be studied: How does our pain become God's pain and how does God's pain appear in our pain? In speaking of 'God's pain', I am liberating myself from the compulsory concepts of the patriarchs: God as dictator, God at the head of hierarchical thought, God as omnipotent—I find these theological notions of the patriarchs distasteful and despicable. And an unchanging, eternal God, who is utterly self-sufficient and beyond need and vulnerability cannot, or, at least, can only cynically, answer the question of human suffering. Such a God must be prosecuted and our desire to defend God disappears. Under the spiritual terms of the patriarchs, under the theology of the omnipotent God, the argument about theodicy is still the best that can emerge. In attempting to introduce God's pain, I am setting this false concept right. I am not speaking of anything that God could avoid or abolish. When we speak of the pain of God, then we no longer see God in a purely masculine presentation. God is then our mother who cries about what we do to each other and about what we brothers and sisters do to animals and plants. God consoles us as a mother does, she cannot wave away pain magically (although that occasionally happens!), but she holds us on her lap, sometimes until we stand up again, our strength renewed, sometimes in a darkness without light. To call this darkness the 'darkness of God', to be able to call it this, is the real difficulty of a theological discussion after the Holocaust: not to yield this darkness to an anti-God, to a different, dualistically opposed, principle, that is *the* challenge of theology after Auschwitz.

God cannot comfort us if she were not bound to us in pain, if she did not have this wonderful and exceptional ability to feel the pain of another in her own body, suffering with us, existing with us.

[Dorothee Sölle, 'God's Pain and Our Pain' in Judaism, *Christianity and Liberation*, edited by Otto Maduro, Orbis, 1991, pp. 112–114]

GOD'S SELF-GIVING LOVE

*In a similar vein the Anglican theologian **Marcus Braybrooke** argues that belief in God is only credible if God shares our pain. His thinking is part of the movement within Christianity called 'Process Theology'. Process Theology represents a movement away from belief in an all-powerful God to a God whose power is limited by human freewill. Marcus Braybrooke links the idea of a suffering God to the resurrection of Jesus. In this extract he argues that Jesus' death and resurrection is God's vindication of self-giving love. This is how the resurrection can be understood within the context of Christian-Jewish dialogue:*

When he refers to the death of Jesus, John uses the term 'being glorified' and he uses the deliberately ambiguous term 'being lifted up'—this refers both to his being lifted up on the wooden cross and being exalted to God's right hand. The Resurrection then is a way of affirming that sacrificial love embodied in Jesus victorious—it is stronger than evil and death.

This understanding links with the profound effect that thinking about the Shoah or Holocaust has had on my picture of God. If God has a reserve of power, why did he not use it? So many of our hymns apply earthly concepts of power and majesty to God: but if these are our pictures of God, no wonder we feel betrayed by God in moments of agony. For God is not a heavenly magician to rescue us from the consequences of selfishness and sin. Human cruelty breeds suffering and violence. God in his gift of freedom puts the world into our hands. He identifies with those who suffer. His power is the appeal of suffering love, as Canon Vanstone suggested in his moving book, *Love's Endeavour, Love's Expense.*

> Therefore He who Thee reveals
> Hangs, O Father, on that tree
> Helpless; and the nails and thorns
> Tell of what thy love must be.
> Thou art God: no monarch Thou
> Thron'd in easy state to reign.
> Thou art God, whose arms of love
> Aching, spent, the world sustain.

And the Jewish philosopher, Hans Jonas, speaks of the gassed and burnt children of the concentration camps. I like to believe that there was weeping in the heights at the waste and despoilment of humanity. Should we not believe that the immense chorus of such cries that has risen up in our lifetime now hangs over our world...And if not their shadow, certainly the shadow of the Bomb is there to remind us that the image of God is in danger as never before...We hold in our hands the future of the divine adventure and must not fail him, even if we would fail ourselves. God's power is the appeal of the suffering victim to the conscience of the world. Therefore for me, to believe in Jesus is to be overwhelmed by his suffering love for me, to be aware of my share in the world's evil and to identify with Jesus' way of self-giving love. To say Jesus is risen is to affirm that his way of self-giving love is victorious and of the nature of reality. But this is a hope not a certainty—at least in terms of outward proof. To believe in the Resurrection is always an affirmation of faith in the way of Christ despite the evidence of the world's evil, not an arrogant assertion that we belong to a privileged group.

[Marcus Braybrooke, 'The Resurrection in Christian–Jewish Dialogue', in *Common Ground*, 1991, no 1, pp. 28.]

Both Sölle and Braybrooke stress a changed idea of God. **Richard Harries**, *Bishop of Oxford in England, is much more traditional. The following extract has been taken from a dialogue group of Jews and Christians called the Manor House Group. The discoveries and challenges have been written up in a book entitled* Dialogue With a Difference. *Bishop Richard Harries is responding to two articles in that book—one Christian (Marcus Braybrooke) and one Jewish (Colin Eimer) that focus on God suffering with the victims. In contrast, Richard Harries argues that God is not powerless but has the power to create and to bring his creation to its ultimate fulfilment:*

Ivan Karamazov did not think God was justified in creating the world, even though an ultimate harmony might be achieved, if children had to suffer in the process. If that final redemption is brought about by a divine incarnation which has as one of its unintended consequences the teaching of contempt by the Christian church, and a Christian Europe which failed to prevent the Shoah, Ivan Karamazov's point applies with new force both to the creation and the incarnation.

Secondly, continuing Jewish faith in God both in and after the Holocaust is a most powerful witness. Despite the horrendous suffering, despite the elimination of virtually all Jewish life in Germany and so much of Eastern Europe, many Jewish people continue to affirm the existence of the Holy One and work in many practical ways for the realization of his kingdom.

The problem of theodicy is posed by the fact that life is such an inextricable mixture of happiness and misery. If life were entirely a burden, the problem of theodicy would not arise. We would know it was the product of an evil or indifferent power. It is because (at least for some of the time) we experience life as a blessing and want to give thanks to a good creator that the evil we see around us appears as such a contradiction of what we otherwise know. The questions that lie behind traditional theodicy, far from being misconceived, take on, in the light of the Shoah, a new intensity for Christians. The evil we have to face is not just an evil permitted by God but one that came into the world in the wake of Christ's Incarnation. The faith we have to go on is not just our own but that of the Jewish people, who despite everything continue to bless God for their creation.

It is clear that in their respective responses to the problem of evil, Jews and Christians will want to say many of the same things, even though sometimes in different language. Christians talk about God's will to create beings with genuine free choice and the limitations this imposes on what God can do without contradicting his fundamental purpose. The Jewish mystical tradition suggests that God could only make space for human beings by a voluntary withdrawal. Within the all-embracing cape of his presence he makes a small space where he is not, in order that human beings might be with a life of their own. So as Colin Eimer rightly says, God watches over us in pain and anguish as we his loved children damage ourselves and one another. But God cannot simply bale us out when things go wrong. 'Like the earthly parent, all he can do is suffer in silence and be there—accessible to his beloved children should they wish to come to him.' Yet God does do more than this. He is ceaselessly active, seeking to draw good out of evil and inviting us to co-operate with him in the task. He does not do this in a remote and distanced manner but, through his spirit, from within the flux of human events. For he is with us and for us, striving in our striving, suffering in our suffering.

It is the nature of love to enter into and share the suffering of others. With Marcus's emphasis on this, every Christian will agree. One of the valuable insights that has come to me out of my membership of the Manor House Group is the awareness of how much this understanding of God is also present within the Jewish tradition. The question arises, however, whether it is adequate to talk about 'the power of suffering love' without further analysis of the kind of power that quite properly belongs to God as God.

Power is the capacity to achieve certain goals. We all have a certain power as human beings or else we would simply drop down and die. We can use that power in loving or unloving ways, but we cannot escape the fact that we have power. It is a mistake to think of God as being totally powerless. God has all the power that belongs to God as God. He has the power to create *ex nihilo*. He also has the power to recreate. He has the power to work in and through his creation to bring all things to their appointed end. God pours himself into his creation, as W. H. Vanstone's book so movingly explores, but God's reserves of himself are inexhaustible. He ceaselessly works, at every point in the universe, for the fulfilment of his purpose by drawing good out of evil. In short, God is not, in the philosopher A.N.Whitehead's phrase, simply the fellow sufferer who understands. He is God the creator, who, at terrible risk, brings this world into being but who does so with a reasonable hope of bringing it to a successful outcome, that is, the growth, spiritual development and eternal fulfilment of his creatures. Otherwise, creation would have been a totally irresponsible act. It is a wounded surgeon who plies the steel, as T.S.Eliot so vividly put it. But a surgeon is more than someone who shares our suffering. He takes action for our good.

[Richard Harries, 'Theodicy Will not Go Away' in *Dialogue With a Difference* edited by Tony Bayfield and Marcus Braybrooke, SCM Press, 1992, pp. 106–107]

'WHERE WAS MAN AT AUSCHWITZ?'

The extracts so far have all concentrated on the nature of God and where God was during this suffering. A further question remains, and one which continues to be raised in the dialogue: 'Where was the Church in Auschwitz?' Why did the majority of Christians, apart from a few individuals, not resist the Nazis? There is an increasing recognition that the issue of bystanders and rescuers should become an urgent topic for discussion in the dialogue. Why are some people bystanders whilst others risk their lives as rescuers? **Lord Jakobovits**, *the former Chief Rabbi of Great Britain and the Commonwealth, raises this key question in an address at Wawel Castle, Cracow in January 1995: 'Where was Man at Auschwitz?'*

When I am asked, Where was God at Auschwitz?, I too have no answer. Perhaps there is none. Indeed, infinity of suffering cannot be multiplied, whether it affects six million, or one million, or a single innocent life. Every time an infant's life perishes in a cot-death, turning young parents into mourners, the same question arises: "Where was God?"

Maybe the question is inscrutable—in the words of one of our great medieval philosophers: If I knew him, I would be Him; or, if I could comprehend Divine justice, I would myself be Divine.

The real question is: 'Where was Man at Auschwitz?' Where was the humanity of a cultured nation mesmerised by a rabble-rouser, to turn into millions of mass-murderers and their accomplices? Where was Man when numerous civilised nations remained silent and closed their borders to those fleeing from fiendish persecution? Where were the leaders of great faiths when the cries of the tormented evoked no response? Where was Man when millions were shipped here in cattle trucks for the crime of being born as Jews?

Auschwitz has been liberated from the Nazi barbarians. But the world has not yet been completely liberated from Auschwitz. When neo-fascists can still form powerful parties in countries like Russia and Italy, when Nazi propaganda can still be freely disseminated in many parts of the world, and when the cloak of respectability can be claimed by fake historians who deny that the Holocaust ever took place, we have the ultimate evidence that, fifty years on, the legacy of Auschwitz—city of death—is itself not yet dead. If Auschwitz never existed, where—I ask—are my aunts and uncles, my cousins and numerous other relatives, together with most of my teachers and classmates who were deported there?

[Lord Jakobovits, 'Where was Man at Auschwitz?', an address delivered at the meeting between President Lech Walesa of Poland and Heads of Delegations at Wawel Castle, Cracow, 26 January 1995]

COULD IT HAVE BEEN DIFFERENT?

Linked with the question of human responsibility the following extract was provoked by the visit of an English Catholic to Yad Vashem, the Holocaust Memorial Museum in Jerusalem. David Hill (1959–1995), one of the founders of the Exeter and Southwest Council of Christians and Jews in England, asks about human responsibility, but also raises the gender issue:

Because I had seen so much of the horror of the Holocaust vividly displayed in books and film, I was not too shocked by what I saw. Instead I found myself frightened by what humans are capable of. It is also good to remember that it is Men who masterminded it: would it have been the same were women involved in politics at the time?

[David Hill, 'An Annotated Description and Personal Experience of the CCJ Young Adults Israel Study Tour 18–29 July 1993', p. 40, unpublished work]

THE HOLOCAUST AS AN ORIENTATING EVENT FOR CHRISTIANITY

The Holocaust does not merely raise questions about traditional belief in God or the nature of humanity. It has far-reaching theological challenges for Christianity. There are profound lessons which need to be incorporated into Christian history and theology—not least the granting of theological space for the continued existence of Judaism. **Michael McGarry**, *a Catholic theologian, succinctly summarizes four key theological implications for the churches:*

That Christians survived the holocaust is clear; they were not its primary victims. Indeed, too often they were among its perpetrators or bystanders. But after the holocaust, how are Christians with integrity to survive as a blessing for the nations and for the nation of Israel? In other words, how is the holocaust relevant to a fully mature, divinely-willed *surviving Christianity* moving into the twenty-first century? We suggest that the holocaust's world-shaking dimensions move Christian self-understanding in four critical directions.

First, the holocaust is not only a part of Jewish history, but more importantly a part of Christian history. The holocaust is 'an orienting event' in their own self-understanding of what it means to be faithful to God today. From now on, in the post-Auschwitz age, Christian history must include as a significant chapter the experience of the holocaust.

Second, Christians are beginning to recognize that, every bit as much as the holocaust raises theological concerns for Jews, so does it for them. These concerns include the haunting, indeed terror-filled question: What kind of God can we believe in after Auschwitz? From that fundamental question, others come tumbling after: What can prayer mean when children are tossed into burning ovens? Can any post-Auschwitz spirituality be credible that does not take history seriously? What does the Christian gathering around the table of worship mean when it could be—and was—celebrated in the midst of Nazi Germany? And since the Jews have survived, what is the Christian to make of this revelation that God wants the Jews to survive as Jews? And if the Jews are to survive as Jews, what implications has this for the age-old Christian efforts to convert them to Christianity? Here one can see the surface is only being scratched by the *theological* relevance of the holocaust for Christian survival.

Third, Christian survival with integrity means to take with some seriousness the *ethical* implications of the holocaust. That is, what is one to make of the behavior that so few Christians saved their Jewish brothers and sisters in their time of need? What is one to say about courage, about stepping out from the crowd to stop the evil onslaught of Nazism? Somehow Christian survival requires that we carefully look at the experience of the rescuers so that Christians might know how to live with more integrity in the future.

Finally, the holocaust raises for the church its very meaning, the very *definition* of the church in God's plan of salvation. No longer can Christians simply mouth triumphal clichés about God's preferential choice of Christians to the exclusion of Jews (or of other religious traditions for that matter). Many Christians are asking, in this post-holocaust world, 'Can we ever be the same, can we ever understand ourselves in the same way with the same theological, ethical, and historical constructs? Who are we really, after the holocaust?' With some humility, Christians are concluding that their survival with integrity requires that a self-definition reached only in dialogue with their Jewish brothers and sisters can meet the requirements of a post-Auschwitz church.

If the meaning and purpose of Christian survival after the holocaust raises the relevance of the holocaust in historical, ethical, theological, and definitional terms for the Christian, it also leaves the survival of the Christian people with a mandate strikingly similar to that of Jewish survival: that is, 'never again!' As they come to recognize that their own definition must be worked out in dialogue with their Jewish brothers and sisters, Christians also recognize that their ultimate fate is tied inextricably to the fate of their Jewish brothers and sisters. That is, post-holocaust Christian survival entails a divine mandate. That is, God has declared, through the catastrophe, that Jews are to survive *as Jews*. It falls to the Christians, therefore, to help carry out God's will by protecting the original people of God, especially where Jews may be threatened by prejudice, marginalization, and oppression. Most assuredly, Christians under the commanding voice of 'never again!' cannot allow their becoming oppressors again, but also in the post-Auschwitz world they cannot tolerate being bystanders when others may threaten the existence and well-being of the original people of God.

[Michael McGarry, 'The Holocaust' in *Introduction to Jewish–Christian Relations*, edited by Michael Shermis and Arthur Zannoni, Paulist Press, 1991, pp.78–79]

FEAR FOR THE FUTURE

*To conclude this chapter, we turn to the future. **Elie Wiesel**, a well-known writer on his experiences as a survivor of the Holocaust, admits that he fears for the future. When he sees the rise of neo-Nazi groups, the desecration of Jewish cemetries, and the Revisionist denial of the Holocaust he is not hopeful. For him, that which was once thought to be unrepeatable could happen again. Has humanity learned the lessons of the Holocaust?*

Perhaps it would be best not to admit publicly: I feel threatened. I am afraid. For the first time in many years I fear the nightmare may be starting all over again. Perhaps it never ended. We may have lived, since the Liberation, a period between parentheses. And now they are closed again.

Is another Holocaust possible? I often asked my students that question. Most answered yes; I said no. By its dimensions, its scope, the Holocaust was a unique event; it will remain so. I explained to them that the world has learned a lesson, that hate and murder transcend those who take part in them directly: one begins by killing others only to massacre one's own in the end. The annihilation of a people leads inevitably to the annihilation of mankind.

Oh yes, so naive was I that I thought—especially during the early postwar years—that Jews would never again be slandered, isolated, handed over to the enemy. Anti-Semitism, I thought, had died under a sky of ashes somewhere in Poland; we had nothing more to fear; the world would never again be insensitive to our anguish. I was convinced that, paradoxically, men of today and men of tomorrow would be protected by the terrifying mystery of the concentration-camp phenomenon.

I was wrong. What happened could happen again. I may be exaggerating. I may be too sensitive. After all, I do belong to a traumatized generation. We have learned to believe threats more than promises. The disquieting signs are proliferating. The sickening spectacle of an enthralled international assembly celebrating a spokesman for terror. The speeches, the votes against Israel. The dramatic loneliness of this universal people. An Arab king presents his guests with deluxe editions of the infamous Protocols of Zion. The desecrated cemeteries in France and in Germany. The campaigns in the Soviet press. The recent *Retro* wave—a trend among writers, movie-makers and others toward retrospective 'evaluation' of events surrounding World War II—that vulgarizes the experience. The anti-Zionist, anti-Jewish pamphlets that distort our hopes. One must be blind not to recognize it: hate of the Jew has once more become fashionable.

Nothing surprising, then, that in so many places Jewish existence is in jeopardy again. In October 1973, while the Israeli army was experiencing grave, almost fatal reverses, Western Europe, with only rare exceptions, refused its help and, much worse, attempted to sabotage America's aid. Europe gave free hand to the aggressors, accepting in advance Israel's certain defeat, that is to say, its probable liquidation. And now? Will this people, so young and yet so old, survive the next attack, and at what cost? How many times will Israel be called upon to sacrifice the best among its children? How long can a community of men live in a state of seige, inside a hostile environment? Is a posthumous victory for Hitler conceivable?

For those of us who have lived the human and Jewish condition to its ultimate depths, there can be no doubt: at this point in history the Jewish people and the Jewish state are irrevocably linked; one could not survive without the other. We have rarely been as united. And as alone.

And so the notion of a new collective catastrophe no longer seems preposterous. We already know that as far as we are concerned, the impossible is possible. When it comes to Jewish history, there is nothing unthinkable.

I say this reluctantly and for the first time. I have always placed the Holocaust on a mystical level, beyond human understanding. I have quarreled with friends for making certain easy analogies and comparisons in that domain. The concentration-camp phenomenon eludes the philosophers as much as it does the novelists, and it may not be dealt with lightly. I speak of it now, in connection with the present, only because Jewish destiny has once again become subject to discussion.

That is why I am afraid. Images from the past rise up and cloud current events. Blackmail in some quarters, abdication in others. Overt threats, hidden complicities. Friends who suddenly declare their neutrality. Neutrals whose hostility becomes apparent. The enemy who becomes ever more powerful and ever more attractive. If allowed to have his way—and he is—he will become the god of our cursed age, demanding—and obtaining—the future of a people as a sacrifice.

Not that I foresee a situation where Jews would be massacred in the cities of America or the forests of Europe. Not that another universe of barbed wire will be built or new death factories erected, but the pattern is emerging. One does not speak of genocide; one envisages the end of Israel. That is enough to justify my fear. I feel what my father must have felt when he was my age. Thus, for us nothing has changed. The world is indifferent to our death as, in fact, it is to its own. It has forgotten too soon.

I look at my students, and I tremble for their future. I see myself at their age on a continent in ruins. And I do not know what to tell them.

I should like to be able to convince them that in spite of the official slogans, in spite of appearances, our people has friends and allies. I should like to be able to tell them that in spite of the accumulated disappoint-ments and betrayals, they must maintain their faith in man, that in spite of everything, there are reasons for hope. But I have never lied to them, and I shall not start now. And yet…

Despair is not the solution, I know that well. But then, what is the solution? Hitler proposed one. He wanted it to be final, and he was well on his way toward accomplishing his goal while, near and far, God and humankind turned away their gaze.

I remember. And I am afraid.

[Elie Wiesel, 'Why I am Afraid', in *Overcoming Fear Between Jews and Christians*, edited by James Charlesworth, Crossroad, 1993, pp. 7–9]

*In a similar vein to Elie Wiesel, **George Carey**, Archbishop of Canterbury in England since March 1991 and co-President of The Council of Christians and Jews, expresses his concern for the future. The rise of religious intolerance and anti-semitism in Europe is again sounding alarm-bells through the Jewish community, but it ought also to have an impact on the Christian communities. The pile of children's shoes at Yad Vashem is a vivid reminder of our inhuman-ity to others. Are the lessons of the Holocaust too easily forgotten?*

Let us not be self-congratulatory. Much has been achieved in fifty years. But intolerance, anti-semitism, xenophobia and downright jeal-ousy and envy still haunt the face of Europe. Already, refugees in Germany have encountered violence, hatred, even death. Here, in Great Britain, we have seen synagogues daubed with anti-semitic slogans, cemeteries vandalised and Jews vilified by extremists. There is a brittleness in our security which means we must be ever vigilant—and even-handed too. To claim human rights for oneself means acknowledging human rights for others, and not only in one's own country. It means that, as a Christian leader, I will support Israel's right to self-determination, freedom and peace in its own land, but would still argue that the arrangements for those rights should not deny the same rights for others who live there too. CCJ is committed to peace in the Middle East so that Jews, Muslims, and Christians may live together in harmony, justice, and integrity.

There is still much to be done. True friendship based on recognition of our common roots will also recognise important differences. It does not mean ignoring distinction in the wishy-washy goo of a careless tolerance. Integrity of faith is crucial. In my Enthronement Address last year, I made the point that my Christian faith is so important to me that I am compelled to speak of it to others. That's why Christianity is a missionary religion. But it is not a religion deaf or insensitive to the faith of others. Genuine sharing of faith respects others, listens to them, engages in dialogue, and is tolerant and generous. We must expect to be open to change ourselves if we hope ever to change the convictions of others. Too often our world is in conflict because people fail to listen to each other, and refuse to be changed by such encounters. Genuine tolerance involves entering into the pain and differences of others and offers to the others the freedom it insists on for itself.

In one of his sermons, Paul Tillich tells the story of a Jewish gravedigger in a concentration camp who was only allowed to live because he buried the bodies of fellow Jews after they had been shot. One day, fifty Jews were paraded by the side of a huge pit and shot. One by one, their bodies fell down the slope. The soldiers marched away. The gravedigger began his terrible chore, praying as he did so. A whimpering sound was heard. He came across the body of a Jewish girl, mortally wounded, who was giving birth to a baby boy. The child was delivered and the young mother died. With tears streaming down his face, the gravedigger cried, 'It must be the Messiah. Only the Messiah could be born at a time like this.' The story has meaning for both our traditions. The link between the Messiah and the suffering, the link between the Messiah and human destiny. But perhaps that little child was to suffer the same fate as the thousands and thousands of other children who died in the Holocaust and whose tiny shoes remain in Yad Vashem, a silent reproach to man's inhumanity to man. Our concern must be for the generations to come, that they will learn the lessons that we are finding today all too easy to forget.

[Archbishop George Carey, 'Tiny Shoes' in *Common Ground*, 1991, no 1, pp. 9]

FURTHER READING

Berenbaum, Michael. *After Tragedy and Triumph*, Cambridge University Press, 1990.

Cohen, Arthur (edited). *Arguments and Doctrines: A Reader of Jewish Thinking in the Aftermath of the Holocaust*, Harper and Row, 1970.

Cohn-Sherbok, Dan. *Holocaust Theology*, Lamp Press, 1989.

Eckardt, Alice & Eckardt, Roy. *Long Night's Journey Into Day: A Revised Retrospective on the Holocaust*, Pergamon, 1988.

Ecclestone, Alan. *The Night Sky of the Lord*, Darton, Longman & Todd, 1980.

Fackenheim, Emil. *To Mend the World: Foundations of Future Jewish Thought*, Schocken, 1982.

Friedlander, Albert (edited). *Out of the Whirlwind*, Schocken, 1976.

Haynes, Stephen. *Prospects for Post-Holocaust Theology*, Scholars Press, 1991.

Peck, Abraham (edited). *Jews and Christians After the Holocaust*, Fortress, 1982.

Rausch, David. A Legacy of Hatred: *Why Christians Must Not Forget the Holocaust*, Moody, 1984.

Wiesel, Elie. *Night*, Farrar Straus & Giroux, 1960.

CHAPTER FOUR

MISSION

CHAPTER FOUR

MISSION

The word 'mission' rings alarms bells throughout the Jewish community and it is probably the most sensitive area in the Christian–Jewish dialogue. The Council of Christians and Jews, for example, has often found that Jews object to the setting up of a new branch in their area because they fear that the Christians will use it as a tool for missionary activity. There are occasions when this has unfortunately happened because some Christians have misunderstood the nature of dialogue.

There are several reasons for the Jewish fear of missionary activity. The history of Christian treatment of Jews has taught Jews to be very suspicious of any close contact with Christians. For centuries the Church taught that Christianity had replaced Judaism as the true heir to the biblical promises. In rejecting Christ, Jews were seen as blind, ignorant, and even incarnations of the devil. The official Church teaching proclaimed *extra ecclesiam nulla salus*—no salvation outside the Church. This led to an active missionary outreach to Jews (as well as others), eventually culminating in periods of forced conversions, forced baptisms, and a general persecution of Jews. Although there were periods of constructive calm between the two communities, on the whole Christians found affirming the existence of Judaism very difficult. The history of Christian–Jewish relations has been dogged by the Church's understanding of its 'mission'.

In contemporary times, as we will see, the Church's understanding of her mission remains somewhat ambiguous. This means that a degree of suspicion still remains amongst Jews. Has the Church really given up its desire to convert Jews? Do Christians in the end ultimately hope that from the dialogue the Jew will come to belief in Christ? Can Judaism not exist without reference to Christ? These are some of the underlying questions which are raised in many Jewish minds when they meet Christians today. This is not surprising given the degree of missionary activity which continues to be directed specifically at Jewish communities by certain Christian groups. There is by no means a uniform approach to mission and dialogue within Christianity. For many Christians there is still puzzlement over the non-acceptance by Jews of Christianity. Some Christians are involved in the dialogue and do not wish to convert Jews. They understand the Church's mission to be a general mandate to make the world fit for the kingdom of God. Some, like George Carey the Archbishop of Canterbury in England, simply believe that Christians and Jews should both witness to the truth of their own traditions and in openness and love allow the truth to emerge. Others, such as Revd Marcus Braybrooke, feel that mission should concentrate on those with no faith at all or a lapsed faith. Alternatively some, like the theologian Hans Küng, stress the ethical mandate.

One of the most positive and important results of the dialogue is often a greater understanding of why the Jew cannot, and does not, accept Jesus and Christian faith. This has led to a reappraisal amongst some Christians and in some churches of how it is to understand its mission. It has also enabled Jews to appreciate that they can have a new relationship with Christians with no hidden missionary agenda.

H.P.F.

JEWISH UNDERSTANDINGS OF MISSION

Jews do not set out to convert Christians. Instead Jewish mission is based on witness rather than seeking converts. The purpose of Judaism is to live out the ethical and spiritual teachings of Torah and thereby witness to the One God. Torah must be embodied in the life of every Jew. It is a matter of living out the covenantal relationship with God. In the first extract **Tony Bayfield***, director of the Reform Synagogues of Great Britain, highlights the link between mission and Covenant. Although it is written from a Reform perspective, it would be recognized as the traditional Jewish understanding of mission and election. The purpose of Israel's election was that through her, all the people of the earth would be blessed (Gen. 12:3). It is absolutely clear that she has done nothing to deserve this election. There is no worthiness on the part of Israel to justify being chosen. It was an act of grace on the part of God and Israel said 'yes' to the Divine call. There is a further dimension to Jewish witness— witness to the Gentile world means the radiating of blessing and enlightenment*

78

to all nations without the requirement to take on specifically Jewish ways of approaching God. Judaism does accept converts but does not actively seek them. The requirements for conversion, particularly in certain strands of Orthodox Judaism, are very strict. This is partly because it is not necessary to become Jewish to 'have a share in the world to come'. What then is the purpose of being Jewish? What is the Jewish mission?:

What is Judaism for? What is the purpose of being Jewish and remaining as such? Let me suggest this. There cannot, of course, be one answer, reflective of countless people from many generations, living in a diversity of lands and cultures. But nevertheless, I am going to risk a generalisation. The Encyclopedia Judaica referred me to the article on Chosen People. And any discussion on Chosen People is likely to refer at some point to the blessing recited before reading from the Torah. The blessing includes the words 'Who has chosen us from among all people and given us Torah'. There is a familiar gloss which reads that phrase as 'Who has chosen us from among all people *by giving us* the Torah'. In other words, Jewish chosenness and mission have to do with Covenant and fidelity to Torah. The Jewish purpose in life is to live out the spiritual and ethical paradigm that the Torah frames and teaches. Judaism is about accepting the yoke of the commandments, about faithfulness to the terms of the Covenant—a role which can be fulfilled perfectly well without recourse to mass conversion. Of course it does not preclude converts but neither does it require them.

However, I would not want to leave the Jewish mission statement there. I want also to refer to the famous passage in Genesis where the promise is made to Abraham: 'And in you and your descendants shall all the families of the earth find a blessing'. Which in turn makes it, I believe, legitimate—and not merely homage to nineteenth-century Reform Judaism—to refer also to the equally famous prophetic phrase about being a 'light to the nations'. The fidelity is not merely a fidelity for its own sake but should radiate blessing and enlightenment far beyond the family of Israel. Mission has this added dimension.

[Tony Bayfield, 'Mission—A Jewish Perspective' in *Theology*, May/June 1993, pp. 181–182]

Martin Cohen, *a professor of Jewish history in the United States, shares some of Bayfield's ideas. Cohen suggests that the mission of Israel is clearly linked to Israel as community. Israel as a people and a community has an obligation to live out a certain ethical life. As in Isaiah 42, she has been chosen for that* *specific task. This does not mean that she is holier than any other people. God is still the God of all nations. The difference is that Israel's relationship is a particular one with a particular mission. This does not exclude the universal work of God through other nations:*

In the tradition of Judaism, the word 'Israel' bears three simultaneous meanings. It denotes the individual Jew (who in our sacred writings is designated not a Yehudi but a Yisrael), our faith-community and our Holy Land. The individual Jew is the terrestrial source of our faith, the people its corporate embodiment, and the land its millennial nourishment and hope. The subject of the mission of Israel is the faith-community, or, as it is usually called, the Jewish people. Israel the people possesses a distinctive characteristic and bears a special obligation. The characteristic is called the election of Israel; more popularly it is referred to as Israel's chosenness or its status as the Chosen People. The obligation is its mission. Election and mission constitute the inseparable obverse and reverse of the same theological coin.

According to Jewish tradition, Israel's mission is pragmatic and verifiable. Its content is ethical, its orientation societal, its teleology universal. The classical expression of this mission still remains the opening words of the forty-second chapter of the Book of Isaiah:

> He shall make the right to go forth to the nations...
> I the Lord have called thee in righteousness,
> And have taken hold of thy hand,
> And kept thee, and set thee for a covenant of the people,
> For a light unto the nations,
> To open the blind eyes,
> To bring out the prisoners from the dungeon,
> And them that sit in darkness out of the prison house.

Through the ages the concepts of Israel's chosenness and mission have remained central to its theology. Without both, the distinctive dimensions of other theological affirmations in Judaism, including revelation, the covenant, the messianic age and even God, are immeasurably compromised. Until our own times these concepts have occupied a central place in the various orders of Jewish prayer.

[Martin Cohen, 'The Mission of Israel After Auschwitz' in *Issues in the Jewish-Christian Dialogue: Jewish Perspectives on Covenant, Mission, and Witness,* edited by Helga Croner and Leon Klenicki, Paulist Press, 1979, pp. 160–161]

WITNESS TO THE ONE GOD

This stress on 'witness' as the key to Jewish mission in the world is shared right across the spectrum of Judaism. **Pinchas Peli's** *contribution to this chapter is important because he writes from an Orthodox perspective. He analyses the literary meaning of 'mission' as drawn out of two Hebrew words:* Shema *and* ehad. *He is using the technique of midrash. The interpretation here would be one that many Jews would recognize as a traditional understanding of 'mission':*

When you note that the rabbis say in the Talmud: when you write the verse of the Shema on the Torah scroll, on the parchment, there are two letters that you have to write larger: the *ayin* of Shema and the *daleth* of *ehad*. The last letter of the first word and the last letter of the last word make up, according to the rabbis, one Hebrew word, *ed*. *Ed* means a witness. Israel, by its very being, is a witness or, if you wish, a martyr to these three aspects of God as Creator—meaning someone who cares for his creation, who joins with his Creator, someone who does not leave his Creation alone—*hamechadesh b'chol yom ma'assei bereshith*, who, renews everyday the acts of creation. Israel also fulfils the role of Teacher and keeps alive the dimension of God as Redeemer.

[Pinhas Peli 'Hear O Israel: Witness to the One God' in *SIDIC*, vol XVI, no 2, 1983, p. 7]

RESPECT FOR 'THE OTHER'

Witness, then, does not require conversion. Other people are not expected to join Judaism. Christians and Muslims seem to find this attitude harder to accept. **Daniel Polish,** *in a stimulating extract that examines the presuppositions of the dialogue relationship, argues that a conversionary approach to 'the other' presupposes that their faith is inferior and inadequate. For Jews this is not the appropriate way to view adherents of other traditions.*

Jews have been content for Christians and Muslims to have the benefit of faith in the one God and the relationship with the one God without having to do so in particular Jewish forms. Jewish reticence in these areas rests upon a respect for the authenticity of the monotheism of the peoples among whom we live. We feel that their faith, rather than demanding witness from us, itself testifies to the effectivenes with which we have carried the recognition of the oneness of God into the world.

The converse, it must be recognized, implies that Jews, too, be freed of the importunings to adopt the accidents of other traditions. Jews wish to be allowed to preserve their faith in the one God through the forms and in the manner peculiar to them. No doubt it may be harder for Christians—and perhaps, to a lesser extent, Muslims—to accept the possibility of faith without the particular accidents of that tradition. But an appreciation of the essential monotheism represented in Judaism may ultimately make such acceptance possible. The recognition would carry with it the corollary that no conversionary outreach to Jews was necessary, nor even warranted.

To regard the subject of this discussion from a slightly different angle of vision, the act of mounting a conversionary programme against another faith group must imply a sense of spiritual inadequacy of that tradition—that is, a fundamental attitude of contempt. It is fair to ask whether this is a proper way for a group to view another which shares the same essential monotheistic faith. Clearly, the Jewish community has made the fundamental decision that it is not.

[Daniel Polish, 'Jewish attitudes to Mission and Conversion' in *Christian Mission— Jewish Mission*, edited by Martin Cohen and Helga Croner, Paulist Press, 1982, p.160]

EVANGELICAL APPROACHES TO MISSION AND DIALOGUE

We turn now to Christian approaches to mission and dialogue. Naturally, many Christians would disagree with Daniel Polish. If you believe that salvation from hell depends on acknowledging Christ as Lord, then it seems difficult to exclude Jews from missionary activities. Yet, as we have seen, Jews do not understand this 'conversion' emphasis and resent the attitude implied to their faith. So can evangelical Christians participate in the dialogue? Do we only dialogue with people who are liberal, perhaps not rooted strongly in their faith? or does one dialogue only with those who give up ideas of conversion?

The following extracts provide some insight into American evangelical responses. Both are actively engaged in the dialogue there. They express two very different approaches to evangelical mission and the Jewish community. In America the evangelical–Jewish dialogue is further advanced than in Great Britain. In Britain there is very little official contact between evangelical

organizations and the Jewish communities, except perhaps in a missionary
capacity. This is partly due to fear in the Jewish community and the feeling on
both sides that nothing can be gained from the dialogue. In the first extract
David Rausch, *Associate Professor of Church History and Judaic Studies at*
Ashland Theological Seminary in America, carefully and sensitively explains
how evangelicals do not always find witness easy and certainly would not
endorse coercive proselytism:

Contrary to popular opinion, it is not easy for most evangelicals to
witness to their faith. Young and old are bombarded Sunday after
Sunday with their responsibility to evangelize. Often when they speak
to someone about their faith, it is with fear and trepidation and out of a
keen sense of responsibility, religious commitment, and love. In all fair-
ness, evangelical theology teaches that one must not coerce or trick a
human being to 'accept Jesus as their personal saviour', for only the
Holy Spirit of God can 'convict and convince' the unbeliever.
Evangelicals are taught to obey the spirit of God, to use common sense,
to be ethical in witness, and to avoid rude behaviour and angry arguments. In dialogue, Jewish leaders soon found that evangelical leaders
deplored any duplicity in presenting the gospel message to Jewish
people. Deceitful techniques and lack of respect in Jewish evangelism
was mourned by evangelical and Jew alike. Evangelicals insisted that
undue pressure on a prospective convert was out of order and that a
Christian's task was to be a faithful 'witness' to the truth of God's love.
Often when evangelicals speak of missions, they are speaking of their
responsibility to the world-at-large. A recent trend is to support missionary enterprises to unevangelized foreign cultures and to permeate countries closed to traditional missionary approaches.

It is important for the Jewish community to realize that when one
simply asks evangelicals to give up 'witness', one is asking them to give
up their faith and belief. While an evangelical may not attempt to
evangelize the Jewish person next to them, most guard vociferously
their right to do so. One popular evangelical magazine in the spring of
1988 sought to have a debate by evangelical theologians over whether
or not one should witness to Jewish people, only to find that those
who would disparage evangelism completely, were not considered
evangelicals. Nevertheless, evangelist Billy Graham stated some years
ago that he did not agree with missionary enterprises aimed solely at
Jewish people, and the American Jewish Committee awarded this
evangelist with their first National Interreligious Award. The citation

noted that Graham had strengthened 'mutual respect and understanding between evangelical and Jewish communities'. Years before, Billy Graham had received the Anti-Defamation League's Torch of Religious Freedom.

Practically, Jews and evangelicals who are friends have little problem over witness on the personal level. Ironically, Jews often want to know what a Christian believes once mutual respect and an honest relationship have been established. But the fact that evangelism exists, vexes Jewish–evangelical relations. Sometimes a Jewish leader will confess of an evangelical colleague in dialogue, 'I, at times, get the feeling that he would like to convert me'. A few Jewish leaders have totally accepted evangelical (and Christian) mission and witness as part of the Christian faith-principle, but they have clearly drawn the line at 'Hebrew Christians' and 'Messianic Jews'—groups they view as deceptive and untenable.

[David Rausch, Communities in *Conflict: Evangelicals and Jews: Evangelicals and Jews*, 1991, Trinity Press, pp. 105–106]

*David Rausch has outlined the mainstream evangelical response to mission and the Jewish community, but it has often baffled Jewish participants as to why evangelicals believe Judaism is obsolete as a 'saving faith'. **Vernon Grounds**, Professor Emeritus of Denver Conservative Baptist Seminary in the United States, provides an explanation of the evangelical view. The argument is based on the authority of the Bible. The mission to Jews is commanded and justified by the New Testament. In the dialogue Jews expect Christians to listen and understand their interpretation of scripture, likewise evangelicals feel that Jews should listen to their perspective. This extract provides an honest and open explanation of evangelical theology from an evangelical who is engaged in the dialogue in America:*

Why do we teach and preach that Judaism as a religion fails to qualify Jews as non candidates for evangelism? That question is being answered in depth and at length as we carry on our dialogue at this conference. We evangelicals are candidly setting forth the answers which we find convincing though they may not prove at all persuasive to our Jewish friends. I assume, then, that it falls within my province as a participant to give a brief answer which I take to be the New Testament answer.

Alienated from God, by sinful disobedience, Jews, together with all members of the human family, are lost. But in his unchanging faithfulness and fathomless grace God has been redemptively at work in history reconciling the self-estranged race of Adam to himself. In doing that he, long millennia ago, challenged Abraham to enter into a unique relationship with himself and thereby embark on a unique mission. In faith Abraham responded. The subsequent history of Israel issues from the covenant thus established. The Jews, God's chosen people, became the recipients of supernatural truth and an efficacious system of atoning sacrifice. The Israelitish theocracy, however, was simply a framework within which God was providing the possibility of a faith-full and faithful relationship with himself duplicating the Abrahamic pattern. From among these people who were Jews ethnically, he was drawing into redemptive fellowship with himself a people who were Israelites spiritually. Yet he intended Judaism qua religion to be temporary and preparatory, the foundation on which a new faith, a new covenant, and a new relationship would in the fullness of time be established.

[Vernon C. Grounds, 'The Problem of Proselytization' in *Evangelicals and Jews in an Age of Pluralism*, University Press of America, 1990, pp. 206–7]

JEWISH RESPONSES TO CHRISTIAN MISSIONARY ACTIVITY

*In the true spirit of dialogue, there now follows two reactions to Christian mission. Both come from Jews who have participated extensively in Christian–Jewish dialogue—and evangelical-Jewish dialogue in particular. The first text is from **Blu Greenberg**, an Orthodox Jewish woman well known for her writings on the role of women in traditional Judaism. She provides a passionate, heartfelt, honest and frank reaction to Christian mission that focuses on three areas. First, the specialness of her election; second, the perspective of history; and thirdly, the perspective of a community which lives in the shadow of Auschwitz:*

But now there's the other part of me, the real me, in fact, the Jew who knows where she's come from and who tests Christian mission against another whole set of criteria.

First, I react to Christian mission as a Jew who believes that election counts for something. To be born a Jew, to live out my life as a Jew, to marry another Jew, to bear children—these are special gifts. Divine election as a Jew is to me a special calling. I often feel overcome with emotion when I attend a bris, a circumcision ceremony, or one of the ritual ceremonies we are now developing for the birth of infant girls. These events bring out the deepest feelings in me, feelings of continuity, of connection, of community, and the binding ties of the Jewish family. The new infant is more than a child of its parents. He/she is also the latest link in the long chain of tradition. This notion of election is quite different from racism—for it does not deny that one can move in or out, not that one can be reborn to another faith. It simply means that my cool detached thoughts about Christian mission are scrambled by another code—the miracle of being born, not only to biological parents, but to a whole community and to Torah.

Second, I reflect on Christian mission to the Jews from the perspective of Jewish history. I know this general truth: whenever the Good News was combined with power, it became the bad news for Jews. In every era in Christian Europe, the closer Christians got to their sacred texts, the more painful things became for Jews. The more strongly Jesus was believed to have atoned for human sin, the more sins were committed against the Jews.

And third, I see mission through the unique and historically discontinuous event of the Holocaust. I see it through the eyes of a community of survivors—biological survivors, the holy ones, and psychological survivors like myself, whose souls were seared although their bodies were untouched. Irving Greenberg has written 'After the Holocaust, no statement, theological or otherwise, should be made that would not be credible in the presence of burning children'. A most powerful theological criterion, and one that applies to Christian mission to the Jews as well.

The question here is not one of silence of the established church, nor acknowledgement of Christian acts of mercy and loving kindness. It is neither complicity and bystandership nor credible, individual Christian selflessness and sacrifice. Nor is it the relative response of fundamentalists or reformers. These are profound issues and scholars everywhere have begun to deal with them thoroughly. The issue here is much more simple. From the standpoint of evangelical theory on mission to the Jews, the Holocaust offers an opportunity for reality testing. Would those who preach conversion for all Jews really want a world Judenrein, a world free of Jews? Having come so close, we are all forced to ask ourselves that terrible question: what would a world with no Jews really feel like? After the Holocaust, can any well-meaning Christian look into my eyes and make that claim, the call for a kind of "spiritual final solution"?

And more, can Jews really be saved through Jesus? Jesus himself, his original apostles, and any of his followers who might have had one Jewish grandparent somewhere would have all been prime targets for the gas chambers. Or conversely, would any decent Christian have felt a theological victory, had Hitler given the Jews a chance to save themselves by affirming Christ?

[Blu Greenberg, 'Mission, Witness, and Proselytism' in *Evangelicals and Jews in an Age of Pluralism*, University Press of America, 1990, pp. 228–230]

MISSION—THE ERADICATION OF JEWS

Susannah Heschel, a leading Jewish feminist theologian, in a similar vein to Blu Greenberg provides a sharp and succinct reaction to Christian mission. Hitler tried to eradicate all Jews; it seems that Christian missionaries are trying to do the same. For Heschel this attempt to finish the work of Hitler contradicts the moral goodness of Christianity. She believes that Christian mission to the Jews is morally wrong:

There is no doubt within the Jewish community that Christian mission is abhorrent. It is especially disturbing after the Holocaust, because it represents its continuation, a spiritual genocide. Can anyone really believe it is to the greater glory of God that there should be no more Jews left in this world? After the Holocaust, to pursue a Jew to convert to Christianity is to murder a soul. What an easy solution: let all the Jews become Christian—after all, there would be no more anti-Semitism if there would be no more Jews. But, I believe, if there were no more Jews, there would be no more Christianity. How could Christianity declare its moral leadership as the new covenant if Christians had done away with Judaism? What would happen to the God of Israel if there were no more Israel? What a remarkable blindness is displayed by those churches that do not see the holiness of Judaism, the preciousness of being a Jew.

[Susannah Heschel, 'The Denigration of Judaism as a Form of Christian Mission' in *A Mutual Witness: Toward Critical Solidarity Between Jews and Christians*, edited by Clark Williamson, Chalice Press, 1992, p. 45]

A JEWISH RESPONSE TO THE DECADE OF EVANGELISM

Jonathan Gorsky, *a British Orthodox Jew actively involved in Jewish education as well as the Christian–Jewish dialogue, explains why a Jew finds converting to Christianity so difficult. In this article he expresses the full dynamic of what it means to be Jewish—it is more than a set of beliefs. For him, Christian missionaries have not understood this dynamic; neither have they comprehended the fundamental principles of Jewish identity and community. His article provides an eloquent and thought-provoking response to Christian mission in the light of the Church of England's declaration that the 1990s should be a 'Decade of Evangelism':*

Judaism is profoundly troubled by the mystery of the incarnation. The perplexity is ultimately spiritual, but the concept is in striking contrast to the assumptions of Jewish religious life. Evangelists who believe that the central obstacle to their endeavour is textual or dogmatic have neither listened nor understood. The matter is of deeper significance. Furthermore, Judaism is the fabric of a communal life, indistinguishable from the most important personal relationships, which colour our memories and our psychological development. To reject the faith is not merely to exchange one set of beliefs for another; it is a most complex and perilous journey engaging every aspect of one's life and relationships and creating in the process conflict, tension and great pain.

The ultimate hope of Judaism is that life will be restored to the holiness of primeval creation; every sabbath is seen as an insight into this resanctified universe, a foretaste of the 'world to come'. The world will be guided by the Messiah, the anointed one of God, and traditional Jews await his coming at the beginning of the redemption which will be the end of days. If we return to our liturgy, we find several references to the Messiah, but even in the most traditional prayer books the Messianic role cannot be described as central. (Reform and Liberal Judaism no longer expect a Messianic figure at all: they emphasize an ultimate age when prophetic visions of peace, harmony and justice will be realised.) Redemption is indeed of focal importance, but emphasis is upon God as the ultimate redeemer.

A similar pattern is discernible in prayers recited on festivals that recall events when human intervention was clearly crucial in effecting deliverance. Moses merits a single, incidental, reference in the Passover narrative, the Haggada, that Jews recite together on the first two nights of that festival. The biblical narrative, of course, is radically different. The divine name does not occur in the biblical book of Esther, but prayers recited on the relevant Jewish festival abbreviate the narrative and focus upon divine providence.

The Jewish soul is imbued with a longing for both transcendence and the intimacy of the divine presence; in consequence there has been a tendency to diminish the redemptive role of major religious figures, even those of the greatest spiritual stature.

The pattern is also discernible in the Jewish conception of Atonement and the spirituality of the High Holy Days, the penitential period of the religious calendar. The High Holy Days, referred to as the Days of Awe, are permeated by a sense of human inadequacy and divine judgement, and even the angels tremble before the Judge of all the earth when the great shofar (rams' horn) is sounded. The presence of the transcendent God is emphasized in the imagery of kingship, fusing distance with omnipotence, but there is, equally, a longing for that same transcendence, in the presence of which every creature is restored to the plenitude of its ultimate holiness, for it finds its source and its place in the presence of God its Creator.

Transcendence coexists with a sense of the divine compassion, even at a time of judgement and accentuated awareness of fragility and sinfulness. At a focal point in each service we stand together and sing very quietly: 'Our father, our king, be gracious to us and answer us. For we have no goodly deeds. Be with us in your charity and compassion and grant us your salvation.'

For Jewish tradition, man in his sin experiences both distance and intimacy. When Adam and Eve stand bereft in the garden, they are about to go into exile. Adam retains his sense of the wonder of life and names his wife Chava, for she is the mother of all the living. In a moment of extraordinary tenderness, God not only makes garments for Adam and Eve, but he also dresses them, as a mother dresses her children before they go out into the cold.

In the Book of Samuel (2 Sam. 12:13) we encounter David after he has received a rebuke from Nathan the prophet. 'And David said unto Nathan: "I have sinned against the Lord"; and Nathan said unto David: "The Lord hath put away thy sin: thou shalt not die".' Rabbi Elijah of Vilna, one of the greatest Rabbinic sages, notes that in the Masoretic text there is a blank space after David's utterance. He was forgiven after his brief confession because God heard his silence and knew the depths of his broken-heartedness.

Between penitence and grace lies a cloud of unknowing. A contemporary Rabbinic authority, Rabbi J.B. Soloveichik, has evoked the essence of Yom Kippur, the Day of Atonement, in his poetic description of Moses standing on Mount Sinai after the disaster of the Golden Calf. Moses had been instructed that no man was to accompany him, nor was anyone to be seen on the mountainside. Sinai is silent and desolate and as Moses scans the rocks he finds nothing. He stands and shivers as the starlight fades at the break of a new day. God does not appear: he wants Moses to seek him in prayer and supplication. God is present in a cloud and is with him. A distant faint sound is heard as Moses trembles. It enunciates the qualities of God's compassion that define forever the penitential liturgy of the days of Awe. Before Moses hears he has to stand alone in the unbroken silence of a dark desert night. This is the age-old world of Baal Teshuva, the man of penitence returning to his God.

It is possible to express this world in the abstract language of the theologian, but to do so is to lose sight of the depth and power of the encounter that is graven indelibly in the remembrance of all who have known the Days of Awe. *Homo religiosus* cannot shed his faith and embrace the world of another as a man changes his garments after the heat of the day has passed. His memories, his language, his deepest relationships and his childhood recollections are embedded in the landscape of traditional life: his spiritual longings are defined forever by the liturgy that gave them form in his earliest years. A Rabbinic gloss on the Joseph story has Joseph about to embrace the culture of Egypt: he draws back suddenly when he is overcome by a sudden recollection of the face of his father. When I study the photograph albums that are my family history, I see the faces of Eastern European Jewry, and I know their dignity, their scholarship, and their suffering amidst the remorseless poverty of Polish Jewish life. I am very different from them, but my spiritual life has been defined by their world, and the names of the Jewish towns of pre-Holocaust Europe wake memories and associations that are irrational and utterly unexpected.

Two years ago, I visited Germany for the first time, to attend a conference of the International Council of Christians and Jews. I expected that my journey would be uneventful; almost half a century had passed since European Jewry had been devastated by its greatest catastrophe, and the people I would meet were of a new generation, who had grown up in a post-war Europe. I had heard of the thousands of young Germans who made cultural pilgrimages to the sites of the concentration camps and I wished to be with them and to understand. I recalled speaking to a group of teenagers from the German School in London; they had an unusual maturity and were deeply concerned about neo-Nazi outrages and racist attacks in their homeland. They wanted to know what I felt and I gradually discovered that, like me, they were burdened by the past. They also felt unsettled by the events of their country's recent history.

The conference took place in a retreat on the edge of the Thuringian forestland in the former Eastern Germany, not too distant from Frankfurt. Frankfurt was a major centre of pre-war Jewish life and the home of what is now described as modern Orthodoxy. As we drove through its streets I could scarcely believe that Rabbi Hirsch's community was no longer and his great synagogue would never again be thronged with worshippers. As we travelled into the country, road signs indicated that Fulda and Hildesheim were close by. One could almost hear Jewish boys and girls of sixty years ago going for Passover rambles, singing their songs and being young together.

I have a great affinity with the Hassidic practice of private prayer in a natural environment but here, in Thuringia, I prayed in a quiet corner of the residence or in my room in the evening. I did not walk in the gardens or the forestland as I usually would. The grounds were pleasant and peaceful, but I felt a sense of utter desolation.

The conference concluded with a reception and concert at the Wartburg, an eleventh-century fortress built on a commanding hilltop overlooking the forest. It is a massive structure that is illuminated at night when its grey stone is visible for miles around.

During the Nazi period the SS used the fortress as an icon of the thousand-year Reich. The stronghold is the incarnate essence of absolute and naked power, infused with the romanticism of its magnificent forest setting. It is the living spirit of the explosive forces that erupted into modern civilization and swept aside its fragile rationality. The sounds of the 'Horst Wessel Song' and Nuremburg, the broken glass and the surging flames, are present and held there forever. How much I had read and how little I knew until I stood in this place.

Night was drawing in and I left the hall to say my afternoon prayers. I gazed at the early sunset and the darkening forest and recalled the dread of the psalmist when the face of God was hidden from him. I could not stand in prayer here; the words lost their meaning and were empty and void. I returned to the hall as the concert came to an end and the gathering applauded the musicians.

The past is a part of me and I had not known. Today, when Jewish men and women read of neo-Nazism, of Zhirinovsky and of Fascist ministers in a major European democracy, when swastikas are once again daubed on our synagogues and our Moslem and Hindu friends suffer violation and abuse as they walk through our streets, we recall our families and our people only fifty years ago. When I visit my synagogue's religion school I sit with the children to help them with their Hebrew and listen to their teachers' stories. I feel the presence of hundreds of thousands of Jewish children who sat with their teachers in similar classrooms all over Europe, before their world was engulfed in darkness and despair.

Can it really be, after all of these things have come to pass, that Jewish faithfulness should disappear from the countries of Europe and the holiness of our traditional life should be no more? Can anyone really desire that Jewish children will no longer learn Hebrew and take joy in the stories of our people? That Shabbat, Pesach and the Day of Atonement will cease to be the sacred times of the year, and the Torah will no longer be chanted in our synagogues?

[Jonathan Gorsky, 'A Jewish Response to the Decade of Evangelism' in *The Way*, vol 34, no 4, Oct 1994, pp. 288–292]

'NO' TO THE CONVERSION OF JEWS

In the light of some of these arguments, many Christians feel that Jews should not be required to convert. **James Parkes** *(1896–1981)—an Anglican priest and theologian, one of the greatest pioneers of Christian–Jewish dialogue and amongst other things a founder of the Council of Christians and Jews in Britain—argued throughout his life that it was wholly inappropriate to convert Jews to Christianity. His life was dedicated to combating anti-Semitism and calling on Christians to acknowledge their anti-Jewish history. Many of his publications explored the problems involved in Christian and secular anti-Semitism. He was especially sensitive to German policies in this area. The following extract is taken from a book published by him in 1948. His attitude here is remarkable when one realizes that he was writing at a time when the Christian ecumenical movement had barely begun. He was one of the first Anglican vicars to suggest that there should be no mission to Jews. In this respect he was ahead of his time and found himself marginalized by the majority of Christians:*

I would like to make clear at the beginning that, though I shall have much to say of co-operation between the two religions, I do not desire to undermine the integrity of either. A Christianity without the Cross is as emptied of meaning as a Judaism without Torah; and it is because a religion based on the Cross and a religion based on Torah, as each has historically developed, are today in any honest interpretation incompatible that Christianity and Judaism are rightly two religions. I do not regard Judaism as an immature Christianity, still less as a religion whose creative vitality and truth have ceased to exist. In this time and generation, not only do I not desire to see the conversion of all Jews to present forms of Christianity, but I do not seek the union of the two religions.

[James Parkes, *Judaism and Christianity*, The Camelot Press, 1948, p. 12]

CHRISTIAN MISSION AFTER AUSCHWITZ

We have already seen from Susannah Heschell's extract how important the Holocaust is in this area. The Holocaust challenged the Church to re-think much of its theology including its approach to mission and the Jews. That process of re-thinking is still continuing and is nowhere near complete. Some theologians are formulating a new Christian theology of Judaism, believing that theological changes are necessary in different areas such as Christology, soteriology, and ecclesiology. As the Catholic theologian **Gregory Baum** *writes in the following extract, the Church has all but given up its mission to Jews but still has much more theological thinking to do:*

After Auschwitz the Christian churches no longer wish to convert the Jews. While they may not be sure of the theological grounds that dispense them from this mission, the churches have become aware that asking the Jews to become Christians is a spiritual way of blotting them out of existence and thus only reinforces the effects of the Holocaust. The churches, moreover, realise the deadly irony implicit in a Christian plea for the conversion of the Jews; for after Auschwitz and the participation of the nations, it is the Christian world that is in need of conversion. The major churches have come to repudiate mission to the Jews, even if they have not justified this by adequate doctrinal explanations. We have here a case, frequently found in church history, where a practical decision on the part of the churches, in response to a significant event, precedes dogmatic reflection and in fact becomes the guide to future doctrinal development. Moved by a sense of shame over the doctrinal formulations which negate Jewish existence, the churches have come to recognise Judaism as an authentic religion before God, with independent value and meaning, not as a stage on the way to Christianity.

[Gregory Baum, 'Rethinking the Church's Mission after Auschwitz' in *Auschwitz: Beginning of a new Era?*, edited by Eva Fleischner, Ktav Publishing House, 1977, p. 113]

THE UNIQUENESS OF CHRIST?

One enormous problem remains: what about Jesus? How do Christians make sense of those New Testament texts that stress the need for mission? **Marcus Braybrooke**, *an Anglican theologian and vicar in Oxford, England, recognizes the problem and attempts to grapple with it. He has been actively involved in Christian–Jewish relations in Britain and the wider international inter-faith dialogue. He argues that because the proclamation to preach the gospel to all nations is so firmly rooted in Christianity, Jews should not expect rapid change. Any progress will be slow; however there are those Christians who recognize that God's salvation is available to everyone regardless of the faith tradition they belong to. For them, Judaism is a legitimate path to God without faith in Christ:*

Traditionally Christians have made claims for the uniqueness of Jesus Christ as the only saviour. They have believed with scriptural warrant that it was their responsibility to share that salvation with others—'to the Jew first and also to the Gentile' (Rom.1:17). Jesus' parting words to his disciples were, according to Matthew's Gospel, 'Go forth therefore and make all nations my disciples, baptize men everywhere in the name of the Father and the Son and the Holy Spirit (28:19) or, according to the Acts of the Apostles, 'You will bear witness for me in Jerusalem, and all over Judaea and Samaria, and away to the ends of the earth' (1:8). Both formulations, especially the Matthean verses with their trinitarian reference, clearly do not go back to Jesus himself. Yet those most committed to mission are unlikely to adopt a critical approach to scripture. For some 'fundamentalist' Christians, the conversion of the Jews will herald the second coming of Christ. Because the responsibility for mission is so deeply rooted amongst many Christians, Jews sometimes expect a more rapid change of attitude than is possible. It is unrealistic to expect the churches just to abandon the call to mission, as one draft of the 1988 Lambeth

Conference document on the 'Way of Dialogue' seemed to suggest was possible.

When in late 1985 and early 1986, because of the publicity given to campaigns by 'Jews for Jesus', especially on university campuses, the issue threatened to endanger the growth of dialogue, the Council of Christians and Jews issued a statement with the approval of major church leaders. It affirmed that 'true dialogue involves mutual respect and precludes any attempt to entice or pressurize the partner to convert from one religion to the other'. It deplored any form of deception in evangelization and targeting of Jews for special missionary activity, although it recognized that groups actively engaged in evangelism were not under the control of the main churches. The statement went on: 'Throughout the centuries Christians have understood the concept of witness in various ways. Many Christians today believe that it is important to develop an understanding of witness or mission which takes into account our present recognition of God's saving activity among other religious faiths, and of the special relationship between Christianity and Judaism'.

[Marcus Braybrooke, *Time to Meet: Towards a Deeper Understanding Between Jews and Christians*, SCM Press, 1990 pp. 97–98]

JEWS ARE TO SURVIVE AS JEWS

We have looked at evangelical Christians who are still committed to mission and we have briefly examined those liberal Christians who want to accept Judaism without requiring conversion. We turn now to a Catholic response which seeks to work within a traditional framework yet suggests that Jews should survive as Jews. Writing as a Catholic theologian involved in the dialogue in America, **Michael McGarry** *provides a careful argument which may provide a fruitful way forward in not only Catholic–Jewish relations but also the wider Christian–Jewish dialogue. He argues that for theological and biblical reasons the Church should make an exception in its conversion programme. He suggests that Jews should no longer be the subject of Christian missionary activity. The Holocaust has mandated that Jews should survive as Jews and not as forerunners to faith in Christ:*

I propose the following as a fruitful direction for Catholic theological thinking to proceed in making a positive exception in the Church's conversionist dimension of mission:

Since the Shoah, Christians ponder ever more deeply the meaning of Jewish survival in the world. In many ways, the Jews survive despite Christians' best (or worst) efforts at eliminating them through ghettoization, conversion, and pogroms. Furthermore, the atheistic Nazi effort to annihilate the Jewish people was unsuccessful—they survived. What does this mean for Christians? Part of Christian and Jewish faith is that God is revealed through history. Not everything in history reveals God, nor is all history revelatory. But when God speaks, it is in and through history that the Divine Voice is heard. The survival of the Jews to this day, even and especially through the Shoah, must now be interpreted as a positive sign that God continues to love them and call them as his/her own. The Christian answer to the 'why' of Jewish survival must be that God wants them to survive, not as a pawn in a Christian theological chess game, but as a people called and chosen. Simply put, Christians are coming to believe that God does not want a world without Jews. After Auschwitz, following the will of God, we Christians do not want a world without Jews. Indeed, we have already noted that one of the most sacred retrievals of the new Catholic–Jewish relationship is the affirmation that God has not abrogated God's covenant with the Jewish people. This belief bears, I believe, a consequence, indeed a mandate, that Christians are not to eliminate the Jews from the face of the earth even by conversionist programs. The Jews are the sign, a sacrament, that our God is faithful to his/her covenant by not seeking to convert them.

Furthermore, in a post-Auschwitz world where the possibility of European Jewish annihilation almost became a reality, would it serve Christian belief in the God of Jesus that there be no Jews, even by all of them becoming Christians? I suggest not for the following reasons:

Christians hold, with all their heart, that Jesus stands as the forever valid sign and sacrament of God's saving action. That they are called as individuals to respond in community is the particular privilege and vocation of the Church, which itself stands as a sacrament to this belief. But as believers of both Testaments know and proclaim, God calls people not only as individuals, but also as communities. The Holy One's call in and through community is as irrevocable and unavailable-to-renegotiation as God's call to the human heart is. Thus, must we not now affirm that God's-call-in-community requires a sign and sacrament to be real to and for the world?

The Jewish people, I submit, stand as the necessary sacrament and sign of this fuller message. God's electing them through Moses does not end, even with the definitive coming of salvation which Christians recognise in the Jew Jesus. If they today seek to convert the Jews, Christians are systematically attempting to eliminate the sacrament and sign that the Holy One calls humans communally as well as individually.

Furthermore, if by a convert-making enterprise Christians ever eliminate the Jews as a recognisable people in the world, as a nation faithful to the call they hear through the Torah, then Christians will obscure their own doctrine of God's faithfulness to election. That is, if the world sees an end to the Jewish people, then the world may rightly conclude that God's election is only for a time until some other groups obliterates it by conversion. What Christians witness to is that, by the gracious love of the Holy One, Jewish election has been opened to the nations through Christ—a branch grafted on, as Paul put it (Rom. 11:17f.).

From a theological perspective such as suggested above, the Church can, must, make the Jews an exception in evangelization not because of any timidity or lack of faith, not because of guilt or interfaith politeness, but precisely because it believes passionately what has been revealed: that salvation is God's work, not human work, that God chooses whom God wills for the Reign of God and that the Holy One has chosen the Jews and has not gone back on that word.

[Michael McGarry, 'Interreligious Dialogue, Mission, and the Case of the Jews', in *Christian Mission and Interreligious Dialogue*, edited by Paul Mojzes and Leonard Swidler, Edwin Mellen Press, 1990, pp. 109–111]

SOME OFFICIAL CHURCH STATEMENTS

The changing attitude to mission and the conversion of Jews is now reflected in both the official Church statements and the attitude of particular Church leaders. Although there has been no renunciation of all mission directed at Jews, there has been a clear message that God's covenant with the Jews remains valid. The ambiguity remains over whether Christians can still convert Jews— particularly in the statements from the World Council of Churches.

The Catholic Church

The first part of this section provides extracts from three different Catholic Statements. The Catholic Church has explicitly and officially rejected any attempts at coercive proselytism or the setting up of societies with the sole aim of converting Jews. God's covenant with the Jews remains valid. This is a remarkable statement given that it was made in 1965 at a time when the Catholic Church was reluctant to participate in the Christian ecumenical movement:

As holy scripture testifies, Jerusalem did not recognise the time of her visitation (cf. Luke 19:44), nor did the Jews in large numbers accept the gospel; indeed, not a few opposed the spreading of it (cf. Rom. 11:28). Nevertheless, according to the apostle, the Jews still remain most dear to God because of their fathers, for He does not repent of the gifts He makes nor of the calls He issues (Rom. 11: 28–29). In company with the prophets and the same apostle, the church awaits that day, known to God alone, on which all peoples will address the Lord in a single voice and 'serve Him with one accord' (cf. Isa. 66:23; Ps. 65:4; Rom. 11:11–32).

Since the spiritual patrimony common to Christians and Jews is thus so great, this sacred Synod wishes to foster and recommend that mutual understanding and respect which is the fruit above all of biblical and theological studies, and of brotherly dialogues.

['Declaration on the Relationship of the Church to Non-Christian Religions' (Nostra Aetate, no.4, 28 October, 1965)]

The following document was prepared by **Tommaso Federici** *at the request of the Vatican. The overall document was much longer than the passage reprinted here; however this section provides the clearest pronouncement that the Catholic Church rejects all forms of proselytism:*

The Church thus rejects in a clear way every form of undue proselytism. This means the exclusion of any sort of witness and preaching which in any way constitutes a physical, moral, psychological, or cultural constraint on the Jews, both individuals and communities, such as might in any way destroy or even simply reduce their personal judgement, free will and full autonomy of decision at the personal and community level.

The time of methods of enforced conversion of Jews, imposed catecheses and compulsory sermons imposed by Christian majority powers has come to a definitive end and has been disowned and deprecated. But the latent danger still exists that popular religious writing and the behaviour of Christians may put pressure on Jews, both individuals and groups. This contradictory way of acting (which must always be rejected) is still expected by some to lead to 'conversion', while those who engage in it are unwilling to bring about their own 'conversion of heart' to God and their brothers.

In fact it is openly recognised in the Church today, as has been repeatedly and insistently confirmed by the Second Vatican Council, that 'conversion' understood as passing from one faith or religious denomination to another, belongs in the setting of the inalienable right of freedom of religious conscience, since it is an inviolable process involving the interaction of God's grace and man's response.

Consequently, attempts to set up organisations of any sort, particularly educational or welfare organisations, for the 'conversion' of Jews must be rejected.

[Tommaso Federici, 'The Mission and Witness of the Church', in *Fifteen Years of Catholic–Jewish Dialogue 1970–1985: Selected Papers*, Libreria Editrice Vaticana, 1988, pp. 57–58]

The following section from **Guidelines** *spells out the presuppositions of any dialogue. The key for both sides must be mutual respect. Even through that dialogue and respect for the other, the Church maintains her right to witness to the world. It is clear that any witness should not give offence:*

From now on, real dialogue must be established. Dialogue presupposes that each side wishes to know the other, and wishes to increase and deepen its knowledge of the other. It constitutes a particularly suitable means of favouring a better mutual knowledge and, especially in the case of dialogue between Jews and Christians, of probing the riches of one's own tradition. Dialogue demands respect for the other as he is; above all respect for his faith and his religious convictions.

In virtue of her divine mission, and her very nature, the Church must preach Jesus Christ to the world (Ad Gentes, 2). Lest the witness of Catholics to Jesus Christ should give offence to Jews, they must take care to live and spread their Christian faith while maintaining the strictest respect for religious liberty in line with the teaching of the Second Vatican Council (Declaration Dignitatis Humanae). They will likewise strive to understand the difficulties which arise for the Jewish soul — rightly imbued with an extremely high, pure notion of the divine transcendence—when faced with the mystery of the incarnate Word.

[Guidelines and Suggestions for Implementing the Conciliar Declaration Nostra Aetate, 1 December, 1974]

Pope John Paul II's Historic Visit to Rome's Synagogue

The visit of Pope John Paul II to the Great Synagogue in Rome in 1986 was a remarkable event—it was the first known visit by any Pope ever recorded. During his address to the community he spoke about the joint witness of Jews and Christians:

Jews and Christians are the trustees and witnesses of an ethic marked by the Ten Commandments, in the observance of which humanity finds its truth and freedom. To promote a common reflection and collaboration on this point is one of the great duties of the hour... In doing this, we shall each be faithful to our most sacred commitments and also to that which most profoundly unites and gathers us together.

[Pope John Paul II in his address to the Jewish community in the Great Synagogue of Rome, 13 April 1986]

The Anglican Community

The following excerpt has been taking from the Lambeth Document 'Jews, Christians and Muslims: the Way of Dialogue'. In it the diversity of Christian responses to Judaism are acknowledged and outlined. In spite of these very different approaches, the Church is united in rejecting unwarranted proselytism and coercive missionary activity:

Within this sharing there are a variety of attitudes towards Judaism within Christianity today. At one pole, there are those Christians whose prayer is that Jews, without giving up their Jewishness, will find their fulfilment in Jesus the Messiah. Indeed some regard it as their particular vocation and responsibility to share their faith with Jews, whilst at the same time urging them to discover the spiritual riches which God has given them through the Jewish faith. Other Christians, however, believe that in fulfilling the Law and Prophets, Jesus validated the Jewish relationship with God, while opening this way up for Gentiles through his own person. For others again, the holocaust has changed their perception, so that until Christian lives bear a truer witness, they feel a divine obligation to affirm the Jews in their worship and sense of God who is, for Christians, the Father of Jesus. In all these approaches, Christians bear witness to God as revealed in Jesus and are being called into a fresh, more fruitful relationship with Judaism. We urge that further thought and prayer, in the light of Scripture and the facts of history, be given to the nature of this relationship.

All these approaches, however, share a common concern to be sensitive to Judaism, to reject all proselytising, that is, aggressive and manipulative attempts to convert, and, of course, any hint of anti-Semitism. Further, Jews, Muslims and Christians have a common mission. They share a mission to the world that God's name may be honoured.

Christians and Jews share one hope, which is for the realisation of God's Kingdom on earth. Together they wait for it, pray for it and prepare for it. This Kingdom is nothing less than human life and society transformed, transfigured and transparent to the glory of God.

['Jews, Christians, and Muslims: The Way of Dialogue' from The Lambeth Conference, 1988]

The World Council of Churches

In 1988 the Sigtuna Report of the World Council of Churches affirmed the following advancements in Christian understandings of Jews and Judaism. The statement affirmed the following:

1) that the covenant of God with the Jewish people remains valid,
2) that anti-Semitism and all forms of the teaching of contempt for Judaism are to be repudiated,
3) that the living tradition is a gift of God,
4) that coercive proselytism directed towards Jews is incompatible with Christian faith,
5) that Jews and Christians bear a common responsibility as witness to God's righteousness and peace in the world.

Further on in the Sigtuna document, the uniqueness of Christ is affirmed yet not at the expense of the validity of Judaism. We see here the first clear indication of what theologians have called 'double covenant theology'; namely that Judaism and Christianity are two parallel and legitimate ways to God.

We rejoice in the continuing existence and vocation of the Jewish people, despite attempts to eradicate them, as a sign of God's love and faithfulness towards them. This fact does not call into question the uniqueness of Christ and the truth of the Christian faith. We see not one covenant displacing another, but two communities of faith, each called into existence by God, each holding to its respective gifts from God, and each accountable to God.

We affirm that the Jewish people today are in continuation with biblical Israel and are thankful for the vitality of Jewish faith and thought. We see Jews and Christians, together with all people of living faiths, as God's partners, working in mutual respect and cooperation for justice, peace, and reconciliation.

['World Council of Churches Consultation on the Church and the Jewish People: Report', Sigtuna, 1988, pp. 8 & 10]

The Orthodox Church

The final extract has been taken from a paper delivered at a World Council of Churches' meeting in Budapest in 1989. It provides an valuable insight into how the Orthodox Church responds to the plurality of faiths. Her mission is defined in terms of an ethical witness with other faiths to bring about the kingdom of God:

Our relationship with God and our mission to the world cannot be separated from our relationship with our neighbour. In the pluralistic societies of today "my neighbour's faith and mine" do not simply co-exist, they interact and correlate. In fact, we always remind ourselves in our ecumenical pilgrimage that the unity of the church and the unity of humankind are interdependent and that there exists a growing interaction between the living faiths. We have also come to realise that the transformation of the world and the building of the world community are no longer a one-way track. It implies mutual openness, mutual listening and a common partnership.

['Unity and Mission in the Context of the Middle East', a paper delivered to the Plenary Commission on Faith and Order, Budapest, Hungary, 1989.]

FURTHER READING

Bosch, David. *Transforming Mission: Paradigm Shifts in Theology of Mission*, Orbis, 1991.

Cohen, Martin & Croner, Helga (edited). *Christian Mission—Jewish Mission*, Paulist Press, 1982.

Cohn-Sherbok, Dan. *Issues in Contemporary Judaism*, Macmillan, 1991.

Croner, Helga & Klenicki, Leon (edited). *Issues in the Jewish–Christian Dialogue: Jewish Perspectives on Covenant, Mission, and Witness*, Paulist Press, 1979.

Keshishian, Aram. *Orthodox Perspectives on Mission*, Regnum Lynx, 1992.

Lubarsky, Sandra. *Tolerance and Transformation*, Hebrew Union College Press, 1990.

Mojzes, Paul & Swidler, Leonard (edited). *Christian Mission and Interreligious Dialogue*, The Edwin Mellen Press, 1990.

Motte, Mary & Lang, Joseph (edited). *Mission in Dialogue*, Orbis, 1982.

Solomon, Norman. *Judaism and World Religion*, Macmillan, 1991.

Williamson, Clark (edited). *A Mutual Witness*, Chalice Press, 1992.

CHAPTER FIVE

ISRAEL

CHAPTER FIVE

ISRAEL

The land of Israel has always been a focal point for Jews, Christians, and Muslims. Jews believe it to be the land God gave his people; Christians acknowledge it as holy because Jesus lived and died there; and Muslims revere Jerusalem as the third holiest city in Islam. For the majority of Jews today, whether religious or secular, Israel is central to their identity; a necessary safe-haven from a world that has often shunned and persecuted them. The twentieth century has certainly taught this much.

Judaism teaches that the land was promised to Abraham by God in the Hebrew Scriptures. It is a promise which forms the central thread throughout Jewish scriptures and writings. If the prophets wished to call Israel to repentance, they would often threaten God's withdrawal of his presence and the loss of the land. There has always been a Jewish presence in the land even during the periods in history when the majority of Jews were exiled from it; nevertheless the hope of a return to the land was a constant reality in Jewish thought and prayer. In the Orthodox siddur there is a prayer for the peace of Israel as people, sung during the shabbat service 'Establish abundant peace upon Your people Israel forever, for you are King, Master of all peace. May it be good in Your eyes to bless Your people Israel at every time and every hour with Your peace.' There is also a prayer for the welfare of the state of Israel, the first line of which reads, "May He who blessed our fathers, Abraham, Isaac and Jacob, bless the State of Israel and make the glory of His kingdom manifest in the land which He sware unto our fathers to give us." Israel as land and people is central to synagogue liturgy and religious life.

For Christians, the land is special, holy, because it was the place of Jesus' birth and death. It was the place on earth where God chose to Incarnate Himself in human form and provide salvation for the world. The Christian attachment to the land tends therefore to be spiritual and theological rather than a terrestrial one. There has traditionally been little concern for the physical land, except as a place of spiritual pilgrimage. Since the foundation of the State of Israel in 1948 there has been a gradual shift towards an overt concern for the current situation, particularly *vis-à-vis* the Palestinians. Alongside this shift there has also been, in some churches, a recognition of the importance of Israel for Jewish self-identity. Although it is not possible to separate totally the political from the religious, the extracts in this chapter will focus primarily on the religious significance of the land.

Often when Jews and Christians come to dialogue there are tensions *vis-à-vis* the land. Christians are often unable to appreciate fully the importance of Israel for Jewish identity, whilst Jews cannot comprehend some Christians who exclusively identify with the Palestinian cause. This has, and continues, to cause tension in Christian–Jewish relations. Things are changing now: the peace accord between the Israeli Government and the PLO might ease this tension. However, thinking through the significance of the land remains a difficult theological and political issue. The following extracts capture some of the main positions in the debate.

H.P.F.

CENTRAL TO IDENTITY

In the first extract **Harold Kushner**, *a Reconstructionist Rabbi in the United States and popularist religious writer, explains that Jewish attachment to the land goes beyond religious, political and social boundaries. It is emotional and perhaps irrational, and yet that attachment is central to Israel as people and land. The two are inextricably linked. Kushner is typical of much diaspora North American Jewry. His commitment to Israel is passionate and as an American citizen he expects the United States Government to do everything it can to support Israel:*

Over the years, I have found that the issue that puzzles non-Jews the most about Judaism is the role that Israel plays in our minds and souls. It has no analogue in the Christian world. It cannot be compared to the Catholic's feelings toward the Vatican, or the Lutheran's to Germany. It is different from the emotional attachment of Italian-Americans to Italy or Irish-Americans to Ireland. The ancestors of most American Jews came from Europe, not Israel. Few of us can trace our ancestry back far enough to identify a forebear who lived in the Middle East.

Moreover, the attachment is emotional, not nostalgic or theological. It cuts across all religious and social borders. Religious and nonreligious Jews, orthodox and liberal, rich and poor are more united by their love for Israel than by any other single subject on the Jewish agenda (except perhaps antisemitism). How shall we understand this?

The attachment is not political. Every Jew I know makes a distinction between the idea of a Jewish homeland in Israel (to which we are passionately and wholeheartedly committed) and the political state of Israel (of whose government we may or may not approve—not that different from most Americans who are totally committed to the idea of America as a democracy but may think that the policies of a current president are misguided). American Jews are citizens of only one country, the United States.

Neither is the attachment religious; nonreligious Jews feel as strongly about Israel as do our more religious neighbors. (For many of them, love of Israel virtually is their religion.) Nor is it exactly historical; statistically, more Jewish history has happened outside Israel than within its borders, from the giving of the Torah in the Sinai desert to the codifying of the Talmud in Babylonia to the philosophical writings of Maimonides in Spain and the insights of Freud and Einstein in Europe.

What, then, is the nature of this attachment? Partly, our love for Israel, like all love, is irrational and does not lend itself to being explained and understood. But parts of it, I think we can understand.

When God and Israel entered into a Covenant at Sinai, God asked the people to live a distinctive lifestyle, to be a model nation, and the people promised that they would. What was God's part of the Covenant? What did He promise in return? Not a life of ease and splendor. God's promise was, first, a sense of His presence, the feeling that we were a unique, special people, and second, that we would have *a land of our own*. And later in the Bible, when the prophets want to threaten Israel with the worst fate imaginable as a punishment for faithlessness, what do they say? They warn Israel that God will withdraw His presence from them and make them ordinary, and that they will be driven out of their land.

Israel symbolizes for us the idea that we are a people, not only a belief system. It has been one of the recurrent themes of this book that Judaism is rooted more in community than in theology. A theology can exist in the pages of a book. It can be adhered to by individuals wherever they may live, and those individuals may choose to gather in a church from time to time to affirm their solidarity. But a people is not an abstraction; a people has to live somewhere. Marriage as a legal concept can be confined to the pages of the law codes, but when a man and a woman get married, they have to find a home and furnish it.

We relate to Israel in such a complicated fashion in part because the notion of Israel overlaps several otherwise distinct ideas. On the one hand, Israel is a state, a political entity, with a Jewish majority but a significant Moslem and Christian population and representatives of other religions as well. (Israel contains one of the major shrines of the Baha'i faith and has welcomed a number of Southeast Asian Buddhist refugees.) But at the same time Israel is the homeland of the Jewish people, even those who do not live there and are uncompromised citizens of another country. The blue and white flag with the six-pointed star on it, the anthem *'Hatikvah'* (The Hope), are the flag and anthem of the state of Israel but also the flag and anthem of the Jewish people worldwide. They have a Jewish–religious significance as well as an Israeli-political one. When a Jewish organization opens or concludes a meeting singing *'Hatikvah'*, it is as members of the Jewish people, not as citizens of Israel, that they do so. (Had the state of Israel chosen as its national anthem the 137th Psalm—'By the waters of Babylon we sat down and wept when we remembered Zion … If I forget thee, O Jerusalem …'—the psalm would still have been a religious poem and page from Scripture even while serving as an anthem of a political entity.)

In traditional Jewish sources, the term *Israel* is used interchangeably for the land and for the people. When I officiate at a wedding, the ceremony calls for the groom to say to the bride, 'Be thou consecrated unto me by this ring as my wife, according to the laws of Moses and Israel', that is, the Jewish people, the children of Israel. To avoid confusion on the part of the congregation, lest they think that Jewish weddings follow the laws of the state of Israel rather than the Commonwealth of Massachusetts, I instruct the groom to say, '...according to the law of Moses and the Jewish people'.

Beyond that, the existence of the Jewish state of Israel is an expression of the world's willingness to let the Jewish people live. It is nearly impossible for non-Jews to appreciate the meaning of the scar that the Holocaust, and the centuries of persecution leading up to it, have left on the Jewish soul. I don't know of any other people that wakes up virtually on a daily basis wondering if the world will let them live. Perhaps African-Americans, perhaps members of other oppressed minorities share this sense of vulnerability. But after the Nazi experience, Jews understand that no matter how economically successful or socially integrated we are, we can never feel totally secure. Even as I write this, the newspapers carry reports of prominent politicians expressing opinions verging on the antisemitic, of sick minds denying that the Holocaust ever happened, of synagogues being vandalized and skinheads threatening violence against Jews and others whom they dislike. When the children in my congregation would hear about such things and be frightened, I would try to reassure them that there are sick and mixed-up people in all countries, but in America, unlike Nazi Germany, the government and the police are on our side and are working to protect us. International acceptance of Israel delivers that same message on an adult, global level. It says to us, 'Despite the haters and the sick minds out there, there is a place for the Jewish people in the world.'

This, I suspect, is why so many of us react so defensively when Israel is criticized: because we are always afraid that criticism will lead to a withdrawal of approval of Israel's right to exist at all. It is not paranoia on our part to note the disproportionate amount of energy the United Nations puts into judging Israel. It is not hypersensitivity on our part to notice that no other country is called on continually to justify its right to exist. (Does anyone call on the dismantling of Pakistan and giving the land back to the tens of millions of Hindus who were displaced when a Moslem state was created there in 1947?) There can certainly be valid criticism of the actions and policies of modern Israel; I have engaged in no small amount of it myself. But because of its symbolic importance to us, we become sensitive to the difference between saying, 'Israel is not perfect; it should be pressed to improve', and saying, 'Israel is not perfect; therefore it should not be protected against its enemies, it should be taken away from its Jewish inhabitants and given to others.' The first is geopolitical commentary; the latter is antisemitism, punishing the Jewish state for things that other states would not be held accountable for.

[Harold Kushner, *To Life: A Celebration of Jewish Being and Thinking*, Little, Brown & Company, 1993, pp. 243–249]

Kushner stresses the 'emotional' links between Judaism and the land. **Moshe Greenberg**, *an Orthodox Jew living in Israel, is much more rational. He traces the historical identification with the land and argues that the State is essential for Jewish survival in the post-Enlightenment age:*

The possession of land, the possession of a land in sovereignty and freedom was, in classical Judaism, an indispensable condition of self-fulfillment—fulfillment of that pattern of life which was fundamentally communal and social and involved not merely the individual but joined him or her to fellow Jews. That fulfillment necessitated a land in which Jews exercised sovereign control and enjoyed the freedom to live the pattern of life given in the Torah.

Dispossession and powerlessness, which resulted from the political and military disasters that befell the Jews twice in their ancient history, generated a life-giving protective response whose core was a burning metaphysical hope of return and restoration. This hope was grounded in the idea that it was a divine necessity to restore Israel, and a line can be traced from Ezekiel to the mystical idea that in the exile of His People God Himself is exiled. It was necessary for God's self-vindication that the scattered, defeated and degraded people who went by His name be restored. Something of His dignity and glory is diminished, and therefore the restoration of the Jewish People is a restoration of full divine dignity as well.

The vision of the messianic righting of wrongs, its idea of restoration in the Land, is monarchic because that was the political order of states and countries in which Jews moved and first found themselves—sovereignty was embodied in a sovereign. Hence the messianic hope clung to the figure of a sovereign, a king like David.

The sense of the election of Israel and its moral superiority was nurtured on a quasi-ascetic personal and social life in which the discipline of the Torah was generally accepted in the Jewish Diaspora. This gave a psychological compensation for the political helplessness of the Jews, as if to say: 'Although we are helpless in our external relationships, we are totally in control of ourselves and are not falling apart spiritually.' Through a regimen of spiritual exercises in the name of law, Jews generated internal energy and morale; through the acceptance of an ascetic pietism, it was possible for Jews to maintain, in the face of universal contempt, a sense of their worth. The Promised Land became a symbol of redress of all wrongs. The contrast between the sense of Israel's self-worth and the external contempt it received would vanish when the People would be restored to the Land; all that was awry would then be set right.

The European Enlightenment had as its professed goal the brotherhood of humanity and acceptance of the equality of all human beings, including Jews. Particularly the Jews of Western Europe, where the Enlightenment began and flourished, regarded it as a new solution to the Jewish problem. They hoped that Jews would no longer be considered outcasts but be fully accepted as part of humanity—the problem of Jewish existence in the Diaspora thus might be settled by gradual acceptance of the notion of universal brotherhood and the realization of such slogans as

'Liberty, Equality and Fraternity.' But the course of events quickly brought Jews to despair of finding in the European Enlightenment a solution to their anomalous existence. They found that even if they gave up messianism and limited their identity to its minimal features as a religious community, that was not a sufficient surrender of particularity to enable the gentiles of Europe to accept Jews as equals. Consequently a movement of 'auto-emancipation' arose. Jews said, 'As we are not being emancipated or given equal status by the nations, we must act for ourselves.' The outcome was a movement of national liberation combined with a Jewish form of Irredentism which came to be called Zionism.

In the past, the Jewish will to live generated the messianic hope of redemption and the unifying ascetic discipline of life by Torah. These two now were transmuted in Zionism: instead of messianism came the idea of redemption (reconstruction and normalization) of the people through redemption (recovery and revitalization) of the Land—by peaceful means it was originally hoped, but eventually by force despite the reluctance of many Jews to use it. In place of the discipline of law came the mobilization of spirit, energy, idealism and material to create a state. The same kind of ascetic self-discipline that was characteristic of Jewish piety throughout previous centuries in the Diaspora, could be seen in the stoical, Spartan life of the balutzim (pioneers) on communes in the Land of Israel during the first part of this century.

In other words, Jews took their destiny into their own hands and stopped hoping for a supernatural solution to their predicament. It was a break with the Diaspora strategy of survival which advocated quietistic endurance of the status quo as part of an understanding with God: Israel would not press for the messianic age, and God would make Diaspora life just tolerable. This understanding broke down in Europe during this century, and a Jewish state offered the best hope for Jewish survival and self-fulfillment. Such self-fulfillment needed a land in which a full range of responsibility for our individual and communal lives could be exercised in accord with the classical concept of Jewishness. Jewishness is not a matter merely of individual expression— it is expressed in the total life, including the political arena, and only in a Jewish state can the struggle to realize Judaism as an all-embracing teaching for life, *torat hayyim*, be carried forward. Here Jews are on their own in a decision-making position on all aspects of life.

To this day it is only in the State of Israel that Jews have to deal as a people with the problems, institutions and temptations of power— economic, political, and military. These issues, which are at the heart of mature societies, can be dealt with Jewishly only here; Diaspora Jewish communities leave them to the secular, gentile political order. In France Jews do not have to run a prison system and a police force for the Jews of France and face the problems of how to rehabilitate prisoners or control riots. Only here can Judaism be challenged to see whether it has an answer, not only a better answer but any answer, to such questions in its store of values. Only her can Judaism's applicability to the complex problems of modernity be tried. I give three such examples:

1. The problem of a democratic political system, endowing the people with power and responsibility and protecting the minority from the tyranny of the majority. Does the Jewish heritage suffice? Will it meet the test of a democratic society?

2. Pluralism, accepting the co-existence and legitimacy of a variety of life patterns and values—given that these various life patterns all share the common goal of upholding the State. Short of legitimating groups whose aim is to destroy the State, can Jewish heritage sustain, justify and enhance the ideal of pluralism?

3. The challenge of equality under the law of sexes and creeds, including varieties of the Jewish religion and, of course, ethnic groups among its citizens.

The great value of the Land and the State is that they allow the ultimate experiment with Judaism, testing whether Judaism can supply the ideology and wisdom to engage modernity. This involves a severe restraint on messianism, that is, on the view that the State of Israel is the beginning of the eschaton, the beginning of the final age—in Aramaic *athalta degeula*, the beginning of redemption—a concept incorporated in the prayer for the State composed by the Chief Rabbinate.

This messianic view of the State in effect is a mandate to pursue national egotism, because all rules are suspended if we are living at the beginning of the final age—all normality, rationality and common morality are suspended if we are living in the eschaton. My view of the State as the great experiment to see whether Judaism can face the rest of politics, economics and social amelioration in modern terms demands a restraint of messianism. We cannot say what current history means, we cannot interpret it in terms of reward and punishment, in terms of the covenant idea literally understood. Military victories are not simply portents of divine approval or a license to do what national egotism would lead us to. Defeats are not simply portents of divine disapproval or warnings to be more single-minded, not to say fanatical, in observance of the rituals of Torah.

Jews have a pattern of life consecrated by a religion containing tenets, precepts, rules and admonitions which are socially positive. Judaism lends significance to the daily life of the individual and the community. Although this pattern of life does necessitate a living space, and a living space means recognized and reasonably secure borders, the significance of Judaism ought not be reduced to defending specific borders nor tied to a particular definition of the geographic boundaries of the Jewish State.

[Moshe Greenberg 'Theological Reflections—Land, People and the State', *Immanuel 22/23*, 1989, pp. 26–29]

Jonathan Romain *writes from the perspective of a Reform Jew living in Great Britain. Within his extract he has quoted the resolution issued by the Reform Synagogues of Great Britain (RSGB) during their conference in 1988. The resolution is remarkable because traditionally Reform Judaism has distanced itself from both the Zionist movement and the state of Israel. For Reform Jews today Israel is seen as part of their identity and a necessary haven from persecution:*

At the RSGB Annual Conference in 1988, a resolution on Israel was passed unanimously which declared:

'Meeting in Annual Conference in the fortieth year of the State of Israel the Reform Synagogues of Great Britain reaffirms its total support of the Jewish people's right to it own independent State within secure borders.

The members of the Reform Synagogues of Great Britain regard the State of Israel as a unique expression of our people's faith and history. It is the homeland of our people as well as home to our spirit and our soul. We are concerned partners in the struggle for its peace, its security and its future.

The RSGB calls upon its constituents to renew and increase their efforts to strengthen the State of Israel, especially through *aliyah* and through support for the Israel Movement for Progressive Judaism. We believe that by strengthening Israel we will also enrich Jewish life in the Diaspora through close contact with the land, the people, the language, the history and the problems of modern Israel; in turn, a strong Diaspora will manifest the universal values of Judaism and constitute the primary source and strength and support for Israel leading to the Diaspora and Israeli Jewry working together in harmony towards the achievement of Judaism's Messianic hope".

For Reform Jews today, Israel has a multi-faceted significance: it is the scene of much of the early religious history of Judaism; its memory has been enshrined in Jewish prayer for the last two thousand years; it is one of the few places in the world that has had a continuous Jewish presence since biblical times; it has witnessed a remarkable re-awakening of Jewish consciousness in modern times; it holds an increasingly large percentage of the world's Jewish population; it is a haven for Jews suffering persecution in any other country; and it has become a centre of Jewish creativity and achievement. Without doubt, it occupies a special place in the hearts of all Reform Jews.

[Jonathan Romain, *Faith and Practice*, Reform Synagogues of Great Britain, 1991, p. 202]

CHRISTIAN PERSPECTIVES ON THE LAND

The Christian approach to the land is very different from the Jewish one. This is evident from the extract by **Marcel Dubois**, *a Catholic priest at the Ecumenical Theological Fraternity in Jerusalem. Naturally, there is no sense that Israel is part of being a Christian: instead for Christians there is no particular homeland in this world; the emphasis tends to be on Israel as a place of pilgrimage:*

For Christians, as such, there is no homeland in this world. The entire earth has become the holy land. For Christianity, Jerusalem remains a spiritual center, the holy place par excellence, but this link with the city does not involve any terrestrial possession or national belonging. After Constantine, when the Roman empire became officially Christian, Jerusalem, with all its holy places, the holy sepulchre in particular, became a spiritual center of devotion and pilgrimage.

In short, throughout history we can see that, despite some aspects of Byzantine rule or of the Latin kingdom, Jerusalem is not a political or even a terrestrial reality at all for Christians. To the Christian faith, this city is, at the same time, both a holy place sanctified by the mystery of salvation which took place in it, and a symbol of another, transcendent and spiritual, reality, the celestial Jerusalem, ultimately the sacrament of the kingdom of God, whose Christ is the Lord.

So we can observe the process of spiritualization of the meaning of Jerusalem which has resulted in the ambiguity, or the ambivalence, of 'sacramentality'. We have observed this oscillation between the two dimensions of Jerusalem, according to different emphasis: celestial or terrestrial, eternal or temporal, transcendent or immanent. For Christianity, beginning with Christ himself and the early Christian community, Jerusalem is no longer the center of a nation in this world, a terrestrial homeland, because the church is universal, extended to the whole 'oikumene', including all nations, all races, all cultures, all civilizations. This means that Jerusalem is, above all, a spiritual reality. Thus, in the book of Revelation, Jerusalem appears as a bride coming down from heaven, as a city in the heavens (Rev 21). And in the first epistle of Peter, the church is a temple, a spiritual construction of which Christians are the living stones. In such a perspective, Jerusalem is a new and heavenly city beyond space and time, the center and the symbol of the kingdom of God in eternity.

This new significance of Jerusalem for Christianity is so evident and so fundamental that, during the middle ages, even at the time of the crusades, the terrestrial pilgrimage to the holy land was considered vain and useless. According to this medieval conception, the true home of a Christian is the celestial Jerusalem. Such was already the thought of many church fathers, like Gregory of Nyssa, Jerome, and Augustine. The kingdom of God is inside your heart, and the only true pilgrimage should be an interior one; the only urgent itinerary is the road to holiness, whose goal is the meeting with God in the Jerusalem of the heart.

We find a typical and beautiful manifestation of this spiritual meaning of Jerusalem in the Christian liturgy for the dedication of the churches. As a temple in which dwells the divine presence, every church is a symbol, more precisely a sacrament, of the celestial Jerusalem, and also a symbol of the temple which is in every baptized person. This liturgy includes all the terminology of the Bible which relates to the dedication of the temple or the sanctity of Jerusalem— *'urbs Sion unica'* (unique city of Zion) and *'mansio mystica'* (mystical home), *'condita caelo'* (built in the Heaven) and prayers, antiphons and hymns filled with references to the book of Revelation.

This poetic symbolism is magnificent: the city of Jerusalem is indeed the model of every church, but it refers, in the final analysis, to the celestial Zion. One must beware of suppressing the realistic existence of the symbol in order to preserve the transcendence of the meaning. This was too often the tendency of the fathers of the church: a tendency to a kind

115

of Platonism, a platonizing way of considering the signified reality without paying enough attention to the consistency of the symbol.

The mistake would be to stress so much the purely spiritual meaning of Jerusalem that one would come to forget that this city is also a city of this world, with a worldly and terrestrial life, a day-to-day history, flesh-and-blood citizens. Here we touch the very root of the attitude of some Christians who, in this present-day situation, fail to attach any terrestrial or existential value to the fact that Jewish identity and Jewish destiny are connected with the historical Jerusalem. In such an approach, Jerusalem retains its beautiful spiritual significance but, as a sacrament without matter, a eucharist without bread and wine, a poem without reference.

A balanced conception of the relationship between place and history, between past and memory, could overcome such a danger. It could be said, on this point, that Christian pilgrims rediscover the role of spiritual memory in the approach to the holy places. To visit a site or a landscape of the Hebrew Bible or the gospel is an occasion for remembering, just like the custom of the Jewish people during the celebration of Passover: *'Be'khol dor va'dor ...'* 'In every generation one is obliged to regard himself as though he himself had actually gone out of Egypt ...' The recollection of the very night of the exodus is a way of being present at its permanent actuality. In the same manner, a pilgrimage to the holy places of the Bible is an occasion to recollect, to remind, to re-present, to make present, through the memory of faith, the actuality of the deeds and events which took place there.

We could express this 'sacramental' attitude by quoting a verse from the book of Genesis: *'Vayifga bamaqom'* (28:11). And [Jacob] touched the place." You know whom Jacob encountered during this night and what is the significance of *'Maqom'* in Jewish tradition. Jacob got in touch with God; he touched God through the place, whereupon stood the ladder connecting earth and heaven. Such an expression aptly describes the pilgrimage to Jerusalem: an experience in which the pilgrim, on this spot, in the earthly framework of this city, remembers the reality of the presence of God for our faith.

[Marcel Dubois, 'Israel and Christian Self-Understanding' in *Voices From Jerusalem*, edited D. Burrell and Y. Landau, Paulist Press, 1992, pp. 86–88]

THE CELESTIAL CITY IN ORTHODOX TRADITION

Many Christians either see the land as a place of pilgrimage or as a spiritual image. The spiritualizing of Jerusalem is a popular way that Christians use the 'Old Testament' so Jerusalem as the celestial city is found in most Christian traditions. It figures prominently in the Eastern Orthodox tradition. The Orthodox theologian **George Papademetriou** *illustrates this well. There is virtually no interest in the earthly Jerusalem. Instead the focus is on the theological significance of the city rather than its historical importance. The city becomes the sign of eschatological fulfilment and the final goal:*

The notion that this new Jerusalem is the initial Paradise reestablished or the Christian Church, especially in its triumphal aspect, is the typical point of view represented by the theology and the exegesis of the Orthodox Church. 'The Jerusalem of above is no other than paradise,' said Gregory of Nyssa expressly. 'Hasten to have your name inscribed in the heavenly Church,' wrote Saint Makarios of Egypt, 'in order that you may be found at the right hand of the Most High. Hasten to enter the Holy City, into Jerusalem made peaceful and very high, where Paradise is.'

Celestial Jerusalem, Paradise, and Church form a unity in the theological thought of the exegetes of the East, of whom some admitted the total identification of these realities, and others characterized the Church as 'the image of this city of God' (Eusebios of Caesarea) or the New Jerusalem as the type (the model) of the Church (Andreas). Whatever may be said of it, celestial Jerusalem is the object of the desires of the Christian, as the earthly Jerusalem in the Old Testament was the most desired place for the exiled Jews. Psalm 136: 5–6 expresses the Jewish sentiment in the following words:

If I forget you, Jerusalem,
may my right arm dry up!
May my tongue be stuck to my palate
if I lose the memory of you,
if I do not put Jerusalem
at the peak of my joy!

For the Christian, the celestial Jerusalem becomes the ardently desired object evoked by this Psalm. The road to this city of Paradise has been opened by Jesus Christ. In an ecclesiastical chant for the Great

Monday of the Orthodox Church, we read: 'Lord, you are going to your Passion willingly, and you said to your apostles as you went along the way: "Here we are going up to Jerusalem and the Son of Man will be delivered up, according to what is written of him." Then let us go, also; let us accompany him, with a purified spirit, let us be crucified with him, and let us die with him to the pleasures of life in order that we may live with him and that we may hear him say: "I am no longer going to Jerusalem to suffer, but I go up toward my Father and your Father, my God and your God, and I will cause you to come up toward Jerusalem with me, into the kingdom of heaven".'

In another paschal hymn, the poet is talking to the Church and to the Mother of God and says: 'Shine forth, shine forth, New Jerusalem; for the glory of the Lord is risen on you. Rejoice, and hope, Zion; and you pure Mother of God, rejoice in the resurrection of your Son.'

We shall sum up what has been said before about the place of Jerusalem in the theological thought and in the life of the Orthodox Church. The historical understanding of the city of Jerusalem given by the ancient Church, in spite of the explication of its destruction by the Romans, continues to be in the consciousness of Orthodox peoples the 'Holy Land' which draws pilgrims to it; in Byzantine iconography, Jerusalem very early took on considerable importance. But in the theological thought of the East, we have noticed a tendency to pass from history to theology. It is not the earthly Jerusalem which shaped the object of theological developments, but the celestial Jerusalem, the eschatological Jerusalem. This celestial Jerusalem is presented, at the same time, as an eschatological hope and as a living reality in the actual (earthly) Church militant.

The differences between Judaism and Christianity can be seen here. For both, Jerusalem is the final goal, and, as such, Jerusalem constitutes a message of full hope for our world which is a world without hope. For Judaism, this goal is to be attained in the future, whereas for Christians, it is the realization that it already has begun in the Church and will be consummated at the end of time.

[George Papademetriou, Essays on *Orthodox Christian–Jewish Relations*, Wyndham Press, 1990, pp. 82–84]

'THIS PROPERTY BELONGS TO GOD'—THE SIGNIFICANCE OF THE
LAND FOR PALESTINIAN CHRISTIANS

*One of the most difficult issues vis-à-vis the state of Israel is the relationship
between Jews, Palestinians, and the land. It is this issue which causes most tension
in the diaspora Christian–Jewish dialogue. The land provokes much passion as
Christian groups tend to be either fervently pro-Jewish or pro-Palestinian.*

*It seems clear to me that Palestinian and Jewish voices must each be heard
if the Christian–Jewish Dialogue is to be credible. It is important for all sides
to listen to the pain of 'the other' and to seek a deeper understanding of
their different perspectives. This cannot mean total agreement or syncretism but
granting theological space to 'the other'. Peace and reconciliation cannot be
imposed from outside, particularly from 'the West'. As further progress is made
in the Middle East Peace Process, perhaps Jews and Palestinians will feel more
able to meet and share their respective religious world-views. This has already
begun through small local dialogue groups, but it is not the norm.*

Naim Ateek *is a representative of the indigenous Palestinian Christian
community and one of the few Palestinians who has been involved in the dialogue.
For him, as for his Palestinian sisters and brothers, the land is seen ultimately as
the property of God. The land is of supreme importance to Palestinian Christians
because it is the place where they were born and represents their natural homeland.
It is also the place where God provided salvation for humanity through the person
of Jesus Christ. By their continued presence in the land they see themselves as the
faithful witnesses to the event of the resurrection:*

One of the most beautiful customs that a visitor can observe among
Arabs in the Middle East is the way they give recognition to God's
ownership of the land. When people build their houses, many of them
ask the builder to engrave on a stone in bold Arabic one of two phrases
that will usually appear above the front door of the house: either *Almulk
lillah*, which means 'property belongs to God', or *Hatha min fudli Rubbi*,
'this house has been built as a result of the beneficence of my Lord'.

Having conceded that all of life and all land belong ultimately to
God, Palestinian Christians, like all other Palestinians, cherish the land
and are loyal to it because it is the land of their birth and the land of
their ancestors. It is their homeland, *watan*.

Those of us who have been born and brought up in Israel–Palestine
recognize that it is indeed a privilege to have been born in the land
that has witnessed some of the greatest events of history. The land is

sacred to the three monotheistic religions—Judaism, Islam, and Christianity. Each in its own way, and by using its own vocabulary of faith, must express the significance of the land to its adherents and to the millions who choose to visit it.

As part of a theology of liberation for Palestinians, I would like to call attention to the significance of the land for its Christian population, especially at a time when the presence of indigenous Christians is rapidly dwindling because of emigration. There are three significant things that define and inspire Palestinian Christians' devotion to the land:

The Land of Palestine Hosted the Great Event of the Incarnation

Jesus was born in Bethlehem, grew up in Nazareth, was bapitized in the Jordan River, lived most of his life in the Galilee, was crucified, died, and was buried in Jerusalem. Jesus Christ's resurrection took place in Jerusalem. Therefore, the first witnesses to the Resurrection were Palestinians; the Church was born in Palestine as the early disciples and followers of Jesus were Palestinians. In Jerusalem on the day of Pentecost the Holy Spirit was poured out, the Gospel of the living Christ was first proclaimed in Jerusalem, and from Jerusalem his witnesses went out to the ends of the earth.

The Palestinian Christians of today are the descendants of those early Christians, yet this is no cause for *hubris*. With a humility that befits their Lord, they accept it as a privilege that carries with it a responsibility for service. Palestinian Christians of today are the present generation of that great cloud of witnesses to Jesus who came before them, and who will, God willing, come after them until Christ comes again. They and their ancestors have maintained a living witness to Jesus and his Resurrection from the beginning of the Church, and they should see themselves dynamically continuing such a witness in the land, witnesses to the Resurrection.

The Witness of Our Land to Scripture

A seminal biblical scholar of the nineteenth century, when visiting Palestine in 1860–61, called it a 'fifth Gospel'. He saw a "striking agreement of the texts with the places, the marvellous harmony of the Gospel ideal with the country." The direct personal knowledge and experience of the land of the Bible can supplement the accounts of the Gospels by enriching and deepening the faith and devotion of the believer.

In his *Catechetical Lectures*, St Cyril of Jerusalem (*c.* 304–386) considered the various places of Palestine as bearing a true witness to Christ. Such sites as the Jordan River, the Sea of Galilee, and the Mount of Olives were for him an eloquent witness to Jesus Christ. What was true for St Cyril, the archbishop of Jerusalem in the fourth century, is still true today in the experience of countless pilgrims. Palestine is a fifth Gospel to them. Indeed, the faith of the pilgrim can come alive through visiting holy sites, from being where Jesus had been, and walking where he had walked. It is, however, equally important for Christian pilgrims to meet the living stones of the land—the Christians. To visit the holy sites is a very moving experience for many; meeting the 'holy' people can be a very rewarding and enriching experience for both. Visiting museums can give a person an important sense and appreciation for the past; but to visit the churches of the land, to worship with the indigenous Christians, and to meet them personally can give the pilgrim both a sense of appreciation for the present and an invaluable experience and insight into the life of the living and pulsating Christian communities of the land, who with their ancestors before them have borne a continuing witness to Christ for the last two thousand years.

Indigenous Christians who are privileged to live in Israel–Palestine today have a responsibility to Christian pilgrims from all over the world—to make their pilgrimage a revitalizing experience of their faith. Their responsibility and privilege is to be host to their brothers and sisters from abroad.

Jesus Christ, Prince of Peace

Christians believe that the message of the only true authentic peace first resounded from the hills of Bethlehem:

> Glory to God in the highest,
> and on earth peace
> among men (and women) with whom he is pleased!

Palestinian Christians, therefore, recognize their responsibility as peacemakers. As will be made clear in chapter 6, they should be actively involved in the work of justice, peace, and reconciliation, calling to remembrance the words of Jesus,

> Blessed are the peacemakers,
> for they shall be called sons (and daughters) of God.

[Naim Ateek, *Justice and Only Justice*, Orbis, 1989, pp. 112–114]

THE ENCOUNTER WITH LIVING JUDAISM

Naim Ateek highlights the importance of Christian pilgrims meeting the indige-nous Arab Christians in the 'Holy Land'. It is important also to remember the other indigenous Christian groups. Often very small Christian communities have managed to survive for centuries: the Greek Orthodox Christians, the Armenians, the Copts, the Ethiopians, the Latin Catholics, the Greek Catholics—to name but a few. They are all small, yet significant. Encountering the diversity of Israel is important. For every Christian group, there are numerous different Jewish groups. The following extract from **David Hill** *(1959–1995), an English Catholic and co-founder of the Exeter and Southwest Council of Christians and Jews in England, stresses the diversity of Judaism. It comes from his unpublished reflections on his first and only visit to Israel as part of a Young Leader's study Tour with the Council of Christians and Jews. His encounter with Orthodox Jews in Israel itself was to have a profound impact on him. His reflec-tions succinctly capture the atmosphere of Shabbat and indirectly the importance of Christians encountering the dynamic expressions of Judaism:*

Friday evening: to the Western Wall:

The site at the Wall is fascinating and moving. Hundreds of men in black coats and hats, all swaying and reading and chanting. Some were chatting, some were dancing. All were happy. Lots of onlookers, everyone friendly.

The wall has a separate area for women. This was less populated (though crowded nonetheless) which reflects the Jewish law which places no burden of duty on a Jewish woman to pray.

Meah Shearim and the Tisch:

After the first meal of Shabbat, to Meah Shearim for a Tisch. This is a ceremony where, in liturgical format, the remains of the Rabbi's Shabbat meal are eaten by his followers. The Rabbi is seen as the source of all spiritual life and the crumbs from his Shabbat meal have a special significance—part of the Kabbala (mystical tradition). The songs were quite extraordinary: chanting like a football crowd, a great rush of men in black and gold with long side locks all very excited and happy. There were little boys shouting the songs too.

I was fascinated by the enthusiasm and zeal of his community. Some would say it is fanaticism, but I see little of exception in the belief, especially when seen in context of the traditional Christian (non-Protestant) belief in the *real presence*.

Tour of synagogues in west Jerusalem:

This is an area of traditional Judaism—orthodox, but not ultra-orthodox. The synagogues of the Sephardic areas are very small, big enough for perhaps 20 men. Some with no space for women. Many, particularly from Syria, are intricately decorated inside. Each synagogue will have its own courtyard wherein lives the community: Ashkenazi, Iraqi, Syrian, Jerusalem. Each has its own particular way of praying. All are basically the same form however, and all are orthodox. We looked into about ten synagogues in a tiny area, some with fifty worshippers, some with just ten. The Sephardi communities are very tactile in their liturgies: much kissing of the scrolls, much blessing of each other.

What a contrast to the Great Synagogue: cathedral like proportions, with a beautiful cantor who sang the service while the rest read along in their books.

[David Hill, from 'An Annotated Description and Personal Experience of the Council of Christians and Jews Young Adults Israel Study Tour, 18–29 July 1993', unpublished material]

THEOLOGICAL PROBLEMS AND ISRAEL

We have looked at the Jewish commitment to the land and some of the political problems within it. We now link these issues with the overt theological problem. In this commissioned piece for the Reader **Ian Markham** *(lecturer in Theology of Religions and Philosophy at the University of Exeter, England) argues that a traditional faith can help the dialogue and not hinder it. In this respect, he is typical of a growing number of participants in the dialogue (for example, David Novak in New York and Keith Ward in Oxford) who want to affirm their own faith and yet explore both the similarities and differences between the faith traditions. Remarkably Ian Markham illustrates this approach by examining the role of providence with respect to the State of Israel. For most people talk about Israel as a divine action seems very unhelpful, however he believes that this could provide the way forward.*

What sort of God do we believe in? To many the God of Interfaith dialogue is quite different from the God revealed in Scripture. The Interfaith God must not do anything to offend any other religious traditions. So Christians are told that the particularity of the Incarnation must go; Muslims are chastised for daring to talk about the final and infallible revelation of God in the Qur'an; and Jews are

123

frowned upon if they have the temerity to imagine that they are a covenant people who have been given Israel. Mutual understanding for those involved in dialogue seems to need the eradication of difference. The final revelation of Jesus for Christians or the Qur'an for Muslims seems denigratory to other claims to revelation; a covenant revelation involving a land leaves the Palestinians as a people opposed to God. The only solution, so it seems, is to reduce theology to a bare minimum, John Hick's 'Real'—an objective entity about which we know nothing.

But perhaps there is another way. Instead of denying difference; we should confront the differences and search for the similarities. When traditions agree, then it is good evidence that it is revealed from God; disagreements should be understood and grappled with. God is the Creator of the whole world so it is highly likely that God has made himself known to the whole world. By listening and learning from each other we can move forward in our own faith. And when it comes to the topic of 'what sort of God do we believe in', the three traditions speak with one voice: 'we believe in a God who is active and intervening, a God who cares for his people, a God far removed from the impoverished Interfaith God'.

Israel, ironically, illustrates this agreement. The theme of the Land dominates the Hebrew Bible. It is a land that God promised to Abraham (Genesis 12); it is a land that God gave to suffering people who were oppressed in Egypt (Exodus 3); and it is from the land that God both exiles and then returns the Jewish people (Isaiah 45). The God the Jewish people discovered is a God of history who requires of his people the highest ethical standards. Christians and Muslims inherited this idea of God; and the story of God's dealings with the Jewish people documented in the Hebrew scriptures became a part of the Christian and Islamic traditions.

Both traditions supplemented this inheritance by particular and distinctive links with the Land. For Christians, God himself was born, taught, and most amazing of all, died in Israel. For Muslims the Prophet made the *Isra*—the night journey on a winged horse to Jerusalem. It was from Jerusalem that Muhammad ascended through the Seven Heavens. God, so it seems, has made Israel a sacred place for all three Abrahamic faiths.

Many sensitive believers in all three traditions are shocked by the idea of providence. A God controlling history seems rather strange in a post-Enlightenment age where history is explained by political, social and economic factors. What are the mechanisms by which God works? And if God intervenes in human affairs occasionally, then why does he not do so more often? So many nations are suffering; why doesn't the omnipotent, loving God of theism intervene and relieve that suffering?

These are difficult questions. The temptation is to surrender this shared vision of God and turn God into the Creator, who simply provides the framework in which we all exercise our autonomy. However, it is important to resist this temptation. Instead we should grapple with our tradition. And as we do so, the following picture emerges. Primarily (although not exclusively) God's agency is through the hearts and minds of those who are open to him. God cannot both respect that freedom and constantly override it. God enlarges vision and frustrates evil. Prayer opens us to the divine perspective; prayer for others is the hope that the gentle and firm persuasion of love can transform the other's perspective.

As we reflect on the events of this century, I am certain that the emergence of the state of Israel is a divine action. It took many millions of people to see that a Jewish homeland is a necessity. One of the many horrific elements to the holocaust experience was the discovery that a Jew who was settled for many centuries in Europe was not allowed to consider it home. There was no security here. And the Jew had nowhere to go. The Jews, it seemed did not belong anywhere. It was wholly right that the world finally realized the Jewish aspiration for a small patch of the globe to be theirs.

Yet our scriptures also teach that God expects the highest ethical standards of his people. The Palestinians have their own tragic story. They are victims of national and global insensitivity. We must find a way of embracing the Palestinian. It looks as if Israel is required by God to become an experiment in the affirmation of diversity. The survival of the state depends on the accommodation of different religions, diverse languages, and contrasting ways of life. Secularists insist that tolerance requires a rejection of religion: for Israel this is not an option. Israel will always attract the religious. Europeans managed to achieve tolerance by insisting on uniformity; this too is not an option. The Jewish, Palestinian, and Christian communities subdivide into hundreds of different cultures all coexisting in Israel. Many of these communities are very small, and understandably paranoid. Israel must find a new way; she must discover tolerance by embracing diversity.

To interpret events in Israel providentially does not add to the problems, but in fact can become the foundation of hope. We hope because we trust. We trust because we are called to live our lives open to the leading of God.

[Ian S. Markham, Professor of Theology, Liverpool Hope University and author of *Plurality and Christian Ethics*.]

THE VATICAN RECOGNIZES THE STATE OF ISRAEL

Until recently the Catholic Church had not recognized the state of Israel de jure. *It had only recognized it* de facto. *This had caused considerable tension and misunderstanding in Catholic–Jewish relations. Whilst huge progress was being made in other areas of the relationship, particularly in Catholic teaching, the issue of the status of Israel remained a sore point. In December 1993, the Vatican formally recognized the State of Israel. Although this may be viewed solely as a political move on the part of the Vatican, there are major theological implications. Not least the repudiation of the myth of the Wandering Jew. Since the time of Augustine the Church had taught that the Jews had lost their land for rejecting Christ. As a result of their refusal to accept Christ they had been destined to wander the earth until the end of time. The significance of the recent recognition of the State of Israel should not be underestimated.* **Geoffrey Wigoder,** *an American Jew who is actively involved in the Jewish–Catholic dialogue, has summed up this significance in an article published in the Jewish Chronicle:*

Seen in its historical perspective, yesterday's scheduled signing of an agreement of mutual recognition between the Vatican and Israel, with the declared intention of exchanging ambassadors in the near future, is a revolutionary development.

Ninety years ago, Theodor Herzl had an audience with then Pope Pius X, who told him: 'If you come to Palestine and settle your people there, we shall have churches and priests ready to baptise all of you.' Thereafter the Vatican was consistent in its hostility to Zionism, while trying to get a foot back into the Holy Land.

With the expulsion of the Muslim Turks in 1917, the Vatican lobbied for the Mandate over Palestine to be given to a Catholic power and not to Protestant Britain. When the British were about to leave in 1947, it managed to have the internationalisation of Jerusalem incorporated in the UN partition proposal. After 1967, the Vatican worked for an internationally guaranteed status for Jerusalem and the holy places. All these efforts proved to be non-starters, but this did not put an end to the Vatican's hope of establishing a presence in the Holy Land.

After the creation of the State of Israel in 1948, the Vatican refused even to utter its name. When the Israel Philharmonic Orchestra played before Pius XII in 1954, the Vatican communiqué stated that he had received 'a group of refugee Jewish musicians', while Paul VI spent a whole day in Jerusalem in 1964 without uttering the 'I' word.

The change in attitudes began in the late 1960s, when Israeli Premiers and Foreign Ministers were received by successive Popes. In the early 1980s, the present Pope, John Paul II, not only referred to Israel by name, but also stressed the right of the Jews to a secure homeland. The failure of the Holy See to accord *de jure* recognition before now has been one of the main obstacles in the international dialogue between Jews and Catholics. It appeared even more important to world Jewry—especially those living in countries with Catholic majorities—than to Israel, for whom the issue was never a priority. Whenever the Pope met Jewish leaders, in the Vatican or on his travels, they invariably put relations with Israel high on the agenda. Dutch Jewish leaders refused to meet him until the issue had been resolved.

Jews long suspected that the refusal to recognise Israel was due, at least in part, to theological considerations. The Roman Catholic Church had always taught that the Jews had been exiled from their land as a punishment for not recognising Jesus and would not return until they had done so. However, the Vatican's claim that this was not the problem was confirmed in an official statement in 1987, which asserted that the obstacles were purely political. Fear of reprisals by Arab countries—in which there are many Catholic and Church interests—played a major role. The Vatican frequently stressed that relations with Israel could be established only after the question of Palestinian refugees and the status of the West Bank and Jerusalem had been resolved. Then, 18 months ago, the Vatican announced that it was willing to negotiate an agreement, with the eventual intention of exchanging ambassadors. The negotiations dealt with local matters, such as the legal status of the holy places and of Catholic communities in Israel, and their exemption from taxation. There was no mention of the status of Jerusalem and other 'big problems'.

The sudden change was the result of the Israel–Arab peace process, launched in Madrid at the end of 1991. The Vatican foresaw the likelihood of major changes in the Middle East and did not want to be left out. Moreover, with Israel establishing relations with Russia, India, China and Egypt, and talking to many Arab states, the Vatican's position was no longer tenable. In the event, the non-Catholic churches kept a close watch on the Vatican's efforts to strengthen its position in the Holy Land. These churches have always been jealous of the Vatican and expressed the fear that the Catholic Church might achieve some preference. The Israeli government has been at pains to pacify these churches and assure them that any concessions to the Catholics would apply equally to all other churches.

For Israel, the importance of the Vatican's recognition lies in its message of legitimacy that will be carried to Catholics the world over. For Jews, the significance is in the implicit acknowledgement and rectification of a long, historical and theological distortion. Indeed, there is a profound symbolism in the mutuality of the agreement, in which the Jewish state has officially recognised the Vatican.

[Geoffrey Wigoder, 'Israel-Vatican Agreement Signals an End to "theological distortion" by Catholic Church', *Jewish Chronicle, 31 December,* 1993, p. 7]

THE WORLD COUNCIL OF CHURCHES

The following extract has been taken from an official statement of the World Council of Churches, made in 1982. To express such a statement is an amazing achievement given the diversity of Christian world-views which make up the World Council of Churches. It quite clearly affirms the importance of Israel for Jewish self-identity and expression:

2.4: Through history there are times and places in which Jews were allowed to live, respected and accepted by the cultures in which they resided, and where their own culture thrived and made a distinct and sought-after contribution to their Christian and Muslim neighbours. Often lands not dominated by Christians proved most favourable for Jewish diaspora living. There were even times when Jewish thinkers came to 'make a virtue out of necessity' and considered diaspora living to be the distinct genius of Jewish existence.

2.5: Yet, there was no time in which the memory of the Land of Israel and of Zion, the city of Jerusalem, was not central in the worship and hope of the Jewish people. 'Next year in Jerusalem' was always part of Jewish worship in the diaspora. And the continued presence of Jews in the Land and in Jerusalem was always more than just one place of residence among all the others.

2.6: Jews differ in their interpretations of the State of Israel, as to it religious and secular meaning. It constitutes for them part of the long search for that survival which has always been central to Judaism through the ages. Now the quest for statehood by Palestinians—Christian and Muslim—as part of their search for survival as a people in the Land, also calls for full attention.

2.7: Jews, Christians and Muslims have all maintained a presence in the Land from their beginnings. While "the Holy Land" is primarily a Christian designation, the Land is holy to all three. Although they may understand its holiness in different ways, it cannot be said to be "more holy" to one than to another.

['Ecumenical Considerations on the Jewish–Christian Dialogue, Geneva, 1982' in *The Theology of the Churches and the Jewish People*, World Council of Churches Publication, 1988, pp. 39–40]

INTER-FAITH RELATIONS AND THE DIALOGUE IN ISRAEL

*The two official Church statements above are representative of those communities which live outside the land of Israel. They are involved in a very different form of the Christian–Jewish dialogue from those living in the land itself. The final extract focuses on the dialogue-scene in Israel itself. In it **David Rosen** highlights the fact that the dialogue in Israel is very different from any Western dialogue. He locates this difference in the non-democratic and pre-modern outlook which is the experience of most of the religious communities in Israel. David Rosen has had many years of experience in interfaith relations and works as an Orthodox Rabbi in Jerusalem and a member of 'Clergy for Peace'. He is a key figure in the international scene of Christian–Jewish relations, having negotiated with the Vatican on its recent recognition of the State of Israel. He is passionately committed to the improvement of Jewish–Arab relations and dialogue between the indigenous communities in Israel:*

Jerusalem today is a mosaic—a beautiful mosaic—made up of individual little squares/components, each separated from those around it by a cement border—often quite impenetrable. Most religious communities in Jerusalem live in splendid isolation of the others. This is partly due to theology and politics but it seems to me that the mind-set is primarily determined by sociology.

The observer notes with some perplexity that within Jerusalem's different Christian denominations, for example, social relations are often strained. However, even when they are not, there is rarely any theological dialogue. Such an idea is often viewed with horror. I believe that this reserve stems substantially from what may be described as a pre-modern view of the world.

Each of these denominations believes that it alone is the authentic bearer of true Christianity and that Christianity is the only ultimate truth. For them it is obvious that there cannot be more than one truth. Therefore, if I am right, the other cannot also be right. Thus, as I am the only right one, then what can any other denomination, let alone faith, have to offer me? The only basis for our exchange is persuasion or polemic.

A pluralist approach that actually seeks out and supports dialogue as a process of growth and enrichment is generally a modern expression born out of an acceptance and even affirmation of the diversity and pluralism of contemporary life. The long-standing Arab Christian communities in the Holy Land, as well as its much larger Arab Muslim population, are overwhelmingly of a mind-set that may be described as pre-modern. For the majority, pluralism is at best an undesirable necessity and inter-religious dialogue is a waste of time, if not worse.

However, the same goes for the vast majority of Jews in Israel. Israel is something of an optical illusion. She is a modern democracy and has made amazing strides in science, technology, and the arts. This is all the more remarkable when one takes into consideration not only that Israel is located in a highly undemocratic region, but also that the vast majority of Israelis do not come from democratic, pluralistic cultures. I refer not only to the majority of Israel's Jews who came from Islamic lands, but even those from Eastern Europe. Moreover, given the military, political and economic pressures that could have torn a mature democracy asunder, the development and maintenance of Israel's democratic institutions is even more impressive.

Israel's Declaration of Independence guarantees freedom of religious expression to all. Assuredly, most of the State's founders genuinely believed in this principle. It is to Israel's enormous credit that despite the conflict in which she was born and has had to contend, she has ensured equality of franchise, the rule of law and not only the freedom of worship, but even the advancement of the different religious minorities in the State, in accordance with her Declaration of Independence.

However, I believe it is fair to state that most Jewish Israelis, precisely because of their pre-modern cultural background, see the principle of freedom of religion as a favour which the magnanimous majority provides for its minorities as long as the latter know and keep their place. For the vast majority of Israeli Jews, there is no logical reason whatsoever, why they should encourage a growth of religious expression of other Faiths.

We should not forget that well over ninety per cent of Jewish Israelis have never met a Christian—especially not a modern Christian. Even when Israelis travel abroad and meet non-Jews, they rarely encounter believing Christians. Most Israelis take their image of a Christian from the long and tragic historical experience. A Christian is widely seen as someone who wants at best to steal my soul, if not to actually wish me physical harm. And even if most Israeli Jews see Islamic 'fundamentalism' as the greatest threat and may well recognise it as such for Christians also, this does not wipe out the historic suspicion of Christianity. The burden of the past weighs heavy on all religious groups in our land. It is not unusual (as was the case during the Gulf War) to hear pejorative references to the crusades or to the most intolerant periods of Islamic rule. All of us in the Middle East see ourselves as victims; as the 'other', in some way.

Interfaith relations here are often at best a fragile matter of 'live and let live', in which the members of each group, believing in their exclusive claim to "truth", are prepared to tolerate the existence of others. There is some social intercourse amongst representatives of the different denominations at official gatherings, but hardly anything that touches the lives of the rank and file and little or no theological exchange. That is not to say that there is no cooperation between people from different communities. According to a survey by the Abraham Fund, there are over two hundred organizations in Israel promoting Jewish–Arab coexistence. Moreover, where communities have been able to grow up alongside each other relatively unvitiated by the political tensions, such as in parts of Galilee, Haifa, Acre and in Jaffa and Beer Sheva, one finds significant cooperation and joint ventures. Yet most of this takes place on a 'secular' basis and rarely involves the most religiously committed elements from either community.

The major religious presence that has laboured in the interfaith vineyard has been disproportionately Christian, but not primarily from the Arab Christian communities. The principle religious impetus for interfaith relations has come from expatriate theologians and scholars. Their predominant western background reflects again the importance of the socio-cultural factors that lend themselves to interreligious dialogue. Yet, despite their limited number, their significance must not be underestimated. The non-Arab Christian presence in Israel has served as a small but significant bridge between communities. Also they have a great number of contacts among pilgrims and fact finding tours. Their role is of great importance in developing greater understanding between Christian Arabs and their Jewish fellow citizens.

[David Rosen, 'Letter From Jerusalem' in *Common Ground*, no 1, 1994, pp. 20–21]

FURTHER READING

Burrell, David & Landau, Yehezkel (edited). *Voices From Jerusalem: Jews and Christians Reflect on the Holy Land*, Paulist Press, 1992.

Cohen, Naomi (edited). *Essential Papers on Jewish–Christian Relations in the United States*, New York University Press, 1990.

Davies, W. *The Territorial Dimension of Judaism*, University of California Press, 1982.

Eckhardt, A. Roy & Eckhardt, Alice. *Encounter With Israel: A Challenge to Conscience*, Association, 1970.

Gordan, Haim & Gordan, Rivca (edited). *Israel/Palestine: The Quest for Dialogue*, Orbis, 1991.

Heschel, Abraham Joshua. *Israel: An Echo of Eternity*, Farrar, Straus & Giroux, 1967.

Hoffman, Lawrence (edited). *The Land of Israel: Jewish Perspectives*, Notre Dame Press, 1986.

Parkes, James. *End of an Exile: Israel, the Jews and the Gentile World*, Micah Publications, 1982.

Rottenberg, Isaac. *The Turbulent Triangle: Christians, Jews and Israel*, Red Mountain Associates, 1989.

Rudin, James. *Israel for Christians*, Fortress, 1983.

CHAPTER SIX

THE JEWISH JESUS

CHAPTER SIX

THE JEWISH JESUS

The nineteenth century marked the beginning of 'the quest for the historical Jesus'. Christian scholars by using various historical-critical methods sought to uncover the historical figure from the layers of Christian tradition in the Gospels. Even though the research has gone through particular waves and trends, there has been a general recognition that Jesus should be located within one of the diverse Judaisms of his day. In this endeavour, Jewish scholars have now taken seriously the historical Jesus research and are making distinctive contributions to this field.

The extracts in this chapter highlight how Jews and Christians view the Jewish Jesus. It will soon become apparent that the extracts are taken from the Western dialogue. In Israel itself there is very little interest in the figure of Jesus amongst the predominantly Orthodox Jewish communities. This is perhaps not surprising given the fact that their faith can function adequately without any reference to him.

However, for those who are engaged in Christian–Jewish dialogue the figure of Jesus remains fascinating. There are Jews who feel sufficiently unthreatened in the dialogue to express their views on Jesus. While some Christians find the Jewish 'no' to Jesus puzzling, often the dialogue has led to a rediscovery of the Jewishness of Jesus. This chapter will show that generally Jews have no difficulty with the Jewish Jesus but they do reject the Christ of Christian faith. It is one thing to accept Jesus as a great Jewish prophet, but quite another to accept him as the Second Person of the Trinity.

H.P.F.

JESUS FROM A JEWISH PERSPECTIVE

*For **Aubrey Rose**, a British Jew involved in the dialogue, Jesus is part of Jewish history and his contribution should be written into the Jewish experience. This does not entail, for him, the recognition of the Christ of Christian faith but the incorporation of Jesus in a totally Jewish way—without any Christian influence or pressure. Jews will not be able to accept Jesus as both God and man, but can accord appropriate respect for him:*

Jews have been fascinated by the figure of Jesus since his birth. He lived as a Jew among Jews for his recorded life, spoke Hebrew and Aramaic, was seen as a Jew by non-Jews. In the last 100 years many Jewish scholars have written about him. The story of Jesus is part of Jewish history. I would like to see his story incorporated in that history, so that, in my view suitable respect can be accorded to him, just as other Jewish figures are respected in other faiths. At the same time I would like to see the Jewish people respected by the ending of attempts to undermine its coherence by the activities of Christian missionaries.

It may be difficult for Christians and for some Jews to accept anything that I have to say. I also have problems of understanding. I do not know, when a Christian says, Lord, who is meant. A true Christian will see Jesus as the singular emanation of God, to the exclusion of all others. Hence my problems, as Jesus is treated both as God and as man at the same time. Is this possible?

There are Jews who, even today, cannot bring themselves to mention the word Jesus, so painful is it because of the terrible persecution committed in his name. My mother, raised in Poland, told me she heard a priest in church there rouse the people to fury against the Jews because of the death of Jesus. This behaviour of the Church remains the main cause of past and current anti-Semitism, which can even prevail in a country where few Jews are present. Those teachings provided fertile ground for the assault on the Jewish people from 1933 to 1945.

That same anti-Semitism would also affect Jesus and his followers if in some way, as Jews, they were physically amongst us today.

There is no doubt but that there are massive differences of doctrine between Judaism and Christianity, as to sin, priesthood, marriage, divorce, the path to salvation. There are similar problems within each religion—violent differences, where one group of Christians will call other Christians anti-Christ, where one group of Jews will never set foot in certain synagogues and refuse to acknowledge their Ministers by the title Rabbi. Jesus, who preached above all love and forgiveness, yet who was angered by hypocrisy, would call them all vipers and hypocrites.

What Jesus did have, as other great religious leaders had, was a sense of the Eternal. He knew true reality was beyond space and time. He knew that he himself was a voyager between two worlds, in fact he was aware of both worlds all the time, in touch with both worlds constantly, and tried to help others in their individual voyages between here and there. He knew that the physical was merely an emanation of the spirit, hence his insistence on the search inwards to find the Kingdom, the *Malchut*, of God.

[Aubrey Rose, 'Jesus, the Nazarene—a Jewish View', *Common Ground*, 1990, no 1, pp. 3–32]

THE DIFFICULTIES OF A JEW TALKING TO A CHRISTIAN
ABOUT JESUS

Lewis Eron, *associate Rabbi at Temple B'nai Abraham in Livingston in the United States, has written widely on the area of Christian–Jewish relations. He shares Aubrey Rose's interest in Jesus as part of Jewish history. Jesus as a Jew contributes to an understanding of the diverse expressions of Judaism in the first century* CE. *However, for Lewis Eron this is as far as it goes. It is not necessary for Jesus to be written into the Jewish tradition in the way that Aubrey Rose would suggest. For him, the key issue remains a Christological one: Jesus the Christ becomes a way to God for Christians but not for Jews. He suggests that the dialogue could fruitfully explore the ways in which God is present in the Torah for Jews and in the person of Christ for Christians:*

The centrality of Jesus to Christian faith, as well as centering in Jesus most of the leadership archetypes of the Hebrew Scripture from the writings of the earliest Christians on, has no simple parallel within Judaism. Kingship, prophecy, sacrifice, redemption, priesthood, messianism, apocalypticism, discipleship, and so on are among the many topics that find their focus in Jesus in Christianity but have no such single focus within the Jewish tradition.

In addition, Jesus, particularly in the guise of the proclaimed Christ, becomes a way of access to God for Christians. This topic could open up a spiritual aspect of our dialogue. As Christians find God through

Jesus, Jews find God through Torah. Investigating this aspect of the dialogue surely needs to bring the partners beyond the historical question of Jesus' understanding of the Law and into the deeper questions of how one approaches God. What is one to do or to believe? What does it mean if one considers God's word incarnate in a flesh-and-blood human or in a book? What does it mean that this book itself has a history and that it grew over time? How does the presence of God's word in a continuing Torah tradition in the Jewish tradition function with respect to Jesus in the Christian?

There is also a particular Jewish interest in Jesus as a historical figure. Some modern Jewish scholars and authors have taken an interest in Jesus in the same way that they have with Jewish figures, such as Elisha ben Abuya, Josephus, David Reubeni, various mystic teachers, and messianic pretenders. This reflects their search for new models of leadership in persons outside of the 'normative' Jewish tradition during a period of radical change in the structure of Jewish personal and communal life. As a Jew studying Jesus and the earliest Church in a Jewish context, I do not approach the issue as part of a primarily religious quest. Jesus and the writings of his apostles are for me examples of the broad span of Jewish religious and philosophic experiences of the first centuries BCE and CE. Jesus of Nazareth is of course interesting as the inspiration of a vast religious movement; so too is, for example, the more elusive Teacher of Righteousness of the Community of the Qumran scrolls. Jesus of Nazareth, a Jew of the first century, is for me—Lewis Eron, a Jew of the twentieth century—of interest and concern mainly insofar as I am interested in the history of my people in late antiquity. Jesus and his followers are a few of the many who attract my interest.

[Lewis John Eron, 'The Problem of a Jew Talking to a Christian about Jesus' in *Bursting the Bonds: A Jewish–Christian Dialogue on Jesus and Paul*, Orbis, pp. 23–24]

WHO DO YOU SAY THAT I AM?

The next extract is very different from the two above. It is taken from the perspective of a Polish Jew, **Byron Sherwin**, *who experienced the Nazi occupation of Poland in the 1940s and the annihilation of Polish Jewry. For him, Jesus can be none other than a Polish Jew who shares the suffering of contemporary Polish Jews and seeks refuge from the Nazis:*

Jewish children do not spend much time thinking about Jesus, but, as a child, I did. Growing up in the years after the Holocaust and knowing the fate of Polish Jews, it is perhaps not surprising that I thought of Jesus as a Polish Jew. As a young child, I knew that Jesus died a terrible death, and I knew that millions of Polish Jews died horrible deaths. As a child, I had even heard Hitler called the 'anti-Christ', and he was compared to Pontius Pilate. Therefore, since a child I have pictured Jesus dressed like and living like a Polish Jew. Such a view of Jesus as a Polish Jew is also found in the artwork of two of the greatest Jewish artists to come from Poland: Marc Chagall and Maurycy Gottlieb.

I picture Jesus as a tortured, wandering, wounded Polish Jew crawling in pain into the doorway of a Polish Catholic home during the Nazi occupation and asking for refuge. A small child finds him and calls his parents: 'Mommy, Daddy,' says the child, 'there is a wounded Jew at the door asking for help, and he says his name is Jesus.' The parents come to the door and ask: 'Are you a Jew? Are you Jesus?' And the man replies, 'Who do you think that I am?'

[Byron Sherwin, 'Who do you say that I am? (Mark 8 v.29): A New Jewish View of Jesus' in *Journal of Ecumenical Studies*, Summer–Fall 1994, 31:3–4, p. 267]

THE CHRISTIAN REDISCOVERY OF JESUS' JEWISHNESS

Coming to terms with the Jewishness of Jesus has been a relatively recent development for Christians. As mentioned in the introduction, Christian scholars have been engaged in historical Jesus research since the nineteenth century. Until then the overt recognition of the Jewishness of Jesus was rare, deemed irrelevant to Christian faith. It was often assumed that because Jesus founded the Church he was a Christian. On occasions it has been known for Christian preachers to talk about Mary taking Jesus to Church! However, there is a growing awareness in the Churches of Jesus' Jewish roots. In this respect **Daniel Harrington***, a Catholic New Testament scholar, provides a clear and helpful summary of Jesus' ministry. He locates Jesus within the prophetic tradition as an itinerant preacher who proclaims the imminent kingdom of God:*

The context of Jesus' teaching was Judaism. To be even more precise, its context was first-century Judaism in the land of Israel. Thus there is a basic level on which Christians and Jews can agree about Jesus of Nazareth. That Jesus the Galilean was born, lived, and died in the land of Israel in the early part of what we now call the first century CE cannot be doubted. This Jesus was a Jewish teacher, though of a some-what unusual type. He taught by means of short sayings and parables, which could be easily remembered and then recited from memory. He attracted disciples, who came to learn from him and to be with him. While Capernaum may have been his base of operations, much of his teaching ministry involved traveling from place to place and relying on the hospitality of local people. His first followers were encouraged to share his itinerant ministry of preaching God's kingdom and healing the sick.

Much of his teaching recorded in the gospels breathes the air of first-century Judaism. Though now expressed in Greek, those teach-ings incorporate Semitic idioms and words, presuppose conditions that prevailed in the land of Israel, and respond well to translation back into Aramaic or Hebrew. Jesus seems to have taught in Aramaic, though like other Jews of his day he knew Hebrew, may well have spoken some Greek, and had exposure to Latin. As he taught various audiences in Galilee, he readily appealed to their familiarity with sowing seeds (see Mark 4:3–9, 26–29, 30–32), baking bread (see Matt. 13:33), hiding treasure (see Matt. 13:44), fishing (see Matt. 13:47–50), and so forth. All these activities were so familiar to Jesus' audiences in the land of Israel during the first century that they needed no explana-tion. By appealing to the everyday experiences of his audiences, Jesus was able to lead them to further reflection on the person of God, the kingdom of God, and God's dealings with his people.

The content of Jesus' teaching is firmly rooted in Judaism as it is expressed in the Hebrew Bible and the Jewish tradition. The God of Jesus can be approached as a loving Father. This God created and sustains all things. This God has entered into a special relationship with the people of Abraham, Isaac, and Jacob. This God has special concern for the poor and the outcast. There is no doubt: The God of Jesus is Israel's God.

Along with other Jews of his day, Jesus looked to the time when God would intervene in his people's history and when all creation would acknowledge the sovereignty of God. This decisive moment in human history, or rather the end of human history as we know it, is what is meant by the expression 'the kingdom of God'. Preparation for God's kingdom requires repentance and constant vigilance. Not all Jews in the land of Israel at Jesus' time necessarily shared this sharp sense of God's imminent intervention. Moreover, Jesus himself seems to have been concerned with showing how God's kingdom was already inaugurated and with tempering speculations about the precise time of the kingdom's arrival. Nevertheless, it remains clear that the phrase that summarizes Jesus' teaching is the line from his own prayer: 'Thy kingdom come' (see Matt. 6:10; Luke 11:2).

The context of Jesus' teaching was Judaism in the land of Israel in the first century. Jesus was a Jewish teacher. He spoke Aramaic, used the methods of Jewish teachers of his day, and spoke basically to other Jews. His teachings about God, God's kingdom, and God's dealings with his people were thoroughly Jewish. About such matters, Jewish and Christian scholars can agree.

[Daniel J Harrington, 'The Teaching of Jesus in His Context' in *Interwoven Destinies*, edited Eugene Fisher, Paulist Press, 1993, pp. 11–14]

AN EVANGELICAL PERSPECTIVE ON JESUS THE JEW

*The quest for the historical Jesus has made its mark on the broad spectrum of Christianity. The next extract by **Marvin Wilson** is a good example of a scholar of the evangelical persuasion who has incorporated the insights into the Christian faith. He is more specific in his location of Jesus, i.e. as a Pharisee. As he points out, much of Jesus' teaching has parallels in the rabbinic writings of the Talmud:*

The life and teachings of Jesus reveal a deep commitment to the Jewish beliefs and practices of his day. He was born of Jewish parents (Matt. 1:16) and circumcised on the eighth day in accord with Jewish Law (Luke 2:21). As a boy he celebrated Passover (Luke 2:41–43), and as a youth he learned by interacting with various Jewish teachers, all of whom were amazed at his understanding (Luke 2:46–47). Frequenting the synagogue from Sabbath to Sabbath as was his custom at the start of his adult ministry (Luke 4:16), Jesus was exposed to a wide range of Jewish thought. To be sure, first-century Judaism was far from mono-lithic. Pharisees, Sadducees, Essenes, Zealots, and other sects dotted the religious landscape. It would appear, however, that the teachings of Jesus show closest affinity to that of the Pharisees. To a certain degree—but not exclusively—the rabbinic teachings of the Talmud reflect this Pharisaic teaching. It has been estimated that one can find parallels in rabbinic literature to perhaps as much as ninety per cent of Jesus' teach-ings. Though this estimate is doubtless excessive, current research on the Synoptic Gospels is revealing in increasing measure a profoundly Jewish setting for the words of Jesus.

Furthermore, Jesus' early followers were Jews. Less than three scant years after Jesus launched his public ministry, a nucleus among them would found the primitive Christian assembly. Jesus discipled his followers in the fashion of a typical first-century itinerant teacher of Judaism. Not in synagogue classrooms but on hillsides, in fields, and in remote locations this Galilean carpenter's son clustered many pupils about him. Jesus was articulate, and drew much of his rich teaching material from the Hebrew Scriptures and from rabbinic traditions familiar in his day. But he also taught directly, on his own authority, which sometimes resulted in the inability of his disciples to understand (Mark 4:10–13). Though the company was often wider than the Twelve (Luke 6:13; 10:1), Peter, James, and John, an inner circle of three, become most prominent in the Gospel narratives. But in addition to the common people Jesus discipled, some of his chief followers were Jewish leaders (John 12:42; 19:38–39). In sum, the ministry of Jesus was focused; in his words, he came to find the 'lost sheep of Israel' (Matt. 15:24).

[Marvin Wilson, *Our Father Abraham*, Eerdmans, 1989, pp. 40–41]

THE ANOINTED ONE

Many Christians continue to be puzzled by the Jewish non-acceptance of Jesus as their messiah. Isn't it obvious that he fits the Old Testament expectations of the messiah and fulfils all the prophecies? The article by **Stuart Rosenberg**, *a rabbi and scholar of the dialogue, clarifies the biblical understanding of the messiah. His interpretation is representative of Jewry on this issue, and he himself is a distinguished American Jewish scholar in these matters. Judaism, in even its diverse expressions today, recognizes that the biblical figure of the messiah was an anointed person—usually a prophet, a priest, or a king. The anointing was performed on them to indicate that they had a divine 'mission'. As Rosenberg points out, this did not imply any divine or super-human qualities:*

The biblical idea of the messiah is, nevertheless, rooted in the primary meaning given to it in the message and teachings of several Hebrew prophets. In the Bible, a 'messiah', literally 'the anointed one', was the product of the prophetic belief that after the destruction of the Temple of Solomon (586 BCE), God would restore his people to the land, under the rule of a descendent of the house of David. But the word 'messiah' must be understood from its original biblical context. Anyone who was selected by God through his prophets to be the ruler of his people was regarded as 'his messiah'—the anointed one. In this way, Saul, Israel's first king, was called 'the Lord's anointed', and so were other kings like David and Zedekiah. Even King Cyrus of Persia, whom the Second Isaiah regarded as God's agent for destroying Babylonia and restoring Israel to its land, is called 'God's anointed one' (45:1). Always, and in every biblical case, the 'anointed one' is a human, not a divine being. And as for the connection to King David, Bible readers will remember that when the first Babylonian exile was indeed terminated and the people restored to their land, it was Zerubbabel, of the house of David, who led the restoration.

Clearly, from the Hebrew Bible itself, there is no warrant whatever to consider the Jewish idea of a messiah in superhuman terms, or to endow 'the anointed one'—*mashiach*—with any of the miracle-making attributes which his first Jewish disciples had ascribed to Jesus of Nazareth. Not a single word in the Hebrew Bible, Jewish scholars aver, can be brought forward as proof that Jesus Christ was already pointed to in Hebrew Scriptures, long before his own arrival in time. To arrive at that kind of messiah—a messiah with a capital 'M'—who would become the Christian Christ, we have to look elsewhere.

[Stuart Rosenberg, *The Christian Problem: A Jewish View*, Hippocrene books, 1986, pp. 33–34]

JESUS AS MESSIAH?

During the post-exilic period, the Jewish concept of messiah developed into the expectation of a single figure who would liberate the people from oppression. That figure was not conceived of in divine terms. This is particularly significant for the Jesus-period and may shed some light on the Jewish 'no' to the messiahship of Jesus. During the first century BCE and CE the Jewish people were living under Roman occupation, with all the tensions that it entailed. There was an increased expectation of liberation. **Randall Falk**—*Emeritus Rabbi at Congregation Ohabai Sholom in Nashville, America—locates the disagreement between Jews and Christians in what did not materialize during, or immediately after, Jesus' lifetime—namely, that Jesus did not liberate his people from Roman occupation. This would again be a widely held view within Jewry today:*

When Jesus lived in Judea, the Romans occupied that tiny land. It was a very cruel occupation. The soldiers were billeted in the country and were not considerate in their treatment of the natives. The taxes enacted by the Romans were a heavy burden, and the people lived in poverty and fear. So again, in the first century of the common era, Judeans prayed for a Messiah. This was what many Jews were looking for when Jesus appeared on the scene. It seems that Jesus probably was a charismatic leader of the people, one who was respected as a rabbi, a teacher. Jesus probably attracted a following who hoped that he was the promised Messiah. But Jesus lived and died without enabling the people to overthrow the Roman rule and live in freedom. Many of his Jewish disciples no longer felt that he was the Messiah, the anointed one who would free the country. There were others of Jesus' followers who predicted his imminent return for the fulfilment of the messianic hope.

It is important to recognise that the disagreement about Jesus as Christ is not over what Jesus taught or did, but rather about what did not occur during his lifetime. Jews accept Jesus as teacher and as prophet, not as Christ or Messiah. Orthodox Jews still look forward to the coming of the 'Mashiach' who will bring God's kingdom on earth with the establishment of a free Jewish nation in Palestine. The orthodox believe that will come about through a Messiah, not through political or military action. Liberal Jews interpret the prophecy still differently and look forward no longer to the coming of an individual Messiah, but rather to a messianic age, a time when all the children of God, living by God's moral law, will together establish God's kingdom on earth.

Another aspect of the Christian understanding of Jesus is also difficult for Jews. Jews do not accept Jesus as *the* son of God, but rather as *a* son of God, because Jews believe that all human beings are children of the one God.

[Randall Falk, 'Understanding Our Relationship to Jesus: A Jewish Outlook', in *Jews & Christians: a Troubled Family,* Walter Harrelson and Randall M. Falk, Abingdon Press, 1990, p. 105]

THE JEWS HAVE NOT REJECTED THEIR MESSIAH

Hyam Maccoby, *lecturer at Leo Baeck College in London, is one of the few Jewish scholars in Britain who has published in the area of New Testament*

*studies. His main thesis, as shown below, is that Paul and not Jesus was the
founder of Christianity. He locates Paul as the one who developed the Jewish
concept of messiah from a human being into a divine figure. Thus for Hyam
Maccoby the Jews have not rejected the Jewish Jesus; rather they have rejected
the claims for his messiahship—based on the fact that the kingdom of God did
not arrive as Jesus had prophesied:*

How the title 'Messiah' became changed into a divine title from its
Jewish meaning of 'anointed king of the House of David' is a question
that requires long and patient enquiry. My own view, and that of many
other scholars, is that this change was initiated by Saint Paul, who
should therefore be regarded as the founder of the central trend of
historical Christianity. It should never be forgotten that Paul never
knew Jesus in the flesh. The full doctrine of the Trinity did not
develop until the fourth century, and there were always some
Christians who opposed the divinization of Jesus. Jesus himself, I
believe, would have regarded this development with great sorrow,
since he accepted Jewish monotheism, and would have regarded
any worship of himself as God a contravention of the First
Commandment. Many Christian scholars too have come to the
conclusion that Jesus did not regard himself as divine. The belief in his
divinity, in my view and in that of the Christian theologians who
produced the book *The Myth of God Incarnate*, has had sad consequences in history, including the tragic split between Judaism and
Christianity and the persecution suffered by the Jews in Christian
countries. Because Jesus was regarded as God, the Jews, wrongly
regarded as his opponents, were also deemed to be the enemies of
God, and therefore as allies and acolytes of Satan. The diabolization of
the Jews in Christian medieval Europe was the precursor of the Nazi
Holocaust.

In historical fact, the Jews did not reject Jesus. They regarded his
messianic claim with great hope, as in the case of other messianic
claimants. The only Jews who opposed Jesus were those, like the High
Priest, who stood for the interests of the Roman occupation. It is the
greatest mistake in New Testament studies to think that the High
Priest was the supreme Jewish religious leader—rather like the Pope
in the Catholic Church. The teaching authorities of Judaism were the
leaders of the Pharisees, such as Hillel and Gamaliel. The latter, indeed
is highly praised in the New Testament as 'respected by the whole
people' (Acts 5:34). The High Priest was not only a Roman appointee

and police chief, and therefore regarded as a quisling, but was also a Sadducee, and therefore to the masses, a heretic. It is ludicrous that such a person should be represented (as in the Gospels) as the guardian of orthodox Judaism. To the Pharisees, the High Priest was only a ceremonial official in charge of the Temple rites, a task for which his personal inadequacies did not disqualify him.

When the Kingdom of God prophesied by Jesus did not materialise, this was considered to be the refutation of his messianic claim. Jesus was rejected not by Jews, but by events. At the same time, there is nothing in Judaism that prevents Jews from continuing to regard Jesus as a brave martyr in the cause of a primary Jewish idea, the Kingdom of God on earth prophesied by the Hebrew Prophets.

Moreover, there is nothing in Judaism that opposes the existence of Christianity as a separate religion, with Jesus as it Teacher. Judaism is a universal religion, but not a universal church. The covenant at Sinai is the way in which Jews worship the One God, but they do not regard it as the only way. The previous Noachic Covenant between God and the whole of mankind was not abrogated by the Sinaitic Covenant between God and Israel. Proselytes are welcomed into Judaism, but not as a matter of salvation, since salvation may be attained outside Judaism. The kind of pluralism that Judaism has always advocated is the key to reconciliation between Judaism and Christianity. If the Jewishness of Jesus were fully acknowledged and understood, Christianity's exclusiveness and claim to unique salvific power could be tempered sufficiently to allow for the validity of other faiths.

[Hyam Maccoby, *Jewish Views of Jesus*, Faith in Dialogue Series, Centre for Inter-Faith Dialogue, Middlesex University, 1995, pp. 17–18]

GOD'S YES IN THE JEWISH NO

*The Christian theologian **Jürgen Moltmann** wishes to take seriously the Jewish 'no' to Jesus and to incorporate it into his theology. He argues that a helpful way forward in Christian–Jewish relations is to see Jesus as the instrument of redemption for the Gentiles. Jesus was 'the messiah' in the sense that he opened up the Jewish God to the Gentile world. In that sense, he argues that Jews may be able to accept Jesus as the messiah without negating their own covenant with God through Torah. He, like an increasing number of theologians, uses Romans 9–11 to reconstruct an adequate Christian theology of Judaism:*

146

When the *Jewish no* to the Messiahship of Jesus is not based on resentment or bad will but on an 'incapacity', as Buber says, then there is no
reason for Christians to deplore this no or to make a rebuke out of it.
The no of Israel is not identical to the no of the nonbelievers, who are
everywhere. It is a special no and must be respected as such.

In the Israel chapter of Romans 9–11, Paul saw Israel's no as the will
of God. Israel is 'hardened', not because it says no; rather it can do
nothing but say no because it is 'hardened' by God. To be 'hardened' is
not to be rejected. It is a historical, not a final, act of God. It is an act for
a definite purpose, as the Moses–Pharaoh story shows. To what purpose
does God burden all of Israel with the incapacity for the yes of the faith
in Jesus? The purpose is that the Gospel passes on from Israel to the
Gentiles and 'the last' become the first. Without the Jewish no, the
Christian Church would have remained an inner-Jewish, messianic
revival movement. But together with the Jewish no, the Christian
community made the surprising discovery that the Spirit comes to
Gentiles so that Gentiles are directly led to Christian faith without
previously becoming Jewish. The mission to the nations, which Paul
himself began, is a direct fruit of the Jewish no. He also made this very
clear to the Christian community in Rome, which consisted of Jews
and Gentiles. Paul writes, 'As regards the gospel they are enemies of
God, for your sake; but as regards election they are beloved for the sake
of our forefathers' (Rom. 11:28). One can therefore rightly say, 'We will
only have left the Christian anti-Judaism behind us, when we theologically succeed in finding something positive in the Jewish no to Jesus
Christ.' This 'positive' lies in the mission to the nations, out of which the
Church arises. It is not only something positive that one makes out of
the negative but it is, according to Paul, the will of God, which has
become revealed in the Jewish resentment of the gospel. Therefore, the
Jewish Christian Paul can indeed deplore the Jewish no and mourn for
his own people (Rom. 9:2–5), but at the same time also praise the yes of
God, which is revealed out of this no: 'Their failure means riches for the
Gentiles' (Rom. 11:12) and 'their rejection means the reconciliation of
the world' (Rom. 11:15).

By no means can it be said that God has finally rejected the people
of his choice—then he would have to reject his own choice (Rom.
11:29)—and has sought a new people for himself with the Church.
The promises of Israel have not passed on to the Church, the Church
does not oust Israel from her place in the history of God. In the
perspective of the Gospel, Israel has in no way become like all other

people. And finally, with its no, Israel is also not a historical witness for the judgement of God and not only a warning for the community of Christ. Exactly because the Gospel has come to the people because of the Jewish no, it will return to Israel. The 'first will be the last'. Everything runs in its direction. For Paul, this was an apocalyptic 'mystery': 'a hardening has come upon part of Israel, until the full number of the Gentiles come in, and so all Israel will be saved; as it is written, "The Deliverer will come from Zion, he will banish ungodliness from Jacob"' (Rom. 11:25–26). This 'Redeemer' of Israel for Paul, the Christ of the Parousia, the Messiah, comes in the glory of God and his name is Jesus. The Jewish no, which Saul embodied with particular fervor against the early Christian communities, was overcome through a vocational vision of the crucified one in the glory of God. Therefore, Paul directs his hope for his people to the Redeemer, who comes in glory 'from Zion'. He expects from the Redeemer no conversion of the Jews or their coming to Christian faith but rather Israel's redemption and resurrection from the dead: 'What will their acceptance mean, but life from the dead?' (Rom. 11:15). The redemption in glory happens not only to the last surviving generation but across the times of history to all dead together 'in one moment'. The redemption hope of the Apostle refers to all of Israel in all times. His practical answer to the Jewish no is not an anti-Judaism but the evangelization of the nations. For him, this evangelization also brings the day of redemption closer to Israel.

If the Christian yes, which in the Jewish no discovers the positive and the will of God, is to be sought for in this direction, then this is also the approach to a 'Christian theology of Judaism' or to a Christology, which is not anti- but pro-Judaistic. But this is only possible for Christian theology when Jewish theology tries to understand the mystery of Christianity on the basis of Jewish no. It is indeed an unreasonable demand 'after Auschwitz', but it must also be a theological question for faithful Jews: What will of God expresses itself in the mission and propagation of Christianity? Through the mission of the Gospel, the name of the Lord is made known to the ends of the earth and the Christian world daily prays together with Israel for the consecration of the name, the doing of the will, and the coming of the Kingdom of God! Can Israel not see, even with all respect for the Jewish no, Christianity as the *praeparatio messianica* of the nations, like Maimonides did, and with that, recognize the way of its own messianic hope in Christianity?

Would not the messianic preparation of the nations for the coming of the redemption be without basis if it did not come from the Messiah himself? From his future he comes through his Gospel into the present and opens the people through hope for the redemption of this non-redeemed world.

[Jürgen Moltmann, 'Christology and the Jewish–Christian Dialogue', in *New Visions: Historical and Theological Perspectives on the Jewish–Christian Dialogue*, edited by Val A. McInnnes, Crossroad, 1993, pp. 89–92]

SOME OFFICIAL CHURCH STATEMENTS

There has been widespread recognition of the Jewishness of Jesus amongst individual Christians, but this recognition has also been reflected in official Church statements. Extracts from documents of the Catholic Church and the World Council of Churches have been reprinted here:

The Catholic Church

Jesus was born, lived and died a Jew of his times. He, his family and all his original disciples followed the laws, traditions and customs of his people. The key concepts of Jesus' teaching, therefore, cannot be understood apart from the Jewish heritage. Even after the Resurrection, Jesus' followers understood and articulated the Christ Event through essentially Jewish categories drawn from Jewish tradition and liturgical practice. An appreciation of Judaism in Second Temple times is essential for an adequate understanding of Jesus' mission and teaching, and therefore that of the Church itself.

Jewish Society in Jesus' Time.

The Judaism into which Jesus was born and in which the early Church developed was characterized by a multiplicity of interpretation of the Scriptures and of Jewish tradition. These combined with external cultural and political pressures, such as the attractiveness of Hellenism and the heavy burden of Roman occupation, to lead to the formation of numerous sects and movements. Such groups included the *Sadducees*, who were closely associated with the Temple priesthood, held to a literal interpretation of the Bible and tended to cooperate with Roman rule; various groups of *Pharisees*, who developed a uniquely flexible mode of interpreting Scripture and held doctrines opposed by the Sadducees; *Essenes*, who strove for a life of abstinence and purity in a communal setting and viewed the established Temple priesthood as violating the Torah's sacrificial law (among the Essenes would seem to be the authors of the Dead Sea Scrolls); various other apocalyptic circles, who felt the End was near and the redemption of Israel from foreign oppression at hand; revolutionary movements such as the *Zealots*, who advocated violent rebellion against Rome; and various political groupings, such as the *Herodians*, who were supporters of the existing political situation and collaborators with Rome. Given the pressure of Roman occupation, these movements existed in a state of flux and tension rather than as neatly discrete groups.

Pharisees and Sadducees:

The Pharisees and Sadducees are the two groups perhaps most frequently mentioned in the gospels, often as Jesus' opponents in particular debates. Here, it is important to emphasize that these groups were quite often at odds with one another and, especially in the case of the Pharisees, often divided among themselves on key issues as well.

In Jesus' lifetime the Pharisees were a popularly based lay group, whose main concern was bringing the people as a whole to a level of sanctity and observance of the Torah then understood as being virtually equivalent to that expected of the Temple priesthood. The Sadducees, allied with the aristocracy and the Temple hierarchy, rejected the innovative interpretations of Scripture offered by the Pharisees and understood religious observance to be defined by literal adherence to the written text of the Bible.

The gospel portrayal of the Pharisees and Sadducees is influenced by the theological concerns of the Evangelists at the time the texts were set in writing some generations after Jesus' death. Many New Testament references hostile or less than favorable to Jews and Judaism actually have their historical context in conflicts between local Christian and Jewish communities in the last decades of the first century (*Notes*, IV). Gospel depictions of conflict between Jesus and groups such as the Pharisees often reflect the deterioration of Christian–Jewish relations in this later period, long after the time of Jesus. So it is at times difficult to ascertain Jesus' actual relations with these groups.

Still, some things are known which drastically change the traditional understanding of Jesus' relationship with the Pharisees. First, his teachings are closer to those of the Pharisees than to those of any other group of the period, and relatively distant from the biblical literalism that characterized the Sadducees. Secondly, the Pharisees were known to be divided among themselves on key issues, principally between the followers of Beth Hillel and those of Beth Shammai. The latter generally took a more strict interpretation of the law and the former a more lenient approach, from what we know of the two movements from later rabbinic materials. Jesus' interpretations, in the main, would appear to have been closer in spirit to those ascribed by later tradition to the 'House' of Hillel. Certain of the conflicts between Jesus and 'the Pharisees' as depicted in the New Testament then, may well reflect *internal* Pharisaic disputes, with Jesus siding with one 'side' against the other.

['Guidelines and Suggestions for Implementing the Conciliar Declaration Nostra Aetate', 1974]

III. Jewish Roots of Christianity

12. Jesus was and always remained a Jew; his ministry was deliberately limited 'to the lost sheep of the house of Israel' (Matt. 15:24). Jesus is fully a man of his time, and of his environment—the Jewish Palestinian one of the first century, the anxieties and hopes of which he shared. This cannot but underline both the reality of the incarnation and the very meaning of the history of salvation, as it has been revealed in the Bible (cf. Rom. 1:3–4; Gal. 4:4–5).

13. Jesus' relations with Biblical law and its more or less traditional interpretations are undoubtedly complex, and he showed great liberty toward it (cf. the 'antitheses' of the Sermon on the Mount: Matt. 5:21–48, bearing in mind the exegetical difficulties—his attitude to rigorous observance of the Sabbath: Mark 3:1–6, etc.).

But there is no doubt that he wished to submit himself to the law (cf. Gal. 4:4), that he was circumcised and presented in the temple like any Jew of his time (cf. Luke 2:21, 22–24), and he was trained in the law's observance. He extolled respect for it (cf. Matt. 5:17–20) and invited obedience to it (cf. Matt. 8:4). The rhythm of his life was marked by observance of pilgrimages on great feasts, even from his infancy (cf. Luke 2:41–50; John 2:13; 7:10 etc.). The importance of the cycle of the Jewish feasts has been frequently underlined in the Gospel of John (cf. 2:13; 5:1; 7:2; 10:37; 10:22; 12:1; 13:1; 18:28; 19:42, etc.).

It should be noted also that Jesus often taught in the synagogues (cf. Matt. 4:23; 9:35; Luke 4:15–18; John 18:20, etc.) and in the temple (cf. John 18:20, etc.), which he frequented as did the disciples even after the resurrection (cf., e.g., Acts 2:46; 3:1; 21:26, etc.). He wished to put in the context of synagogue worship the proclamation of his Messiahship (cf. Luke 4:16–21), but above all he wished to achieve the supreme act of the gift of himself in the setting of the domestic liturgy of the Passover, or at least of the paschal festivity (cf. Mark 14:1, 12) and parallels; John 18:28). This also allows for a better understanding of the 'memorial' character of the Eucharist.

['Notes on the Correct Way to Present the Jews and Judaism in Preaching and Catechesis in the Roman Catholic Church', 1985]

The World Council of Churches

We recognize that Jesus Christ both binds us together and divides us as Christians and Jews. As a Jew, Jesus in his ministry addressed himself primarily to Jews, affirmed the divine authority of the Scriptures and the worship of the Jewish people, and thus showed solidarity with his own people. He came to fulfil, not to abrogate, the Jewish life of faith based on the Torah and the Prophets (Matt. 5:17). Yet Jesus, by his proclamation of the dawn of the eschatological kingdom, call of disciples, interpretation of the Law, messianic claims, and above all his death and resurrection, inaugurated a renewal of the covenant resulting in the new movement of the early Church, which in important ways proved also discontinuous with Judaism.

[World Council of Churches Consultation on the Church and the Jewish People: Report, Sigtuna, Sweden, 1988, p. 9]

A PASTORAL LETTER FOR ADVENT FROM A CATHOLIC BISHOP

The Pastoral Letter issued by **Christopher Budd** *is significant because of its sensitivity to the living faith tradition of Judaism. His letter was read in every Catholic Church throughout the South-West Diocese of England on the first Sunday of Advent 1994. Its importance lies in how he deals with the particular biblical readings for Advent and the continuing links with the Jewish people. He draws upon official Catholic teaching for his authority:*

In Advent we celebrate the divine promise, both fulfilled and yet to come. It is a time of preparation for Christmas when we remember the first coming of God's Son; and it is also the time when our minds are directed by this memory to Christ's second coming at the end of time.

The first sentence of today's Old Testament lesson explains what is special about the season of Advent, 'The days are coming—it is the Lord who speaks—when I am going to fulfil the promise I made to the House of Israel and the House of Judah.'

As we listen to the 'Law and the Prophets' read in our churches week after week, we can come to an appreciation of the status and dignity of that people from whom the Old Testament Scriptures have come to us. After centuries of bullying and vilifying our Jewish brothers and sisters, Christians and Jews are entering into a new and positive era of friendship.

We do have different beliefs about the Messiah—for Christians, Jesus the Christ is the fulfilment of the promises God made to the houses of Israel and Judah; for the Jews the Messiah is a human figure who ushers in an age of peace and justice in the here and now. We need to ponder with true regret that the one we accept as the Messiah, truly God and truly man, we have often used to bring not peace and justice, but pain, injustice and destruction on many of our fellow human beings, particularly the Jewish people.

Jesus himself, his mother Mary, the Apostles and Disciples were Jewish. The Jewishness of Jesus is very obvious in the Gospels, perhaps mostly in Matthew; but it is Luke's Gospel which we begin reading today, that tells us that Jesus was circumcised and was presented in the Temple in Jerusalem, as far as we know like any other Jewish boy of his time. The other Gospels mention Jesus worshipping in both Temple and Synagogue, observing the Great Feasts, keeping and criticising the Law, like any other Rabbi of his time.

The death of Jesus and the death of millions of Jews this century are tragically and inextricably linked. For centuries Jews have been pilloried, persecuted and blamed for the death of Jesus. The charge of deicide or killing God was levelled against them—this was fertile soil in which the evil of Nazism took root with such catastrophic effect.

The teaching of deicide is to be firmly rejected. Historically, Jesus was killed by crucifixion, a Roman penalty; theologically, the Churches have taught that the death of Jesus was within the purpose of God and that he died to save us all; morally, it is wrong to blame a whole people for the supposed sins of their forbears. This false teaching that in someway all Jews were responsible for the death of Jesus has only recently been corrected, especially by Pope John XXIII. Vatican II took up the theme at his prompting. However, some of our prayers and hymns still have traces of this prejudice.

The New Catechism of the Catholic Church emphasises the unique relationship between Jews and Christians. (CCC, *passim*, esp.839) Christians and Jews are linked together at the very level of their identity.

The Catechism nowhere suggests that God's loving choice of the Jews has been diminished in any way by their unwillingness to accept Jesus as their Messiah; but it goes on to make it quite clear that God's dealings with the Jews remain a constant source of blessings.

Christians are indebted to the Jewish people for so much: No Jews—No Jesus—No Bible—No Liturgical tradition. The first part of the Mass is based on the synagogue service and even the Lord's prayer itself is made up from phrases which Jesus would have heard in the synagogues of his time.

Jesus had much in common with the Pharisees: the doctrine of the resurrection of the body, forms of piety, like almsgiving, fasting and prayer, addressing God as Father; the priority of the commandment to love God and our neighbour. Paul always considered being a Pharisee as a title of honour.

The Catechism in various ways invites Catholics to see their faith as inseparably bound to the pattern of Jewish faith as expressed in the Old Testament, the faith and practice that nurtured Jesus. We are also bidden to understand that the faith and practice of the Old Testament, though now greatly revised and understood, is what nurtures Jews of today.

Pope John Paul recently reminded us that Israel remains the chosen people, the pure olive on which were grafted the branches of the wild olive which are the Gentiles. Christianity and Judaism come from the same root but have grown in different and distinct ways. Slowly we are learning that we do not have to squabble over which of us God loves best.

As we listen to the words of Isaiah during this Advent, we have an opportunity of coming to understand and love that people from whose stock came the One who was born for us. This could be a fruitful way of using our Advent celebrations to prepare for the birth of Jesus at Christmas.

[Rt. Revd Christopher Budd, 'Pastoral Letter for 1st Sunday of Advent 1994 about our Links with the Jewish People', 10 November 1994]

IMPLICATIONS FOR CHRISTOLOGY?

Jacobus Schoneveld, a pastor in Holland and General Secretary of the International Council of Christians and Jews, reflects on what Christians have learnt through fifty years of encounter with Jews and Judaism. He argues that there are far-reaching implications for Christianity if it is to take seriously the Jewishness of Jesus. For him, Jesus as a loyal Jew validates the Jewish way to God. The challenge is whether the Church will make the necessary theological space for the continuing existence of Judaism as a legitimate and valid faith. The recognition of Jesus the Jew can, for Schoneveld, provide the way forward for a profound acceptance and appreciation of Judaism:

The challenge emerging from this history of defamation, hatred, persecution and murder and from the darkness of the Shoah is this: Can the Church find space in its own faith for an attitude which sees the Jewish people as loved and accepted by God, notwithstanding the fact that it does not share its confession about Jesus Christ? Is there theological space in the Church for the way the Jewish people sees itself before God, although its self-understanding contradicts the Church's deepest conviction? Can this conflict be overcome?

Considering the resurrection of Jesus in connection with the question concerning our relation to the Jewish people we find that the resurrection is the vindication of Jesus as a Jew, as a person who was faithful to Torah, who—as so many of his Jewish brothers and sisters—had taken upon himself Jewish martyrdom in sanctification of God's name. The resurrection of Jesus cannot mean anything less than the validation of the Torah and the vindication of God's beloved people called to serve God.

But why, then, has this deep conflict come about? The majority of the Jewish community did not perceive that which had happened to Jesus as the decisive turning point in history, and did not share the conclusions drawn from it by the early Christian community, nor were they convinced that Jesus was the Messiah, since in no way was the new order coming about. At this point we meet the Jewish 'no' to the claims made by the church for Jesus. As Marquardt has pointed out, this Jewish 'no' is an expression of Jewish faithfulness to the Torah, to its God-given calling. This is the dignity of the Jewish 'no' to Jesus. Jews know that as long as the world is not redeemed, and the image of God has not yet become visible in the whole of humanity, they have to remain faithful to the Torah. I think that Jewish 'no' to Jesus, which Paul has described as 'a hardening that has come upon Israel' now has to be valued positively by the church as being the hard shell that protects the precious pearl of faithfulness to the Torah in a world that is still awaiting redemption.

Through the events around Jesus of Nazareth a new gate, in particular for non-Jews, has been opened to the way of the Lord which began with Abraham (Genesis 18:19) and which will find its final destination in the kingdom of God. The Church must make it completely clear that she has not replaced Israel nor taken over its vocation. Both Israel and the Church await the fulfilment of the Torah, when the image of God will be visible in the whole of humanity.

By defining the relation between the Church and the Jewish people in this way we can overcome this age-long conflict and find a way to co-operate which will bear fruit for the world of today.

[Jacobus Schoneveld, 'Christians in Conflict and Dialogue with Jews', *Common Ground*, 1994, no 2, pp. 25–26]

IMPLICATIONS FOR JUDAISM?

As the previous extract highlighted, acceptance of the Jewish Jesus does have implications for Christianity. What about for Judaism? **Hans Küng** *suggests that Jews may wish to incorporate Jesus into their tradition. By this he is not suggesting that Jews should accept the Christ of Christian faith. For him, if Jews do incorporate Jesus into their history, the key Christological issue remains: 'Who was Jesus? Was he more than a prophet?'*

It is not impossible that in the future more Jews will come, with a struggle, to acknowledge Jesus as a great Jew and witness of faith, and perhaps even as a great prophet or teacher of Israel. The gospels rightly have a unique fascination for numerous Jews. They show to the Jew many possibilities lying within the Jewish faith itself. And cannot Jesus be understood almost as a *personal symbol of Jewish history?* The Jew Marc Chagall constantly depicted the sufferings of his people in the figure of the Crucified. We might see it in this way: Does not the history of this people with its God, this people of tears with life, of lamentation with confidence, culminate in this one figure, Jesus? Is not his history a striking sign of the crucified and risen Israel?

In all this, however, there remains the one disturbing question: Who is Jesus? More than prophet? More than the Law? Is he even the Messiah? A Messiah crucified in the name of the Law? Must the discussion come to a complete end at this point? Here perhaps the Jew particularly could help the Christian to conduct the *discussion* on Jesus afresh, as we suggested, not from above, but *from below*. This would mean that we Christians too should strive to consider Jesus from the standpoint of his Jewish contemporaries. Even his Jewish disciples had to start out first of all from Jesus of Nazareth as man and Jew and not from someone who was obviously the Messiah or even the Son of God. It was only in this way that they could raise at all the question of the relationship of Jesus to God. And for them, even later, this relationship did not consist of a simple identification with God, which might have meant that Jesus was God the Father. Perhaps Jews could also help us Christians to understand better those central New Testament statements on Jesus and particularly his honorific title, which have an obvious background in Early Judaism.

Be that as it may, if we start out from Jesus of Nazareth as man and Jew, we shall be able to go *a good part of the way together* with unbiased Jews like my distinguished colleagues in this volume. And it may be that in the end of our journey together, Jesus will appear remarkably different from what the long Jewish–Christian disputes have led us to expect.

[Hans Küng, 'Christianity and Judaism' in *Jesus' Jewishness*, edited by James Charlesworth, Crossroad Publishing, 1991, pp. 268–269]

A DIALOGUE BETWEEN A JEW AND A CHRISTIAN ON JESUS

The final extract is taken from a book which has reproduced a dialogue on Jesus between an Orthodox Jew, **Pinchas Lapide**, *and the New Testament scholar,* **Ulrich Luz**. *The book itself aims to address from a Jewish and Christian perspective three distinct theses that: Jesus did not declare himself to his people as Messiah; the people of Israel did not reject Jesus; and Jesus never repudiated his people. In the final chapter, under the title of 'Prolog for tomorrow', the authors bring together their conclusions. Part of these conclusions are reprinted here. They reflect an honest dialogue—a rare openness—given the long hostility between Jews and Christians:*

PINCHAS LAPIDE: It is true: as a Jew among Jews, Jesus was not unique. As teachers of Torah and interpreters of Scripture, other rabbis also contributed their special insights and ideas to the overall wisdom of Israel. Thousands of his fellow Jews died as religious heroes and martyrs on Roman crosses like the one on which he lost his life. As messianic prophets, others called for repentance in the face of the new age which was expected to dawn any day. And more than a dozen messianic contenders were crucified.

Even the debate about Jesus' messiahship within Judaism after Golgotha was not exceptional. Whereas his suffering and ignominious death became proof of his failure for some, for others the same passion became a clear indication that God had accepted his self-sacrifice.

It is equally true that only in the case of the Nazarene did his disciples experience him as the resurrected One; and as a result, that he would return as Messiah became the certainty of their existence. It is no less true, moreover, that this certainty soon crossed the borders of Israel to become the certainty of salvation which called innumerable Gentiles away from their idols to the living God of Abraham, Isaac, and Jacob.

Last but not least, it is an indisputable fact that Jesus of Nazareth—and he alone—became a person of vital significance for millions of believing Christians whom he has helped, and continues to help, to a better life, an undying hope, and a peaceful death.

If the Hebrew good news of the boundless love of God, which Isaiah calls 'salvation' (Isa. 49:6), would have reached the four corners of the world in the name of a Greek philosopher or a Roman orator, most Jews would have had serious misgivings. But since this spread of monotheism throughout the Western world was accomplished in the name of a pious, God-fearing Jew, the story of its influence cannot remain irrelevant for Israel.

Granted, some of the more open-minded will now ask whether the figure on the church's crucifixes is actually still identical with the man from Galilee. How did the believing Nazarene become the Savior in whom others believed, the proclaimer become the proclaimed, the earthly Son of man become the heavenly Son of God, the preacher of the Sermon on the Mount the bringer of salvation? In short, how did the Jesus of history become the Christ of faith?

Certainly the proliferation of legends, the free rendering of texts, and the process of mythologizing have played a significant role in exalting the humble Nazarene; and yet, after discounting all Hellenization and foreign elements, we are left with an irreducible residue that resists demythologizing. 'A certain something', Martin

Buber calls it, for which Jesus deserves 'a great place ... in Israel's history of faith'; a place that 'cannot be described by any of the usual categories'—which in the end can be understood as an acknowledgement of the 'mystery of Jesus'.

Son of God, Redeemer, Son of David, Lord, Master, Servant of God, and a dozen other titles, which only a few in Israel took literally, are basically nothing more than the spontaneous attempts of the reticent rural folk of Galilee to give expression to their amazement. They simply wanted to express verbally that they believed him, that they were willing to learn to trust in God—blindly and without question, as he did.

A generation later, far from Jesus' homeland, in a totally different religious environment, this confusing polyphony gave rise to a theology which placed its faith in him, intensified Jewish enthusiasm to the point of Greek veneration, and eventually exalted him to Savior of the world.

Did the initial community believe too little? Or did his later disciples believe too much? Who recognized him? Who mistook him? Or was it faith (Eph. 3:17) that after Easter transformed him into something he had never been, nor could have been?

Any Jewish scholar who examines the New Testament will find that Jesus was undoubtedly a Jew—not just a marginal Jew, nor a lukewarm, *pro forma* Jew, but a true Jew, whose spiritual roots rose out of the prophetic core of Israel's faith, that he was closely related to the Pharisees, that he was a Galilean, and that, on top of everything else, he was a master in the art of telling parables. But to maintain that he was only a Jew, or only a Pharisee, or nothing but a wandering preacher, would be the height of unbiblical arrogance. Moreover, it would contradict one of the basic principles of those same Pharisees, which asserts that negative testimony is not allowed. In Israel no one can state before a court what an accused person has *not* said, or done, or been involved in. There is just as little ground for anyone today to testify who Jesus was not. Using the sources at our disposal we can attempt to determine who Jesus was, what he accomplished, and which sayings were most likely his. But what he became after Easter Sunday for believing Jewish Christians and later for the Gentile church in addition to and beyond this remains an untouchable prerogative of faith that belongs to the mystery of the church.

ULRICH LUZ: If Jesus was a true Jew who confessed the God of Israel and believed in him, who perceived himself as being sent to the people of Israel and to no one else, a Jew who was a human being, who would have felt decidedly strange in the divine heights to which Greek theology later elevated him, a Jew who, according to you, kept the Torah (p. 92), then the primary question is not whether Jews can consider Jesus their brother, the way many in Jesus' own lifetime did and many today still do. Rather, the question is whether the Christian churches can rightfully appeal to Jesus, not merely as *one* of their brothers, but as *the* beginning, the foundation, and the goal of their faith. The primary question is certainly not whether Jesus belongs to Judaism, but rather, whether we as Christians have not so transformed Jesus that we can reclaim him only if we transform ourselves.

Is there a trajectory that can proceed from Jesus to Christendom? Is there a trajectory from the man Jesus to the second person of the Trinity? Is there a path from the mission of Jesus to Israel to the mission to the Gentiles? Is there a line from Jesus' expectation of the kingdom of God to faith in Jesus' saving death, his death on our behalf for the forgiveness of sins, and the mystery of the resurrection? Is there a line from Jesus' faithfulness to the Torah to the Pauline statement that Jesus is the end of the Law (Rom. 10:4)?

Put in still another way: Is the identity between Christian faith and Jewish faith so great that—to use a catchword of Shalom ben Chorin in a different context—Jesus can be 'fraternally shared in fraternity'? Or is the difference between Jews and Christians, as well as between contemporary Christendom and its origins, finally so great that it would be better for us not to gloss it over with a Jesus we hold in common? Has what you refer to (p.114) as the 'irreducible residue' of the earthly Jesus, which firmly resists all mythification, deification, and theologizing, really remained decisive for the Christian faith, or is it in fact the myth—the Son of God, the bringer of salvation, the Christ of faith—of greater importance? Is the spread of Christian monotheism in the western world, which you gratefully acknowledge as God's way, not a *de facto* de-Judaizing of the God of Israel? The primary question for us Christians must be: can *we* call upon Jesus as *the* (not merely one!) ground of our faith at all?

This question contains much explosive material. In one of our conversations we once stated that because of what has happened in our history it was high time that a Jewish–Christian dialog be conducted with Judaism taking the offensive and Christianity the defensive. Actually it is really a pity that you did not radically pursue the offensive. I find your approach a sort of offensively executed defense, but not a real offensive (even though at several points the course such an offensive would take becomes apparent). This being the case, I would like to anticipate something of the coming dialog, or at least mark the points at which it must take place and indicate several basic factors that I have incorporated into my position and that characterize it.

I am convinced of three things: *First, Christianity must appeal to Jesus*—not merely to the 'that' of his coming, not merely to his name, which can be filled with almost any content desired—*if it wants to endure* without allowing itself to be transformed willy-nilly by anyone and by every historical epoch. It *must* appeal to Jesus, as long as it continues to affirm that God acted historically in Jesus and not merely in our momentary faith experiences and ideas.

Second, I am convinced that appealing to Jesus cannot be painless and without consequences for us in the present; rather, it demands that our churches modify their theology and practice.

Third, I believe that it is possible for the church to appeal to Jesus; that is, there is a trajectory from Jesus to Christ, from the kingdom of God Jesus anticipated to faith in his saving death and resurrection, from his own understanding of Torah to the Christ of Paul who is the end of the Law (Rom. 10:4). I am convinced—to take up a point that must perhaps continue to remain controversial between us—that Jesus according to his own self-understanding cannot simply be classified as *one* among many pious Jews, who may have expressed and enriched the faith of Israel in an exemplary fashion. Rather, it is my conviction that a response to Jesus involves taking a position on his claim of having been given a *unique role* and a *unique commission* by God. That is to say, a response to Jesus that affirms him and his message, yet considers him merely *one* of many in the great series of fathers of the Jewish faith, does not, in my opinion, do him justice; moreover, it contains a negation at least of his claim of wanting to be more, decisively more, than just another prophet or teacher of Torah among many. This does not exclude the possibility that the Christian responses to Jesus, i.e. the post-Easter confession of his uniqueness and indispensability, have at many points forgotten or supplanted the concrete form of his activity and have spiritualized, theorized, and idolized him, thereby also making him harmless. However, the basic *dimension* of the post-Easter response to Jesus appears to me to correspond with his own claim.

Perhaps you may now think: 'These crafty Christians! First they agree completely, even admitting that Jesus was not the Messiah; then they smuggle his messiahship back in through the back door, larger, even more unassailable—because it is more indefinable—than it was before!' No! That is not my intention. I do not mean that Jesus considered himself to be the Messiah in the theo-political sense anticipated by Israel, but something completely different. I also do not mean that the rejection of Jesus' claim in any way imposed guilt on, or contradicted the basic confession of, the Jewish faith. To the contrary, I agree with you now as I did before, that a Jewish affirmation, at least of *certain* Christian responses to Jesus, would have led to a contradiction of the basic confession of Israel's faith. Israel *can* not follow the way of freedom from Torah, because God *gave* (not imposed as a burden!) *them* (not the Gentiles!) the way of Torah. Moreover, even with Christ, the way of Israel must, because of the Law, still remain a different way than that of Gentiles, if God is not to be accused of not keeping his word. As I see it, even Paul would have said this. Especially from the perspective of Christian theology, so it seems to me, there must be a *particular* way for Israel to follow. Beyond this it is also my opinion that Israel's rejection of certain Christian responses to Jesus can truly raise fundamental questions for us Christians, perhaps because our responses to Jesus actually contradict his own self-understanding.

[Pinchas Lapide and Ulrich Luz, *Jesus in Two Perspectives: A Jewish–Christian Dialog*, Augsburg, 1985, pp. 112–115 & 157–161]

FURTHER READING

Bivin, David & Blizzard, Roy. *Understanding the Difficult Words of Jesus: New Insights from a Hebraic Perspective*, Center for Judaic–Christian Studies, Dayton, 1983.

Charlesworth, James (edited). *The Messiah: Developments in Earliest Judaism and Christianity*, Fortress, 1992.

Charlesworth, James. *Jesus Within Judaism*, SPCK, 1988.

Dunn, James. *Christology in the Making*, SCM, 1989.

Falk, Harvey. *Jesus the Pharisee: A New Look at the Jewishness of Jesus*, Paulist Press, 1985.

Lapide, Pinchas & Küng, Hans. *Brother or Lord?* Fount Books, 1977.

Lee, Bernard. *The Galilean Jewishness of Jesus*, Paulist Press, 1988.

Moran, Gabriel. *Uniqueness: Problem or Paradox in Jewish and Christian Traditions*, Orbis, 1992.

Rivkin, Ellis. *What Crucified Jesus?* SCM Press, 1984.

Sanders, E P. *Jesus and Judaism*, SCM Press, 1985.

Young, Brad. *Jesus and His Jewish Parables: Rediscovering the Roots of Jesus' Teaching*, Paulist Press, 1989.

Zannoni, Arthur (edited). *Jews and Christians Speak of Jesus*, Fortress, 1994.

CHAPTER SEVEN

SCRIPTURE

CHAPTER SEVEN

—

SCRIPTURE

The study of Scriptural texts has been very fruitful in furthering Christian–Jewish dialogue. Joint Bible-study sessions attract large numbers of participants. It is here that adherents of both faiths can engage with the thoughts and beliefs of the other faith community. The expounding of the Scriptures brings alive an ancient but holy text; providing a path to a deeper understanding of the faith and tradition of 'the other'.

When Jews and Christians come to study the Bible together they notice firstly, that each is using very different types of exegesis and secondly, their shared Scriptures are in a different order. The Hebrew Bible begins with the Book of Genesis and ends with II Chronicles; the Christian Old Testament begins with Genesis and ends with the book of Malachi. The order of the Christian Scriptures is theologically significant because the theme of the last few verses of Malachi leads immediately into the opening theme of Matthew's Gospel—the preparation of the 'coming one'. The Christian soon discovers that the meaning of the Book of Malachi changes if it is placed between the book of Zechariah and the Psalms as it is in the Jewish Bible. This raises many questions. Does the text in Malachi refer to Christ? What did the original writer mean? These are some of the questions which Jews and Christians have to wrestle with when studying a text, particularly a text that is found in both Scriptures.

The Book of Isaiah provides another good example of different interpretations of the same text. For example, in Isaiah 53 Jews would understand the 'suffering servant' to be Israel itself whereas many Christians would see it as a prophecy about Jesus. The challenge which comes from the dialogue is whether Jews and Christians can allow space for their respective interpretations of Scriptural texts without imposing only one meaning upon it.

It is also important for Christians to recognize that the Jewish tradition did not end with the Hebrew Bible. A wealth of rich and diverse interpretation can be found in the Talmud and Mishnah. Some of the interpretations in them belong to rabbis who were contemporary with Jesus. There are interesting parallels between the sayings of some of these rabbis and the teachings of Jesus. This will become apparent shortly.

H.P.F.

HOW A RABBI READS THE BIBLE

*The first extract provides a valuable insight into the different ways that a Jew might approach the Bible. **Jonathan Magonet**, the director of Leo Baeck College in London, England, highlights two key strands of Jewish exegesis:* midrash *and* aggadah. *As he so eloquently demonstrates in his illustrations, there are many interpretations of a text—what the rabbis have called 'the seventy faces of Torah'. This is often in contrast to some Christian exegesis which seeks to impose one single 'true' interpretation on a text.*

For many Jews the Bible is a living, dynamic organism that should be studied in its original language (Hebrew). Each word is carefully analysed to ascertain its meaning and its context. Traditionally, no word in the Hebrew Bible is without significance; there must be a reason why one particular word is used instead of another. In addition, the reader will ask questions of the text and read between the lines. Often the Bible accounts are one way conversations, so it is important to establish the other side. As Jonathan Magonet shows, the distinctively Jewish approach to the text is always to ask questions:

Midrash

They called this work of interpretation *Midrash* from a Hebrew word meaning to 'search', hence 'to seek out' the word of God. Indeed one of the names of the Synagogue was *Bet Hamidrash* (House of Study) from its function as a place for education of young and old alike. They divided *Midrash* into two types. The first is called *Halachah*, 'law'— though the real meaning is much wider as it comes from a word meaning 'walk', the way a person should walk and conduct himself/herself before God in the world. In *Halachic midrash* they expounded and developed the commandments contained in the Pentateuch (the Five Books of Moses), interpreting them to fit every aspect of the life of the individual and community—for they saw as their task the building of a model society, an example of the kingdom of God on earth in which every individual had his/her particular role to play. But since 'law' only covers one dimension of life, there was a second type of *midrash—Aggadah*, 'narrating', which incorporated moral and ethical teachings, legends and stories of the Bible characters, folklore and custom, cautionary tales and jokes, all the multiple dimensions of mystery and wonder, drama, adventure, tragedy and humour, awe and love that make up the richness of a religious life.

Getting Behind the Words

But better than explain these terms, one should see them in action to learn the way the Rabbis read and understood the Bible. Let us begin with a familiar statement that clearly belongs within the field of *Halachah*. 'Honour your father and mother'. Firstly the Rabbis had the advantage of going behind this rather imprecise word 'honour' to the Hebrew *Kabed* which derives from a word whose original sense is 'heaviness, weight'. It moves on to the meaning 'glory', as the words of Isaiah: 'Holy, holy, holy, is the Lord of Hosts, the whole earth is full of His glory!' (Isaiah 6:3). Here the threefold 'holy' emphasises the 'otherness' of God, his 'transcendence'. 'Glory', however is that which gives 'substance, weight' to a person in the eyes of others and in some passages in the Bible may refer to wealth or power or wisdom. Hence 'glory' for Isaiah is that aspect of God which man can encounter and know in the world, the 'immanence' of God, His power, His 'presence'. All of which helps explain the 'weight' to be given to parents who shared with God in the creation of the child. But how is this 'honour' to be expressed? The answer of the Rabbis is surprising: 'What is honour? Give them food and drink, give them clothing and shelter, bring them in and take them out!' They concentrate on the responsibilities of a child to support the parents in their old age, spelling out the minimal duties that must be performed. But what of the other aspects of 'honouring'? Here one must recognise a Rabbinic principle that no words of scripture are redundant, and even apparent repetitions must be studied to derive new ideas. For they are aware that another verse in the *Torah* speaks of this relationship. Leviticus 19:2 reads: 'Let each man "fear" his mother and his father, and keep My Sabbaths, I am the Lord your God'. Again the word 'fear' must be understood in its *Hebrew* sense, ranging from fear in the presence of danger to 'reverence' and 'awe' in the presence of the holy. But what is the 'fear' meant in this verse? The Rabbis spell it out: 'Do not stand in their place, nor sit in their place; do not contradict their words (in public and thus embarrass them) and do not humble them in any way'. Thus here they find the myriad aspects of human behaviour and attitude that mean respect for parents. These are not the only teachings of the Rabbis on this subject, but they show how from this sort of starting point, both practices and principles can be derived.

However our passage can yield a further piece of *Halachah*. For the Rabbis were always quick to notice the juxtaposition of two paragraphs, or sentences or even phrases, as a potential source for learning something. Why is the command to fear mother and father placed next to the one about keeping God's Sabbaths? Their answer: So as to resolve the difficult problem of the limits of the responsibility to honour parents and obey them. 'It is taught: could it be that because of respect for parents one is permitted to desecrate the Sabbath on their orders? No! That is why Scripture says explicitly: Let each one fear his mother and his father *and* keep My Sabbaths. *I am the Lord*—that is to say, they too are obligated to honour Me; so one's duty to God is greater than one's duty to one's parents in this matter'. Once the principle is established the Rabbis go on further: 'Whence do we know that if a father tells his son to make something ritually impure, or not to return lost property to its rightful owner, that the son should not obey? From this same verse, and keep My Sabbaths, for all are obligated to honour Me.' Wherever the honour due to God may be damaged by obedience to parents, whether in ritual matters or in any ethical behaviour, then one has the responsibility to make the honour due to God a first priority.

Getting Behind the Stories

If we turn now to *Aggadah* perhaps the richest strain is found in the Rabbinic way of reading the Bible stories. Any curious statement, unusual spelling of a word, gap in the narrative, become the excuse to fill in the story, point a moral or indulge in some whimsical interpretation. What happened to Balaam's famous talking donkey after the episode was over? It died! Why? Two reasons are given. So that people would not see it and recall Balaam's humiliation, for to shame a man in public is tantamount to killing him. Or, alternatively, because the princes of Moab were present, and if the talking donkey had gone on living, they were bound to start worshipping it! What was the real crime of the builders of the Tower of Babel? One suggestion that the Rabbis brought nearly two millenia ago is as apt a commment as any on the values of today's technological society. When a worker fell off the Tower during its construction, nobody noticed or worried, but when a brick fell off, all went into mourning! Why does it say that 'Noah walked with God' (Genesis 6:9) but to Abraham God says 'Walk *before* Me!' (Genesis 17:1)? It is like a king who has two sons. To the child he says: 'Take my hand and walk with me', but to the one who has grown up he says: 'Walk before me'. In that simple distinction the Rabbis speak volumes about the moral uprightness of Abraham, and the necessary self-respect, dignity and independence they see granted to the truly God-fearing man.

The Seventy Faces of Torah

The examples are endless, and the body of interpretation that has grown around the *midrashim* themselves is also vast. The classical *midrashim* flourished over a period of about a thousand years. But the creativity of Jewish Bible exegesis did not cease with it. In the Middle Ages figures like Rashi and Radak commented on the Bible seeking the simplest meaning and the *midrashic* ones as they educated new generations not only of Jews, but also indirectly, of Christians—for the great European translations of the Bible leaned on their commentaries to explain the Hebrew text. Philosophers and grammarians like Abraham Ibn Ezra helped found the basis for a proper scientific linguistic analysis of the text. Others found in the Bible the source of mystical doctines, of philosophical speculations—in short, every generation brought the best of its contemporary knowledge and wisdom to the task of interpreting the Bible for their time.

When the Rabbis said 'There are seventy faces of *Torah*', they had in mind this infinite variety of interpretation and teaching stored up within it; every verse, word, even letter being a potential source for enlightenment. Every letter? Why not? What is the first letter of the *Torah*? 'Bet' ('b') at the beginning of the word '*bereshit*' 'in the beginning'. And the last letter of the Torah? '*Lamed*' ('l') at the end of the word 'Yisrael' at the end of the book of Deuteronomy. Put these two letters together and they spell '*bal*' meaning 'nothing'. Turn them around and they spell '*lev*' which means 'heart'. So if you serve God in the consciousness that you are 'nothing' yet try to serve Him with all your 'heart'—then it is accounted to you as if you had kept all the *Torah* between that first and final letter.

[Jonathan Magonet, 'How A Rabbi Reads the Bible', in *Catholic Gazette*, vol 68, no 4, April 1977, pp. 24–25]

HOW A CHRISTIAN READS THE BIBLE

In contrast Christians approach the Bible differently. However as the theologian **Monika Hellwig** *insists, correctly, there is no uniform Christian approach to the study of Scripture. There is no universal Christian method of interpretation but many different ways of handling a text. Some Christians would stress as much as possible the literal interpretation while others acknowledge the cultural influence of the original writer on its composition. It is important for Jews (and many Christians) to appreciate this diversity within Christian exegesis:*

Reflection on the Christian creeds and the structure of liturgies since early days suggests that the Bible as a record of events really begins for Christians with the gospels of the New Testament and looks back from there into the Hebrew Scriptures for interpretative categories. It is true that in the extant literature of the first Christian centuries the term 'the Scriptures' means exclusively the Hebrew Bible, while Christian writings of the beginnings are more generally referred to as 'the apostles'. Nevertheless, there can be no doubt that for the Christian community history is founded upon and interpreted by Jesus of Nazareth and the Christian story begins there. It is, of course, on this unrecognized fact that some of the crassest false judgments by Christians against Jews have been based. For many centuries Christians have spoken and written as though any Jew in good faith would necessarily conclude from the Hebrew Scriptures to the messiahship of Jesus. The corollary of this is that those who remain Jews are in bad faith, and that the Jewish community has no right to exist as a contemporary with the Christian.

The more general recognition of the inner logic of the Christian use of the Hebrew Scriptures has now penetrated sufficiently into the circles of systematic theologians that it would not be respectable or acceptable to establish the Christhood or messiahship of Jesus on such grounds today. There is, in other words, a general acknowledgement by those who have studied theology that the Hebrew Scriptures have as their primary meaning that which is discerned therein by Jewish piety and tradition—a meaning that is complete without the New Testament. The meaning that Christians discern there, in the light of their experience of Jesus the Jew and his impact on their world, is a reinterpretation, not the primary and evident meaning of the Hebrew texts themselves. Obvious as that may be to modern Scripture scholars and to Jews, it has been accepted slowly and reluctantly by theologians and is by no means shared even now by all the Christian people or their pastors. Yet it is a basic and crucial area of advance for the Christian–Jewish dialogue because Christians cannot take Jews seriously until this is established.

The question of the Bible as the record of God's dealings with his people in history functions somewhat differently in the Christian–Jewish relations with respect to the Hebrew Scriptures and with respect to the New Testament. With respect to the Hebrew Scriptures, a strictly fundamentalist interpretation of what is written there gives the Christian substantial foundation for taking the Jewish tradition and stance seriously. It is otherwise with a fundamentalist interpretation of the New Testament—for instance, the references to the Jews in John's gospel, the infancy narratives of the gospels of Matthew and Luke, all the accounts of the passion and death of Jesus, the resurrection narratives, and a number of the miracle stories, as well as many Pauline passages. In all of these cases a fundamentalist reading necessarily condemns contemporary Judaism as inauthentic, possibly even insincere, simply because the fundamentalist reading sees the messiahship of Jesus (and perhaps even the divinity claim) as authenticated by overwhelming and publicly verifiable evidence. It is only a more nuanced and critical reading of the New Testament, with its claims of what happened in the heart of Israel in the life, preaching, death and resurrection of Jesus, that there lies any possibility of granting good faith on the part of Jews then and now in their rejection of the Christian claims for Jesus.

In case this is not clear enough, perhaps some examples should be given. A fundamentalist reading of passages in the Pentateuch will indeed lead a Christian to say that God's election rested upon Abraham and his offspring forever, that the land of Israel is given by God to Israel in perpetuity, and that God has made with the children of Israel a covenant in perpetuity that can never be abrogated. The Christian reading, however, cannot and will not stay with the Hebrew Scriptures but will continue into the 'New Testament' to learn God's word concerning the outcome or fulfilment. A fundamentalist New Testament reading will yield the understanding that 'God can make children of Abraham out of these stones here' (Matt. 3:9), and that 'You (the followers of Jesus, whether Jews or Gentiles by birth) are now the people of God, who once were not his people' (1 Pet. 2:10). This thesis will be amplified and reinforced by further search of the

New Testament, and suggests on a literal reading that God indeed is faithful to his promises but that the 'true Israel' which falls heir to those promises is identified with Jesus, the faithful remnant, and those who have gathered around him. So the fundamentalist reading, which seemed so promising in relation to the Pentateuch, ends by excluding all legitimate claims for Jews who remain Jews after the Jesus movement separates itself from the national identity of Israel and from the Temple, the Law and the Land.

In this author's experience, Jews who engage in the dialogue are not always aware of this. It frequently happens in conventions and workshops that some of the Jewish participants will be at pains to elicit from the Christian partners an endorsement of a very fundamentalist interpretation of focal passages of the Hebrew Scriptures, particularly those relating the land of Israel to the covenant of God with the Hebrews. Yet, if they succeed they drive the Christian partners to an equally fundamentalist interpretation of the problematic passages of the New Testament by the inexorable logic of the Christian perception of Scripture. This perception views the New Testament, and the gospels in particular, as the core of the record of God's dealings with the human community, and therefore as the last bastion to resist critical analysis. If other parts of the Scriptures are to be taken in a pre-critical literal understanding, then all the more so must the New Testament, which seems to discern the followers of Jesus as the 'true Israel' inheriting the promises, leave other Jews in sinful schism. Clearly, there is no real 'take-off point' for a profitable Jewish—Christian dialogue that does not rest upon a critical study of Scripture. A meaningful dialogue can begin when the Bible is recognized not as a literal account of what happened, but as a collection of interpretations of what happened. This allows for a legitimate variety in the approaches to and interpretation of the same reality.

When we turn from the Bible as a record to the quest for revelation in the Bible, there are again some preliminary distinctions to be made. To the Christian, the Bible is not the revelation of God simply, but rather the testimony of the revelation of God. To the Christian, Jesus is the central revelation of God—Jesus with his Hebrew piety, his Jewish sense of covenant and election, his Jewish sense of God as caring Father and simultaneously as all-powerful Master of the universe, his Jewish longing for the reign of God to be fully realized, his Jewish understanding of community within the covenant of God. What Christians have claimed from the beginning is not so much that Jesus has brought revelation to the Gentile world, but that in his person he is the revelation of the Father and the outreach to all nations.

Beyond this initial affirmation there are distinct differences between Protestants and Catholics, and among Protestants there is a variety of positions. Best known of these latter is the extreme version of the Lutheran stance, *sola scriptura*; it is by the Bible alone that we have access to revelation, because it is the only trustworthy witness. The Catholic understanding is more inclusive: the Bible is one expression of the witness of the Church to revelation. In this understanding, Jesus centrally mediates the encounter with God; the Church as the collectivity of those who have been touched by him mediates the encounter with Jesus (who is the revelation or encounter with God) in its community life, its values, its rituals, its prayer; and among the ways that these are passed on or communicated is that collections of writings, canonized in the early centuries of the Church and left intact since then, which includes the collection of the Hebrew Scriptures (in its more inclusive form) and the collection of the writings 'of the apostles' (actually a collection of very early Church documents incorporating the traditional preaching of the 'good news of Jesus as the Christ' handed down by the apostles). Thus, for Catholics, the Bible is not the only trustworthy witness; it is the apostolic community as such that is the only ultimately trustworthy witness, and it is the Church as a whole that holds the responsibility for transmission and interpretation. Yet the Bible holds a privileged place, precisely because the corporate discernment of the Church has selected these documents and no others as the most solemn literary testimony to the revelation of God. While the Bible itself requires Church interpretation, the texts taken as a whole also function as a criterion of orthodoxy of subsequent developments in the tradition.

Thus, for Christians the Bible holds a central position as testimony of the self-revelation of God. It is held to be inspired. For most Christians this does not mean that every word is thought to have been, so to speak, dictated, but rather that the whole message conveyed is that which God wills to have conveyed. It is also held to be inerrant, which follows logically from the claim of divine inspiration, but this does not mean that all actual information in the Bible is correct. Inerrancy rather means that the Bible unfailingly testifies to the self-revelation and the call of God. It is accepted by almost all Christians that the various writers of the biblical texts took for granted the science, geography, history, astronomy and so forth of their time. If their perceptions were incorrect in these matters, this is thought to be unimportant inasmuch as it does not interfere with the religious or spiritual message of the text.

[Monika K. Hellwig, 'Bible Interpretation: Has Anything Changed?' in *Biblical Studies: Meeting Ground of Jews and Christians*, Paulist Press, 1980, pp. 174–178]

GENESIS 32: READING A SHARED BIBLICAL TEXT

In the following extract **Henry Knight**, *writing as a Christian academic, provides a concrete example of a joint textual study. The text is Genesis 32:22–32 where Jacob prepares to meet his estranged brother Esau. Notice how, in analysing the text, the author has made use of Jewish exegesis—asking the questions! In the post-Holocaust world, Knight sees the story of Jacob as a legitimate parallel to the estrangement between Jews and Christians:*

What might Jews and Christians discover if they met over a shared biblical text in an honest and forthright attempt to interpret a text that each honored as the Word of God? Would either have anything to offer that the other could receive with appreciation and insight? Could either offer an interpretation that the other might recognize as the Word of God or an authentic interpretation of God's Word? More specifically, what would happen if Jews and Christians met over a text that mirrored their experience as estranged children of Abraham? That is, what would happen if Jews and Christians met over and through a text that reflects the kind of encounter this question ponders?

Such a text is Gen. 32:22–32 (23–33, as numbered in Jewish translations), wherein Jacob anticipates meeting his brother Esau from whom he has long been estranged. In the shadows of Auschwitz, this meeting takes on increased significance. The specific encounter initiated in this midrash is undertaken in the tragic light cast by the Christian legacy of supersessionism. What follows is a single voice in this encounter—a Christian one—offered at the threshold of the Jabbok, self-consciously on the post-*Shoah* side of the history of Jewish-Christian relations.

Who (or what) was the *ish*, the one with whom Jacob wrestled during the night on the banks of the Jabbok? Was it the guardian angel of Esau, as the sage, R. Hama b. R. Hanina, has suggested? Was it Esau, the estranged brother, sneaking into the camp under the cover of darkness? Was it fear personified? Was it guilt? Was the stranger the haunting and stalking shadow of Jacob's father, Isaac? Was the stranger

174

God? Was the *ish* Jacob himself, that is, the other side or sides of Jacob? Who or what was encountered that night?

At the Jabbok, Jacob prepared for meeting his estranged brother on the following day. He sent his family across the river out of harm's way, and prepared to wait and rest. However, nightfall brought not rest but struggle. An unnamed stranger, an *ish* (literally, a man), came and wrestled with Jacob through the night, putting his hip out of joint in the struggle. When dawn approached, the assailant asked Jacob to let go. Jacob resisted, demanding to be blessed in return. So the figure asked for Jacob's name, which Jacob offered freely. At that point, with Jacob making his identity known to the stranger, Jacob found it returned to him transformed. He received a new name, 'Israel', meaning, according to the text, that Jacob had striven with God and with human beings and had prevailed.

Jacob, now Israel, held his grip long enough to ask for the name of the one with whom he struggled, but he received only a question—asking Jacob why he wanted to know. Jacob's question was met by another question that forced him to search more deeply within himself: Why did he want or need to know? Once more, Jacob had to face himself, even as he faced the *ish*, in that return question. There the encounter ended, and the stranger blessed Jacob. Following the struggle, Jacob named the place Peniel/Penuel—face of God— meaning, as the story explains, that Jacob had seen God face-to-face and lived. Afterwards, Jacob left the place, limping because his thigh had been injured in the struggle. Ahead of him lay the morning and his encounter with Esau.

Whatever else happened that night, Jacob struggled with himself, with his own identity and legacy. Elie Wiesel, in his commentary on the story, contends that Jacob wrestled with himself, the other Jacob, hidden from view: weak, vulnerable, and dependent on his mother Rebecca. He met and wrestled with the one who felt unworthy of everything he was and had—and perhaps even resented the one who, with his mother's help, bore a history of deception and manipulation, trickery, and misrepresentation, as well as the favored blessing of his father. He was the one who had taken his brother's birthright, who had tricked his blind father, yet who seemed never to initiate a thing. According to Wiesel, this Jacob fearfully anticipated the morning encounter with Esau. Surely, then, whatever else Jacob wrestled with that night, it included, even if it was not limited to, the legacy and identity he brought to that river bank. Jacob wrestled with a lifetime in one night.

Is it any wonder that Jacob's opponent remained unnamed in the story? Was it God? Was it his conscience? His fear of his brother? His brother? His bother's spirit? Was it Jacob's shame? His alter ego? Must it even be just one of these options? Could it be all of them? Does it even matter which of these it was? By remaining unnamed, the *ish* could be any one of them or all of them. It could be some at one point in Jacob's lifetime and memory; it could also be others at some other time in his pilgrimage. To be sure, the one encountered remained, even as it remains now, shrouded in mystery.

Jacob asked for the intruder's name. Instead, he received a question: 'Why do you want to know?' Jacob's request was returned to him, and then he received a blessing. What happened in between? Did the returned question become the occasion for further wrestling? Perhaps Jacob, then, inquired more deeply about his own motives in the encounter: Why did he want to know the intruder's name? Did he want to control the *ish*, which he would be able to do if he learned the name? Did he want to master the encounter and the one whom he encountered? Was he playing a power game of mastery and deceit even in the wrestling? Did Jacob care about the stranger's reality or simply his own welfare? Perhaps the question was ironic, in effect, asking Jacob, 'Do you really need to ask? Certainly, you know whom you have encountered!' The reader can only wonder. Nothing more was said between them, at least nothing recorded in the text. The story reports only that afterward Jacob named the place 'Penuel/Peniel', the face of God.

Why name this place the face of God? The story says because in that place Jacob met God face-to-face and lived. Does that not imply that God was the assailant? The word used for assailant was *ish*, which is not a name used for God. Neither was the word *Malach* (angel) used, although that word is used in other texts that interpret or refer to this one (e.g., Hos. 12:5), lending increased ambiguity to the encounter and its interpretation. Given what the text reports, then, why name the place Peniel/Penuel?

The story suggests a change. The old Jacob—the one who was the trickster, the deceiver, the supplanter—might have stolen the chance to name the other, just like he once usurped his brother's birthright. Up to this point in the story, the text even relates that Jacob had come hoping to placate his brother and redirect Esau's anger—especially after years of fearing reprisal, even death (Gen. 32:20). In this episode, however, Jacob respected the limit. Jacob was satisfied not having the

176

name of the other, yet somehow knowing in the encounter that he had been wrestling with God as well as with his past, his trickery, his pain, his deception, his shame. He left what or whom he encountered open and rich: never just God or just the past or just fear or just shame. And yet, never without any of them.

Jacob had encountered, among other things, a legacy of shame and fear, and *in all that* he encountered God as well. They went together, inseparably. The struggle with everything he encountered brought change and a new name, a new identity—though not without cost. Whatever else Jacob encountered that night, it included the history he brought to the river bank. So, Jacob named the place, that is, the encounter, not the one encountered.

[Henry Knight, 'Meeting Jacob at the Jabbok: Wrestling with a Text—A Midrash on Genesis 32:22–32', in *Journal of Ecumenical Studies*, 29:3–4, Summer–Fall 1992, pp. 451–460.]

READING THE NEW TESTAMENT FROM A JEWISH PERSPECTIVE

Is there any value in Jews reading the Christian New Testament? Not so long ago the answer would have been a resounding 'no'. This century has seen an emerging interest by Jewish scholars in studying New Testament passages, primarily because they shed some light on the diversity of first century Judaism. However, to supplement this academic pursuit, there are some rabbis who believe that a Jewish reading of the New Testament can illuminate theologically both Judaism and Christianity. Not only can Jews gain a deeper understanding of the developing rabbinic traditions, but they can enable Christians to appreciate the Jewish roots of Jesus' teaching. **Leonard Kravitz**, *Rabbi and Professor of Midrash and Homiletics, succinctly highlights the reasons why such activity is important for Jews:*

How, then, should the Jewish reader respond to the New Testament? Remembering that he reads the book as an outsider, the Jewish reader still finds great beauty in some passages and great problems in others. He sees evidence of what was the belief of the early Church, and what is the basis of belief for contemporary Christendom. As he knows that the Judaism of our time developed from rabbinic Judaism, so he surmises that present-day Christianity has evolved further, which is to say that it differs from early Christianity. He can see how the teaching of Jesus can serve as the core of Christian faith, even while he himself is not convinced by it. He can come to appreciate Paul's efforts in spreading Christianity beyond the confines of Palestine, though he as a Jew would not agree with many of Paul's statements.

In saying that, the Jewish reader does not intend to challenge the Christian's faith, for, in a sense, faith can never be challenged. Faith is, as Paul so beautifully put it, 'the substance of things hoped for, the evidence of things not seen' (Heb. 11:1). That which is hoped for cannot be contravened, and that which is not seen but yet believed cannot be disproven. As a Jew, he too hopes, and as a Jew, he too believes. Having read the New Testament, he now has a clearer idea of that which the Christian hopes for and that in which he believes.

[Leonard Kravitz, 'A Jewish Reading of the New Testament' in *Biblical Studies: Meeting Ground of Jews and Christians*, ed. Lawrence Boadt, Helga Croner, & Leon Klenichi, Paulist Press, 1980, p. 94]

A RABBI LOOKS AT THE LORD'S PRAYER

*The following extract puts into practice some of the points raised by Leonard Kravitz. Here we have **Jakob Petuchowski** of the Hebrew Union College, Cincinnati in America reading the Lord's Prayer from a Jewish perspective. In so doing, he has brought insights from and found parallels with Rabbinic Judaism. He highlights the similarities between Jesus' prayer and the Jewish prayer,* Kaddish *which is recited regularly in Jewish homes and synagogues:*

'Thy name be hallowed'

Names have meaning, occasionally even for us today. In ancient times, they were considered to be even more important, for name denoted essence, nature, character. When Moses asked to know God's name, he was told, '*Ehyeh asher ehyeh*', 'I am the One who is always present ... This is My name for ever, and this is My title for all generations" (Exod. 3:14–15). Another name by which God was known to Biblical Israel was 'The Holy One of Israel'.

The Hebrew word for 'holy' has the sense of being other, of being something out of the ordinary, of being totally different. Rudolf Otto has written perceptively of what 'the Holy' means. On one hand, it is the *mysterium tremendum*. It overpowers us and terrifies us. On the other hand, it is *fascinans*. It fascinates us, it attracts us, and it causes us to relate to it. Rudolf Otto has gathered his material about 'the Holy' from all kinds of cultures and religions, and he noticed a strong similarity in the various perceptions of 'the Holy.' He also discovered that, on a very primitive level, 'the Holy' has no necessary connection with the moral and ethical realm.

The intimate connection between holiness and ethics, between the holy God and the moral demands made upon humanity, would seem to have been the great contribution which the Hebrew Prophets made to human civilisation—as, for example, when Isaiah said:

> The Lord of hosts is exalted in judgment,
> and the holy God is sanctified in righteousness.
> (Isa. 5:16)

The hallowing, the sanctifying of God's name, of His essence, therefore, means that His moral qualities, as it were, are to be imitated by us humans in ever widening dimensions. Thus the Prophet Ezekiel, speaking in God's name, said:

> Thus will I magnify Myself, and I will sanctify Myself,
> and I will make Myself known in the eyes of many nations;
> and they shall know that I am the Lord.
> (Ezek. 38:23)

That, of course, is the terminology we encounter at the very beginning of the *Qaddish* prayer ('Magnified and sanctified be His great name') and in the Lord's Prayer ('Thy name be hallowed'). And it follows quite logically that in *both* prayers, the petition for the coming of God's Kingdom is placed immediately after. God's Kingdom will be established on earth, once God's holiness is perceived by all His human children, and once those human children will endeavor to live their lives in accordance with God's will.

'Thy Kingdom come'

It will have been noted that, in Luke's version of the Lord's Prayer, Matthew's phrase 'Thy will be done, on earth as in heaven' does *not* occur. Luke might here be closer to the original. My late teacher, the great Rabbi Leo Baeck, once explained in a lecture that the phrase 'Thy will be done, on earth as in heaven' is not an additional *petition* at all, but merely a gloss on the phrase 'Thy kingdom come'. When a Jew hears the words 'Thy kingdom come' he understands at once what the kingdom of God is all about. It implies many things, to be sure. But, for a Jew, it goes without saying that the 'Kingdom of God' means our doing God's will on earth. Yet when the Gospel was preached to the pagans of antiquity, they had no prior notion of what the words 'Kingdom of God' mean, although they were, of course, familiar with all kinds of *other* human kingdoms. For their benefit, therefore, the words 'Thy will be done, on earth as in heaven' were added as an *interpretation* of the phrase 'Thy kingdom come'.

Perhaps we need not even posit a pagan audience for whose benefit that explanatory gloss was added. For while it is true that, in most versions of the *Qaddish* prayer, no explanation of what is meant by 'May He establish His kingdom' is added, there is one version of the *Qaddish*—recited both at a funeral and at the joyous occasion of completing the study of a whole tractate of the Talmud—that spells out in some detail what the eschatological expectations of Pharisaic–Rabbinic Judaism were in connection with the coming of God's Kingdom:

> Magnified and sanctified be His great name
> in the world which will be renewed,
> when He will resurrect the dead
> and raise them up to life eternal,
> when He will rebuild the city of Jerusalem,
> and establish His temple in her midst,
> when He will uproot idolatry from the earth,
> and restore the worship of the true God to its place.
> Then the Holy One, praised by He, will reign
> in his sovereignty and in His glory.
> May that be during your life and during your days,
> and during the life of the whole Household of Israel,
> speedily and at a near time,
> and say ye: Amen.

Here, too, although at much greater length than in Matthew's version of the Lord's Prayer, we have a 'spelling out' of what is meant by the coming of God's Kingdom.

[Jakob Petuchowski, 'A Rabbi Looks at the Lord's Prayer', in *New Visions: Historical and Theological Perspectives on the Jewish–Christian Dialogue,* ed. Val McInnes, Crossroad, 1993, pp. 105–108]

THE SERMON ON THE MOUNT

*The article above has taken a look at part of the Sermon on the Mount, namely the Lord's Prayer. Petuchowski has identified certain parallels between Jesus' teaching and developing Rabbinic exegesis. In similar vein **Eugene Fisher**, Director for Catholic–Jewish Relations National Conference of Catholic Bishops (working in America), looks at other sayings from the Sermon on the Mount. Like Petuchowski, he brings into focus the parallels between the teachings of the Pharisees and Jesus' own preaching on the kingdom of God. The similarities are striking. Much of what Jesus said in his Sermon can be located firmly within first century Pharisaic Judaism. His discussions with the Pharisees were part of the ongoing debates of his day on how far some of the commandments of the Torah should be extended:*

The Sermon on the Mount (Matt. 5–7; Luke 6) represents a collection of some of Jesus' most famous sayings as preserved by the early Church. It is rightly considered to contain the core of Christian moral teaching.

The Sermon, properly understood, reveals the close similarity between rabbinic Judaism and Christianity in the moral sphere. For both the Sermon and the Talmud begin with the Hebrew Torah as their starting point. And both apply the principles of the *middoth* for interpreting the spirit of the Law.

The Beatitudes, for example, find their source in the Hebrew Scriptures and have parallels in the Talmud. The second, 'Happy are the lowly (humble, meek); they shall inherit the land', is found in Psalm 37 as 'The humble shall have the land for their own, to enjoy untroubled peace' (verse 11). The following saying from the Talmud captures much the same spirit as the Sermon on the Mount:

> Isaiah said, 'Sovereign of the Universe, what must a man do to be saved?' God said to him, 'Let him give charity, dividing his bread to the poor, and giving his money to those who study Torah; let him not behave haughtily … If he humbles himself before all creatures, then will I dwell with him (Isa. 57:15). I testify that he who has these qualities will inherit the world to come; whoever has Torah, good deeds, humility and fear of heaven'. (*Pesikta Rabbati*, 198a)

Note that here is not an earthly kingdom but the spiritual Kingdom of God that is promised to the humble of heart.

For 'Blessed are the peacemakers' the Talmud has this, among others:

> Elijah said to Rabbi Baruka, 'These two will share in the world to come.' R. Baruka then asked them, 'What is your occupation?' They said, 'We are merry-makers. When we see a man who is downcast, we cheer him up. When we see two people quarrelling with one another, we try to make peace between them.' (*Ta'an* 22a).

In the Sermon, then, Jesus does not oppose Rabbinic Judaism. He does not seek to create his own Torah ('teaching') but to interpret, as do the Pharisees, the spirit of the one Law of God. We should take him seriously when he points out within the Sermon itself: 'Do not imagine that I have come to abolish the Law or the Prophets ... Not one *yod* [the smallest letter of the Hebrew alphabet], not one tittle [a small curl on the end of certain letters]' (Matt. 5:17–18).

The Sermon, like much of Jesus' teaching, appears in the light of the Talmud to be an application of the Pharisaic concept of the 'oral Torah'. The rabbis felt that this oral law contained the means by which the written law could be reinterpreted from age to age. The concept is to some extent similar to the Catholic Church's notion that the 'tradition of the Church' by which the written word of God is to be authentically interpreted. The major difference is that the measure of authenticity of the oral Torah is not so much that the interpreter stands in a line of succession with the original biblical authors but that the interpreter follows precisely the rules of interpretation (*middoth*).

The concept of an oral Torah emphasises the importance of the spirit of the Law, of proper intention (*kavanah*) over mere externalism. The oral Torah tradition was bitterly opposed by the Sadducees of the temple party, who felt that one must follow the written Law only. The Pharisees argued this way:

> It matters not whether you do much or little, as long as your heart is directed to heaven (Ber. 17a).
> The Torah that is practised and studied for its own sake is a Law of love. The Law (followed) not for its own sake is a Law without love (Suk. 49b).

Much of what Jesus says in the Sermon can best be understood within the context of internal Pharisaic discussion over the meaning of the oral Torah through which the written Torah was to be interpreted. The reasoning behind Jesus' ruling on divorce (Matt. 5:32), for example, is found in Matthew 19. Here, Jesus is applying the *peshat* or 'literal' form of interpretation that was favored by the school of Rabbi Shammai. Marriage, for him, means that 'the two are one body' and that only God can end the relationship. Jesus gives as evidence for his position the passage in Genesis 2:24: "For this reason a man shall leave his father and mother and cling to his wife." The record of the Pharisaic discussion as preserved in *Mishnah Gittin* 9:10 shows that Jesus is quite close to the *peshat* interpretation of the Shammaites. He is not opposing rabbinic Judaism as such, but taking a stand within its broad context.

Jesus' teaching on adultery (Matt. 5:27) also has a close Talmudic parallel:

> It is written, 'The eye of the adulterer' (Job 24:15). Resh Lakish said, 'The eye: lest you think only he who sins with his body is an adulterer. He who sins with his eye is also an adulterer' (*Lev. R., Ahare Mot* 23:12).

Likewise, the saying, 'If anyone orders you to go one mile, go two miles with him' (Matt. 5:41) finds its rabbinic parallel. Hillel was once approached by a poor man to whom he gave a horse. Unable to find a servant for the fellow, who was 'of good family,' Hillel himself "ran before him for three miles," in order to restore his sense of self-worth.

[Eugene Fisher, *Faith Without Prejudice*, Crossroad, 1993, pp. 47–49]

THE EPISTLE OF JAMES FOR JEWS AND CHRISTIANS

*So far in this chapter the parts of the New Testament which have provoked most interest from the Jewish–Christian dialogue have been the Gospels. However **John McDade** argues that the epistle of James should be seen as a Christian halakah. The epistle reflects the Jewish emphasis on hearing and doing the Law. The epistle of James has always been controversial within Christian circles. Martin Luther (the Reformer, 1483–1546) described it as an 'epistle of straw' for it lacked the great Pauline themes of grace and faith. It is true that the Letter of James has a quite different approach to faith than that of Paul. However, McDade argues that it is much more like that of Jesus:*

At the end of the Sermon on the Mount, we are told that the proper reaction to the teachings of Jesus is 'hearing and doing' (Matt. 7:24–27): the knowledge gained is to flow into practical expression, so that 'true knowledge' can be contrasted with the kind of wrong 'doing', characterised by the tax-collectors, Pharisees, scribes and pagans. Betz characterises the Sermon as an 'epitome' of the theology of Jesus, in ways which are applicable also to the Epistle of James:

> (The epitome's) function is to provide the disciple of Jesus with the necessary tools for being a Jesus theologian. 'Hearing and doing the sayings of Jesus', therefore means enabling the disciple to theologize creatively along the lines of the theology of the master. To say it pointedly: the Sermon on the Mount is ... theology to be intellectually appropriated and internalized, in order to be creatively implemented in concrete situations of life.

If we are right in thinking that the Epistle represents a collection of teachings which, like the Synoptic compilations of Jesus' words, takes us close to the piety of the earliest Christian communities and to the forms of oral traditions behind the Synoptic Gospels, then the impulses behind its composition are shared with those of the Sermons of Jesus in Matthew and Luke. The Epistle, too, has the character of an 'epitome', albeit incomplete, and coming from James and not from Jesus: it may be thought of as an epitome of the basics of practical living for Christian Jews for whom the Torah is interpreted and fulfilled in the Messianic teaching of Jesus. In particular, the Epistle makes even more explicit than the Synoptic Gospels the programme of "hearing and doing" as the characteristic of discipleship within "the royal law" given to Moses and interpreted by Jesus.

The emphasis in the Epistle is, of course, practical: how to live in trials (1:2); in temptation (1:12); with single-mindedness (1:8); with fervent prayer (5:17 ff.); with confession of sins to one another (5:16); with respect for the poor (2:2 ff.) and with a correct perspective on the condition of the rich (5:1 ff.); with patience (5:7 ff.); with due control over the tongue (3:3 ff.) and with heavenly wisdom (3:13 ff.). But its central teaching is on the need for faith to find expression in actions (2:14 ff.): an intellectual belief in God is insufficient—even the demons can make the great confession that 'God is one'! (2:19). 'Faith by itself, if it has no works, is dead' (2:17). True piety, by contrast, comes to the relief of the helpless, the orphans and widows in their distress, and keeps a moral distance from evil-doing (1:27). This is a theology, not of inner experiences, but of the hands and the body as the *locus* of religious observance. It regards religious living as a pragmatic and existential task in which moral behaviour shapes the heart. In this respect, it is eminently Jewish in character, a piece of *Halakhic* wisdom, a traditional Jewish instruction on piety and behaviour which avoids the speculative and mystical dimensions of religion. Jacob Neusner describes the characteristics of this type of Jewish *Halakhic* teaching:

> Halakhah is normally translated as 'law', for the halakhah is full of normative rules about what one must do and refrain from doing in every situation of life and at every moment of the day. But halakhah derives from the root *halakh*, which means 'go', and a better translation would be 'the way'. The halakhah is 'the way': the way man lives his life; the way man follows the revelation of the Torah and attains redemption. For the Jewish tradition, this 'way' is absolutely central.

It is not unreasonable to see the Epistle as a Christian *Halakhah*, a delineation of how the Torah interpreted by Jesus is to be lived. The Epistle teaches how to live obediently within what the author calls "the perfect law, the law of liberty", "the royal law" (1:25; 2:8): this can only be the Torah expounded by Jesus, the Law of the Kingdom of God. What the Epistle of James offers is instruction on Christian *Halakhah* or discipleship: the terms can be used interchangeably and accurately, since if we ask what Christian discipleship is, it can only be a pattern of life whose regulative norm is Jesus' observance of the Torah, the *Halakhah* of his religious practice which becomes the definitive law of the Kingdom (2:8).

James speaks unreservedly with a sense of the union of the two dispensations, and ought to be heard more attentively at this stage of the Church's history. Hence its continuing importance for a Church whose identity needs to be strengthened by a deeper engagement with the impulses which lie at its foundation. The Epistle of James, far from being peripheral to that project, may in fact be one of the most significant and non-polemical witnesses to that dimension of the Church which we call the *ekklesia ex circumcisione,* and which we usually ignore.

[John McDade, 'The Epistle of James for Jews and Christians', in *SIDIC*, Vol. XXVII, No. 1, 1994, pp. 6–7]

INTERPRETING A DIFFICULT TEXT

One can see that Jews and Christians can learn much from each other. However, the history of anti-Semitism has found much inspiration from the Christian Scriptures. How might Christians deal with some of their difficult texts regarding Jews and Judaism? For many Christians involved in the dialogue passages in John's Gospel seem to be the most difficult. It is a gospel which contains contradictory images of Jews. On the one hand John writes that 'salvation is of the Jews', on the other he writes that 'the Jews' are 'the children of the devil'. One of the most difficult passages for Christian–Jewish dilaogue, and inter-faith relations in general, is John 14:6; the declaration that no one comes to the Father except through Jesus. How does one interpret such a text in the light of the new rapproachment between Jews and Christians? **Gareth Lloyd Jones**, *an Anglican priest and lecturer in Christian–Jewish relations in Bangor, makes some helpful points. He writes from a historical–critical perspective and taken on board the insights of New Testament scholarship.*

One Way?

> Thomas said to him, 'Lord, we do not know where you are going; how can we know the way?' Jesus said to him, 'I am the way, and the truth, and the life; no one comes to the Father but by me'.
>
> (John 14:5–6)

Together with the claim in Acts 4:12 that there is salvation in no one else except Jesus Christ, John 14:6 is a key confessional statement for Christians. These two verses provide the basis for the stock question which anyone engaged in inter-faith discussions must be prepared to answer: 'Do you or do you not believe that Jesus is the *only* way to God?' Both are often quoted to support unbridled statements about the exclusiveness of Christianity and the damnation of unbelievers. For the dialogue-minded Christian, the problem which they pose is not the derogatory anti-Jewish polemic characteristic of the rest of John and Acts, but the insinuation that God does not hear the prayer of a Jew. From the Jewish standpoint, they imply a sweeping denial of the validity of the Torah as a means of access to God because they appear to state categorically that Christianity has superseded Judaism. In dealing realistically with this difficult text two considerations merit attention.

The first is concerned with the nature of the statement 'no one comes to the Father but by me'. These words are included by John in a section of the gospel usually referred to as the Last Discourse, in which Jesus addresses his disciples in a lengthy monologue (13:31–16:33). Theories about the origin of this Discourse vary considerably. Some commentators believe that it contains a verbatim report of what Jesus said at the Last Supper and on other occasions. Accordingly the words must be regarded as part of the original Christian message dating back to the time of Jesus. Another view is that John's portrayal of Jesus was not intended to be historical. James Dunn, for example, thinks 'it is hardly likely' that the claims Jesus makes about himself 'were already in place from the beginning of Christianity'. This conclusion is supported by the fact that the Johannine Jesus is so different from the Jesus of the Synoptics. For example, the unequivocal claim he makes in John, when he speaks of God as his Father and refers to himself in the 'I am' sayings as 'the bread of life', 'the way', 'the truth', etc., are nowhere to be found in the other three gospels. Also, in John Jesus uses long, complex discourses in which he frequently speaks of himself, whereas in the Synoptics he uses pithy sayings and epigrams, and rarely refers to himself.

This difference in style and content of Jesus' teaching has led scholars to postulate that John's gospel contains the theological reflection of a later age put into the mouth of Jesus. Barnabas Lindars feels that the 'conclusion is inevitable that John writes at a time when the living memory of Jesus is fading, and so the portrait of Jesus is becoming more stereotyped and shaped by dogmatic considerations.' The Last Discourse may well contain actual sayings of Jesus which the evangelist used to develop a particular theme, but in its final form it resembles the sermon or homily of the Synagogue. It is, in all probability, John's own composition, and as such it inevitably blurs the distinction between history and interpretation. It reflects the doctrinal concerns of an age later than that of Jesus.

The titles which Jesus gives himself in the Fourth Gospel, and the claims which he makes, were first applied to him by early Christians like John the Evangelist in an attempt to convey what significance he had for them. They are essentially confessional, and therefore historically conditioned, as all creeds are. Furthermore, they belong to the language of worship, adoration and affirmation. They come to the fore between 80 and 90 CE when Judaism and Christianity were fiercely competing for adherents. This confessional nature of John 14:6 should be borne in mind for it has significant ramifications for inter-faith dialogue. The comment of N.A. Beck with reference to the exclusive claim of Acts 4:12 is applicable also in this context. 'Salvation for the Christian is in the name of Jesus. This is a matter of confession that any Christian, indeed every Christian, is entitled to make. When it is clearly presented as a statement of faith rather than as a general statement of fact (which presumably could be verified by empirical means!), the anti-Jewish polemic is lessened at the same time that the Christian confession is highlighted.' Knowing that for Christianity Jesus provides access to the Father does not preclude the possibility that the Torah does the same for Judaism.

The second point which must be recognised when pondering this text is the continuing validity and vitality of Judaism. Are we, because of a theology of Christian uniqueness, to disregard historical evidence and insist that Judaism does not provide access to God? Are we, with the Anglican *Alternative Service Book's* Good Friday prayer to lump Jews together with 'all who have not known' God? The great Jewish philosopher and theologian Franz Rosenzweig answers this question when he notes the exact wording of John 14:6 and offers his own interpretation of it. 'What Christ and his Church mean within the world—on this point we are agreed. No one *comes* to the Father—but the situation is different when one need no longer come to the Father because he *is* already with him. That is the case with the nation of Israel (not the individual Jew). The development of Judaism passes by Jesus, to whom the heathen say "Lord", and through whom they "come to the Father"; it does not pass through him.' In view of the anti-Judaism present in the rest of the gospel and the constant emphasis on supersessionism, it may be debated that this is what John really meant. Nevertheless, Rosenzweig is surely right in saying that Israel (though not every individual Jew) knows the Father and has access to him. He admits that others, who are not already with God, will be brought to him only through Jesus Christ, but this means of access is not necessary for those who already have one in the Torah. The one who already *is with the Father* has no need to come. Hair-splitting exegesis perhaps, but surely worth noting.

[Gareth Lloyd Jones, *Hard Sayings: Difficult New Testament Texts for Jewish-Christian Dialogue*, CCJ publication, 1993, pp. 36–38]

THE GREATEST COMMANDMENT

*The final extract has been taken from a collection of textual studies by a Reform Rabbi (**Michael Hilton**) and a Dominican priest (**Gordian Marshall**). The two have been engaged in joint Bible studies. Their results have been brought together in a book entitled* The Gospels and Rabbinic Judaism. *The book is based on real dialogue sessions which they have led. This particular passage looks at the topic of eternal life. It begins with a question posed to Jesus in Matthew 19:16–30 on what one must do to inherit eternal life. Together Michael Hilton and Gordian Marshall highlight the parallels and differences between Jesus' response and Rabbinic ideas contemporary with Jesus:*

Notice the question: 'Teacher, what good deed must I do, to have eternal life?' This is a very different type of question to 'What is the great commandment?' It is a naive question, asking for a simplification of the law. This man seems a little like the convert in text 3 who wanted to be a high priest.

But consider Jesus' reply here. 'Why do you ask me about what is good. There is one who is good ...' Everything is now open to question. In the previous texts it was taken for granted God has given his Torah, and the questioner wanted Jesus to interpret it. But here the questioner is almost inviting Jesus to give an alternative to the Law, *his* way of getting to eternal life. Jesus rejects this way of thinking, and replies that if the man would enter life, he must keep the commandments.

In the rabbinic tradition, the question of eternal life was very closely tied to ideas of orthodoxy and heresy, as can be seen from the following texts:

Mishnah Sanhedrin 10.1
All Israel has a share in the world to come, for it is said (Isa. 60:21) 'Your people also shall be all righteous, they shall inherit the land for ever; the branch of my planting, the work of my hands that I may be glorified.' And these are those who have no share in the world to come: he who says that the resurrection of the dead is not from the Torah; he who says that the Torah is not from Heaven, and an apostate. Rabbi Akiva says: Also he that reads the heretical books, or that utters charms over a wound and says, (Exod. 15:26) 'I will put none of the disease upon you which I have put upon the Egyptians: for I am the Lord who heals you.' Abba Saul says: Also he who pronounces the Name of God with its proper letters.

'Having a share in the world to come' is an equivalent phrase to 'inheriting eternal life'. The idea was not whether a person would go to heaven or hell, but whether a person would be resurrected or not. Having said all Israel will have a share in the world to come, the Mishnah then gives a fascinating list of those who will not have a share. The word translated 'apostate', *epikoros*, referred to someone who did not keep the commandments—and this links very closely to Jesus' reply about keeping the commandments. The first one mentioned is he who says that the resurrection of the dead is not from Torah—he who denies the resurrection will have no part of it. As we shall see, most scholars suggest that it was the Sadduccees who are here being criticised—which would place the origin of the text before 70 CE.

This Mishnah clearly reflects various debates current among Jews in the first two centuries. Can you have a share in the world to come if you don't believe in it—or if you deny the Torah is from heaven? One debate reflected here is that between the Sadduccees and Pharisees. The Sadduccees were known to have denied that the Torah contains the doctrine of the resurrection of the dead—the Pharisees disagreed. After the year 70, when the Sadduccee party no longer existed, it was the pharisaic view which was followed by the Rabbis. In our Gospel passage the debate is also about how one achieves salvation—but the issues are different. The link between 'the world to come' in the rabbinic text and 'eternal life' in Matthew 19:16 raises complex issues of interpretation which is possible only to summarise very briefly here. Regardless of the term eternal life (which has the connotation of the successful completion of life), the man seems in fact to be asking 'How do I live in the right way?' This is precisely what is referred to in much of the Gospel usage of the phrase 'The kingdom of Heaven' or 'The kingdom of God'. It may well be wrong to regard the kingdom of heaven as an afterlife or a non-earthly kingdom—better to translate kingdom as 'Rule'—'The Rule of Heaven' or of God, and this can be as effective here and now as anywhere else: in the 'Our Father', it says 'Thy kingdom Come *On Earth* as in heaven'. It refers to living according to his rule here and now: it seems to be assumed that somebody who does that will receive a reward of eternal life. In rabbinic literature too, the phrase 'kingdom of God' normally refers to the perfection of this world of ours, as in the third-century *Aleynu* prayer, which is said in every Jewish service:

All shall accept the yoke of your kingdom: and you will reign over them speedily, and for ever and ever: for yours is the kingdom, and for all eternity you will reign in glory ...

The kingdom of God here is the kingdom of God on earth, which all peoples must strive to build.

Jesus' questioner, having been told God has given the commandments, seems to want to keep only part of them—he wants Jesus to make a selection for him. He is not looking for a fundamental principle to remind him of all of them, but asks 'Which must I keep?' Perhaps a current debate also lies behind this text—but it is difficult to be certain, because there is no immediate background discussion. Matthew 19 begins with a move from Galilee to Judaea. The questions which arose there were—divorce, little children, and then this. The man seems to want to keep only part of the commandments, and Jesus tells him he has to keep them all. Strangely, when he gives the list of the Ten Commandments, he does not mention the first five, the ones which relate to God, only those relating to us. Then the young man says, 'I've done all this! What more do I need to do?' This is where it becomes more obvious that our text reflects a current debate, because it seems to set up various artificial questions. Where does the Law come from? How much is relevant? Do I need anything beyond it? Once again Jesus is prepared to go further than the law's demands: this time the suggestion is that he should go and sell his possessions. The young man goes away feeling very sad.

The idea of being *prepared* to use all one's wealth in the service of God is paralleled in Sifre on the Shema. The phrase, 'With all your might' represents the Hebrew *meodekha*: one rabbinic idea interpreted this to mean 'With all your money'. This is not as fanciful as it appears, because *meod* literally means 'muchness', which could be taken to indicate your greatness in this world, i.e. your resources, your possessions. The Jerusalem Talmud reports that it was enacted that nobody should give to charity more than one fifth of his wealth: however, the passage continues with a tale of a man called Monobaz, who gave away everything he had to the poor, and said, "I have gathered treasures for the world to come" (cf. Matt. 19:21). The Monobaz in this passage has been identified with the ruler of the Persian client kingdom of Adiabene in the second half of the first century CE. Monobaz' father Izates had converted to Judaism.

Our Gospel texts here, then, show Jesus at his most 'rabbinic', engaged in lively debate, and answering some of the same questions as the Rabbis. At no point does he clearly contradict Jewish teaching, but twice he shows a willingness to go beyond it—in love of enemies, and giving away one's wealth.

[Rabbi M. Hilton and Gordian Marshall, *The Gospels and Rabbinic Judaism*, SCM Press, 1988, pp. 31–34]

FURTHER READING

Beck, Norman. *Mature Christianity: The Recognition and Repudiation of the Anti-Jewish Polemic of the New Testament*, Associated University Presses, 1985.

Büchmann, Christina & Spiegel, Celina. *Out of the Garden: Women Writers on the Bible*, Harper Collins, 1994.

Fornberg, Tod. *Jewish–Christian Dialogue and Biblical Exegesis*, Uppsala University Press, 1988.

Greenspan, Frederick (edited). *Scripture in the Jewish and Christian Traditions: Authority, Interpretation, Relevance*, Abingdon, 1982.

Lodahl, Michael. *Shekhinah/Spirit: Divine Presence in Jewish and Christian Religion*, Paulist Press, 1992.

Magonet, Jonathan. *A Rabbi Reads the Psalms*, SCM Press, 1994.

Magonet, Jonathan. *A Rabbi's Bible*, SCM Press, 1991.

Neusner, Jacob. *What is Midrash?* Fortress, 1987.

Thoma, Clemens & Wyschogrod, Michael. *Parable and Story in Judaism and Christianity*, Paulist Press, 1989.

Thoma, Clemens & Wyschogrod, Michael. *Understanding Scripture: Explorations of Jewish and Christian Traditions of Interpretation*, Paulist Press, 1987.

Williamson, Clark & Allen, Ronald. *Interpreting Difficult Texts: Anti-Judaism and Christian Preaching*, SCM Press, 1989.

CHAPTER EIGHT

SALVATION

CHAPTER EIGHT

SALVATION

Jews and Christians share a common hope for the redemption of humankind. Both acknowledge that personal salvation can be achieved in the here and now and that full redemption for the world is yet to come. Both await the messianic fulfilment at the end of time, whether conceived of in terms of a personal messiah or a messianic age. However, despite these similarities, there are fundamental differences in Jewish and Christian concepts of salvation. Although the same terminology is often used, Christians and Jews have different frameworks into which this language fits.

For Judaism, salvation is available to Jews in this life through their faithful observance of Torah. Jews prefer to use the phrase 'have a share in the world to come' rather than 'salvation'. Redemption—a share in the world to come—is available through the quality of Torah-living and not through belief in a particular saviour-figure. Contrary to popular Christian stereotypes, faith not works is the key to personal redemption in Judaism. Good deeds are important as a means to faith but they are not a substitute for it. Redemption is not earned through the quantity of good deeds but through faithfulness to God. Torah is the instrument by which Jews express their faith in God. In terms of other faiths, Judaism recognizes that the righteous of all nations 'have a share in the world to come'. Redemption is available outside the Jewish faith by faithfulness to God through a person's particular religious tradition. As we will see shortly Judaism stipulates that for Gentiles to become 'the righteous of the nations' there are seven laws, the Noahide Laws. These laws provide the minimum requirement by which non-Jews can share in the world to come.

For Christianity, traditionally, salvation is only possible through Christ. The Church believes that Jesus' death on the cross was the once-for-all sacrifice that, in some mysterious sense, atoned for the sins of humanity. Traditionally, personal salvation is attained through the conscious acceptance of Christ as saviour and Lord; therefore those without Christ face eternal damnation. This is technically called an exclusivist approach to salvation. Today, however, two alternative Christian approaches to other faiths have emerged. These are the inclusivist and pluralist positions. Instead of seeing other religions as demonic, some Christians want to affirm them. There are nuances within inclusivism and pluralism, but in general it would be fair to say that inclusivists argue that the creator God is working through every religion. Christ is saving the adherents of other religions without them realizing. When Christians encounter a person from another faith, they are to assume that God is working anonymously through Christ in their lives. This is the official position of the Catholic Church. On the other hand the pluralist theologian would affirm that salvation is available apart from belief in Christ. Each religious tradition can effect salvation for its adherents if they turn from self-centredness to God-centredness. Although many Christians are sympathetic to pluralism, the official position of most Christian churches is either exclusivist or inclusivist.

H.P.F.

JEWISH CONCEPTS OF SALVATION AND REDEMPTION

In this first extract the dialectic in Judaism between faith and works is clearly explained. **Daniel Breslauer**, *a Jewish scholar involved in the dialogue in America, outlines the importance of works as the preparation for redemption. Faith is the necessary condition for 'a share in the world to come'. Jews do not earn salvation. They prepare themselves for it through their good deeds and their faithfulness to God through adherence to Torah. The quality of one's life in faithfulness to Torah is important, not the quantity of good deeds:*

While redemption is a future, undisclosed hope, salvation is a gift made immediately accessible in the present. Through Jewish teachings and instructions—through Torah—a Jew becomes a *ben Olam Haba* (son of the world to come, i.e., member of those worthy of salvation). While Torah is the means to salvation, the measure of a person's worth is not the quantity but the quality of Torah living. Some people attain in one moment of self-sacrifice what it takes others a lifetime to achieve. Faith rather than works is primary as the story of Elazar ben Durdia makes clear. Elazar ben Durdia was a well-known reprobate who frequented every house of ill repute. Once after traveling far to a famous courtesan he was moved to repent and cried aloud until his heart broke and he died. A heavenly voice at once declared, 'Rabbi Elazar ben Durdia is a ben Olam Haba'. In amazement Rabbi Judah the Prince remarked: 'Not merely is a penitent accepted into the world to come but he is also called rabbi' (TB *Ta'anit* 16a). The highest merit a person can acquire depends on the movements of faith, not on quantitative accumulation of deeds.

Judaism posits a subtle connection between personal salvation and national redemption. Transformed human beings do become the basis for God's gracious redeeming act. Joshua ben Levi living in a time of Roman domination and suffering under Roman seige once demanded when the Messiah would come. The answer was given through Psalm 95:7 'Today, if only you would harken to God's voice' (TB *Sanhedrin* 98a). A world obedient to God is a world in which messianic fulfillment is more possible. A Hasidic rabbi once commented on 1 Samuel 20:27, 'Why has not the son of Jesse come ...either yesterday or today?' (Martin Buber, *Tales of the Hasidim*). The messianic redemption has not occurred because we today are no different from what we were yesterday. Personal acceptance of religious responsibility becomes the prerequisite for God's redemption of the entire national body.

The Jew does not *earn* either salvation or redemption, but Jewish deeds are understood as the *preparation* for each. Torah prepares an individual to turn in faith to God; the turning of individuals to God prepares the way for God's gracious act of redemption. The stress in Judaism is on discovering *opportunities* in personal life for the response of faith and *opportunities* in political life for God's reaching out of redemptive power. This emphasis on the need to create opportunities, to prepare the way for both human response and divine activity, helps explain why Jews find the existence of the modern State of Israel so important in the context of both salvation and redemption. The Jewish State is first and foremost a spiritual opportunity. Within its borders a Jew can experience an all-embracing Jewish life. Sabbaths and holidays, laws regarding the land of Israel itself, communal obligations and social injunctions from Torah can be fulfilled in a Jewish political setting. Zionism is not a human attempt to usurp the divine prerogative. It rather offers a unique opportunity for faithful turning to God and the unique challenge of constructing a political system ready to respond to the divine redemptive act. Modern statehood is thus neither the fulfillment of messianic hopes nor a substitute for individual salvation. It is rather a reflection of modern political realities which dictate that neither salvation nor redemption can be possible without a concrete framework of Jewish existence, a framework which must be assured in these post-Holocaust days by a secure national body and communal structure.

Christians in dialogue with Jews often confuse this emphasis on the need for concrete opportunities in which personal salvation and national redemption can take place with a humanistic arrogance. True ecumenical sharing can begin only when the spiritual element of the Jewish hope for salvation and redemption is clearly understood. Christians need to realize that Judaism stresses deeds as a means to faith, not as substitutes for it. Salvation is made possible because God graciously gave a Torah in which opportunities for a faithful turning to God are numerous. The Jew does not earn salvation by multiplying large quantities of sterile actions. Only one action, faithfully performed, is sufficient. God's grace, however, has made the faithful turning possible through the instrument of Torah.

A second important issue in the Christian–Jewish discussion concerns life in an unredeemed world. The Jew refuses to acknowledge that this world of war and tension is God's promised redemption. The biblical messianic expectations are still unfulfilled from the Jewish point of view. Life in an unredeemed world, however, does not preclude *individual salvation*. The Jew finds personal self-fulfillment possible even in a world which is not yet touched by God's final act of political redemption.

A final point needs to be made. Torah presents the Jew with opportunities for turning in salvific faith. All human beings, however, are graced with opportunities of their own. At the very least the seven divine instructions given to Noah provide non-Jews with such opportunities. A basic Jewish presuppostion is that the righteous from all nations inherit the world to come (cf. TB *Sanhedrin* 105a). While redemption may be national and particular, salvation because it is individual and personal is universal. The Jew denies salvation to no human being. Religious traditions may vary, but salvation is possible for the non-Jew no less than for the Jew.

[S. Daniel Breslauer, 'Salvation: A Jewish View' in *A Dictionary of the Jewish–Christian Dialogue*, edited by Leon Klenicki & Geoffrey Wigoder, Paulist Press, 1984, pp. 180–182]

THE RELATIONSHIP BETWEEN SIN AND REDEMPTION

*Breslauer has focused on Jewish concepts of redemption and salvation. He has not made any mention of sin. The next extract is written jointly by two Jews who are also involved in the dialogue—**David Berger**, a historian, and **Michael Wyschogrod**, a philosopher. Their contribution is important because it succinctly explains to the Christian the relationship in Judaism between sin and salvation. Traditionally the notion of being 'saved from sin' is a Christian one. In Judaism human beings have a good inclination and a bad inclination. There is no concept of 'original sin' (as in Christianity), rather people have the freedom to choose to follow their good or their bad inclination. When a Jew follows the bad inclination and 'sins', redemption for that person comes through repentance:*

For Jews, the view that the six million victims murdered by the Nazis went directly from Hitler's ovens to eternal hell-fire is morally offensive. It must be noted that the certainty of damnation without faith in Jesus is understood not as a function of the individual's sin but rather as a fate preordained by the sin of Adam, whose fall and guilt are carried by all human beings at birth, making them worthy of hell even before they have had a chance to sin at all.

Judaism, too, takes sin very seriously. From the beginning, the Hebrew Bible documents man's recurring disobedience to the commands of God and the punishments meted out to him as a result of his disobedience. It is true that Judaism does not interpret the sin of Adam to mean that every subsequent human being starts his career with the verdict of guilty entered against him. Nevertheless, the Bible, as well as subsequent Jewish history, shows that sin is an ever-present human temptation to which we succumb far too often. The prophets of Israel interpret the various calamities that befall the people of Israel as the result of the people's sin. Similarly, the rabbis interpreted the destruction of the Second Temple in 70 CE as resulting from Israel's sin.

It is further true that sacrifice plays an important role in the forgiveness of sin. The Temple in Jerusalem, built on the spot where Abraham prepared to sacrifice his son Isaac until commanded, at the last moment, not to do so, was and remains the holiest spot on earth for Jews. It is plain to any reader of the Pentateuch that God commanded a whole system of sacrifices to play a role in the atonement of sin. Because this is so, there is no doubt that the destruction of the Temple in 70 CE (not to speak of the earlier destruction) was a great problem for Judaism. What effect would the discontinuation of the sacrifices have on Israel's relationship with God? Could sins be forgiven without sacrifices? Could Judaism survive in exile, without a Temple and with Jews living in many different countries?

Before going any further, we must now speak of the traditional Christian explanation of how the death of Jesus took the place of the sacrifices offered in the Temple so that no further Temple sacrifice has been needed since this final sacrifice. This view is most clearly expressed in Hebrews 9:13–14, where we are told:

> For if the blood of goats and bulls and the sprinkled ashes of a heifer have power to hallow those who have been defiled and restore their external purity, how much greater is the power of the blood of Christ, a spiritual and eternal sacrifice; and his blood will cleanse our conscience from the deadness of our former ways and fit us for the service of the living God.

The argument is that the sacrifices brought in the Temple had only limited efficacy because they had to be repeated periodically, while the death as a sacrifice of Jesus was perfect and was therefore the sacrifice to end all sacrifice.

Judaism rejects this view on simple grounds. The God of Israel forbids human sacrifice. Again and again, in the Hebrew Bible, God condemns the sacrificing of children to Moloch with particular vehemence (e.g., Leviticus 18:21, 20:2–5 among others). While God's command to Abraham to sacrifice Isaac perhaps established in principle God's right to demand human sacrifice, his last-minute intervention established his firm desire that not human beings but animals be sacrificed to him. Once this is grasped, it becomes impossible for the faith of Israel to accept the account of a human sacrifice as conforming to the will of God. It can be argued that the death of Jesus was not a sacrifice in the sense in which human sacrifice is forbidden, since it was voluntary on his part and those who killed him did not do so for the sake of bringing a sacrifice. But if that is so, then the death of Jesus can only be considered a sacrifice metaphorically and cannot substitute for, and certainly cannot terminate, the sacrifices specifically commanded by God in the Hebrew Bible. Many Jews and Christians see the reestablishment of the State of Israel as the beginning of the redemption of the Jewish people as foretold by the prophets of Israel.

These same prophets foretold the rebuilding of the Temple and the resumption of the sacrifices (e.g., Zechariah 14:21, Isaiah 60:7, Malachi 3:1–4), a resumption for which traditional Jews have prayed since the time of the destruction. These prophecies in themselves indicate that the Hebrew Bible never envisioned any event that would make the reestablishment of the sacrifices in Jerusalem unnecessary, and if this is so, then the death of Jesus cannot be considered the sacrifice to end all sacrifice.

Nevertheless, the seriousness of sin and the need for its forgiveness remain. For the Christian mind, this is accomplished by the death of Jesus. How does Judaism deal with this problem?

It does so through the idea of repentence. It is the basic teaching of God in the Hebrew Bible that God does not will the death of the wicked but their repentance (Jeremiah 18:1–10). Ezekiel 18:21–23 expresses this most clearly:

> It may be that a wicked man gives up his sinful ways and keeps all my laws, doing what is just and right. That man shall live; he shall not die. None of the offenses he has committed shall be remembered against him; he shall live because of his righteous deeds. Have I any desire, says the Lord God, for the death of a wicked man? Would I not rather that he should mend his ways and live?

Repentance involves recognizing that one has done wrong, being sorry for having done so, and asking God sincerely to forgive one's sins. Any Jew who does so will be forgiven by God.

Many scholars consider repentance a higher and more spiritual relationship to God than the offering of sacrifice. Frequently, the great prophets of the Hebrew Bible criticized those who brought sacrifices while continuing their evil deeds (e.g., Amos 5:21–22). The conclusion that these scholars draw from the prophetic denunciations of sacrifice without repentance (repentance not only means saying you're sorry, but also changing your conduct) was that the prophets considered sacrifice primitive and unnecessary. The truth is that the prophets denounced sacrifice without repentance, but they deeply respected sacrifice combined with repentance. The prophets had the highest respect for the Temple and its divinely ordained sacrifices, and expressed great sadness about the time after the exile when Israel could no longer fulfill its sacrificial obligations (Hosea 9:4).

But that time came, and while we reject the view that the prophets considered sacrifice unnecessary even while the Temple stood, we cannot overlook the emphasis that the prophets laid on repentance. It is perhaps in Psalm 51:18–21 that the matter is best summed up. The Psalm starts with the expression of a sense of sin which weighs heavily on the writer. He begs God to cleanse him of his sin and then continues:

> For thou delightest not in a sacrifice that I would bring; thou hast no pleasure in burnt offering. The sacrifices of God are a broken spirit; a broken and contrite heart, O God, Thou wilt not despise. Do good in thy favor unto Zion; build thou the walls of Jerusalem. Then wilt thou delight in the sacrifices of righteousness, in burnt offering and whole offering; then will they offer bullocks upon thine altar.

When sacrifice is posssible it is necessary, though useless without repentance (the 'broken spirit' and 'wounded heart'). When sacrifice is not possible, God forgives those who sincerely repent.

Judaism thus looks to God for forgiveness. In his infinite mercy God waits for man's return to him, and when this happens, God forgives all his sins. The rabbis taught that not only are the sins of a repentant sinner forgiven, they are turned into virtuous deeds. So great is the power of repentance.

[David Berger and Michael Wyschogrod, Jews and Jewish Christianity, Ktav, 1978, pp. 54–59]

THE SEVEN LAWS OF THE CHILDREN OF NOAH

Judaism allows for genuine faith in God to exist in other religious traditions. There has always been a positive attitude to those people who were referred to as 'God-fearers'. It was during the second and third centuries CE, possibly as a reaction to Christian views of mission and salvation, that Judaism formulated a strict code of practice to clearly define how a non-Jew can attain redemption. The Seven Laws of Noah, the Gentiles being the children of Noah, were formulated. These laws are explained and outlined in the next extract by **Chaim Clorfene** *and* **Yakov Rogalsky**, *two Orthodox Jews. These seven Laws of Noah are believed to be inherent in human nature:*

1. With respect to God's commandments, all of humanity is divided into two general classifications: the Children of Israel and the Children of Noah.

2. The Children of Israel are the Jews, the descendents of the Patriarch Jacob. They are commanded to fulfill the 613 Commandments of the Torah.

3. The Children of Noah comprise the seventy original nations of the world and their branches. They are commanded concerning the Seven Universal Laws, also known as the Seven Laws of the Children of Noah or the Seven Noahide Laws. These Seven Universal Laws pertain to idolatry, blasphemy, murder, theft, sexual relations, eating the limb of a living animal, and establishing courts of law.

4. All Seven Universal Laws are prohibitions. Do not wonder at this. Negative commandments are of a higher order than positive commandments, and their fulfillment, which takes more effort than positive commandments, earns a greater reward.

5. Men and women are equal in their responsibility to observe the seven commandments.

6. It is a matter of dispute as to when a person becomes responsible for his or her actions under these laws. One opinion holds that it depends on the intellectual development of the individual. According to this opinion, as soon as a child has attained the maturity to understand the meaning and significance of the Seven Universal Laws, he is obligated to the fullest extent of the law. The other opinion is that a boy reaches the age of legal responsibility at his thirteenth birthday and a girl at her twelfth birthday.

7. The Children of Noah are permanently warned concerning the Seven Universal Laws. This means that ignorance of the law is not a valid defense. One cannot claim, for example, that he did not know that idolatry was one of the seven commandments. Nor can he claim that he did not know that bowing down to an idol constitutes idolatry. (He can, however, claim that he did not know that such-and-such was an idol, for this is not ignorance of the law.) Therefore, one is duty bound to study the Seven Universal Laws to the best of one's ability and to teach the knowledge of them to one's children.

8. When one of the Childen of Noah resolves to fulfill the Seven Universal Commandments, his or her soul is elevated. This person becomes one of the *Chasidei Umot ha-Olam*, the Pious Ones of the Nations, and receives a share of the Eternal World. The Holy Scriptures call one who accepts the yoke of fulfilling the Seven Universal Laws a *ger toshav*, a proselyte of the gate. This person is

permitted to live in the Land of Israel and to enter the Holy Temple in Jerusalem and to offer sacrifices to the God of Israel.

[Chaim Clorfene and Yakov Rogalsky, *The Path of the Righteous Gentile*, Targum Press, 1987, pp. 40–41]

CHRISTIAN CONCEPTS OF SALVATION

Turning now to Christian concepts of salvation we find **Hans Ucko**, *the Executive Secretary for Christian–Jewish relations for the World Council of Churches, contrasting (as he understands it) Jewish and Christian concepts of salvation and redemption. He highlights the diverse understandings of salvation within Christianity: from salvation as expiation to salvation as the liberation from injustice. At the end of his extract he divides these diverse concepts into two main models: the exemplary theory of atonement whereby one is saved through following Christ's teaching; and the objective theory of atonement whereby salvation is effected by Christ's work:*

Salvation is described in the New Testament through a variety of images. Jesus' proclamation that salvation was at hand was always woven into his teaching of the kingdom of God. Here salvation has a religious and communal, individual and social dimension. It is both a present and future reality. After Easter the death and resurrection of Jesus Christ becomes the dominant image of salvation. The Golgotha event became identified with salvation. But nobody had noticed that salvation was at hand. Although salvation takes place in history— 'suffered under Pontius Pilate, was crucified, died and was buried'—it yet happens without and outside any human involvement. Those people who contribute actively to the death of Jesus are extras, spectators at a cosmic drama of salvation where there is no room for any human contribution. We are invited to collect the fruits of salvation, but we are unable to share with the Saviour in his saving act. Suddenly, without our knowing it, the table of salvation is set before humanity.

Judaism accords a major role for the Jewish people in the drama of salvation. Israel is to contribute to it. The salvation offered by God to Israel takes place in history, but Israel must not only look upon it as a spectator; Israel must be prepared, and equipped, to play their part. When the angel of God passes over the homes of the Israelites, it is because they have prepared themselves for salvation by spreading the blood of the lamb on the door-posts. When with his strong and powerful hand the Lord saves the people from the power of Egypt, the people are prepared to let salvation take place. They have given thought to what they are to bring along for their salvation. Bread for the way. As it turned out they could not wait until it was leavened. They take the kneading bowls in their mantles on their shoulders. They bring along their belongings and go out of Egypt, and salvation takes place. In the desert of Sinai salvation takes place as Israel lifts the Torah upon its shoulders. Israel simply stands by. Salvation is Israel going out of Egypt and into the world with the Torah scrolls on its shoulders. Without the words of Israel, 'All that the Lord has spoken, we will do' (Exod. 19:8), there would be no salvation.

Thus salvation in the Jewish tradition is not primarily a theological concept, related to a theological understanding of the human predicament. It is not primarily deliverance from sin and sinfulness and a fallen world, or an antidote to original sin. It is not an escape or a striving towards the Beyond. The earth is not an alien place where human beings do not belong. Salvation means being set free to be involved in this world because there is none other, only this earth, which is part of God's creation.

In the tradition of the church there are several ways of interpreting the concept of salvation. One sees salvation as the process by which human beings, through the death and resurrection of Christ, are restored to the image and likeness of God. Another focuses on the distinctive significance of Christ's death as expiation for human sin. Christ dies for our sins; the forgiveness of our sins is the result of his death. Our debts are wiped out. Christ came to repair the damage caused by Adam and to make us, as it were, go back to square one, back to Eden. The going back to Eden leans on a tradition, well documented from the middle ages but probably older. Here salvation is deliverence. We are being lifted out of life, freed from a corrupt world, where violence reigns and poverty, hunger and disease are rampant. Salvation means the possibility to enjoy a heavenly kingdom beyond and away from this 'vale of tears'. Salvation becomes something separate from ordinary human life, a distinctive religious phenomenon. Such images of salvation as the regaining of a lost state of mind, a lost paradise or the return to Eden, are utopian. They have little to do with liberation from injustice, from hunger and thirst, from nakedness and imprisonment. Such an interpretation of the work of Christ turns the attention of Christians to the past instead of orienting them for the present and the future. It contradicts the meaning the Bible gives to the interventions of God. When God intervenes, he does not re-establish or restore, but he creates anew. God's interventions in history are meant to bring about a new humanity, making us truly human, our becoming what we are supposed to be, 'the image of God', in communion with our Creator.

Salvation as liberation is yet another interpretation of salvation, based on the heritage from the Jewish tradition which sees salvation as involvement. In Christian thinking the attention is turned to the person of the earthly Jesus, his preaching, action and religious attitudes. Following Jesus is salvation. Salvation concerns the whole person, has to do with social justice, is liberation from oppression and exploitation. Salvation is a total event and embraces society and social structures. Ethics and salvation are interlinked.

In the Jewish tradition salvation is dependent on conversion and a life in accordance with the Torah. The aim of salvation is the creation of a holy people marked by righteousness and peace. The rabbis said that creation was not really completed until Israel, saved from Egypt, received the Torah in Sinai, and shouldered the yoke of the kingdom of heaven and walked away as a people of God, assigned to be instruments of peace and righteousness. When the people at the foot of Mount Sinai say, 'All that the Lord has spoken we will do', they signal their preparedness to mirror God in the world. Because of that affirmation now salvation is at hand.

In the church there have been at least two ways of interpreting the mission of Jesus as a way to salvation, two dominant Christologies among many others, with two distinct emphases. 'One was to follow and imitate what Yeshua taught and lived and the other was to be "saved" by what Yeshua the Christ did for those who believed in him as raised from the dead. In shorthand, the former could be called the "teaching Yeshua" and the latter the "taught Christ" or the "Christ of faith".'

[Hans Ucko, *Common Roots, New Horizons*, World Council of Churches Publication, 1994, pp. 88–90]

SACRIFICE: THE RESTORATION OF HUMANITY'S RELATIONSHIP WITH GOD

At the heart of Judaism and Christianity lies some notion of sacrifice. In both traditions sacrifice provides a symbol for connecting a person to God: it makes possible repentance and a restored relationship with God. **John Lyden**, *writing*

as an American Evangelical Lutheran, provides a sympathetic explanation of how sacrifice functions in the two faiths. Jewish and Christian notions of sacrifice and salvation were affected by the destruction of the Temple in 70 CE. This event provided a key shift in their understanding of atonement. For Judaism, sacrifice was not necessarily to be viewed as an external religious ritual but a matter of the heart—in line with the biblical prophetic tradition. For Christianity, Jesus became the sacrifice which replaced all Temple sacrifices. Christ's death became the sacrifice which provides for personal repentance. The point of departure between the early Jewish Christians and Pharisaic Judaism was twofold. Firstly, the Christians made Jesus' death the atoning sacrifice; and secondly, they made it universal in scope rather than particular:

The link between the Jewish and Christian views of atonement lies in the concept of sacrifice. The notion of sacrifice seems very distant from most modern Western people, but that may be because they do not understand its purpose. Many people seem to view cultic sacrifice as a practice of superstitious primitive peoples who think that their gifts can placate the divine wrath or make up for their sins. Viewed as such, sacrifice indicates an amoral understanding of God's justice and human guilt.

However, this interpretation misunderstands the nature and purpose of sacrifice. Primarily, it is neither propitiation of the gods' anger nor satisfaction for sin but a medium whereby the worshippers are related to the divine, a 'ferry-boat between heaven and earth'. This is true of all religions that have used sacrifice, including the religion of ancient Israel. They performed sacrifices as part of the process of atonement, but they did not believe that their sins were magically removed when an animal was slaughtered on the altar, as if something took place that made their own moral actions irrelevant. Rather, sacrifice was understood as the ritual that symbolically connected them to their God, thereby providing the external basis for effective repentance. Sacrifice is not then to be viewed as an alternative to repentance but as that which makes it possible. Godfrey Ashby noted that 'expiatory sacrifice should never be seen as a rival to other means of response, such as expressions of repentance, but as the provided vehicle for confession and reparation.' Sacrificial acts show the penitence of the sinner and give concrete expression to his or her desire to repent. In this way, the sacrifice is part of the process whereby the sinner is reconciled to God.

This understanding of the process of atonement was forced to change when the Second Temple was destroyed in 70 CE. The Jews soon realized that they would somehow have to preserve their religion without the temple sacrifices. The rabbis turned to the fact that sacrifice was never effective as an external rite in itself, as if it could 'automatically' cleanse people apart from their own repentance. Atonement cannot be effective without the genuine expression of sorrow for sin and a sincere desire to reform. The rabbis therefore put forward the view that atonement is now made possible through the individual confession of sins, apart from any cultic ritual. The high priest no longer confesses for the people on Yom Kippur; now it is the duty of all Jews to confess their own sins. This confession is no longer externalized in ritual form but in deeds of lovingkindness done for one's neighbor. The way to this life of righteousness and love is to be found through following the Torah.

The rabbis supported this view by quoting the prophet's words that 'God desires mercy and not sacrifices'. However, this is not meant to imply a rejection of sacrifice as such. One should realize that, when the prophets said God took no delight in the offerings of Israel, this was only a rejection of sacrifice performed without the right intention. Ashby noted: 'The call from the prophets is to perform sacrifice, not to abolish it. It is sacrifice emptied of its content and detached from its context that is denounced by prophets and psalmists. To have condemned all offering of sacrifice would have been, in effect, to have condemned all public worship.'

Likewise, in quoting the prophets, the rabbis were not claiming that sacrifice was immoral or undesirable. They were simply trying to deal with a situation in which they could no longer offer sacrifices, which forced them to develop a new understanding of atonement. Therefore, they stressed the human intention to repent that underlay the sacrifice and that remains in effect even without the cult.

This does not mean that the idea of sacrifice has completely disappeared from Judaism. The prayer service itself was constructed as a form of sacrifice so that, as the rabbis said (quoting Hos. 14:2), 'we will offer the fruit of our lips'. Furthermore, traditional Judaism looks forward to a restoration of physical sacrifice in the new Jerusalem, demonstrating that the cult had a role that has remained unfulfilled since the destruction of the temple. Michael Wyschogrod has claimed that the cultic aspect of Judaism cannot be replaced by ethical and rational categories, because a 'religion must make it possible for the holy to appear to the believer' as it does in cultic worship. Without the cult, the 'personal relationship with the lawgiver' is lost. In his view, Judaism has retained sacrifice as part of the process of atonement, in that the commemoration of the cult (which includes the hope for its renewal) is 'itself a form of the practice of the cult'. There is a sense, then, in which Judaism has continued to be a religion of sacrifice, even though the sacrifice is no longer offered physically. Repentance requires some form of 'sacrifice' as its external expression, just as sacrifice requires repentance as its internal basis. Neither can exist without the other.

Sacrifice is also essential to the Christian concept of atonement. The first Christians were Jews who were familiar with the temple cult in Jerusalem as the means of atonement. Therefore, it is not altogether strange that they applied the language of sacrifice to the death of Jesus. They believed that Jesus was like the high priest at the temple, interceding with God on their behalf, making a holy offering to overcome the gap that separated them from God. Like the high priest, Jesus did not provide a substitution for their own moral efforts to atone for their sins. Like other Jews, the first Christians believed their own repentance was essential to appropriate the value of the sacrifice. This does not mean that they thought the purpose of Jesus' sacrifice was merely to prompt them to repent; rather, they believed his sacrifice provided the external form in which their desire to repent and be forgiven was expressed.

In the Christian view, Jesus' sacrifice and human repentance are inseparable, so atonement occurs in one's own personal appropriation of Jesus' work. The Christian identifies with Jesus' work through faith in him; hence, one's own obedience and suffering is included in the acceptance of his suffering on one's behalf. Jesus is in this sense not a *substitute* for us, who acts without our participation, but a *representative* of us who reconnects us to God. The first Christians believed that sacrifice requires our response of repentance to be effective, just as repentance requires sacrifice. The two are concurrent in early Christian thought just as they are in Judaism, because the Christian view evolved out of the Jewish concept of sacrifice.

Although the Christian view of atonement was rooted in Judaism, there were still differences in the way the doctrine developed in the two traditions. One obvious difference between the sacrifice of Jesus and that offered by the high priest is that the former offered up his own life as the sacrifice. One might claim that this idea clearly separates the Christian view of atonement from the Jewish view, but this is not strictly true. The idea that one may suffer for the sins of another is found already in Isaiah 52–53, the "suffering servant" poem to which the early Christians so often referred. Even before Jesus' lifetime, other Jewish writings proposed the idea that the death of martyrs could atone for the sins of Israel. The idea was developed more extensively during the period of persecution in the first and second centuries CE.; one can find numerous references to it in the Jewish literature of the times. It was believed that the righteous ones who die for their faith not only cleanse themselves from sin but are also able to intercede with God on behalf of all Israel. In this sense, their lives are a sacrifice for the sins of others. Even though this idea was formulated most explicitly in texts written after Jesus' lifetime, it did not appear then for the first time, so it is probable that the early Christians were familiar with it. The belief in the atoning power of Jesus' death, then, is not discordant with Judaism, for it evolved out of a Jewish understanding of martyrdom as a form of representative atonement.

In spite of this similarity, however, there were two crucial differences that separated the early Christian conception of atonement from the ideas of other Jews: it made the death of one individual *the* central act of atonement, and it made this atonement *universal* in scope.

First, by making the death of Jesus central, Christians separated themselves from those Jews who either had no personal relationship to Jesus or could not see why he had to be the central means of salvation from sin. Christians claimed that Jesus was central to salvation because he was the messiah, but this claim involved a view of the messiah that was very different from the typical Jewish view. In the view of most Jews, the messiah was to be the agent of God's rescue of Israel from suffering, not one who atoned for their sins. Christians, however, viewed the mission of the messiah as sacrificial, first and foremost. Only through his death and resurrection could he redeem Israel. By reinterpreting the concept of the messiah and applying it to Jesus in this way, the first Christians gave a significance to his death above all other atoning sacrifices.

Second, the messianic significance attributed to Jesus' death led to the view that the atonement he brought is universal in scope. The first Christians expanded the message of salvation beyond the boundaries of Israel in that Jesus was said to have died for the sins of everyone in the world. It was this idea that made the mission to the gentiles possible, and very soon the idea was being translated into terms that made sense to them. There were already many popular myths of gods who die and are reborn to bring new life to the world, and the gentiles may have understood Jesus' death in such mythic terms.

At the same time, we should realize that the sacrificial concept of Jesus' death was not developed in response to gentiles ideas but, rather, as a Jewish conception of the righteous one who reconciles us to God by his sacrifice of suffering and death. Although the centrality and universality attributed to Jesus' death distinguished Christian views from those of non-Christian Jews, these ideas did not negate the Jewish form and content of their understanding of his sacrifice. If we do not understand the Christian view of atonement as originally Jewish, we cannot explain its development within the primarily Jewish community of the early Christians.

[John Lyden, 'Atonement in Judaism and Christianity' in the *Journal of Ecumenical Studies*, 1992, vol. 29, no. 1, pp. 48–52]

CATHOLIC PERSPECTIVES

We turn now to two Catholic perspectives on salvation and redemption. The Catholic Church is the largest Christian community in the world. It is also fairly traditional: it definitely wants to develop the concept which we found in Ucko's extract which stresses the saving of humanity by the Christ of faith. Since Vatican II (1965), it has had this understanding of the Christian tradition and on the other hand a positive and affirming attitude to Judaism. The first extract spells out the official Catholic position vis-à-vis salvation and Judaism. The second seeks to move one step further in its acceptance of Judaism. The first is written by **Johannes Cardinal Willebrands**, *the first president of the Pontifical Council for Religious Relations with Jews, and the second by* **John Pawlikowski**, *Professor of Social Ethics at the Catholic Theological Union in Chicago in the United States:*

Salvation and redemption are, in fact, among the most significant themes of our common deposit of faith. The *Notes* (I:7) recognized the primacy of this theme, and at the same time they indicate the necessity of further reflection. Stating that the church and Judaism cannot be seen as two parallel ways of salvation, they understand parallelism in the sense of classic mathematics, according to which parallel lines will never meet. However, we hope to share, at least at the end of times, the salvation which God has reserved for all the righteous, as the psalm says: 'This is the gate of the Lord, the righteous shall enter through it' (Ps. 118:20). In that sense I understand also the words of Jesus: 'So there shall be one flock and one shepherd' (John 10:16). In the

Guidelines we affirmed the church must witness to Christ as the redeemer for all, 'while maintaining the strictest respect for religious liberty in line with the teaching of the Second Vatican Council (Declaration *Dignitatis humanae*)' (*Guidelines*, 1).

I wanted to make these remarks in order to show how much our theme is a delicate one. Indeed, at the same moment in which we express in very similar ways and terms our conception of salvation and the action of our saving God, we cannot but recognize that there are a certain number of substantial divergences which are characteristic for each part. Both of us, in fact, implore salvation from the Father with the same words: *Hosha-nah* ('Save, us O God!'), and the Jews end the celebration of *Sukkot* with the day of *Hosha-nah Rabbah* or 'of the Great Hosannah', imploring to be inscribed and sealed in the book of life. We Christians repeat the same invocation in the eucharistic celebration, which is the memorial of Christ's passover and implies also the salvific memorial (*zikkaron*) of Israel's liberation from Egypt, and of every subsequent event of salvation. Thus we cannot do without the salvific categories of Judaism to understand and express our religious identity, even as we cannot but recognize that Jesus, our savior, 'was and always remained a Jew' (*Notes*, III, 20). In the proclamation of and reflection on the mystery of salvation great importance is given to the prophecies of Isaiah, especially the last part, called Deutero and Trito Isaiah, about the mission of the suffering servant and the universality of salvation, offered to all peoples. In traditional Jewish exegesis these expressions are applied to the people of Israel in its totality, while the Christian exegesis reads in these chapters the prophecy about the suffering and glorious Christ. These two exegeses are not contradictory. Saint Paul, in his meditation on Isaiah, will write to the Romans that God's saving plan does not change and Israel keeps its proper function: 'God does not change his mind about whom he chooses and blesses' (Rom. 11:20). Though in different ways, Christians and Jews know the vocation of a chosen people, but this does not mean that other peoples are rejected. We adore the endless mercifulness of the Almighty, Blessed be his Name, in his mysterious plan of salvation, designed for all humankind. In every human being we respect the image of the creator and we wait in faithful hope and adoration for the day that 'all Israel will be saved' (Rom. 11:26), 'for he will come like a rushing stream, which the wind of the Lord drives. And he will come to Zion as redeemer' (Isa. 59:19–20).

The theological theme of salvation is not the only one that can be presented from two different sides, the Jewish and the Christian. There are two other important and characteristic themes, such as messianism, the word of God, prayer, exegesis, and in particular the typos, *the covenant*. Entering together into these different issues in an attitude of humble openness to search for the will of God, Father and savior, we will each learn to know better the religious identity of the other in its characteristic traits, growing in mutual respect and esteem for those religious values which are common to both of us.

[Johannes Cardinal Willebrands, *Church and the Jewish People*, Paulist Press, 1992, pp. 152–154]

In this second extract **John Pawlikowski** *formulates an understanding of salvation which is sensitive to the continued existence of Judaism. Salvation, meaning wholeness, is attained through human reconciliation with God. That wholeness is as yet incomplete. Christ's salvific work continues the process which was begun at Sinai but,* importantly, *it does not replace God's covenant with the Jews:*

I would begin with the premise that the term 'salvation' in its root meaning means wholeness. In this sense it is quite legitimate to assert that the understanding and experience of the Christ event brings to the human community the promise and partial fulfillment of salvation. The human community can achieve wholeness or salvation only insofar as it attains total reconciliation both with God and with humankind. This process of reconciliation began at the level of community with the revelation of God in the Sinai covenant. It was developed at the individual level starting with the Pharisaic revolution and achieved a significant new phase in the Christ event. The ultimate contest between humanity and divinity had been settled in a harmonious fashion, at least in principle. Pride had been fully vanquished. The human community could now more easily accept its dependence on God as a gift, for God had acknowledged the dignity of humanity through his presence in the Son Jesus. The working out of this 'settlement in principle' still lies ahead of us. That is why we must assert that salvation remains an incomplete process in practice. But the revelation in the Incarnation coupled with the revelation of Sinai has given humankind the blueprint and the power to achieve full wholeness as individuals and as the basic community of the children of God.

213

The Christ event completed the process of stripping away the barriers to the full understanding of how the human community could assert its dignity and at the same time acknowledge its dependence on the Creator God. The fundamentally sinful condition of humankind could be overcome. The only qualification I would make to the traditional notion of Christ as Savior is that this salvific dimension must be seen as the culmination of the process begun with Sinai and not as a replacement for the Sinai experience. Without an understanding of the communal dimensions of reconciliation and the link between ultimate reconciliation and human history—the core of the Sinaitic revelation—the notion of Christ as Savior becomes truncated and in the last analysis significantly distorted.

[John Pawlikowski, *Christ in the Light of the Jewish-Christian Dialogue*, Paulist Press, 1982, pp. 133–134]

NOT ONE COVENANT, BUT TWO

*The next extract is taken from a famous book written by **Franz Rosenzweig** (1886–1929), entitled* The Star of Redemption. *It is a central text for any study of the Christian–Jewish dialogue. He was writing as an Orthodox Jew committed to the improvement of Jewish–Christian relations. He was the first theologian to conceive of the 'double covenant' theory. In this work, he argues that both Judaism and Christianity have partial insights into the truth. They represent different but legitimate covenantal paths to God. They are not to be fused into one tradition but are to exist side by side. His theory has implications for a theology of mission because if both are legitimate faiths then there is no mandate to 'convert' the other. There are Christian theologians, such as James Parkes and Paul van Buren, who would endorse Rosenzweig's idea of a double covenant:*

Before God, then, Jew and Christian both labor at the same task. He cannot dispense with either. He has set enmity between the two for all time, and withal has most intimately bound each to each. To us [Jews] he gave eternal life by kindling the fire of the Star of his truth in our hearts. Them [the Christians] he set on the eternal way by causing them to pursue the rays of that Star of his truth for all time unto the eternal end. We [Jews] thus espy in our hearts the true image of the truth, yet on the other hand we turn our backs on temporal life, and the life of the times turns away from us. They [the Christians], for their part, run after the current of time, but the truth remains at their back; though led by it, since they follow its rays, they do not see it with their eyes. The truth, the whole truth, thus belongs neither to them nor to us. For we too, though we bear it within us, must for that very reason first immerse our glance into our own interior if we would see it, and there, whilst we see the Star, we do not see—the rays. And the whole truth would demand not only seeing its light but also what was illuminated by it. They [the Christians], however, are in any event already destined for all time to see what is illuminated, and not the light.

And thus we both have but a part of the whole truth. But we know that it is in the nature of truth to be im-parted, and that a truth in which no one had a part would be no truth. The "whole" truth, too, is truth only because it is God's part. Thus it does not detract from the truth, nor from us, that it is only partially ours. A direct view of the whole truth is granted only to him who sees it in God. That, however, is a view beyond life. A living view of the truth, a view that is at the same time life, can become ours too only from out the immersion into our own Jewish heart and even there only in image and likeness. As for the Christians, they are denied a living view altogether for the sake of a living effectiveness of the truth. Thus both of us, they as much as we, we as much as they, are creature precisely for the reason that we do not see the whole truth. Just for this we remain within the boundaries of mortality. Just for this we—remain. And remain we would. We want to live. God does for us what we want so long as we want it. As long as we cling to life, he gives us life. Of the truth he gives us only what we, as living creatures, can bear, that is our portion. Were he to give us more, to give us his portion, the whole truth, he would be hoisting us beyond the boundaries of humanity. But precisely as long as he does not do this, just so long too we harbor no desire for it. We cling to our creatureliness. We do not gladly relinquish it. And our creatureliness is determined by the fact that we only take part, only are part. Life had celebrated the ultimate triumph over death in the Truly with which it verifies the personally vouchsafed truth imparted to it as its portion in eternal truth. With this Truly, the creature fastens itself to its portion in eternal truth. In this Truly, it is creature. The Truly passes as a mute mystery through the whole chain of beings; it acquires speech in man. And in the Star it flares up into visible, self-illuminating existence. But it remains ever within the boundaries of creatureliness. Truth itself still says Truly when it steps before God. But God himself no longer says Truly. He is beyond all that can be imparted, he is above even the whole, for this too is but a part with him; even about the Whole, he is the One.

[Franz Rosenzweig, *The Star of Redemption*, 1970, Holt, Rinehart and Winston, pp. 415–417]

SOME OFFICIAL CHURCH STATEMENTS

There are few official Church statements which overtly address the topic of salvation—particularly vis-à-vis Jews and Judaism. Two extracts have been chosen here, one from the Lutheran Church and one from the Catholic Church. Although perhaps not going far enough in stating that Jews can receive salvation without Christ, they do grant some degree of theological space for Judaism. The Lutheran Church statement outlines what Jews and Christians can learn from each other's concepts of salvation:

The Lutheran Church

Jews put great emphasis on faithfulness whereas our own emphasis is more on salvation. However, these are emphases rather than clear distinctions. Jews speak of salvation (God loved the patriarchs, chose their descendants, and gave them the covenant on Mount Sinai. (cf. Deut. 10:12ff.). 'Christians strive to be faithful (that I might be his own and live under him in his kingdom and serve him in everlasting righteousness, innocence, and blessedness'—Explanation of the Second Article in Luther's *Small Catechism*). The following paragraphs comment on characteristic terms and concepts used by Jews and Christians when they speak of salvation and faithfulness.

One of the striking differences between Jews and Christians lies in their understanding of the human will. Jews hold that human beings are created with two inclinations, an inclination for good and an inclination for evil. As sons and daughters of the covenant, Jews are urged to choose life and blessing rather than death and curse (Deut. 30) and to keep the commandments of God. It is presupposed that they have the freedom to make this choice.

Christians, on the other hand, hold that they cannot even believe in Jesus Christ unless the Holy Spirit has called them by the Gospel. Before conversion the human will is in bondage to sin. After conversion believers live in tension between slavery and freedom.

When Jews speak of sin, they refer to multiple acts of commission or omission, violations of individual commands. Christians have a more comprehensive view of sin and see it as a power that enslaves. Individual sins are symptoms of the rule of sin in a person's life.

Jews seek to be faithful to the God of the Covenant, and their calling is to live the commands that have been given in the Torah. The concept of corresponding importance for a Christian is faith, or trust in the gracious promises of God. While faith is a free gift, every believer is freed for faithfulness, a life of obedience and discipleship. Paul has expressed well the paradoxical relationship between faith as gift and faithfulness as task: 'Work our your own salvation with fear and trembling for it is God who works in you to know and do his will' (Phil. 2:12–13).

For Jews the covenant given to Moses on Mount Sinai is still the basis for membership in the redeemed people. Christians confess that they have been incorporated into a new covenant people through the merits of Jesus Christ.

Jews underscore the importance of obedience here and now, within the covenant community. Christians speak of past liberation from sin, world, and flesh, but they anticipate and look forward to the completion of salvation when God will be all in all, and sin and death will be no more.

Christians can learn much from Jews about faithful living for God and the neighbor in everyday life in this world. 'Faith' too easily becomes escape from vocation and reliance on 'cheap grace'. A faith without faithfulness is no real faith. We hope that Jews might see through our faith the central importance of a gracious God, who calls, gathers, enlightens, and sanctifies the whole church.

These words are a preliminary attempt to understand and to detect divergent emphases. We are not called to judge each other, but to learn from one another about both salvation and faithfulness.

[*Stepping Stones to Further Jewish–Lutheran Relationships* edited by Harold Ditmanson, Augsburg, 1990, pp. 88–89]

The Catholic Church

From Nostra Aetate:

The Church of Christ acknowledges that in God's plan of salvation the beginning of her faith and election is to be found in the patriarchs, Moses and the prophets. She professes that all Christ's faithful, who as men of faith are sons of Abraham (cf. Gal. 3:7), are included in the same patriarch's call and that the salvation of the Church is mystically prefigured in the exodus of God's chosen people from the land of bondage. On this account the Church cannot forget that she received the revelation of the Old Testament by way of that people with whom God in his inexpressible mercy established the ancient covenant. Nor can she forget that she draws nourishment from that good olive tree onto which the wild olive branches of the Gentiles have been grafted (cf. Rom. 11:17–24). The Church believes that Christ who is our peace has through his cross reconciled Jews and Gentiles and made them one in himself (cf. Eph. 2:14–16).

Likewise, the Church keeps forever before her mind the words of the apostle Paul about his kinsmen: 'they are Israelites, and to them belong the sonship, the glory, the covenants, the giving of the law, the worship, and the promises; to them belong the patriarchs, and of their race according to the flesh, is the Christ' (Rom. 9:4–5), the son of the virgin Mary. She is mindful, moreover, that the apostles, the pillars on which the Church stands, are of Jewish descent, as are many of those early disciples who proclaimed the Gospel of Christ to the world.

As holy Scripture testifies, Jerusalem did not recognize God's moment when it came (cf. Luke 19:42). Jews for the most part did not accept the Gospel; on the contrary, many opposed the spreading of it (cf. Rom. 11:28). Even so, the apostle Paul maintains that the Jews remain very dear to God, for the sake of the patriarchs, since God does not take back the gifts he bestowed or the choice he made. Together with the prophets and that same apostle, the Church awaits the day, known to God alone, when all peoples will call on God with one voice and 'serve him shoulder to shoulder' (Soph. 3:9; cf. Isa. 66:23; Ps. 65:4; Rom. 11:11–32).

['Declaration on the Relation of the Church to Non-Christian Religions', *Nostra Aetate*, 28 October 1965]

A DIALOGUE BETWEEN A JEW AND A CHRISTIAN ON SALVATION

*The final extract represents an honest and frank dialogue between **Pinchas Lapide**, an Orthodox Jew and New Testament scholar, and **Karl Rahner** (1904–1984), the Catholic theologian. The dialogue is remarkable in its ability to recognize the difference of 'the other' and yet retain respect for his religious tradition:*

LAPIDE: That Jesus had a central role to fulfil in the divine plan of salvation (which is largely unknown to me) through which the West has been led to faith in the one God in his name is beyond every doubt as far as I am concerned. If Paul is right (in the quotation from Isaiah [59:20] that he transforms into a reference to the parousia of Christ in Romans 11:26), and the coming redeemer turns out to be Jesus, then all of Israel will surely welcome him as the anointed of the Lord. 'Until he comes' (1 Cor. 11:26), we both live in hope that must remain open as long as God does not give us certainty. Just as hard to dispute would be the possibility that God could surprise us both as he has already done so often, 'for my thoughts are not your thoughts, neither are your ways my ways, says the Lord' (Isa. 55:8).

RAHNER: Everyone lives in a dialectical relationship with his fellow human beings. He recognizes the other to be as he is and still has expectations, hopes and demands that the other has not yet fulfilled. So you must indulge me (if I may formulate it so sharply) if I were still to expect that you would be baptized in this present age.

LAPIDE: I accept your hope in the same spirit of love and concern for the salvation of my soul in which it is meant—although I cannot share in it. Likewise I nurse the hope that when 'the Son himself will also be subjected to the [Father] …, so that God may be all in all' (1 Cor. 15:28), on that day 'all of them may call on the name of the Lord and serve him with one accord', as it says in *Nostra Aetate* in the words of Zephaniah (3:9), and that you also, dear Father Rahner, and your fellow Christians will become such monotheists as understood by Judaism.

RAHNER: Naturally, as long as you are a Jew in your convictions, you must hope that Christian monotheism will distance itself from an incarnational alliance with Jesus and in this way, as you formulated it, God will be all in all. You must hope for that out of your conviction, as you must grant me the opposite conviction.

LAPIDE: I would nevertheless want to go beyond mutual toleration. For me, Jesus is no insignificant person, one of many rabbis in Galilee. For thirty years I have occupied myself with him, his teachings, and the history of his impact. But many riddles remain unanswered, some of his features I see only in blurred outline, and his precise identity eludes all research. It is certain for me that he is a bright light of Israel and belongs to the great teachers of humankind. When in church you glorify God with 'halleluja' and conclude your prayers with the Hebrew word 'Amen', when Hebraic vocabulary and Hebraic modes of thought run through your theology and your liturgy like a red thread, that is not the least of his merits. The Catholic New Testament scholar Franz Mussner writes: 'Jesus makes humanity "Jewish" insofar as humanity was Christian and becomes Christian, for through him the Jewish categories of thought and faith came into the consciousness of people and works like a fermenting sourdough.' If the conversion of humanity to Israel's God is the penultimate goal of world history, the Christianization of a billion people—which happened in Jesus' name—is a significant step forward in the direction of this salvation. It is true that I can not acknowledge Jesus as the Messiah of Israel nor as the redeemer of a still unredeemed world. However, that God availed himself of him in order to being about a step forward, a progression on the way to redemption, is a fact of more profound theological consequence. I can also not accept his birth as God's incarnation (in the Christian sense of the word) but his exemplary human existence as vere homo, which has much to say to us both, can help us to a deepened, more noble human existence. This is and remains the basis for continuing dialogue.

RAHNER: What you say is an approximation of the Christian teaching about Jesus, an approximation that I can greet only thankfully. For myself, I would still perhaps suppose that behind your relativism in the interpretation of Jesus there is something else lurking that, if I may formulate it explicitly, you would still reject. However finally and ultimately I must still say once more, first: because Jesus himself promised me God's absoluteness in an irreversible way (which means, that God in his works can neither retreat from this promise nor trump it), everything is already included for me in this future irreversibly by Jesus, both in terms of the further possibilities of religion and of my own existence as well, even though I don't know in detail what is already implied. And second I would say: if I believe in Jesus in this way as the irreversible and victorious self-promise of God, I have already actually reached that which the Church's theology of Incarnation teaches. For even in this theology of Incarnation that which is of absolute importance for the Jewish monotheist, and possibly also for the Muslim, is not denied—namely, that God and the creature are two different realities and they remain unmixed even in Jesus with total unity between divinity and humanity.

LAPIDE: I am grateful to you for this clarification. For fifteen hundred years the average Jew has been of the opinion that 'becoming human' and 'incarnation' signify for the Christian that the creator of the universe shrank himself completely into the human body of Jesus, in a manner of speaking, in order to become totally flesh and blood. Such a notion for the Jew, however, borders on idolatry or the deification of the creature. It is high time to demolish such faulty interpretations and misunderstandings, which are frequently more semantic than theological in nature, through a candid exchange of ideas. It could be that we will then discover that the chasm which separates Jews and Christians from one another is not half as deep as our forefathers had assumed.

RAHNER: To that I would say the following, which you may regard as a compliment to the Jews if you like. For me the Incarnation, properly understood (which doesn't signify an identity between divinity and creatureliness, but rather a nevermore dissolvable union between the promising God and creaturely promise), is in a certain sense, and naturally only so, an almost self-evident matter. Especially when for me the end of the creature is only fulfilled by God when the creature, without disappearing, reaches God again— precisely in Jesus and in the deifying grace that comes to people. However, the Incarnation, so understood, occurs precisely in Jesus the Jew (and not in a Buddhist or in some otherwise mystical way), and thus the irrevocable promise of God in history, as opposed to some mystical experience, is given precisely in Jesus the Jew as nowhere else. That is the matchless and exciting conviction of Christianity. I would almost say that the scandal in the Christian message is not a Christology, but rather a Jesus-oriented Christology. To an Indian, for instance, it is self-evident that there is a divine humanity in human being as a whole. And that is not simply false. For as a Christian I say that the eternal God communicates himself through the uncreated grace that we name the Holy Spirit to every person who will not be damned eternally, then a universal divine humanity is also somehow envisioned. But for me as a Christian the fact still remains that there is a historical self-promise of God in the event of a concrete person and that this happened in Jesus and (please pardon the banality) not in Prussia or India. And this is the concrete experience of

Christianity, which cannot be deduced speculatively. This self-promise happened in Judaism.

LAPIDE: That may belong to the mission of Israel. For if we, 'the fewest of all peoples' (Deut. 7:7), were called to transmit to the world the monotheistic faith, the Bible, and the ethos of the prophets as the God-given service to the people of the world, then perhaps Jesus also belongs to those 'gifts' that we were destined to bear and pass on. Could you imagine that this mission of Israel's extends even unto the future, that further redemptive tasks await us?

RAHNER: I am no prophet. So strictly speaking I must allow your question to go unanswered. But naturally I hope that Israel helps the balance of humanity to believe further in a prophetic monotheism of God the Father and also Jesus.

[Karl Rahner and Pinchas Lapide, *Encountering Jesus—Encountering Judaism: A Dialogue*, Crossroad, 1987, pp. 81–86]

FURTHER READING

Borchsenius, Poul. *Two Ways to God: Judaism and Christianity*, Vallentine Mitchell, 1968.

Braybrooke, Marcus. *Time To Meet*, SCM Press, 1990.

Buber, Martin. *Two Types of Faith*, Macmillan, 1951.

Hick, John & Knitter, Paul (edited). *The Myth of Christian Uniqueness*, SCM Press, 1987.

Hillman, Eugene. *Many Paths*, Orbis, 1989.

Jacob, Walter. *Christianity Through Jewish Eyes*, Hebrew Union College Press, 1974.

John Paul II, *Crossing the Threshold of Hope*, Jonathan Cape, 1994.

Klenicki, Leon & Neuhaus, Richard. *Believing Today: Jew and Christian in Conversation*, Eerdmans, 1989.

Novak, David. *The Image of the Non-Jew in Judaism*, The Edwin Mellen Press, 1983.

Solomon, Norman. *Judaism and World Religion*, Macmillan, 1991.

Sullivan, Francis. *Salvation Outside the Church?* Geoffrey Chapman, 1992.

Van Buren, Paul. *A Theology of the Jewish–Christian Reality: Part 3*, Harper & Row, 1988.

CHAPTER NINE

WOMEN

CHAPTER NINE

WOMEN

The feminist challenge to religion has been very significant on both Judaism and Christianity. The role suggested for women varies greatly from community to community. Within the Reform traditions, and some of the Protestant Churches, women can occupy positions of leadership either as rabbis or ordained ministers/priests; however within the Orthodox Jewish, Eastern Orthodox Christian and Catholic traditions, this is not the case.

In Reform and Liberal Judaism a woman can perform all the ceremonies in the synagogue and fully participate in those duties which are designated to rabbis. These women have received a good grounding in Torah and Tradition. They are counted as part of the *minyan* and are able to recite community prayers and the mourners *kaddish*. The awareness of gender issues has meant a change from exclusive to inclusive language in the new Prayer Book of Liberal and Progressive Judaism (only brought out in 1995).

In Orthodox Judaism the status of women is governed by *halakah*. There are numerous issues which are being raised in Orthodox circles—from issues of women's prayer groups, roles of leadership in the community, marriage and divorce proceedings, to the religious education of Jewish women. Jonathan Sacks, Chief Rabbi of the United Hebrew Congregations of the Commonwealth, in 1993 instigated a survey and report to be compiled on the status and concerns of Jewish women. This has naturally opened up perhaps far more than was expected. Some, but very few, of the recommendations of the report have been implemented so far. That may take some time. As many Jewish women have pointed out, the status of women in *halakah* has a mixture of negative and positive elements. On the negative side they cannot form part of a minyan or hold leadership roles. On the positive side, for example, marital rape is prohibited and the husband can be found guilty on the basis of the wife's uncorroborated testimony. The three most significant areas of Judaism *niddah* (governing sexual relations), *hallah* (observance of kashrut), and *nerot* (symbol of Shabbat and Holy Days) are entrusted to women; and the raising and educating of children in the faith is entrusted to them.

Judaism then, particularly Orthodox expressions, tends to focus on the role of women rather than the theological challenges raised by the feminist cause. There is less interest in examining the male concept of God than one finds amongst Christian groups. Even Jewish feminists worry more about praxis than theology. Perhaps this is currently the fundamental difference between Jewish and Christian feminists.

In Christianity the role of women in the community varies. In many of the Protestant churches women are able to be ordained as priests or ministers. In Orthodox and Catholic Christianity, and some fundamentalist groups, women are prohibited from such roles. This means that they are unable to perform certain rituals like the Mass or Eucharist, Baptism, a wedding ceremony, or the last rites and anointing of the dying. The pressure for change in these denominations is considerable. However unlike Judaism, Christian feminists are not simply seeking institutional change but a theological change too. They believe that their experiences as women are excluded by the male dominated God-talk. The Christian revelation has primarily been interpreted by men. For some women even the idea of a male saviour is problematic.

The dialogue between Jewish and Christian women remains largely a new venture—particularly in Great Britain. Still less is there any real dialogue between Orthodox Christian and Orthodox Jewish women. These are areas which will undoubtedly unfold in the coming years. Women benefit from involvement in the dialogue in two ways. First, they can discuss their concerns as women challenging their respective traditions; and secondly they can bring a different perspective to the wider Christian–Jewish dialogue. Such meetings break down the stereotypes that women often have of each other—it is surprising how much misinformation there is on both sides. It is vital that women express their emerging feminist theology so that it is open to the critical assessment of 'the other'. This is particularly important where some Christian feminist theology seems to have as its shadowside a new form of anti-Judaism.

H.P.F.

WHY CHRISTIAN–JEWISH FEMINIST DIALOGUE?

Deborah McCauley, a Catholic feminist writer, identifies two main purposes of Jewish–Christian feminist dialogue. First, to bring gender issues into the dialogue and second, to provide a forum for Jewish and Christian women to discuss the challenges which they bring to their respective traditions. Although these women meet out of a common concern to change their patriarchal traditions, their experiences are often very different. One of the key issues she addresses is how women might 'survive as feminists in patriarchal religions'. Not only that, but how can the wider Christian-Jewish dialogue benefit from feminist insights—particularly when that dialogue has been dominated so far by men:

Jewish–Christian feminist dialogue seeks to address what are, to date, two different endeavours: on the one hand, to bring a feminist perspective to interreligious dialogue about the relationship between Judaism and Christianity; on the other hand, to encourage interreligious dialogue between Jewish and Christian feminists. Whilst interaction between Jewish and Christian feminists has been going on for some years now, what brings together most Jewish and Christian feminists thus far is our common bind as feminists and our mutual interest in feminist critiques of Judaism and Christianity. Although the feminist values bringing us together may be the same, our religious world views and historical experiences as women within our religious traditions are *not* the same. Except for the bond of feminism and the need to share feminist insights about our respective religious heritages through the inevitable overlap in our historical and theological explorations, Jewish and Christian feminists have been passing each other like ships in the night; inured to the problem of the historical relationship between Judaism and Christianity, while failing to confront and resolve these problems with other feminists through interreligious dialogue as Jews and Christians. As a consequence, the problem of anti-Semitism in the women's movement and the undercurrent of anti-Judaism in feminist commentary and scholarship are becoming more acute and are dividing Jewish and Christian feminists from each other. Jewish and Christian feminists, as Jews and Christians, are equally affected by the history of our traditions' mutual estrangement. The bond of feminism and the fact that Jewish and Christian feminists are a minority in our religious traditions are no longer sufficient reasons for us to overlook the fact that our efforts to eliminate sexism and misogyny in our religious traditions often inadvertently perpetuate religious prejudice between Christians and Jews.

What feminism has to contribute to interreligious dialogue and the need for interreligous dialogue between feminists is the dual focus of Jewish–Christian feminist dialogue. The first question bringing together many Jewish and Christian feminists was (and still is), 'How might we survive as feminists in patriarchal religions?' From the encounters initiated by this question has developed the recognition for the need of Jewish–Christian feminist dialogue on interfaith relations. Feminists now turn their energies, commitment, and talent to such a dialogue, but find themselves at the stage of the 'incipient issue'. We straddle three conflicting hurdles: contemporary feminist scholarship on religion and culture, the abysmal history of Jewish–Christian relations over the millennia, and the grist of Jewish–Christian dialogue as defined thus far by the men who have gone before us.

From the 1960s to the present, interreligious dialogue between Catholics and Jews has been based on scholarship and theology and has been limited, for the most part, to clergy. Today, dialogue is still primarily in the hands of clergy—*male* clergy: neither the Roman Catholic Church nor Orthodox and (until February of 1985) Conservative Judaism ordain women. As a consequence, very few women today are involved in Jewish–Christian dialogue. In addition, the almost exclusive focus on scholarship in interreligious dialogue has precluded the participation of many women, although this exclusion is not consciously deliberate. Historically, scholarship has been reserved for men in both the Christian and Jewish traditions. Christianity has propagated a world view dominated by mind–body dualism, with men as the minds and women as the bodies. In Judaism, the study of *Torah* and *Halakkah* traditionally have been reserved for men, with women as the enablers. Because women have been excluded from the processes which have given normative shape to our religious traditions—and to the values and world views which our traditions express—women have not been able to challenge until now those elements in our traditions which foster anti-Judaism and misogyny. Like Catholic–Jewish dialogue since the promulgation of *Nostra Aetate*, the involvement of women in the dialogue process is, in the words of the prophet Jeremiah, a 'new thing in the earth' (Jer. 31:22b).

Some who are drawn to interfaith dialogue between Jewish and Christian feminists are feminists actively committed to

Jewish–Christian relations. Many more are Christian and Jewish feminists who are coming to interfaith dialogue for the first time out of
their deep commitment to their own religious traditions and out of
their need to find encouragement and support from feminists in other
religious traditions, who, like themselves, are actively working to
achieve equality for women and co-responsibility within their faith
communities and religious institutions. Most are not clergy or scholars. Most do not possess 'Rabbi' or 'Reverend' before their name, with
'PhD' bringing up the rear for good measure. As a consequence, most
feminists concerned with interfaith dialogue with other feminists and
with those already engaged in interreligious dialogue do not possess
the credentials necessary to gain access and to influence the dialogue
process that has been established almost exclusively through the channels of academic and religious institutions.

Out of their experiences as feminists within their religious traditions, some Jewish and Christian feminists of faith are now working
together to create a genre of interreligious dialogue that will help to
refocus the issues dominating the history of Jewish–Christian relations. We are working to refocus these issues by bringing the hereto-
fore 'alien' factor of *women's* experiences, aspirations, and women's
historical consciousness to interfaith dialogue and to examine, through
feminist hermeneutics, religious practices, and theological concepts
such as 'covenant' that are of particular concern in interfaith dialogue.

The Task Force on Jewish–Christian Feminist Dialogue has a
motto: 'We must understand what was, in order to change what is, and
so effect what is to be'. Many feminists accuse religion of being the
seed-bed for the sexism and misogyny experienced in western
cultures and they trace its origins to a Judaic heritage. Even feminists
who are not 'religious', both Jews and non-Jews, have picked up this
anti-Judaic thrust and internalized it. Those efforts at feminist scholarship which have contributed so much to the self-understanding of
Jewish and Christian feminists have been, to date, the work mostly of
Christians. Tragically, through these same efforts has emerged the
ancient voice of anti-Judaism which operates within Christianity at
best at a subliminal level, and which has been prevalent in the women's
movement since the time of the suffragists, as so blatantly presented in
Elizabeth Cady Stanton's *The Woman's Bible* (1895). Jewish feminists
have had the painful task of making Christian feminists aware of
the often unwitting anti-Judaism reflected in their scholarship and
commentary. Our recognition of anti-Judaism attitudes in Christian

and post-Christian feminists writings has been a major force behind the incipient issue of Jewish–Christian feminist dialogue.

[Deborah McCauley, 'Nostra Aetate and the New Jewish–Christian Feminist Dialogue' in Unanswered Questions, edited by Roger Brooks, University of Notre Dame Press, 1988, pp. 194–197]

FROM EXCLUSIVISM TO INCLUSIVISM

Deborah McCauley writing in the next extract with **Annette Daum** (a Reform Jew and founder of 'Feminists of Faith'), puts into practice some of the points made in her previous article. They highlight how feminists can influence their respective traditions. In this instance they use the concept of covenant as a helpful way forward. It is a theme at the heart of both faiths. They argue that the traditional understandings of covenant in Judaism and Christianity have led to an exclusivist approach to 'the other'. The covenant is central in the biblical tradition—so by returning to this theme feminists can incorporate women's experiences into the faith. Where women have been abused and oppressed their humanity has been violated. Together, through the dialogue, they can explore the ways in which women and men can honour their covenantal relationship with God:

Our traditions' ancient metaphors for covenant have been locked into patterns of interpretation that posit the inferiority of 'Others' through their marginalization, be they Jews, Christians, or women. Further, the metaphors and their history of interpretation have become our *models* for how we believe God would have us live our covenant relationship with each other. Our traditions teach us that God has a purpose in the covenant relationship and that human beings are not yet finished. If we are to begin to incorporate our new maturity about the equality of women and men in relation to each other, and the equality of Christians and Jews in relation to each other, our metaphors for covenant must reflect our new understanding. Our metaphors must enhance—not undermine—our new awareness. If we do not wish to eliminate our traditions' metaphors for covenant, we must *add* to the metaphors and change how *we* (and our descendants) interpret the ones we receive from tradition.

Jewish–Christian feminist dialogue seeks to *refocus* interreligious dialogue on covenant from 'election and exclusiveness' to 'responsibility and inclusiveness'. We are at the beginning of the process of shaping a feminist vision of what the covenant relationship between God and

humanity is and should be and our responsibilities within that relationship. We come to this exploration from different faith traditions which
have to be mutually understood and respected before we can move on
to shape that vision about the covenant relationship. We need each
other because we are both in a covenant relationship with God; we
share the same focus and are a minority within our faith traditions. Our
focus is feminist, and our purpose is to explore how women and men
may equally honor the full integrity of their covenant relationship with
God and with each other, beyond the impediments imposed by a sexist
vision of reality which promotes the covenant relationship of one sex at
the dehumanizing expense of the 'Other's'.

Within the biblical tradition of both Judaism and Christianity,
covenant stands at the heart of the biblical vision of reality. Covenant is
addressed neither to individuals in particular, nor to community in
general, but to individuals within the context of community. Persons
are able to respond to the covenant and to take responsibility *for* the
covenant. Indeed, the word 'responsibility' may be hyphenated to read
'response-ability', the ability to respond. The covenant vision of reality
means for Judaism, as it does for most of Christianity, that humans have
the ability to respond to the covenant and are accountable for *how* they
respond. The biblical vision of who God is and who human beings are
in relation to God and to each other *assumes* that the essence of
humanness, that is, what makes us unique in the 'order of creation', is
our response-ability. If you strip people of their response-ability, you
violate their humanness, their accountability for themselves and their
relationships with others. As such, you strip them of the ability to be
fully accountable for the Image in which they are made.

In human social systems, oppressors control people by *limiting* their
ability to take responsibility for their own lives, first of all, by limiting
the *choices* available to them, and, secondly, by choosing *for* them.
Oppressors assume unwarranted responsibility over the lives of others,
and thus exclude others from sharing in the responsibilities oppressors
have assumed for themselves-over-'Others'. Under patriarchy, women
have been stripped of the fullness of their humanity in relation to men
by the negation of their potential (and obligation) to take full responsibility for themselves and for the world in which they live. The degree
to which a person is stripped of her ability to take authority over her
own life (biologically, politically, economically, religiously) and for the
world in which she lives is the degree to which she has been stripped
of the fullness of her humanity. Such deprivation violates the biblical

model of humanness which is predicated on the assumption that individuals are to be accountable for their lives *because* they are accountable for the covenant relationship. Sexism sins against a woman's right to be a fully responsible human being in the same world she shares with men and for which, in the prescriptive aspect of the biblical tradition, she is told she is fully accountable *with* men: for the image of God is *both* female and male (Gen. 1:27) and to *both* has been given responsibility for the world in which we live (Gen. 1:28–31a), not just bits and pieces of that world according to sex and gender.

If we are going to accept equal responsibility in the covenant relationship, we have to be equal within our faith traditions as actors and participants. How do we, who see response-ability as a focus, assume responsibility sufficient enough to get Jews and Christians to stop fighting over whose covenant is better than whose? How can we have a common witness to the rest of humanity that affirms the best that is within our religious traditions, when women have not been able to assume responsibility commensurate to our humanness within our religious traditions and their institutionalized expressions? As feminists of faith, our common witness, at least for the immediate future, is to help each other, as Jews and Christians, make our faith traditions deal justly with women first.

The reasons why Christianity and Judaism do not deal justly with each other are basically the same reasons why our religious traditions do not deal justly with women. The critique of triumphalistic interreligious dialogue on covenant and feminist critique of covenant in Judaism and Christianity illustrate that the parallels between the two are no mere coincidence, but a pattern deeply ingrained in our histories of interpreting the covenant relationship between God and humanity. *Hesed*, not hierarchy, needs to be our primary interpretative matrix for covenant.

[Deborah McCauley and Annette Daum, 'Jewish–Christian Feminist Dialogue: A Wholistic Vision', in Union Seminary Quarterly Review, Vol. 38, 1983, pp. 165–167]

ANTI–JUDAISM IN CHRISTIAN FEMINIST THEOLOGY

At the end of McCauley's first extract the issue of anti-Judaism in feminist theology is raised. It is of concern to many Jewish and Christian writers that the emerging Christian feminist theology ferments a new kind of anti-Judaism.

*It is often subtle and usually takes the form of either blaming Judaism for patriarchy or proclaiming Jesus as the great liberator of women in contrast to the other Jewish groups of his day. These are themes which **Judith Plaskow**, a Jewish feminist, succinctly outlines in her article below. She has written widely on this theme and poses a number of challenges to Christian feminists—challenges which are being taken seriously:*

The contrast between the God of love and the God of wrath and the condemnation of Jews for the death of the Goddess represent two areas in which feminist treatments of God continue traditional anti-Jewish themes. Anti-Judaism still seems most entrenched, however, in relation to the figure of Jesus, and in particular, feminist attempts to articulate his uniqueness and significance. I find the persistence of anti-Judaism in this area especially significant, given the profound ambivalence of many Christian feminists about the nature and role of Jesus. In the US context, Christian feminist anti-Judaism certainly does not take the traditional forms of reproaching the Jews for rejecting the Messiah or accusing Jews of deicide, for Christian feminists are not always sure who they want to say Jesus was and is. Indeed, the charge of deicide is much more comfortably made in the Goddess context, for the Goddess at least is a clear representation of the sacred, even if not one Christian feminists wish to adopt. Yet in wanting to hold on somehow to the centrality and specialness of Jesus without necessarily making ontological claims about his nature, feminists are forced to focus on his human uniqueness, and this uniqueness is most easily established by contrasting him with his Jewish context.

I first made this point many years ago in relation to the still-popular claim that Jesus was a feminist. As I argued then and still would insist, this claim depends on wrenching Jesus out of his Jewish context and depicting the Judaism of his period in unambiguously negative terms. As one writer on this topic put it, 'At the historical moment when Jesus was born into the world, the status of Jewish women had never been lower.... By the time of Jesus's birth, many decades of rabbinic commentary and custom had surrounded Old Testament literature. And these rabbinic traditions considerably lowered the status of women.' The author then goes on to quote a series of misogynist talmudic passages that may date anywhere from before the time of Jesus to five centuries later.

Such polemical use of rabbinic material to document Jesus's feminism shows no interest in the serious examination of Jesus's actual context. Aside from the fact that the Talmud is more appropriately compared with the church fathers than the sayings of Jesus, rabbinic literature is as varied as the New Testament in its comments about women and its legal treatment of women's issues. As Judith Wegner points out in her book *Chattel or Person? The Status of Women in the Mishnah*, the Mishnah a second-century legal text that lays the basis for the Talmud, is perfectly comfortable treating women in some contexts as full legal persons with the rights and responsibilities of Jewish males, and in other contexts as virtual chattel. To cite one side of this contradiction without the other is like quoting 1 Timothy 2 on women with the implication that it represents the entire New Testament.

Ignoring the complexities of rabbinic literature is just one problem with the Jesus-was-a-feminist argument, however. A more curious aspect of the strategy contrasting Jesus with his Jewish background is that it simultaneously acknowledges and negates the fact that Jesus was a Jew. He was a Jew sufficiently that his supposed difference from other Jews is significant and noteworthy, yet he was not a Jew in the sense that his behaviour counts as evidence for the nature of first century Judaism. If we acknowledge that the Jesus movement was a movement within Judaism, however, then whatever Jesus's attitudes toward women, they represent not a victory *over* Judaism but a possibility *within* early Judaism—a Judaism that was in fact so diverse and pluralistic that it is impossible to state its normative position on anything. The notion of a normative Judaism is a later rabbinic construct that Jewish feminists are trying to free ourselves from, and that we would urge Christian feminists not to adopt in the first place.

The argument that Jesus was a feminist is theologically very interesting for its simultaneous radicalness and conservatism. Obviously, its intent is to awaken the Christian tradition to self-transformation, yet it does so on the basis of an unnuanced and uncritical reading of the New Testament and early Judaism that seeks to proof-text in the service of feminism. It assumes, to use Krister Stendahl's phrase, that contemporary Christians are called upon to 'play "First Century Bible-Land"' and so do as Jesus did, however Jesus's actions are understood. Moreover, though the Jesus-was-a-feminist argument does not depend on explicit claims about Jesus's unique ontological status, it leaves these traditional claims unexamined in the background as a buttress to the feminist cause. It is perhaps not surprising then that traditional anti-Jewish attitudes work their way into this argument, along with other traditional assumptions.

234

I find it especially disturbing, therefore, that the tendency to define Jesus as unique over against Judaism remains even in feminists who do not make use of the Jesus-was-a-feminist argument, who are quite aware of the Christian anti-Judaism, who are freely critical of Christian sources, and who have gone very far in deconstructing notions of Jesus's divinity. Carter Heyward's view of Jesus, for example, as a man of passionate faith who shows Christians the way to live their own lives in relationship to God, but who cannot do it for them, seems to provide very little grounding for traditional anti-Jewish themes. And yet when Heyward tries to state the meaning of the 'dynamic relatedness we call Christ', she says, that Jesus 'seemed to perceive his own work would involve a radical shift in consciousness... from an emphasis on ritual to right-relationship; from salvation as "deliverance-from-enemies" to salvation as "right-relationship-with-God" which might involve deliverance into the hands of enemies.' Here we have the conventional law/gospel, carnal Jew/spiritual Christian dichotomies clearly stated in feminist form—a form that I must say is utterly astounding to me as a Jewish feminist, for what is Judaism about, if not right-relation?

It seems as if the feminist struggle with patriarchal Christologies itself generates a dilemma that leads back into the trap of Christian anti-Judaism. If Jesus is not the Messiah and the incarnate son of God on any traditional interpretation of these terms, then how does one articulate his uniqueness in a way that makes sense out of remaining a Christian? If one is unwilling to make statements about Jesus's ontological status or about God's work in and through him, then maybe it is necessary to make some claim about his specialness as a human being—and how does one do that except by contrasting him with his Jewish context? This is why I said earlier that confronting anti-Judaism forces Christians to redefine the self. Must Jesus be different from every other human being who had ever lived in order for Christianity to make sense? Can Christians value Jesus if he was just a Jew who chose to emphasize certain ideas and values in the Jewish tradition but did not invent or have a monopoly on them? If claims about Jesus's specialness are intrinsic to Christianity, then is there any way to make these claims that does not end up rejecting or disparaging Judaism as their left hand?

I think the persistence of anti-Judaism in feminist work—sometimes even in the writing of feminists who have explicitly addressed the problem—is clear enough. Since, as I said earlier, I see the issue of anti-Judaism as one aspect of the larger issue of how we create communities that honor diversity, I must at least touch on the complex political context in which Jewish and Christian feminists of good will approach this issue.

In discussing three loci of Christian anti-Judaism in relation to the question of God, I tried to speak in a way that would not deny the kernel of truth in the issues concerning Judaism Christian feminists have raised. The image of a dominating, angry father God is a problem for Jewish feminists as much as for Christian feminists. Jews *have* contributed to the suppression of the Goddess. The early Christian movement was open to women, whether we see that openness in contrast to Judaism or as part of it. Given these kernels of truth, even if Christian feminists engage in a continuing process of consciousness-raising and self-monitoring with regard to anti-Judaism, there always will remain gray areas in the anti-Judaism discussion that will need to be openly talked through with the utmost sensitivity. Christian and Jewish feminists need to be very aware of how we *talk about* and *hear* feminist criticism of Judaism and discussion of Jesus in the light of the past and present history of Christian anti-Judaism.

This history, and efforts to begin grappling with it, raise very different dilemmas for Jewish and Christian feminists. On the one hand, it is very difficult for Jewish feminists to critique Judaism in a non-Jewish context when we know that what we say as internal criticism may appear against us in Christian work. On the other hand, it is obviously essential to our health and well-being as Jewish feminists that we do critique Judaism and seek to transform it. On the one hand, the Hebrew Bible *is* the Christian Old Testament, and Christian feminists have a right to explore and critique the Old Testament—including images of God in the Old Testament—as part of their tradition. On the other hand, Christianity has a history of using the Hebrew Bible in a way that belittles and discredits the people who wrote it, and Christian feminist criticism cannot but be read in that context. On the one hand, Christian feminists have every reason to explore and value Jesus's openness to women. On the other hand, in doing so, they need to take account of the difficulty of talking about Jesus' relations with women without evoking in the hearer negative comparisons with Judaism. On the one hand, I as a Jewish feminist could write a modern critique of Protestant theology without ever having anyone suggest I was anti-Christian. On the other hand, a Christian feminist whose field is Judaism might well find herself in very uncomfortable waters if she chooses to do work on documenting the patriarchal character of Judaism.

[Judith Plaskow, 'Feminist Anti-Judaism and the Christian God', in *Journal of Feminist Studies in Religion*, Vol. 7, No. 2, Fall 1991, pp. 104–107]

JESUS: THE LIBERATOR OF WOMEN?

*In a similar vein the Christian theologian **Katharina von Kellenbach** acknowledges that although the feminist movement has brought significant insights to Christianity, it has as its shadowside a form of anti-Judaism. Often Christian feminists have appealed to New Testament women as models for contemporary female spirituality. This in turn has led to the denigration of Judaism by their laying the blame for the oppression of women on the shoulders of first century Judaism. In contrast, Jesus and the early Church movement are seen as the great liberators of women. New Testament scholarship has shown the situation was far more complex. As von Kellenbach points out, there is little evidence to substantiate the claim that Jesus was a feminist because he 'never openly and explicitly condemned patriarchy':*

Christian feminist theology started in the fifties and sixties with women and men battling for the ordination of women. Since the exclusion of women from power in the church was justified biblically, theologically and historically, men and women started to dismantle these arguments exegetically and historically. Christian feminists *rediscovered* Eve, Sarah, Hagar, the Hebrew midwives, Ruth, Hannah, Mary and Martha, Mary Magdalene, Mary, the Mother of God, Prisca, Phoebe and hundreds of other outstanding women who devoted their energy, creativity and strength to the Christian faith and Church. The equality of women was to be achieved by appealing to the foundations of Christianity. The marginalization of women was understood as stemming from misinterpretation, misunderstanding and corruption of the original revelation. The efforts of Christian feminists were devoted to investigating the 'true meaning', or the liberating intention of the scripture. This approach has two goals: on the one hand, 'herstory' had to be recovered in order to create female role models which could energize and encourage contemporary Christian women. On the other hand, the male establishment in the Church and in academia had to be convinced that sexism cannot be grounded biblically and theologically. The female models uncovered in the Bible and in history were supposed to legitimize the integration of women into the Church as equal members.

This approach, unfortunately, displays anti-Jewish tendencies: the openness towards women in the New-Testament, for instance, is contrasted with the alleged sexism and misogyny of the Jewish environment. This dualism is not fundamentally new. It is merely a continuation of traditional dichotomies such as grace versus law, spiritual redemption versus legalism, freedom versus pharisaic hypocrisy, new versus old. A new contrast is introduced, namely feminism versus sexism.

It is difficult to argue that Jesus was a feminist, because he never openly and explicitly condemned the patriarchy. Feminists claim Jesus as a feminist through his actions, namely his actions against 'the Law'. From Jesus' admittedly liberal attitude towards women, feminists reconstruct that he *deliberately* and *intentionally* transgressed existing misogynist law: for example the Niddah Laws (ritual uncleanliness during menstruation) are contrasted with his healing of the bleeding woman. The statements of some rabbis that one should not talk with a women (Mishnah Abbot 1,5), and that one should not teach a woman Torah (Sotah 3:4) are contrasted with Jesus' contacts with Mary and Martha, the Samaritan woman, Mary Magdalene etc. The baptismal formula (Galatians 3:27–8) is compared with the daily prayer in which a Jewish male gives thanks for not being born a woman, a slave, a pagan (Megillah 23a). This list of contrasts could be made longer. Sentences like 'Against such background, we begin to understand…' or 'The more we find out about the cultural conditions of rabbinic Judaism, the more we realize that... Jesus was deliberately breaking rabbinic customs that were degrading to the self-concept of women', abound in Christian feminist books on Jesus. While it is certainly accurate to describe Jesus as a liberal Jewish male, his 'feminism', that is, intentional actions towards the improvement of the position of women, depends upon a distorted description of misogynist Jewish laws. How is this image of sexist and patriarchal Judaism created?

Perpetuating traditional Christian exegetical methods, Christian feminist theologians assume that rules and regulations, which are recorded in the Mishnah and Talmud, were already in effect in Israel before the destruction of the Temple, before the wars of liberation, before the expulsion of Israel. The historical–critical method, usually the basis of every exegesis, seems to be out of effect when Judaism is concerned. One neither asks whether and how certain rabbinic legal opinions were already in effect six hundred years before the final compilation of the Talmud, nor whether they were ever applied at all.

As a feminist I would further question this method because it bases the actual life situation of women solely on male literature, namely a legal code. Can the actual life situation of Catholic women be deduced from papal encyclicals? Bernadette Brooten's research on 'Women Leaders in the Ancient Synagogue', which is based upon architecture, inscriptions of ancient synagogues, cemeteries, and documents of industry, commerce and social life, leads to considerably different conclusions compared to feminists who use the Talmud as sole evidence for determining the position of women in Israel.

Another problem of this method is, as Judith Plaskow, a Jewish feminist, pointed out, that the rabbis of the Mishnah and Talmud have to be compared with the misogyny of the Church Fathers. Such a comparison would be historically correct. It is, however, avoided. Is it avoided because the Christian tradition would not emerge as the winner in this contest?

[Katharina von Kellenbach, 'Jewish–Christian Dialogue on Feminism and Religion', *Christian–Jewish Relations*, Vol. 19, No. 2, 1986, pp. 34–36]

WOMEN AND JUDAISM: A VIEW FROM TRADITION

*The next section of this chapter looks at what McCauley described as the feminist challenge to Jewish and Christian traditions. Four extracts have been taken: two from Jewish and two from Christian women. They highlight the challenges raised by women to their respective traditions. In the first, for **Blu Greenberg**, an Orthodox Jew who is vocal in the feminist cause, the status of women in Orthodoxy is defined by* halakah. *That* halakah *was formulated by men and governs the position of women vis-à-vis for example prayer, leadership in the community, and marriage and divorce. Greenberg argues that women should be educated in* halakah *to enable them to make their own decisions in the community. Until women are adequately educated their* halakic *status will probably remain unchanged:*

From this brief sketch of the position of Jewish women through the span of many centuries, three principles emerge. Laws concerning woman underwent considerable change; her position was not static. In fact, her status generally improved; most of the legislation concerning women—from biblical through talmudic through medieval—

upgraded her position. Further, her condition was influenced to some extent (e.g., monogamy, inheritance) by the status of women in the surrounding cultures and societies. Rabbinic scholars were responsive to society and in many instances incorporated external social norms into their own legal system.

These principles seem to hold much promise as guidelines for the present and future. Still, there are two basic problems we must acknowledge; first, the Jewish woman always was subjected to disabilities in certain areas of Jewish law, just as all women have been faced with disabilities throughout history. That these disabilities have been codified in halakhic decisions, however, makes it more difficult to engender change. Second, the role of the Jewish woman usually was assigned to her by men. The rabbis had the sole power to determine her rights and obligations, which were presented to her as faits accomplis. In other words, she was kept ignorant of the processes of development of Jewish law.

The feminist movement generates new expectations; it has its greatest impact on Jewish women in these two areas. Like all women, Jewish women will not accept inequalities so readily, comfortable though the status quo may be after centuries of conditioning. Jewish women will begin to recondition themselves to what ultimately will be a more satisfactory situation. Indeed, we are witnessing an increase of Jewish women, learned and faithful, who want to enlarge their religious and ritual expression of Judaism. At present, these women are capable of the full range of human expression and learning; they are not asking to be led out, they are asking to enter Jewish life more fully. To discourage them in their endeavours is to act contrary to the ethics of Jewish law, the ethics of human dignity.

Similarly, Jewish women now must begin to study the processes of legal interpretation and innovation to enable them to emerge from a position of ignorant dependency to one of knowledgeable self-reliance and authority. Women must apply themselves seriously to the difficult demands of Jewish scholarship; perhaps this is the only route that eventually will lead to lasting Jewish liberation.

Just as women are expanding their role in general society, so too Jewish women can expect to play a creative role in influencing rabbinic decisions for our time, not only in the area of women's halakhic status but in all areas of Jewish life.

Some confront these challenges by saying that nothing can be changed. This is certainly not true of Halakhah, which is a living system, an ongoing process. There have been stringent and lenient trends in Jewish law in every generation. By combining common sense and a sensitivity to contemporary needs with a desire to remain faithful to the Torah, rabbis in every generation succeeded in preserving a love for the tradition and a sense of its continuity. It is important to emphasize this fact, for contemporary resistance to change has wrapped itself in a cloak of biblical authority and rabbinic immutability. Rabbi Yannai, a leading amora, teaches us otherwise:

If the law had been given in the form of final rulings, the world could not exist (Rashi explains: it is essential that the Torah can be interpreted in this way or that way). Moses said, 'Master of the universe, tell me which way is the Halakhah.' God answered him, 'Follow the majority'.

That Jewish women are beginning to grapple with the problems is a healthy sign, because halakhic changes never occurred in a vacuum but always in response to real needs. Thus the extent of the change we shall witness will be in direct proportion to the amount of unrest. It will take a lot to recondition both men and women in the Jewish community to these new values. Maybe unrest and rebellion against stereotypes must be considered the greatest merit, and lack of pride and simple obedience the greatest sin. A large part of the responsibility for change lies with Jewish women who must articulate more openly and more clearly their own needs. Current leaders cannot but be influenced by special pleading; this has happened many times in our history.

For the present generation of Jewish women, a clear mandate can be given. In the areas of marriage and divorce, the remaining disabilities should be removed quickly; enough halakhic groundwork has been laid to allow no room for further procrastination. The unequal status of women in the religious courts needs halakhic reinterpretation and repair. There must be a flowering of women's prayer and an encouragement of leadership roles for women in liturgy. And, most important—the means whereby all of these will be wrought—Jewish women must begin to acquire an intensive Jewish education right up through the level of high-quality rabbinic schools, preferably non-sex differentiated, so that each will hear the interpretation of the law in the presence of the 'other', so that they simultaneously grow in understanding of the tradition. Only then will women become part of the learned elite of our community in whose hands is vested the authority, the power, the leadership, and the inspiration.

And eternal Judaism will integrate and grow with such changes because these changes are wholly compatible with the spirit of the fundamental principle of Judaism—that every human being is created in the image of God.

[Blu Greenberg, *On Women and Judaism: A View From Tradition*, Jewish Publication Society of America, 1981, pp. 66–69]

PRISONERS OF HISTORY?

Sybil Sheridan, a Reform rabbi and lecturer at Leo Baeck College in London, looks at three central areas where Judaism has been criticized for its status of women: niddah, challah, *and* hadlakat nerot. *These issues have been explored in a similar way by Blu Greenberg in her book,* On Women and Judaism. *Sybil Sheridan, although working in a different Jewish tradition, endorses Blu Greenberg's exposition of the three halakic requirements of* niddah, challah, *and* hadlakat nerot. *Far from being sources of oppression these* mitzvot *endorse her identity as a woman. The following extract will be helpful to the Christian reader for its sympathetic reading, from a Jewish feminist perspective, of the* mitzvot *relating only to women. Jewish women need not be prisoners of history:*

Niddah

The Laws of niddah go back to the Torah where, in the book of Leviticus (15:19ff.) a woman is charged to separate herself from her husband and touch no one during her menstrual period. Afterwards she must immerse herself in flowing water—a mikveh or a stream—before resuming her normal life. The purpose, in the context of the Torah was clearly one of ritual purity. No man, having touched a menstruating woman could participate in Temple of Tabernacle worship. The laws of niddah themselves are set amongst those of male semen discharge and certain illnesses which prevented a man from entering the Tabernacle precincts. So, logically, once there was no Temple, the laws regarding ritual immersion should no longer be required.

This is what happened in the case of the men, who ceased going to the mikveh, just as they ceased sacrificing, blowing silver trumpets, or doing other things that were required as part of Temple worship. A principle was established, that whatever activities related to the Temple, could not be observed when there was no Temple.

But the women kept on observing the laws of niddah. Why? Firstly, because it gave them space. A man was forbidden from sleeping with his wife during her period and for some days after. It meant a woman was not constantly at the beck and call of her husband; it meant their relationship was not based entirely on sex. Secondly, it gave the women control. A man could not resume sexual relations with his wife until she had immersed herself in the mikveh. It meant that the woman was in charge of the sexual activity of the couple. Although the time for immersion was fixed, it was in her power to go to the Mikveh at that time—or not. You can see why women were loath to give this independence up.

But there is another aspect. The Rabbis required that laws relating to the Temple were to be left in abeyance while no Temple existed, yet the women appear here, to be flouting this. They deliberately continued to observe a Temple law that was now, no longer necessary.

Challah

The law requiring that the dough used for baking should be separated comes from Numbers 15:19–21. It demands that when eating the produce of the land of Israel, a portion should be set aside as 'teruma' a freewill offering to the Lord.

This is not a law specific to women, but the reality certainly by rabbinic times was that the women baked the bread in the home. And logically once the Temple was destroyed the requirement of the offering ceased along with all other sacrifices. Yet the women continued to put aside a portion of the *Challah* they baked for Shabbat,—and not only to put it aside, but also to burn it in, as it were, a surrogate sacrificial offering. Once again, they seem to be flouting the rabbinic principle regarding observance once the Temple had been destroyed.

Hadlakat Nerot

This law does not come from Torah. It is cited in the Mishna (Shabbat 2:1) and does not, at first sight have anything to do with the Temple. It was not originally exclusive to women, but the reality would be, that at the time for lighting the lamp—just before sundown and the beginning of the Sabbath, the men would be in synagogue, offering their afternoon and evening prayers.

It is often said that Christian ritual translated the symbolism of the Temple to the Church; with its priests and vestments, its altar and communion as sacrifice; while Judaism translated it to the home, with the Friday night table decked out as an altar and its ritual of lighting candles, drinking wine and eating bread.

It is not clear how accurate this picture actually is, since much of what we see as 'traditionally Jewish'—for example the two candles, the white table cloth, etc., may well have come to Judaism late in the middle ages via Christianity.

But it is clear that by the Middle Ages for sure, the Sabbath meal was seen as symbolising in some way the Temple sacrifice, and the dispenser of the ritual—namely the woman who prepared the meal, arranged the table and 'declared the Sabbath' by lighting the candles—became for that moment *in loco* High Priest.

The following is a prayer that was composed in the eighteenth century by one Sarah bat Tovim, to be said after the blessing over the Sabbath candles:

> My mitzvah of candle lighting should be accepted as the equivalent of the High Priest lighting the candles in the Temple.

The prayer may be late, but the sentiment could well have been around for centuries before.

It is quite possible that the women who so assiduously kept Mikvah and Challa alive because of their Temple connections attributed to the lamp something also of the Temple ritual—the lighting of the Menorah perhaps?

If this is so—and it is a big if—we see in the three women's mitzvot a studied preservation of Temple ritual that the men had abandoned; of purification, of dedication and of sacrifice.

It suggests a very careful and very independent response on the part of women to the trauma of the times. It suggests that women did not feel themselves bound by the principles that governed Rabbinic Judaism. It suggests that they had an autonomy of thought and action. It suggests they were educated and sufficiently confident in their education to form their own opinions. It suggests they took upon themselves the preservation of the Temple ritual they felt the men were abandoning.

It suggests a very different picture of Jewish women than the one we are often led to believe in, but it is a view that is to be found from time to time down the ages, in the responsa literature. It becomes evident that where the men legislated for women, it was on what the women were actually doing—not on what the law said they should be doing.

For today's women this is very important. It breaks the myth of women leaving the religious life to the men while they got on with the cooking. It implies a deeply spiritual and theologically articulate community of women who felt no need to 'break into' the men's world—not because they were satisfied with their domestic role, but because they were satisfied with their religious one.

For we Jewish women of the late Twentieth Century, it forms a framework upon which to start new traditions, and it gives us a history. It may not be a true history in the factual sense, but then, neither may the rabbinic picture that has so long held sway over the Jewish imagination. It is not the 'facts' that are important in religious history, but the significance attributed to them.

So, are we prisoners of our history? We need not be, if we can accept the limitations of history. We must not be, if Judaism is to advance to include women as equals in tradition. We cannot be if we are to be absolutely honest about the processes of history.

Once we accept that, life can never be the same again. A whole vast new realm of spiritual, of creative, of fulfilling possibility emerges, and this, I believe, will the be the future of our faith.

[Sybil Sheridan, 'Are We Prisoners of our History?' a lecture for Jewish–Christian–Muslim Conference, Bendorf, Germany, March 1995]

THE EFFECT OF THE CHRISTIAN TRADITION ON WOMEN

The next two extracts take up some of the feminist challenges to Christianity. **Sandra Schneiders**, *a Catholic, and Rosemary Radford Ruether, a feminist theologian and professor at Garrett-Evangelical Theological Seminary in the States, are both eloquent exponents of feminist concerns. The first excerpt by Sandra Schneiders outlines the traditional role of women in the churches, especially as seen in the Catholic Church. Traditionally women had been taught that their femininity was a barrier to approaching God. All positions of leadership and influence were held by men. The response of many Catholic women has been to abandon their tradition altogether. Schneiders argues that women should not leave the Church but should reform from within. This is often not easy given the exclusion of women from positions of influence in the Church. The feminist struggle in Christianity, she argues, must go on in three areas: the spiritual, the intellectual, and the political:*

The effect on the religious experience of women of this traditional warping of biblical revelation has been deeply damaging. Both by explicit teaching (e.g. that women are intrinsically incapable of priest-hood solely because they are female) and by innumerable implicit and non-verbal forms of rejections and degradation (e.g. exclusion from public roles in worship; sacramental subjection and dependence on men; exclusion from participation in decision-making and leadership in the Church; denial of theological education, etc.), Christian women have been taught to think of themselves as essentially alienated from God, 'unholy' by nature, dependent on men for all approach to God. A woman 'becomes' holy to the extent that she approaches 'masculinity' (cf. the collect in the old Roman missal for a woman martyr which praises God for giving masculine virtue *even* to members of the 'weaker sex'). Consequently, women have learned to experience their femininity as an obstacle to union with God rather than as a privileged mode of experiencing God. Even the traditional assimilation of women to Mary, the Mother of Jesus, has been a generally negative development. It has been used to idealize women and thus to effectively remove them from participation in the common Christian endeavor, whilst sacralizing their domestic role which has been the most effective tool of domination by a male society. There have been occasional positive notes in Christian tradition's treatment of women, such as the admission of women to Baptism (largely negated by their exclusion from Orders), the exaltation of monogamy (largely negated by the double moral standard in practise) and the recognition of women's religious life (partly negated by the denial to women religious of all forms of self-determination and their total subjection to the ecclesiastical authority of men). But the overall record of tradition is dismal when one considers the truly sublime teaching of Jesus on discipleship. The only honest judgement that can be made is that the Christian community, on the subject of women, has indeed 'nullified the word of God on account of [its] traditions'.

The crucial question at this point in history, when the consciousness of both men and women Christians is rising rapidly despite (or perhaps because of) Rome's consistent efforts to maintain the subservience of women to men in the Church and the effective exclusion of women from full participation in Christian life, is, 'What can be done about an admittedly bad situation?'

The answer, for increasing numbers of women, is to abandon Christianity as a degrading experience. But this is to participate in a 'nullifying revelation' by admitting that the erroneous tradition is more important than the truth of God. If it is sinful to bind the

Word of God by our traditions it is also wrong to abandon the community of revelation because it is in the iron grip of sinful tradition. The answer, it seems to me, can only lie in the reform of the tradition, in the liberation of revelation from the deforming power of false interpretation.

This is not easy, because, first of all, women are officially excluded (by men) from all positions in the Christian community which could give them a real impact on the institutional life of the Church. This disability is compounded by the fact that Christian women are the victims of that ultimate and most devastating effect of prolonged oppression, the projection of self-hate onto one's co-members in the oppressed class. It is, in large measure, *women* who consider women unfit for full Christian participation, who wish to be ruled by men, represented by men, and legislated for by men. Under this double handicap of institutional disenfranchisement and sociological crippling how can women participate in the reformation of Christian tradition and have a liberating influence on a culturally imprisoned community consciousness?

It seems to me that the struggle must go on in three spheres. First, in the realm of the spiritual, women must come to grips with the mystery of the cross which Christian participation in a male Church constitutes for them. The suffering that a woman must undergo as she begins to realize what has been and is being done to her 'in the name of Christ' is unimaginable to those who have not experienced it. For the twentieth century Christian woman, there is no way to avoid the spiritual struggle unto death in which she will learn to pray for her brothers who are crucifying her thinking that they are giving glory to God: 'Father, forgive them for they know not what they do; Lord Jesus, lay not this sin against them.' But until this identification with Christ in his salvific death for his persecutors (who we all are) begins to take place, the Christian woman is not equipped to do battle with the institutionalized sin of the Church.

Secondly, in the sphere of felt knowledge, women (and men) must begin to get over the depth conviction, which resists all rational attack, that the traditional position of the Church on women must be true, must be the authentic Christian tradition. Christian tradition on women is no more true or valid than the persistent Christian tradition of anti-Semitism or of the rejection of the blacks. Both men and women need to study the passages of Scripture which bear on this question, both to correct the erroneous interpretation and to affirm the genuine teaching of revelation, and to interiorize the truth by prayer and practice. The truth will make us free if we give ourselves to it with enough perseverance and faithful love.

Thirdly, all possible political pressure must be brought to bear from within the Christian community to change the present situation of rejection and oppression to one of full acceptance of women. Prudential judgments will have to be made about the advisability of selective and loyal disobedience. And courageous stands must be taken. The responsible and active participation of men in this struggle for justice and holiness is essential. Just as Christian have no choice but to battle actively against anti-Semitism, and whites to struggle against the oppression of blacks, so men do not have a moral choice about joining their sisters in the struggle for justice in the Church.

Man has indeed disjoined what God has created and redeemed together, and out tradition has nullified the Word of God about himself and about us. In recognizing the sinfulness of the present situation in the Church in regard to women we cannot pretend to be sinless ourselves. We can only choose between the attitude of the repentant adulterous woman before Christ and the attitude of her doubly adulterous oppressors.

[Sandra Schneiders, 'Christian Tradition on Women', in *SIDIC*, vol. IX, No. 3, 1976, pp. 12–13]

THE THIRD TESTAMENT

Rosemary Radford Ruether, *well known for her critique of Christianity, expresses difficulty in relating to a tradition that has been shaped almost entirely by men. Even the Christian saviour is a male figure. Christian theology, argues Ruether, needs to listen to the voices of women who have experienced victimization and oppression. Ruether therefore suggests a 'third Testament'—the Testament of women—as the new 'feminist midrash on patriarchal texts'. That 'Testament' must incorporate the voice of women from other communities— whether Jewish, Muslim, or pagan for example:*

As long as one is limited to the historical Bible as canonised by the rabbis and church fathers, there are very few stories, even those about women, that are really written from women's perspectives. Much of the awkwardness of translation that offends esthetic sensibilities, even of those who in principle support inclusive language, seems to me to

arise not merely from the fact that readers and hearers are more familiar with the old language than they are with the new. Rather, the
negativity suggests that, in some more basic sense, the revelations of
the biblical tradition were *male* revelations, not female revelations. This
does not mean that the divinity to which they point is male, but rather
that men received these revelations in the context of male experience
and shaped their telling from a male perspective. In the Hebrew scriptures the key locus of revelation is the flight of a people from bondage,
surely an event in which women also participated. But male heads of
families came to dominate the definition of that people freed by God,
and this definition of Israel ultimately determined the description of
those who received the final revelation at Sinai.

In Christianity we have a first-century rabbi—a member of an
office that excluded women—who became a prophet and critic of
established religious authorities. Betrayed by powers of religion and
state, he was executed by Roman officials as an insurrectionist. This
was a tragedy in which women surely participated as his followers, as
those who mourned his death and cherished his memory as the
Christ. But his prophetic criticism of religion only implicitly, rather
than explicitly, included the sexism of religion. It is male suffering at
the hands of male religious and political authority, rather than female
suffering at the hands of these authorities, that is lifted up as the
salvific paradigm, as the place where God is present in suffering unto
death and the renewing of life. In Hebrew scripture male suffering and
victory in war is a primary focus of revelation. Only once or twice the
female agony in childbirth is compared with this male agony on the
battlefield. But here also it is a male child that is to be born who serves
as a symbol of the renewed Israel. Where, then, is female suffering
taken seriously as the locus of revelations of the divine? Is it possible to
think of women as battered wives, as victims of child abuse, as victims
of rape, as insulted and silenced by patriarchy, as tortured by bound
feet, by clitorectomies, and by a thousand other means of sexual objec-
tification and dehumanization, as the place where the divine descends,
is present in these agonies as healing power, and brings new life?

I have recently been teaching a course on violence towards women.
One of the exercises in the class is a case study in which each student
describes and analyzes some crisis in her life or in the life of someone
she knows. In these case studies, we heard repeated stories of profound
suffering of women, sufferings from which each woman managed to
emerge a stronger and more autonomous human being. In one such

case study a woman described her rape by an unknown man in a ski mask while she was taking trash to a dump near woods. During the rape she became convinced she would die and resigned herself to her impending death. But when the rapist left and she found herself still alive, prone on the ground, she experienced all around herself a sudden and compelling vision of Christ as a crucified woman. As she lay transfixed by this vision, an enormous relief swept over her and she realized that she would not have to explain to a male God that she had been raped. God knew what it was like to be a woman who had been raped.

Such an experience of Christ as a crucified woman, making God present in the agony of a woman who had been raped, has not been thinkable in our religious tradition. If any woman had thought it before, she would not have been able to communicate it to the community of faith, or if she spoke of it among believing women, they would not have been able to make it a part of the tradition of authoritative texts from which the church engages in theological reflection, preaching, and teaching.

This is why the feminist challenge to Christianity cannot find sufficient response in the recovery of neglected texts in the Bible or in inclusive translation. Women must be able to speak out of their own experiences of agony and victimization, survival, empowerment, and new life, as places of divine presence and, out of these revelatory experiences, write new stories. Feminists must create a new midrash on scripture or a 'Third Testament' that can tell stories of God's presence in experiences where God's presence was never allowed or imagined before in a religious culture controlled by men and defined by male experience. This Third Testament is not simply a religion for women. Just as women have been able to experience themselves in the crucified rabbi from Nazareth, men must be able to experience Christ in the raped woman and therefore come to experience the question mark this directs at a male culture in which the tortured female body is regarded as pornographic, rather than the expression of the suffering of God.

This new feminist midrash on patriarchal texts and traditions will not only enter into dialogue and controversy with patriarchal religion. It must also open itself to dialogue with feminist exploration of religion in other traditions. There must certainly be a dialogue between Christian and Jewish feminists, and also with Muslim feminists as well. There must also be a dialogue between feminists engaged in the transformation of historical religions and feminists who break with these historical religions and seek to revive, from repressed memories of ancient goddesses and burned witches, visions of new possibilities for women's spirituality today.

This does not mean that such a dialogue between feminists in historical faiths and pagan feminists will be easy. There are many barriers to communication to be cleared away, questions about the historical interpretation of ancient religions and the relationship of female divinity symbols to modern post-Christian patterns of thought. There are also questions about reverse exclusivism and separatism, as well as about exclusivism on the Jewish and Christian side, which is often reinforced today by accusations from male Jewish and Christian theologians who define feminism as 'paganism' in order to frighten Jewish and Christian women away from any feminist analysis of patriarchal religion. It may be that feminism done in the context of historical faiths and feminism done in the context of religions of nature-renewal are working with different paradigms of religious experience, so that each side lacks, fundamentally, certain categories that the other sees as essential.

It is not at all certain if such a dialogue between these two types of religious feminism is both possible or where it may lead. But what I would like to urge here is that both kinds of feminist religious quest are valid, and each must therefore respect and affirm the basic presence of the divine in and through these several paths. One can dispute about questions of interpretation and their ethical and religious use today. But one cannot dispute that the divine mystery did indeed truly appear in the finding again of Persephone by her Goddess mother, Demeter. It is this new starting point that sets the quest for feminists—whether Christian, Jewish, or pagan—on a new basis.

[Rosemary Radford Ruether, 'Feminism and Jewish-Christian Dialogue', in *The Myth of Christian Uniqueness*, edited by John Hick, SCM, 1987, pp. 146–148]

RACHEL'S TOMB, MARY'S GROTTO

While Ruether wants to supplement the Christian tradition with the experience of oppressed women, others prefer to highlight those women already in the tradition. This final extract is taken from an article written by **Susan Starr Sered**, *currently at the Hebrew University in Jerusalem researching the religious lives of Ethiopian Jewish women. Her perspective provides a practical example* *of how two biblical characters, Rachel and Mary, can express the woman's experience. Jewish and Christian women have made pilgrimages to Rachel's Tomb and the Milk Grotto, respectively, for centuries. Rachel's Tomb marks the place where Rachel died after giving birth to Benjamin; and the Milk Grotto marks the place where Mary and Joseph, with the infant Jesus, rested during their flight to Egypt. These two places can provide a helpful focus for women's experience as mothers. What qualities do Rachel and Mary share with ordinary women? They are mothers who weep for their children and intercede with a male deity on their behalf. That deity gives them special access. There are similarities between these two Jewish women, however Susan Sered is sensitive to the different ways that Jews and Christians have developed these figures: for Jews, Rachel is always a mortal figure whereas for Christians, Mary became 'the Mother of God'—set apart from other women:*

When women pilgrims come to Rachel's Tomb and the Milk Grotto they are visiting sites of holy women who are seen as prototypes of all women. What qualities does Rachel share with mortal women? Surely not her 'hot line' to God. Rather, like real women, Rachel suffers; she is a victim; she dies in childbirth. I propose that this is what Jewish women mean when they say that they visit Rachel's Tomb because Rachel 'understands'. Rachel is the personification of the vulnerability of Jewish women; she is the quintessential sufferer, even rising from her grave to cry for her children. Women visit Rachel's Tomb to cry to/with/for Rachel, who is the weeping mother par excellence.

However, neither the Bible nor the midrash portrays Rachel as passive or open to manipulation. She struggled with the real-life problems of family quarrels, jealousy, and infertility. She stole the idols from her father, argued with her sister, and even asked to die. I suggest that this also may be a reason that Rachel is so popular and easy for women to identify with. Rachel, like all women, suffers, but somehow rises above the tribulations of life and ultimately triumphs, becoming Israel's most successful defender. One further element that must be recognized here is the belief that Rachel shares in the exile of Israel. I would tentatively suggest that women, living in exile in a male-dominated world, identify particularly with the saint whose job it is to accompany her people in their exile.

Mary is seen as the prototype of the Christian woman. Catholic novelist Mary Gordon, in her article 'Coming to terms with Mary', describes her parochial school where girls were encouraged to buy dresses for their senior prom at a store that specialized in 'Mary-like gowns', extremely modest dresses. 'In my day, Mary was a stick to beat smart girls with. Her example was held up constantly, an example of silence, of subordination, of the pleasure of taking the back seat.'

Turner and Turner state that among the people, Mary is always completely 'feminine' by patriarchal standards. She is compassionate, tender, capricious, vulnerable to suffering, maternal, and understanding; she grieves at rather than punishes sin, is aggressive toward those who threaten her children, and takes care of sick people. Her role as intercessor is a weak one: Mary *asks* Jesus to replenish the wine at Cana, she cannot do it herself. Mary Daly rightly emphasizes that Mary is the ideal of the feminine good—passive. But that is not all: Mary also triumphs. Stephan Gudeman, in his study of Roman Catholic saints as folk symbols in a Panamanian village, suggests that, 'Christ and Mary are alike in that they are linked to sorrow and pain, though in different ways. Mary, for women, is a figure of consolation and justification. As a mother, she is an image of birth and life, and she consoles women for all of the pains they bear. Christ is more a figure of persecution... He bears the weight of the world's sorrows, but not in order to release others from these... He represents resignation rather than redemption.' Or, as Gregory Ashe put it in his study of Marian miracles; Jesus' crucifixion was too final; he is too dead. Mary, on the other hand, lives on both as Queen of Heaven and as a frequent and powerful visitor to earth.

Both Rachel and Mary are identified primarily as mothers. Indeed, both are called 'Mother'. Both are seen as weeping for their child/ren. Both are merciful and compassionate and willing to intercede with the [male] deity for their children's sake. Both 'understand'. In short, Rachel and Mary, like earthly mothers, act as intermediaries between their children and both earthly and heavenly fathers who are all too often harsh and punishing. However, unlike most human mothers Rachel and Mary have special access to God's ear. It is said about both that God cannot refuse anything that they ask. Rachel and Mary can be seen as the archetypal feminine figures who manage, in Jungian terms, to surface from the collective unconscious of their respective patriarchal religions. Mary has frequently been viewed by Catholic laity as Co-Redemptrix. Rachel has explicitly been identified with the Shekhina (the female aspect of God), and her name interpreted to mean Ruah-El ('the spirit of God'). Both women are regarded alternately as regular human beings as Scripture demands, and as more or less divine, as (female) folk tradition demands.

There is, however, an important difference in quality between Jewish women's identification with Rachel and Catholic women's identification with Mary. Whereas Rachel remains essentially mortal both in her weakness and in her strength (her noble act of giving Leah the signs is something that any woman could do), Mary, as the Virgin Mother of God, is essentially inimitable. Since the doctrine of the Immaculate Conception officially sets Mary apart from all other women, Mary is an impossible model for Catholic women. I must also stress here that Rachel can be considered a local saint; she has only one shrine, and while all Jews know of her, the cult is largely limited to women living within bus distance of her tomb. Mary, however, playing a necessary role in the scheme of Redemption, is important to all Catholics and has numerous shrines all over the world.

[Susan Starr Sered, 'Two Women's Shrines in Bethlehem', in *Journal of Feminist Studies in Religion*, vol. 2, No. 2, Fall 1986, pp. 16–18]

FURTHER READING

Christ, Carol & Plaskow, Judith (edited). *Womenspirit Rising: A Feminist Reader in Religion*, Harper Collins, 1979.

Fiorenza, Elisabeth Schüssler. *Jesus: Miriam's Child, Sophia's Prophet. Critical Issues in Feminist Christology*, SCM Press, 1995.

Fischer, Kathleen. *Women at the Well*, SPCK, 1989.

Grossman, Susan & Haut, Rivka. *Daughters of the King: Women and the Synagogue*, The Jewish Publication Society, 1992.

Heschel, Susannah (edited). *On Being A Jewish Feminist: A Reader*, Schocken, 1983.

King, Ursula. *Women and Spirituality*, Macmillan, 1989.

O'Neill, Maura. *Women Speaking Women Listening*, Orbis, 1990.

Plaskow, Judith. *Standing Again at Sinai*, Harper Collins, 1990.

Plaskow, Judith & Christ, Carol. *Weaving the Visions: New Patterns in Feminist Spirituality*, Harper Collins, 1989.

Ruether, Rosemary Radford. *Religion and Sexism: Images of Women in the Jewish and Christian Traditions*, Simon & Schuster, 1974.

Shepherd, Naomi. *A Price Below Rubies: Jewish Women as Rebels and Radicals*, Weidenfeld & Nicolson, 1993.

Sheridan, Sybil (edited). *Hear Our Voice: Women Rabbis Tell Their Stories*, SCM Press, 1994.

Umansky, Ellen & Ashton, Dianne (edited). *Four Centuries of Jewish Women's Spirituality: A Sourcebook*, Beacon, 1992.

CHAPTER TEN

A MUTUAL WITNESS

CHAPTER TEN

A MUTUAL WITNESS

The chapters so far have concentrated on the theological differences which separate the two faiths. In contrast, this chapter will look at the practical nature of dialogue. What can Jews and Christians do together? Do they share a common ethic? Do they have a joint witness to the world? As we have seen, there are many different levels to the Christian–Jewish dialogue. The basic level of the dialogue is one of getting to know one another and establishing friendships. This was the major characteristic of the early dialogue. The next level is that of theological dialogue: exploring the similarities and differences of the respective traditions.

The relationship is now moving onto a different level. Jews and Christians are beginning to explore what they can do together for society. Both faiths recognize that there are many issues that can be addressed: poverty and deprivation, homelessness, unemployment, the environment, limited world resources, animal rights, and fair trading. Some initiatives have been taken by groups such as the Young Leadership Section of the International Council of Christians and Jews, in addressing the plight of asylum-seekers and refugees, but such projects are still relatively new.

This chapter, then, explores the Jewish and Christian 'mission' to the world—namely, the proclamation of their shared ethical insights for building the kingdom of God on earth. This vision is part of the prophetic tradition of both faiths and one which, perhaps, neither faith can achieve single-handedly.

H.P.F.

THE INTEGRITY OF CREATION

To start with **David Novak**, *Professor of Modern Judaic Thought at the University of Virginia in America, illustrates how the Judeo–Christian contribution differs yet complements the secular contribution. He argues that Jews and Christians have a joint proclamation to the world in their shared belief in the integrity of creation and human life. He attacks the secular assumption that the only way to overcome religious hostility and conflict is to remove religion from society altogether. He suggests that these secularist presuppositions can be challenged by the joint ethical witness of Jews and Christians. Judaism and Christianity share a general revelation which demands respect for all forms of life within creation. Although these traditions should challenge secular assumptions, Novak still wants a 'secular space' to be respected:*

Jews and Christians have a resource for developing approaches that both respect the integrity of creation and the integrity of the unique human creature therein, one who is in some ways part of it, and in some ways is not. The question, then, is: How can Jews and Christians bring these considerable resources to the world at large?

The first point that emerges from the acceptance of this challenge is that neither Jews nor Christians can do it alone, in our society at least. For in our society today, the usual secularist reaction in dealing with the message brought to society by any particular community is to automatically assume that the message is from a 'special interest group', one whose motives are those of self-interest, even when hidden behind a seemingly altruistic rhetoric. In this view, the task of secular society is to balance the message of one community against those of other communities and to try to find some consensus among all of them. If the secularists involved are still old-fashioned enlightenment rationalists, this consensus will be one in which the rights of the individual remain the ultimate criterion for judging the often conflicting claims of various, particular communities.

Jews and Christians in our society have all too easily fallen into this secularist trap and been naively willing to present their message to the world under the rubric of self interest. The reasoning behind this adjustment is that it is the only way to survive in a secular world. Nevertheless, by so doing, these Jews and Christians have lost sight of who they are and what their message to the world really is. For the true claims of Jews and Christians are based on the doctrine of revelation, which means that they are essentially the recipients of a message about the world, one which is given to them from the only source who can see the world from the perspective of real transcendence—*sub specie divinitatis*. They claim to be the recipients of the word of God, the God who created the world and who promises to redeem it.

When, however, this message is proclaimed by only one community, simultaneously making exclusivistic and triumphalistic claims about itself, claims which more often than not delegitimize all others, the public credibility of the message becomes highly suspect. For the claims of the community on its own behalf are frequently more emphatic than the message proclaimed to and for the world. As such, it appears to be another case of special pleading by one more special interest group in society. By setting itself up to be so categorized and characterized, any religious community eclipses the very intent of its message altogether.

When, on the other hand, Jews and Christians discover their common border that faces onto the world, and devise means for the joint proclamation of certain truths they hold in common, the public credibility of their message increases enormously. It increases because the animosity which, truly but unfortunately, characterized so much of the relationship between the two communities throughout history is now being overcome by these two communities themselves. The secularist assumption, conversely, has been that the only way to overcome interreligious animosity is to essentially remove 'religion'—in reality, that means removing Judaism and Christianity—from public influence altogether.

The religious communities themselves, however, are beginning to accomplish for themselves and for the world what secularism could not do because it demanded what is culturally impossible. When Jews and Christians now have something in common to say jointly to the world, and that message is not one which simply promotes some issue immediately benefiting both communities politically, many of the secularist stereotypes about the necessarily religious character of public animosity are then belied. It is a good deal more difficult to continue reducing the message to a case of special pleading under these new historical circumstances. Moreover, it stands to reason that if something is true for the world at large, that truth should surely have been discovered by more than one community alone.

This joint proclamation of certain truths about the nature of the human person and human community as created historical realities cannot be made, however, in a didactic way. It cannot be done in a way which basically says to the world: We already have the truth, and you must now accept it from us! That method of relating to the moral issues of the world cannot be applied for two reasons.

First, Judaism and Christianity do not operate from the same basis of authority. In both communities, it is not the unmediated voice from scripture which is sufficiently normative, but rather the voice of scripture as interpreted by the traditional community and its structure of authority. Here, at this level, Judaism and Christianity cannot speak with the same voice; both cannot and dare not jointly proclaim 'Thus saith the Lord'. The word of God for Judaism and Christianity, respectively, is materially inseparable from the communal medium who proclaims it. Christians cannot in good faith look to Jewish authorities for the normative meaning of the word of God any more than Jews in good faith can look to Christian authorities for it. The only way this could be done, without total surrender of one religious community to the other, would be some sort of syncretism between the two communities. But the respective traditions of both communities have carefully proscribed those practices which seem to express syncretism. They have been rightly suspicious of syncretizing tendencies because they imply that human creation can ultimately overcome (in the sense of Hegelian *Aufhebung*) what God has originally ordained and revealed.

Judaism and Christianity can jointly proclaim certain normative truths about the human condition—without the surrender demanded by proselytism, syncretism, or secularism—by affirming what Jewish and Christian traditions have taught about general revelation. The latter is historically antecedent to the special revelation each community, respectively, claims as its own basic norm. General revelation still functions even after that special revelation has occurred. For Jews, it is the affirmation of the revelation to the children of Noah, something which extends beyond the revelation of the children of Israel at Sinai. For Roman Catholics and some Anglicans, it is the affirmation of natural law, something which extends beyond the divine law. For many Protestants, certainly those of Lutheran or Reformed background, it is the affirmation of the order of creation, which extends beyond the gospel. In all these traditions, it needs to be added, what is 'beyond' is certainly not what is 'higher' on any scale of value. Quite the contrary, what is more general is lower on that scale, a point that Jews who affirm the divine election of Israel, and Christians who affirm the incarnation, can readily understand. Nevertheless, what is more general and therefore lower is not without any value at all.

This general revelation, which makes itself manifest in certain universal moral principles, is most immediately accessible to human reason. It does not require a covenantal experience wherefrom the religious community proclaims it to the world. General revelation must be discovered within ordinary human experience. It must be seen from within that experience, as creating conditions necessary for authentic human community to be sustained. Yet the religious communities do not dissolve into some general human moral community by affirming these moral principles. They must insist all along that these principles, though *necessary* for authentic human community, are not at all *sufficient* for authentic human fulfillment. That can only be commanded through revelation and consummated by salvation: the ultimate redemption of the world by its creator God.

Although the religious communities of Judaism and Christianity should not legislate this minimal human morality (indeed, when they do they most often retard its social impact, especially in a democracy), they do provide it with an overall ontological context, which is a continuing vision of its original grounds and its ultimate horizon. Without that continuing vision, the very operation of human moral reason, indeed all human reason itself, flounders. Reason cannot flourish for long in an ontological vacuum, namely, in an otherwise absurd universe and in an otherwise aimless trajectory of human history.

The constitution of the relation between God's revealed law and universal moral law is an intellectual operation, conducted not only differently by the respective religious communities themselves, but even by adherents of different theological and philosophical tendencies within those communities. Nevertheless, recognition of the similarity of the problematic, coming as it does out of that which both communities accept as sacred scripture, i.e. the Hebrew Bible, can lead to a new mutuality. Such mutuality allows each community to maintain its own faith integrity in relationship with God, with the members of its own covenant, with the members of the most proximate religion (which I hold is, for Jews, Christianity), and with the world beyond.

The final requirement is that both communities respect with theological cogency the integrity of the secular order. In America, that means respect for the *novus ordo seculorum*, carefully distinguishing its legitimate moral claims from the illegitimate philosophical claims of those who would insist that secularism can be its only sufficient foundation. This respect for the integrity of the secular order, therefore, requires Jews and Christians to eschew those ultra-traditionalist elements in either community which wish to simply annul modernity *in toto* and return to their nostalgic vision of a theocratic polity of some sort or other. Both Jews and Christians should learn from modern history that the only means now available for such a restoration of any *ancien régime* come from fascism in its various guises—the most hideous caricature of the kingdom of God.

Whether the possibility of this new Jewish–Christian relationship will be realized in and for our time will depend in large measure on the theological ingenuity, philosophical perspicacity, and historical insight of leading thinkers in each community. For the most part, their work, both separately and in concert, still lies before them.

[David Novak, 'A Jewish Theological Understanding of Christianity in Our Time', in *Toward A Theological Encounter: Jewish Understandings of Christianity*, edited by Rabbi Leon Klenicki, Paulist Press, 1991, pp. 96–101]

JEWS, CHRISTIANS AND LIBERATION THEOLOGY

Where Novak identifies the need for a Judeo–Christian contribution to society, **Dan Cohn-Sherbok***, a Reform Rabbi and lecturer in Theology at the University of Canterbury, England, believes that liberation theology can provide a basis for Jews and Christians to work together. Liberation theology is a largely Catholic movement which emerged in Latin America and seeks the liberation of all oppressed groups, including an awareness of the interdependence and integrity of all creation. This extract focuses on three key areas for Jews and Christians: the unemployed, the environment, and the status of women. He suggests that liberation theology provides a framework for bringing about God's kingdom on earth; i.e. the means of the redemption of the world. It is a vision which is at the heart of the prophetic tradition of both Judaism and Christianity. Their joint mission is to work for the kingdom of God:*

The Unemployed

As liberation theologians have noted, the unemployed are generally found in the destitute parts of the inner city. Unemployment is a growing problem. Liberationists have therefore directed attention to this deprived group. Gutiérrez, for example, stresses that the church has an obligation to those who are without work: they should be a focus of pastoral and theological activity. Christians must labor on behalf of the:

> underemployed and unemployed, who are dismissed because of the harsh exigencies of economic crises, and often because of development-models that subject workers and their families to cold economic calculations [Gutiérrez 1983, 134].

Such individuals face particular difficulties in coping with their misfortunes. The unemployed do not know what to do with their time, and as a consequence, they are unfulfilled in essential areas: basic human needs for human relationships, for financial income, for social status and identity, and for satisfaction and fulfillment.

Helping those faced with such difficulties should be a high priority. The Jewish community together with concerned Christians can take the lead in assisting those out of work. Recently Christian writers have made a number of suggestions about the kinds of activities that could be undertaken: ways must be sought for creating new work opportunities; labor not traditionally regarded as paid work (such as housework) must be accepted as valid and necessary; new manufacturing enterprises that stimulate the job market should be encouraged; apprenticeship for the young should be reintroduced; jobs need to be spread out through job sharing and part-time work; education must be seen as a preparation for life; voluntary activity should be stimulated and seen as a legitimate means of helping those in need (Handy 1983, 24–25).

In the quest to alleviate distress and disillusionment, Jews and Christians can make substantial contributions to those on the bottom of the social scale. Liberation from frustration and disappointment involves a reappraisal of life and labor: it is a task that can bind together both faiths in the quest for a meaningful life for all.

Feminism

Liberation theology has also been concerned about the plight of women. Feminist theologians have attempted to delineate the biblical traditions encapsulating the liberating experiences and visions of the people of Israel so as to help free women from oppressive sexist structures, institutions, and internalized values. In the view of these writers, women have been and continue to be socialized into subservient roles:

either they are forced into domestic labor or they hold low-paying jobs. Only a few women manage to occupy jobs in traditionally male professions.

> Work segregation is still the fundamental pattern of society. Women's work universally is regarded as of low status and prestige, poorly paid, with little security, generally of a rote and menial character. The sexist structuring of society means the elimination of women from those activities that allow for and express enhancement and development of the self, its artistic, intellectual and leadership capacities [Ruether 1983, 178].

Throughout society, these theologians maintain, the full humanity of woman is distorted, diminished, and denied.

To encourage the restoration of women's self-respect, liberationists focus on a number of biblical themes: God's defense and vindication of the oppressed; the criticism of the dominant systems of power; the vision of a new age in which iniquity will be overcome; God's intended reign of peace. Feminist theology applies the message of the prophets to the situation of women; the critique of hierarchy thus becomes a critique of patriarchy. For these writers, images of God must include feminine roles and experiences, and language about God must be transformed. For Christians, they believe, it is necessary to move beyond a typology of Christ and the church that represents the dominant male and submissive female role. In Church structures women must be given full opportunities to participate at every level, including the ministry. In the civil sphere women must be granted full equality before the law—a stance that calls for the repeal of all discriminatory legislation. There must be equal pay for equal work and full access to all professions. Many liberationists also insist on women's right to reproduction, self-defense, sex education, birth control, and abortion as well as protection against sexual harassment, wife-beating, rape, and pornography.

Similarly, in the Jewish community awareness of discrimination against women has been growing. Over the last two decades a significant number of Jewish feminists have attempted to reconstruct the position of women in traditional Judaism. In the past Jewish women were not directly involved with most Jewish religious activity. Today however Jewish women are trying to find ways to participate fully in their faith. In their attempt to reconcile Judaism and feminism these women are rediscovering various aspects of Jewish life: some study the place of women in Jewish history; others examine religious texts for clues to women's influence on Jewish life; still others redefine and feminize certain features of the Jewish tradition.

In seeking equality with men, these feminists demand that women be allowed to participate in the areas from which they have previously been excluded: serving as witnesses in a religious court, initiating divorce proceedings, being counted as part of a quorum for prayer, receiving rabbinic training and ordination, and qualifying as cantors. For these Jewish feminists, all formal distinctions in the religious as well as secular sphere between men and women should be abolished.

> We have been trying to take charge of events in our own lives and in every area of what we call Jewish life: religion, the community, the family, and all our interpersonal relations [Schneider 1984, 19].

Given this impetus of liberating women from the restrictions of patriarchal structures, there is every reason for Jewish and Christian feminists to share their common concerns.

The Environment

Not only do liberation theologians advocate a program of liberation for all humankind, they also draw attention to human responsibility for the environment: ecological liberation is an important element in their policy of emancipation. Since the scientific revolution, nature has been gradually secularized; no corner of the natural world has been untouched by human domination. Yet in this expansion of material productivity, the earth has been exploited to such a degree that polution, famine, and poverty threaten humanity's very existence.

Liberationists assert that human beings must accept responsibility for the environment.

> The privilege of intelligence....is not a privilege to alienate and dominate the world without concern for the welfare of all other forms of life. On the contrary, it is the responsibility to become the caretaker and cultivator of the welfare of the whole ecological community upon which our existence depends....Although we need to remake the earth in a way that converts our minds to nature's logic of ecological harmony, this will necessarily be a new synthesis, a new creation in which human nature and nonhuman nature become friends in the creating of a livable and sustainable cosmos [Ruether 1983, 87–88, 91–92].

Reform in this area calls for a different attitude toward the natural world; human beings must accept balance in nature as an essential characteristic of the earth's ecosystem. Human intervention inevitably upsets the natural balance; thus steps must continually be taken to restore equilibrium to the earth. In particular, environmentalists point out that care must be taken about the use of pesticides. Habitations previously available to many living creatures have been destroyed; for agricultural purposes, we should attempt to maintain diversity within nature and this requires a careful monitoring of the use of chemical substances.

Pollution too is a major problem in the modern world; industry, urban waste, and motor transport have all adversely affected the environment, and conservationists maintain that adequate control must be exercised over the use of pollutants that infect the air and water resources. Furthermore, environmentalists contend that human beings must take steps to preserve endangered species and avoid inflicting cruelty on wild and domestic animals.

The Jewish community has a role in all these endeavours. That human beings are part of the ecological whole is fundamental to Jewish thought. According to the Jewish faith, we have been given authority over nature; such responsibility should curb the crude exploitation of the earth for commercial purposes. The divine fiat should foster in us a sympathetic understanding of the whole ecological situation engendering for Jews as for Christians an attitude of caring concern for all of God's creation.

Summary

These then are some of the areas in which Jews can unite with Christian liberation theologians to bring about God's kingdom. In pursuit of the common goal of freedom from oppression, committed Jews and Christians can become a saving remnant of the modern world, embodying the liberation message of Scripture. Like Abraham they can hope against a hope in labouring to build a more just and humane world. They can become an Abrahamic minority, attentive to the cry of oppression:

> We are told that Abraham and other patriarchs heard the voice of God. Can we also hear the Lord's call? We live in a world where millions of our fellow men live in inhuman conditions, practically in slavery. If we are not deaf we hear the cries of the oppressed. Their cries are the voice of God. We who live in rich countries where there are always pockets of under-development and wretchedness, hear if

we want to hear, the unvoiced demands of those who have no voice
and no hope. The pleas of those who have no voice and no hope are
the voice of God [Camara 1976, 16].

Throughout history the Jewish people have been God's suffering
servant, yet inspired by a vision of God's reign on earth they have been
able to transcend their own misfortunes in attempting to ameliorate
the lot of others. In the contemporary world, where Jews are often
comfortable and affluent, the prophetic message of liberation can too
easily be forgotten. Liberation theology, however, with its focus on the
desperate situation of those at the bottom of society, can act as a
clarion call to the Jewish community, awakening the people of Israel
to their divinely appointed task. Jewish tradition points to God's
kingdom as the goal and hope of humankind: a world in which all
peoples and nations shall turn away from iniquity and injustice. This is
not the hope of bliss in a future life, but the building up of the divine
kingdom of truth and peace among all peoples. 'I will also give thee
for a light to the nations, that my salvation may be unto the end of the
earth' (Isa. 49:6).

In this mission the people of God and their Christian liberationist
sisters and brothers can join ranks; championing the cause of the
oppressed, afflicted, and persecuted, both faiths can unite in common
cause and fellowship proclaiming together the ancient message of
Jewish liturgy in their struggle to create a better world:

O Lord our God, impose Thine awe upon all Thy works, and let Thy
dread be upon all Thou has created, that they may all form one single
band and do Thy will with a perfect heart.

...Our God and God of our fathers, reveal Thyself in Thy splendour as
King over all the inhabitants of the world, that every handiwork of
Thine may know that Thou has made it, and every creature may
acknowledge that Thou has created it, and whatsoever hath breath in
its nostrils may say: the Lord God of Israel is King, and His dominion
ruleth over all.

Jesus put it more concisely:

Thy Kingdom come,
thy will be done on earth as it is in heaven.

[Dan Cohn-Sherbok, *On Earth as It is In Heaven*, Orbis, 1987, pp. 124–130]

ARE THERE LIMITS TO THEOLOGICAL DIALOGUE?

Jonathan Sacks, the Chief Rabbi of the United Hebrew Congregations of the Commonwealth, shares with Cohn-Sherbok and Novak the stress on respect for creation and human life. He would agree with Cohn-Sherbok that there are areas of practical and social concern where both Jews and Christians can work together. The dialogue has a practical and theological side, but Sacks argues that the ethical dialogue has implications for the theological dialogue. We therefore find the different dialogue levels come together in Sack's work. To illustrate his point he uses the paradigms of exclusivism, inclusivism and pluralism. He argues that these positions may be helpful for dialogue in areas such as 'salvation and redemption', but are morally inadequate responses to 'the other'. He suggests a more appropriate model: 'post-liberal pluralism'. This he defines as 'an open-ended multiplicity of moral ways of life':

Rabbinic tradition records a dialogue between two teachers of the Mishnaic age. Each was asked to provide a statement of the 'great principle' which underlay the Torah. Rabbi Akiva answered by citing the verse, 'You shall love your neighbour as yourself'. Ben Azzai replied that there is a more fundamental principle: 'When God created man, He made him in the likeness of God'. In terms we have been using, Akiva takes as his moral ultimate the complete extension of empathy involved in loving one's neighbour as oneself. Ben Azzai rightly notes that though this may be the end of morality, it is nonetheless not its most basic proposition. Morality has boundaries, and they are set by the recognition that there are certain things one may not do to any human being, whether one loves him or hates him. In the Bible this is grounded in the ontological sanctity of humanity as the image of God. To which ancient rabbinic wisdom added the following comment: 'When human beings create things in a single image, they are all alike. God makes humanity in a single image, yet each of them is unique.'

On this point, the ethical dialogue between faiths imposes a limit on the theological dialogue, and one that needs to be clearly articulated. Three theological positions are usually distinguished. The exclusivist maintains that only his faith is in possession of the truth. The inclusivist maintains that his faith alone is true, but that others unwittingly or partially share it. The pluralist maintains that each faith is its own reflection of the same underlying truth.

If these positions are confined to theology alone, to the vocabulary of salvation, redemption, fate in the afterlife and the like, we can reasonably proceed within the categories they set forth. But if they are taken to entail ethical consequences, then all three must be regarded as inadequate. For if I do not have moral obligations to those I believe to be categorically in error—if I am not prepared to recognise the image of God in the human being as such, independently of his or my theological commitments—then there is at least a possible line from faith to holocaust. The twentieth century has surely taught us this much. I would argue, therefore, as part of any dialogue between faiths, races or cultures, that it seeks to establish, for each of the partners, a morally adequate theory of 'the other', the one who is in God's image though he is not in our image.

To summarise what has been a somewhat extended argument: Jewish thinkers have advocated a form of dialogue in the realm, not of theology, but of ethics, conducted in the 'universal language' of 'common humanity'. I have argued that it is a given feature of modern Western societies that there is no such universal language. We are in an ethical Babel which shows no signs of converging on a single moral vocabulary. But we need not draw from this situation the two most common inferences, that there is a Platonic universal morality underlying the apparent diversity, or that to the contrary there is nothing left to morality than the expression of individual choice.

There is an alternative conclusion to be drawn, sometimes called 'post-liberal pluralism', that there is an open-ended multiplicity of moral ways of life, each set in its own tradition and embodied in its own form of community. It is in the context of such communities, of which the family is the most basic, that the moral enterprise gets under way and is at its most lucid. A central moral task of religions, though not only of religions, lies in building such communities. The sense of the anomie which pervades modernity has much to do with the poverty of secular culture at this intermediate point between the individual and the state. This is the primary moral domain.

The religious ethical endeavour would thus lie in creating persuasive examples of moral communities, each living out its distinctive traditions. Religious leadership can no longer speak to society as a whole on the basis of authority, for that authority cannot be presumed to be accepted by all. But it can speak out of its own experience and example. That too confers a kind of authority, perhaps the only kind for which we can hope in the modern situation.

Dialogue is necessary. Each faith community can learn volumes from others by seeing how they, in quite different ways, build caring communities. As Jews, for example, we have learned much from the Christian tradition of pastoral ministry, and we have incorporated it into our religious life. Long ago, to give another example, the rabbis learned from ancient Roman examples what 'honouring thy father and mother' might mean in practice.

Dialogue has a second aim: to establish a clear sense of the limits of ethical particularism. The growth, throughout the world and in all the major faiths, of religious fundamentalism makes this particularly urgent. Ethics sets boundary conditions for theology. If the unredeemed are not, at some level, objects of moral concern, possessing independent integrity and rights, then faith itself becomes morally untenable.

Dialogue need not be grounded in the belief that, *au fond*, we all share the same faith or the same morality. There is something profoundly moving in such a belief. But there is something equally momentous in the opposite conviction: that our worlds of faith are irreducibly plural yet we have been cast into the same planet, faced with the same questions. Can we live together? Can we learn from one another? Within this vision much is possible. Much, too, is necessary.

[Jonathan Sacks, *Tradition in an Untraditional Age*, Vallentine Mitchell, 1990, pp. 175–177]

TOWARDS CRITICAL SOLIDARITY—CHRISTIAN PERSPECTIVES

Sacks has linked ethical dialogue with theological dialogue. **Clark Williamson**, *Indiana Professor of Christian Thought at Christian Theological Seminary in the States, wants to do the same. However, he advocates a stage beyond mutual witness to mutual influence—what he calls 'critical solidarity'. He suggests that Jews and Christians move to a relationship where they are able constructively to challenge and criticize certain elements of their partner's tradition whilst remaining in basic solidarity with them. He offers three examples of 'critical solidarity' in practice. First, the Church should rid itself of any kind of teaching of contempt for Judaism; second, the Church must accept the Jewish 'no' to the Gospel; and third, the ability to take a critical stance on some Israeli Government policies and yet affirm the importance of the Jewish tradition of the land and learn something from it:*

If there can no longer be a conversionary mission to the Jews, that does not mean that the church no longer has a responsibility to the Israel of God. In this sense, there is a mission to the Jews and that is to enter into a mutually critical and supportive relationship with Jews. On numerous points, the church needs to become more self-critical than it has yet been; on others, and some of them highly sensitive, the church will need to learn how to be critical of Jews and Judaism. The church's first responsibility is to come clean on a number of issues, of which we can discuss here only pitiably few. First, the church needs to rid itself of all vestiges of its traditional 'teaching (and practice) of contempt' for Jews and Judaism. In place of this 'teaching of contempt', it should put a 'teaching of respect' for Jews and Judaism, lest it create a vacuum into which rush seven demons worse than the original. By a teaching of respect, I do not mean a 'philoJudaism' or an unrealistic and untrue idealization of Jews and Judaism, but a corrective to the tradition of contempt and to the stereotypes with which that contempt was under-girded and reinforced. All religions are ambiguous, Judaism no less than any other. But these ambiguities do not serve to distinguish one reli-gion from another. Christians have consistently described Judaism as essentially legalistic, works-righteousness, judgmental, committed to the letter rather than the spirit of faith, and Christianity by contrast as gracious, committed to love and acceptance, and spiritual. Yet Christianity has known all too well of its own legalism, works-right-eousness, judgmentalism, and literalism. Jews have to have an anti-defamation league because for too many millennia the church has been the defamation league. Not only should the church get out of the defamation business, because that is a denial of the very word it is given to proclaim and to live by, it should become the anti-defamation league (putting the ADL out of business) standing up to protect and defend the rights of Jews as of all other persecuted minorities.

Second, the church needs to come clean on the matter of the Jewish 'no' to the church's proclamation. It has been inherited ortho-doxy to interpret this 'no' as a simple and straightforward 'no' to Jesus Christ, and to argue that this 'no' constitutes the reason for the early and categorical separation of Christianity and Judaism from each other. Neither of these claims seems to be true. Initially, Jews were the only people who said 'yes' to Jesus Christ, and they did so without entertaining any thought of thereby leaving Judaism. Until Sabbatai Zvi in the seventeenth century, there were numerous Jews who were thought by at least some of their fellow Jews to be the messiah, yet believing that Sabbatai Zvi was the messiah did not somehow make his followers non-Jews, any more than believing that bar-Kochba was the messiah made Rabbi Akiva a non-Jew instead of the authoritative Talmudic rabbi which he remains. Nor does an early and categorical separation of Christianity and Judaism from each other seem to have happened, else we have to wonder about what the church fathers were fulminating and against what they were legislating well into the middle ages.

The Jewish 'no' is quite real, but it was a 'no' to a displacement ideology of the covenant, a 'no' to a spiritualized and de-historicized understanding of redemption emptied of its this-worldly promises of the end of oppression, war, and injustice, and a 'no' to the claim that salvation was now the property of Gentiles and accessible to Jews only on condition that they turn their backs on the God of the Exodus and Sinai. It was a 'no' to an invitation to join a church that defined itself as a gentile, not a Jewish people, as a universal, not a Jewish, people, as a spiritual, not a carnal, Jewish people, as a replacement (not a replaced) people, and as a superior (not an inferior, Jewish) people. The Jewish 'no' to the Gentile church's ideological distortion of its own gospel results from a firm and staunch decision to remain faithful to the God who had liberated Israel from oppression and who promised so to liberate the whole world. Jews could only reject a church whose message denied the validity of the covenant of Sinai and the importance of fidelity to Torah as of the essence of that covenant.

The *adversus Judaeos* tradition of the church interprets this Jewish 'no' as a willful 'no', 'a willful blindness' to the gospel, the truth of which Jews cannot see because they always 'trifle' when Christians present to them arguments supporting the truth of the Christian faith. Yet Jews, from the apostle Paul to Martin Buber, have consistently contended that their refusal to see the truth of the gospel results not from a voluntary obstinacy but from an inability to see that the world is redeemed. The apostle Paul put this down to God's doing and refused to blame Jews for it, crediting it instead with the fact that the knowledge of the God of Israel had come to the Gentiles (Romans 11:25). This Jewish 'no', as Paul Tillich rightly insisted, is the most profound question that can be put to Christianity. In a sermon Tillich tells the story of some Polish Jews hiding out in a graveyard, hoping to escape the roundups for Auschwitz. In one of the graves a young woman gave birth to a boy, assisted by an old grave digger wrapped in a shroud. When the child was born, 'the old man prayed: "Great God, hast Thou finally sent the Messiah to us? For who else than the Messiah Himself can be born in a grave?" But after three days [he] saw the child sucking his mother's tears because she had no milk for him.' Whereas Christians talk too readily of redemption having come into the world in Jesus Christ, the old Jewish grave digger knew better: 'For him, the immeasurable tension implicit in the expectation of the Messiah was a reality, appearing in the infinite contrast between the things he saw and the hope he maintained. That tension means that if Christians continue to insist on calling Jesus the messiah, they cannot do so except in a sharply dialectical way in which the 'not yet' of liberation is consistently laid alongside the 'already' of the gracious knowledge of God to which Gentiles have been led by Jesus Christ.

A third point on which Christians need to come clean is the way in which Zionism and the fact and actions of the state of Israel make it difficult if not impossible for Christians to participate in the conversation with Jews and Judaism and to change their inherited ideological negativity toward the Israel of God. Two facts are of overwhelming importance. First, the church long made a lot of theological hay out of the destruction of Jerusalem and the Temple by the Roman army, arguing that this geo-political event proved the truth of Christianity. It was this point over which Athanasius accused Jews of 'trifling', and which served as the occasion for the ideology of the wandering Jew whose purpose is to bear the strange witness of unbelief. And it was this concrete, earthly promise of a land, an actual piece of earthly turf, that was one among the many promises the church spiritualized and thereby denied in order to argue that it had been fulfilled in Jesus Christ, who, as the *Epistle of Barnabus* argued, is the 'good land' into which Jews should enter. Thereby the church 'christified', spiritualized the land. Second, the church since 1948 has been faced with a development new in its history, the fact of Jewish sovereignty in the land of Israel. This fact, with all its ambiguities, rubs liberal Christians the wrong way, because liberal Christians want to understand Judaism in Christian terms, specifically as a 'religion' like Christianity, not on Jewish terms as a people some of whom profess the religion of Judaism, but none of whom accept a dichotomy between faith and politics, faith and economics, or between a faith and its 'storied place'. The first, but not the last, rule of dialogue is to accept the other's self-definition in the other's terms, and if Jews in the dialogue have difficulty with this rule, preferring to define Christians as Noachides with a little *shituf* thrown in rather than to accept Christian definitions of themselves in their terms, so Christians have a continuing tendency only to be able to get along with Jews so long as troublesome issues of historical concreteness and particularity can be kept nicely out of sight.

The appeal here is neither for Christians to sanction every action of the State of Israel nor condone the oppression of Palestinians. It is, first, for Christians to cease spiritualizing Israel (and all the other concrete, this-worldly realities of biblical faith) lest we become so spiritual that we are full of 'hot air' (the biblical words for spirit, *ruach* and *pneuma*, refer to air), '*Luftmenschen*', air people, forever floating about fifty feet off the ground. It is, second, to cease and desist our commitment to the doctrine of Jewish homelessness, to the figure of the 'wandering Jew', and to come to terms with the fact that after the Holocaust it is hardly conscionable to continue to insist that Jews live everywhere as a minority trusting in the good will of their gentile neighbors. Since those gentile neighbors have killed half the Jews born in the world in the last eight hundred years, Jews rightly view such suggestions with suspicion. But, because an argument like this is a moral argument, it cuts both ways. Neither can Palestinians be expected to live on the West Bank and Gaza Strip trusting in the good will of the *Bloc of the Faithful* or the government of Israel. It is, third, to recognise that Christians might learn something of real value from the Jewish land tradition. This tradition includes the central notion that Jews live in a moral covenant with the land itself in which it is understood that the earth's fate is determined by our conduct, an understanding too long missing from the Christian tradition but which could now be well reappropriated in this era of ecological crisis. It is, fourth, to recognise that there are many Zionisms that have in common an attachment of faith to the land of Israel, and that still retain the capacity to be brought critically to bear on actions in that land which cause the oppression and suffering of Ishmael, the brothers and sisters of Isaac.

[Clark Williamson, 'Is There a Mission to the Jews?' in *A Mutual Witness: Toward Critical Solidarity between Jews and Christians*, edited by Clark Williamson, Chalice Press, 1992, pp. 131–136]

ORTHODOX CHRISTIAN–ORTHODOX JEWISH DIALOGUE

Thus far the stress in this chapter has been on the contributions that Jews and Christians can make to a secular modern society. However, some Jews and Christians find their shared programme in opposition to modernity. This comes

out clearly in the Orthodox Christian–Jewish dialogue: one of the most excit-
ing developing areas. There has been some dialogue between the Orthodox
communities but it is relatively rare. What can Orthodox Jews and Orthodox
Christians practically do together? **Norman Solomon**, *an English Orthodox*
Rabbi and scholar, suggests that they share a common concern: the challenge of
modernity to their respective communities. In this following article he provides a
report on an Orthodox Christian–Jewish Conference which he attended in
Vouliagmeni near Athens in March 1993. The theme of the Conference was
'Continuity and Renewal'. Solomon points out that it was remarkable in the
wide range of participants from diverse Eastern Orthodox Churches—from
Greeks to Copts, Russians, and Armenians, to name just a few. Solomon
argues that there are three partners in the dialogue: Orthodox Jews, Orthodox
Christians, and the modern world. The challenge of modernity provided a
fertile dialogue ground:

The Greek government and the small local Jewish community overwhelmed us with their hospitality. Athens appeared to have been
'kosherized' in our honour—a feat demanding collaboration from
government, one lone rabbi, and numerous upmarket hoteliers and
restaurateurs.

However, we were not there 'for the Ouzo', but for a ground-
breaking meeting between IJCIC (the International Jewish
Committee on Interreligious Consultations) and the Orthodox
Churches. IJCIC was set up by the World Jewish Congress under the
leadership of Dr Gerhart Riegner in the 1960s as an authoritative
'across the board' Jewish body to engage in dialogue with bodies such
as the Vatican and the World Council of Churches.

For twenty years Dr Riegner cherished the ambition to initiate
meaningful dialogue with the Eastern Churches at a similar high level.
In the West, declarations such as the World Council of Churches'
condemnation of antisemitism (Amsterdam 1948) and Second Vatican
Council's Nostra Aetate n.4 (1965) laid the foundations of a new era
in Christian–Jewish relations for Protestants and Catholics. Would it
be possible to make similar progress in the East?

'Academic' meetings of IJCIC with Greek Orthodox theologians
took place in 1974 and 1979. The epithet 'academic' reflects the hesi-
tancy of the Greek Church as a whole to commit itself fully and theologically to dialogue. Moreover, the Orthodox Churches within the
Soviet Union were unable (their few representatives were subject to
political surveillance), and those in the Middle East unwilling, to

engage in the dialogue. However, some seeds were sown and carefully nurtured—by Dr Riegner, by Metropolitan Damaskinos of Switzerland and by Professor Theodor Sylianopoulos of the Greek Orthodox School of Theology—until the time became ripe, with the regained independence of churches in the ex-Soviet Union, for our 'Third Academic Meeting between Orthodoxy and Judaism'.

This third meeting marked a significant step forward. It was the first to have such broad participation, including Jewish and/or Orthodox Christian representatives from Russia, Rumania, Georgia, Ukraine, Bulgaria, Serbia, Israel, the Armenian and Coptic Churches, as well as from Greece itself and from North America. There was a strongly supportive message from the Ecumenical Patriarch Bartholomaios I of Constantinople, which indicated a commitment beyond the merely 'academic'. Jewish commitment was demonstrated by the presence of Dr Israel Singer, Secretary General of the World Jewish Congress, and a galaxy of distinguished scholars and rabbis.

Under the rubric 'Continuity and Renewal' contentious issues surfaced, including the relation between modernism and tradition, 'super-sessionist' theology, the use and abuse of memory, and the politics of the Middle East. Frank exchanges took place in an atmosphere that was open and constructive, and great enthusiasm was expressed for building on the friendships and foundations we were able to establish.

I was stirred to intervene on the controversial issue of modernism. We had come to Athens as Jews and Orthodox Christians. Yet in reality there were three partners to the dialogue. The third 'partner' is the modern world which envelops us all. We share a 'language'—the common culture and intellectual apparatus of the modern world, without which we could not communicate with each other, let alone engage in serious dialogue.

This 'third partner' contributes four elements to our dialogue. One is the equality before law of all, regardless of religion or ethnic origin. Then there is the application of historical criticism to the sources of our religious traditions, forcing us to ask deep questions about the nature of revelation, and hence of religious authority. Next is the scientific world view, which in many instances contradicts traditional understanding of Scripture, generating conflicts such as that over creation and evolution. Finally, modern philosophy of language demands careful consideration of language when used in a religious context: rather than 'Does God exist?', we ask 'What are we trying to communicate when we use God-language?'

Yet we retain our sense of belonging to faith communities, and continue to cherish our traditional distinctive symbols and rites. The same question thus confronts us all: religious Jews, or Orthodox Christians, how should we engage intellectually with the modern world?

I left Athens confident that many within the Orthodox Churches are confronting such issues, and appreciate the value of doing so within terms of the spiritual heritage that binds them not only to their Western Christian brethren but also to the Jewish people and faith.

[Norman Solomon, 'Three International Inter-Faith Conferences', in *Ends and Odds*, no 51, July 1993]

TILLING THE GROUND OF DIALOGUE: REVIEWING A FERTILE PERIOD

Speaking of fertile ground the final article from **Graham James**, *commissioned for the* Reader, *reflects on the often unexpected, achievements of Christian–Jewish dialogue. His reflections come from the period when he was chaplain to the Archbishop of Canterbury, England from 1987 to 1992. The article begins as an introduction to an extract which appeared in the journal* Manna *in 1993:*

Hans Küng has done us all a service by promoting a succinct apologia for his work on the essence and history of Judaism, Christianity and Islam.

No Peace among nations
Without peace among the religions.

No peace among the religions
Without dialogue between the religions.

No dialogue between the religions
Without investigation of the foundation of the religions.

Theological dialogue can seem sometimes far removed from the demands and pressures of contemporary life. The temptation is always to see what people of faith might do together in areas of social responsibility or civic life rather than to court the pain which comes from discovering just how estranged we may be in our patterns of believing.

Both Judaism and Christianity have a strong tradition of social action. Our common scriptural heritage makes it clear that the initiative in creation and redemption lies with God. Yet human beings are not helpless in their ability to shape the world into a better place. Indeed, the injunction is upon us to be co-workers with God in our care for a world which is His and ours.

There is a Hasidic story which provides a simple, yet profound, illustration of this truth. It is about a disciple of Menahem Mendel of Kotzk, the Kotzker Rebbe, who was disturbed by the state of the world. 'Look,' he said to the Rebbe, 'God created the universe in six days. And he did a rotten job. It's a mess.' 'So,' said the Rebbe, 'Do you think you could have done any better?' 'I..I..I think so' stammered the disciple. 'Yes,' exclaimed the Rebbe. 'Then what are you waiting for? Start working–right now!'

Jews and Christians share a common vision of the transformation of society. They both look to the exodus story as a story of divine deliverance. It is a spur to working together for freedom for victims of persecution, slavery, and racial hatred. Jews and Christians also look to the prophetic tradition as a call to righteousness and justice. God's just and gentle rule will be established as a result of his initiative but he also seeks human response, obedience and co-operation. These themes are taken up in the preaching of the Kingdom of God which Christians regard as central to the message of Jesus Christ.

The exploration of these foundations lies at the heart of dialogue, and through dialogue comes peace between religions, and peace for our world. Judaism and Christianity both recognise the world-changing ability of individuals and small groups. It's not always the mass movement that creates the most permanent changes in human consciousness. That's why small groups beavering away at Jewish–Christian dialogue may be part of a much wider mission. That's why individual leaders in our respective traditions bear a particular responsibility for showing us a path to peace.

The article which follows draws on my experience as an observer and participant in various areas of Jewish–Christian relationship and dialogue in the late 1980s and early 1990s. It was a particularly fertile period when the contacts between our two communities in the United Kingdom at the level of our respective leadership was considerable. It was also the period in which the Manor House Group met regularly. This small group of Jews and Christians, self-selected and making no public statements until producing a book in 1992, produced relationships of great depth between the participants. The book they produced, *Dialogue With a Difference* (SCM Press, 1992) isn't a simple story of friendships but of theological and personal encounter. I know of no comparable equivalent in this area, and it stands as a token of a period of sustained progress in the relationship between Judaism and Christianity in this nation. In writing a review article on the book, I set it in the wider context of the contact between successive Archbishops of Canterbury and Judaism over the same period during which the Manor House Group was meeting. The task in the next decade is not to let these advances in dialogue slip away, but to see them as the foundation for a deeper theological encounter and common social witness.

The smallest university in this country is to be found in the person of the Archbishop of Canterbury. He has the right to confer degrees, a vestige from long-forgotten days when the Papal Legate could grant dispensations from the residence requirements at our ancient universities. The preservation of such eccentricities within the Church of England reflects a national affection for the ancient and archaic. But sometimes the fossils of English life convey surprisingly contemporary meanings.

It was on my second day as a member of the Archbishop of Canterbury's staff in 1987 that I saw this academic relic of the English Reformation put to creative use. The then Chief Rabbi, Immanuel Jakobovits, came to Lambeth Palace to receive a doctorate in divinity awarded by the then Archbishop, Robert Runcie. A Jewish choir sang. Latin prayers were said, incomprehensibly thus neutralising any theological difficulties. The ritual was distinctively Anglican. As the Archbishop's chaplain, I led the procession carrying a mace over my shoulder and bearing a mortar-board. Though I did not know it, even more bizarre ceremonies lay ahead of me.

The Archbishop expected criticism for bestowing a doctorate of divinity upon a Jew. It was only a few years earlier that the first non-Anglican Christian had received a Lambeth degree. There are not many things an Archbishop of Canterbury does or says which escape criticism. This time his reserves of courage were not tested. He received only praise. That was a tribute not simply to the esteem in which the then Chief Rabbi was held, but to the development of Jewish–Christian dialogue in this country. It was a token of the changed relationship between the mainstream Christian churches and the Jewish community.

The existence of the Manor House Group is both a reflection of and one of the hidden contributory factors to this shift in thinking. It is easy to sneer at a self-selected group of people with a liberal cast of mind, secure in each other's company, yet feeling the occasional theological thrill when advancing a daring thought. This book of essays deflates such cynicism, for it combines lucidity with a degree of excitement not commonplace in the literary fruits of dialogue. It is a sort of theological Alton Towers. In each of its four main sections, the first essay, by Tony Bayfield, John Bowden, Marcus Braybrooke and Julia Neuberger respectively, invites us to look over the precipice of a theological roller-coaster which might break off the rails established by our traditions. The descent into danger is modified, qualified, and corrected in succeeding essays, thus assuring us that the ride is safe after all. Only in Alan Race's commentary on Julia Neuberger's article does the ride gain consistent momentum so that there is a sense of the reckless throughout. But there we move into the sphere of prophetic witness, so recklessness is expected.

Most of the contributors to this book are well known to me through my previous work at Lambeth Palace. The Archbishop's chaplain is a sort of private secretary, research officer, liturgical decoration and valet all rolled into one. He is a generalist and anything that doesn't quite fit the usual categories of Lambeth life falls into his lap. He is, like Autolycus in *The Winter's Tale*, 'a snapper-up of unconsidered trifles'.

One such 'unconsidered trifles' was the Archbishop's relationship with Judaism and other faith communities. There are specialists in Christian ecumenism on the Archbishop's staff but no such equivalent for inter-faith matters. Peter Schneider, of blessed memory, was a singular exception in the early 1970s. When I was appointed, however, I was given to understand that inter-faith work would not occupy much of my time. In the event it did, not as a result of any expertise on my part—I claim none—but because the circumstances of national and international life, alongside a growing theological eclecticism, seemed to demand it

Though it doesn't rate a mention in *Dialogue With a Difference*, one factor was the controversy surrounding *The Satanic Verses*. I observed a new energy in the search for dialogue and friendship between the faith communities in this country as a result. It also illustrated the estrangement of religions which have a common ancestry. That strangeness remains even amongst Jews and Christians who trust each other with their deepest thoughts, as in the Manor House Group.

What we share—the Hebrew scriptures, for example—can deceive us into thinking that we hold more in common than we do. John Bowden's passionate call for doctrinal criticism reflects such a distinctively Christian concern that Jonathan Magonet needs to exercise a considerable leap of imagination to comprehend its significance. The living relationship which Jews have with the Bible seems to create in them a natural capacity for implicit historical criticism. Julia Neuberger jumps from the prophetic words of Micah and Isaiah into contemporary issues without any intervening hermeneutic. It is the very thing which would incur the wrath of examiners at most of our Anglican theological colleges, yet is the stuff of many Christian sermons. John Bowden thinks we are not being honest with ourselves. Perhaps, after all, the text is its own interpreter.

The most striking essay in the book is Tony Bayfield's plea for making theological space. He clears the ground so considerably that he is able to acknowledge the New Testament as a book of revelation, 'as a document out of which God speaks to Christians'. There is a generosity here which I find deeply moving. It acknowledges the validity of a distinctively Christian experience of God without yielding to supercessionism. Tony rightly contrasts his perspective with the common Jewish view that Christianity is founded upon a mistake. By comparison, the invincibility of Hyam Maccoby's Judaism is painful to a Christian reader.

In the wake of the *Shoah*, the suggestion that Jews might cause Christians pain is one that seems unacceptable. Yet our dialogue will remain sterile until we recognise this truth. Many Christians now acknowledge just how much pain their past actions and present attitudes bring to Jews. It is lack of contact with the living Jewish community that causes so many Christian priests, preachers and teachers to characterise Judaism as a religion of slavish law observers, puffed up with their own righteousness. Contact punctures caricatures. It is but a preliminary to deeper dialogue.

Within weeks of conferring a Lambeth degree on the Chief Rabbi, the Archbishop addressed the annual meeting of the Council of Christians and Jews. In his address, Archbishop Runcie explored the shared significance of the creation narratives in the Jewish–Christian understanding of the world. The theological bias in this lecture was a significant departure from the neutral language often chosen by the Joint Presidents of CCJ in the past. It heralded what Robert Runcie once called his 'Jewish period', so frequent were his theological forays in this area. In 1988 he preached at the West London Synagogue only days after addressing the *Kristallnacht* Memorial Meeting. He later gave a lecture to the World Union for Progressive Judaism at its biennial international conference. The shift from courteous speeches to theological dialogue was barely noticed in the media, but it shows that the Manor House Group experience was neither unique nor out of touch. There was some nervousness when Robert Runcie was followed by an evangelical, George Carey. In the event, the Jewish community, despite its concerns about the Decade of Evangelism, has discovered the present Archbishop to be a true friend. Hardly anyone expected an evangelical Archbishop to be the first to refuse the patronage of the Church's Ministry Among the Jews. Symbolic actions are important to Jews and Christians alike. The significance of this departure from tradition should not be underestimated. It is an acknowledgement that the fear of Christian missionary effort amongst the Jewish people is understood at the heart of the Church of England's leadership. Jews believe that Christian missionary efforts within their own community are a contemporary extension of the anti-Semitism which led to the *Shoah*. Christians can barely understand how their desire to share the love of Jesus Christ can be comprehended in that way. But it is not Christian comprehension that matters. It is Jewish pain. And the penetration of the pain of Jewish experience into Christian life has led to this archiepiscopal decision. It has been done at a price, and the Jews most involved in dialogue recognise this.

Tony Bayfield describes Judaism as 'a love affair with God'. Many are the Christians who would recognise that as a description of their own religion. It reminds us of the priority of relationships—with God and each other—in our two faiths. Jews existed before the Hebrew scriptures were written. Our twin faiths are rooted in experience of a God who is just but merciful, righteous yet compassionate. Jews and Christians come first. What flows from their experience comes second. The Manor House Group directs us to an encounter between Jews and Christians themselves in which dialogue is a delight, as the Psalmist says, in Psalm 43:4, God Himself is our 'joy and delight'.

[The Rt. Revd Graham James, currently the Bishop of St Germans in the Diocese of Truro, England, commissioned for this book]

FURTHER READING

Bayfield, Tony & Braybrooke, Marcus (edited). *Dialogue With a Difference*, SCM Press, 1992.

Braybrooke, Marcus (edited). *Stepping Stones to a Global Ethic*, SCM Press, 1992.

Cohn-Sherbok, Dan. *On Earth as it is in Heaven: Jews, Christians, and Liberation Theology*, Orbis, 1987.

Ellis, Marc. *Toward a Jewish Theology of Liberation*, SCM Press, 1988.

Küng, Hans. *Global Responsibility: In Search of a New Ethic*, SCM Press, 1991.

Lowe, Malcolm (edited). 'Orthodox Christians and Jews on Continuity and Renewal', Immanuel 26/27, 1994.

Maduro, Otto (edited). *Judaism, Christianity, and Liberation: An Agenda for Dialogue*, Orbis, 1991.

Markham, Ian. *Plurality and Christian Ethics*, Cambridge University Press, 1994.

Papademetriou, George. *Orthodox Christian–Jewish Relations*, Wyndham Hall Press, 1990.

Sacks, Jonathan. *Faith in the Future*, Darton, Longman & Todd, 1995.

Swidler, Leonard (edited). *Toward a Universal Theology of Religion*, Orbis, 1987.

CHAPTER ELEVEN

CHALLENGES FOR THE FUTURE

CHAPTER ELEVEN

CHALLENGES FOR THE FUTURE

Thus far as the editor, I have tried to be impartial. My comments throughout have simply tried to aid understanding of each text. However, I am in fact a participant in the dialogue: I am trying to think through my own faith in the light of the problems raised and explored in this *Reader*. In this concluding chapter I shall briefly reflect on the direction that I think Christians should take. My training is in Christian theology, and it is from this vantage point that I have participated in the dialogue. My reflections are built around the main chapter headings which appear in the *Reader*. Each topic will be dealt with in turn.

H.P.F.

ANTI-JUDAISM

The extent to which elements of anti-Judaism remain in Christian liturgy and theology needs to be addressed. Liturgy and theology affect Christian preaching and teaching. I suggest that the Church constantly needs to assess whether all elements of her supersessionism have been rooted out.

In terms of liturgy much has already been done—particularly in the Catholic Church where for example the Good Friday prayer for 'perfidious Jews' has been replaced. With regard to the Orthodox Churches, Yves Dubois's commissioned article highlighted that such reforms are beginning. It will take time but there are Orthodox theologians, such as George Papademetriou, who are seeking to purge the liturgy of its anti-Semitic elements.

The main focus of the extracts in Chapter 2 addressed the extent to which the Church was responsible for the Shoah. I endorse the comments of Braybrooke that the causes of anti-Semitism are complex. As many contributors have suggested, I believe that it is possible to trace a link between centuries of anti-Jewish teaching by the Church and the emergence of secular anti-Semitism in the twentieth century. The groundwork for Nazism had been prepared in Europe by centuries of Christian anti-Judaism. Judaism as a faith was dispensable. It had no validity apart from the ultimate hope that Jews would embrace Christianity. Two key theological issues remain unresolved: anti-Judaism in feminist theology; and Christian concepts of salvation. The issue of anti-Judaism in feminist theology will be addressed later in this chapter under the heading of 'women'.

Christians, although not directly responsible for the actions of their ancestors, do nevertheless have a responsibility to ensure that the false teaching on Judaism is not propagated in this and future generations. I suggest that each generation has to reassess its theology to ensure that elements of anti-Judaism have not re-surfaced. That constant critical assessment, with the help of the Jewish people, will enable Christianity to move beyond denigration to respect for Judaism. I wish to make some very brief comments concerning salvation and anti-Judaism. In my own article in Chapter 2, I argued that the root cause of anti-Judaism in Christian theology was a particular understanding of salvation. So far the churches have not addressed the implications of their soteriology for their theology of Judaism. Until the churches make theological space for Judaism by accepting it as a legitimate path of salvation, then much anti-Judaism will remain. As long as Judaism is not granted a salvific status in its own right, Christians will continue to see it as an inferior and inadequate faith. This soteriological reappraisal is, I suggest, vital for future relations between Jews and Christians. I explore how this may be achieved in the section on 'mission and salvation'. Yosef Yerushalmi writes: 'For my people is in grave peril of its life. And it simply cannot wait until you have completed a new *Summa Theologica*.' To a certain extent he is correct, but my concluding comment would be that it is imperative for the Church to complete a new *Summa Theologica* if the Christian–Jewish dialogue is to survive.

HOLOCAUST

Numerous theological responses to the Shoah have been made. As we have seen they have ranged from traditional affirmations of God's omnipotence to the 'death of God' theology. Of supreme importance is, as Fackenheim identifies, the Jewish determination to survive and not grant Hitler a posthumous victory. The Church has a responsibility too in ensuring that Hitler is not granted that victory.

Amongst some Orthodox Jews and fundamentalist Christians there is a tendency to use the biblical model of sin and punishment to explain the Shoah. They argue that in some sense it was a punishment for Jewish sin. This suggestion must, for me, be firmly refuted. This biblical model is insufficient to explain the horrendous suffering exacted upon the Jewish people in our century. There are three main problems with that model: first, the suffering is disproportionate to any sin that could have been committed; second, what kind of God are we talking about if such horrendous suffering is meted out to one particular group of people? Third, we are talking about the systematic annihilation of a people which includes innocent children. Any attempt to justify God must take into account these factors. We have to acknowledge human responsibility.

The challenge it seems to me is not where was God, but where was humanity? The perpetrators of the crimes of the Shoah must not be free of their responsibility by transferring the blame to God. Elie Wiesel is right to have fear for the future. When we see again the rise of ethnic-cleansing, we are fearful for the future of minority groups in Europe. We ask not 'where is God?' but, 'where is humanity?' Where is the human protest?

One further word of caution concerning the interpretation of the Shoah. Christians have been urged to incorporate the lessons of the Shoah into their theology. That is certainly necessary. Care has to be shown, as Norman Solomon has suggested, that the Shoah is not Christianized. Care has to be taken to ensure that what was essentially a Jewish persecution is not turned into a Christian suffering. Such elements have appeared in some Christian theologians; not least in the identification of Christ's death with that of Jewish suffering.

MISSION AND SALVATION

I have linked these topics under one heading because the issues are so intertwined. The main challenge which runs through this section, and for that matter most of the *Reader*, is how Christianity can make theological space for Judaism—something which it has rarely done over the last two thousand years. If Christianity is to be credible in the dialogue, it must come clean on the issue of mission. Is there, or is there not, an ultimate aim to convert Jews? Theologically, can the Church provide theological space for Judaism, particularly *vis-à-vis* mission and salvation?

As we have seen the major Church statements have clearly rejected any coercive proselytism and the setting up of organizations which have the sole aim of converting Jews. The Churches have affirmed the validity of God's covenant with the Jews but the logical conclusion of their statements needs to be worked out fully. If the covenant is still valid, surely it has within it the means for Jewish redemption?

For many Christians the belief that Christianity contains the fullest and definitive revelation of God in Jesus Christ necessitates a mission to the world. In addressing this issue today, Christians need to be reminded that the mission of the historical Jesus was confined to Israel during his lifetime (Matt. 10:5). Taking seriously the utter Jewishness of Jesus necessitates some reflection on this. Christians need to ask what was the nature of his mission to the Jews of his day. As many New Testament scholars have highlighted, that mission was based on a call to repentance and a turning back to the ways of Torah. It was a kingdom-centred message. Jesus pointed away from himself to God. He did not proclaim salvation through his own person—that belief was part of the developing post-resurrection affirmation of Christ. Salvation for Jews was always seen by Jesus as faithfulness to Torah. As Chapters 6 and 7 have shown, much of what he said had parallels in the Rabbinic Judaism of his day. If Jews and Christians are to take seriously that message, then salvation for Jews comes through faithfulness to Torah. I do believe that the historical Jesus has a profound relevance for contemporary systematic theology—after all, Christianity has always understood itself as rooted in history. God is seen as acting in history through the incarnation. I believe that the Jewish Jesus challenges previous understandings of mission and for that matter, salvation. It will become clear in the following comments that the two topics are often inextricably linked for Christians.

What then are the implications for the traditional Christian mission to Jews? It means that Christians should enable Jews to be better Jews rather than converting them to Christianity. That would then be in line with the teaching of Christianity's central figure, Jesus. But there is a further dimension. Converting 'the other' has constituted the traditional Christian approach because it is usually linked to a particular understanding of salvation. As I said at the start of this section, if you believe that your tradition has the sole means of salvation then you are obliged to share the truth with others. I suggest that it is unreasonable to link a person's place in the after-life to a particular set of beliefs. First, it is elitist because it requires a correct understanding of complex doctrines; and second, all beliefs are culturally and historically conditioned and those born into the right culture would have a head start.

It is still possible for Christians to hold that Christ is central to Christian faith and yet to allow space for Judaism as a living and salvific tradition. The role of Christ is revelatory rather than soteriological. Christ can be seen as the fullest revelation of God but acknowledgement of that is not essential to salvation. Rather, salvation comes, as John Hick writes in *Disputed Questions* and *Interpretation of Religion*, through the turning from self-centredness to God-centredness. Was this not the essence of Jesus' teaching for the Jews of his day? Mission in terms of converting someone to your tradition is no longer applicable. The witness to 'the other' comes through enabling them to turn from self-centredness to God-centredness through their own distinctive symbols and traditions. This does not mean giving up the quest for truth. Dialogue is about understanding the other, yes; but also seeking a deeper understanding of the truth. This does not imply that we cannot speak of anything meaningful in dialogue. On the contrary Christians, for example, can talk about the importance of Jesus whilst Jews accept this as a valid experience for Christians. But, such openness and trust is undermined if there is a hidden missionary agenda. Each of us, whether Jew or Christian, is still on that spiritual journey for as the Jewish tradition says: 'If we knew everything, we would be God.'

ISRAEL

For Jews there must be a caution over readily endorsing all Christian support for the State of Israel. Some Christians, particularly the evangelical or fundamentalist communities, support it because of their expectations about the End Times. There is little attempt to acknowledge Israel because of its centrality for Jewish identity. Israel is seen as important in so far as God is working out the final plan of the messianic redemption. For these Christians, the purpose of supporting the Jewish return to the land is eschatological—only when the Jews return to Israel can the Second Coming of Christ occur.

There are, however, other Christians who would not accept this particular interpretation. They, like Ian Markham in the commissioned article for this chapter, would see the foundation of the State as part of God's plan for the Jewish people but not in any sense linked to the End Times. The land is seen as a necessary safe-haven for the Jewish people—two thousand years without a land has shown what they have risked for their survival. Israel as an earthly place is seen as essential for Jewish survival.

The challenge for Christianity must be to recognize the importance of Israel for Jewish identity. As we have seen Christianity has traditionally focused on the celestial Jerusalem and given little theological space to Israel as an earthly place. Part of the recognition of Israel for Jewish self-identity must include theological space for the earthly Jerusalem. This process has begun—as expressed in some official Church documents; however many Christians have difficulties in recognizing the State when it clashes with their support for the Palestinian cause.

In the Christian–Jewish dialogue there is often a tendency to side with one political cause over and against another. The way forward is for there to be a genuine listening to the pain of all sides—whether Jewish or Palestinian. It seems clear to me that Palestinian and Jewish voices must each be heard if the Christian–Jewish dialogue is to be credible. It is important for all sides to listen to the pain of 'the other' and to seek a deeper understanding of their different perspectives. This cannot mean total agreement or syncretism but granting theological space to 'the other'. Peace and reconciliation cannot be imposed from outside, particularly from 'the West'. As further progress is made in the Middle East Peace Process, perhaps Jews and Palestinians will feel more able to meet and share their respective religious world views. This has already begun through small dialogue groups in Israel, but it is not the norm.

THE JEWISHNESS OF JESUS

To dialogue on the key figure that separates the two faiths, given the long history of persecution in the name of that figure, is a remarkable achievement. As I see it, there are three areas to tackle in the dialogue with regard to Jesus: the Jewish Jesus, the messiahship of Jesus, and the Christ of faith.

As the chapter has highlighted, Jewish and Christian scholars in the dialogue largely agree on their reconstruction of the historical Jesus. Many Jews are keen to learn more about the Jewish Jesus and for that matter early Jewish Christianity, because the reconstructions shed light on the diversity of first century Judaism. It enables Jews to understand some of the factors behind the development of Rabbinic Judaism in the first century CE. As Aubrey Rose has suggested it may one day be possible for Jews to incorporate Jesus the Jew, as prophet and rabbi, into the history of Judaism. Maybe; but there are some difficulties. For Jews, sensitive to the missionary nature of Christianity, they would not want Christians to think that they have after all accepted the Christ of faith. There is a fundamental difficulty with sources: the only accounts of Jesus' ministry, apart from a couple of brief sentences in Josephus, come from the early Church. The Gospel accounts are coloured by the emerging beliefs about the person of Jesus, and therefore Jews could only ever accept the Jesus reconstructed by New Testament scholars. The final point to make regarding the Jewish Jesus is that Judaism can function perfectly well without him. There is a rich Jewish tradition, the Rabbinic tradition, which developed as a parallel movement to Christianity. It is testimony to another possible interpretation of the biblical heritage. However Jews can, and do, accept Jesus as the figure through whom the Gentiles came to worship the God of Israel.

The second unresolved issue between Jews and Christians concerns the messiahship of Jesus. The question is, it seems to me, 'was Jesus or was he not the messiah of Jewish expectation?' It has puzzled me as to why Christians are so adamant to affirm Jesus as the *Jewish* messiah. Through my involvement in the dialogue and my study of biblical literature I have come to the conclusion that whatever Jesus was, he did not fulfil the messianic prophecies in the Hebrew scriptures. I do believe it is time that Christians listen to the Jewish understandings of messiah and recognize that Jesus did not bring about what was expected. It was not obvious to the Jews of his day during or after his ministry that he was the messiah. Some disciples did later believe that he was the messiah, but it was an affirmation of faith rather than a self-evident fact. I believe that Christians must take seriously the idea that for Jews the messiah could never be a divine figure but only ever a human one. Furthermore, Jesus did not inaugurate a period of peace, nor did he overthrow the occupying Roman army, neither did the general resurrection of the dead occur. These central Jewish messianic expectations were left unfulfilled. Christians perhaps need to acknowledge that Jesus was not the messiah of Jewish expectation. Whatever his significance, it must be located elsewhere.

Christianity cannot function without reference to Jesus; Judaism can. Therefore the contemporary Christological issue for Christians centres on what is an appropriate Christology for the new Christian–Jewish relationship. What about the Christ of faith? Can Christianity develop a Christology which does not have anti-Judaism as its left hand? The challenge for Christianity is summed up succinctly in Jacobus Schoneveld's question: 'can the Church find space in its own faith for an attitude which sees the Jewish people as loved and accepted, notwithstanding the fact that it does not share its confession about Jesus Christ?' In my response to Rosemary Radford Ruether in Chapter 2, I argued that soteriology not Christology was the root of Christian anti-Judaism. It is possible to develop an absolute Christology which is detached from traditional exclusive models of salvation. As Lewis Eron suggested, God can be present in Torah for Jews and in the person of Christ for Christians. As I suggested in my comments on mission and salvation, a Christology for the Christian–Jewish dialogue can be centred on the affirmation that the nature of God was fully revealed in Christ. Conscious affirmation of this revelation is not necessary for salvation. Salvation is dependent on a turning from self-centredness to God-centredness. This Jews achieve through following the *mitzvot* in Torah and Christians achieve through following Jesus.

SCRIPTURE

The fact that Jewish scholars feel comfortable to offer a Jewish reading of the Gospels is a measure of how far the dialogue has progressed. Joint textual study has often proved to be one of the most dynamic areas of the relationship. Such studies seem to attract the largest number of participants.

On both sides, Jews and Christians need to understand that Christianity and Rabbinic Judaism grew up as parallel but separate paths which *both* superseded biblical Judaism. Neither faith can claim the definitive interpretation of that tradition, but through the dialogue can come to an appreciation that there are diverse and sometimes complementary ways of interpreting our shared texts. Each faith must allow 'the other' the space to interpret the biblical tradition in their own distinctive way. However, that interpretation should not be allowed to become a fixed dogma for all people of all ages. The relationship cannot then be equal or true to the historical situation. There must be a recognition that both Judaism and Christianity have their difficult texts. The way forward is, as some study groups have done, to read these texts together with a critical awareness and sensitivity.

WOMEN

The chapter on women raised two main issues: the feminist challenge to Judaism and Christianity; and the anti-Judaism inherent in much Christian feminist theology. The dialogue between Jewish and Christian women has barely begun—certainly in Britain. The situation in the States is somewhat more advanced. The contribution of women promises to be a fruitful dimension to the wider Christian–Jewish dialogue.

The first comment that I wish to make relates to feminist challenges to religion. It has become clear from the extracts that there are issues within both Christianity and Judaism which women of the respective traditions wish to challenge. That in itself is important if it is part of women's experience; however, I would suggest that the women's Christian–Jewish dialogue should not be limited only to feminist critiques. This seems to be the impression given in many feminist writings in the dialogue. It is essential that the dialogue is not seen as purely a critique of religion nor promoting a radical feminist agenda. It should be broader, to include women who are content with their tradition but who can equally bring new insights to the Christian–Jewish dialogue. It is important for women to meet and share their experiences as women. This may mean that they raise challenges to their respective traditions, but it may also mean that some are content with their tradition. To illustrate this point, I have been in dialogue with Jewish women of the Orthodox tradition who are quite happy with their position in the community. This is their experience and it is important to listen to them. They explain what it is like to be an Orthodox woman in a traditionally male dominated community. Or is it really male dominated? That is the point of the dialogue—to discover the nuances within each community regarding its women. It is essential for women to meet and dialogue on a wide range of topics: for example, prayer and tradition—how their respective traditions shape their experience as women; or how particular biblical women express the experience of childbirth, or the loss of a child, or personal prayer to a male God. Another fruitful area would be joint textual study to enhance the insights into some of our shared biblical texts. Those insights may be different from the traditionally male interpretations.

As I said in the introduction to Chapter 9, there are many stereotypical views which Jewish and Christian women hold about each other. There is much misinformation on both sides. One of the most important results of the women's dialogue will be to break down these stereotypes. Whilst on the issue of stereotypes of 'the other', we turn to the second issue raised in the chapter: the anti-Judaism inherent in much Christian feminist theology. It is of grave concern to me that many Christian preachers are propagating a new, subtle form of anti-Judaism. They argue that Jesus, and for that matter early Christianity, was the great liberator of women in contrast to the Judaism of the day. It has been said, in a sermon that I heard, that Jesus liberated women to pray for the first time. What about Hannah in the sanctuary? What about women in the Temple? As Katharina von Kellenbach has pointed out in her extract, Jesus did not overtly challenge the patriarchal structure *vis-à-vis* women. Care has to be taken not to superimpose modern feminist concerns onto the ministry of Jesus. Judith Plaskow raised a significant point in her article, a point worth repeating: 'If we acknowledge that the Jesus movement was a movement within Judaism, then whatever Jesus' attitudes toward women, they represent not a victory over Judaism but a possibility *within* early Judaism.' Christians need to take this point seriously. Must Christianity always define itself by denigrating Judaism? As Plaskow asks later in her extract, 'If claims about Jesus' specialness are intrinsic to Christianity, then is there any way to make these claims that does not end up rejecting or disparaging Judaism as their left hand?' I believe this to be the ultimate question for Christian theologians in our time.

MUTUAL WITNESS

I share the sentiments of the contributors in Chapter 10 and endorse the need for, as Clark Williamson has said, critical solidarity on theological and practical matters. There is, as Sacks suggests, a need to address issues of common concern to humanity. In his extract he writes: 'our worlds of faith are irreducibly plural yet we have been cast into the same planet, faced with the same questions. Can we live together? Can we learn from one another?'

What can Christians learn in dialogue with Jews? The most important is perhaps the acknowledgement that there are profound experiences of God to be found outside of Christianity. The encounter with living Judaism has had far-reaching effects on my own religious quest. My first encounter with Judaism as a living faith, rather than the often stereotypical text-book version, was on my first visit to Israel. It was for me the first time that I had ever stepped inside a synagogue let alone attended a service. It did rather take me by surprise that I as a non-Jew, should experience God in the synagogue.

Insights from particular practices may be helpful in dealing with certain life experiences; for example a look at the liturgy of the Catholic Requiem Mass and the symbols used during the service may be helpful in expressing one's sense of grief and loss. Not least, the length of the service allows some space to work through the different emotions. On the other hand much may be learnt from the Jewish tradition which has a period of mourning called *shiva*. For the first seven days the main mourner is given space to grieve. That grieving is an ongoing process and for seven days that person does not cook, nor do the housework, nor go out of the house. People come and visit, bring meals for that person, and share their memories of the deceased person. In a society which often shuts out any talk of death, such space is crucial. Many Christians would acknowledge that they are often not sure how to behave or how to grieve at such a time. Much can be learned here from the Jewish tradition.

What can Jews learn from the dialogue with Christians? Prayer may be a helpful area. Many Jews would acknowledge that after the Shoah they have difficulty with private prayer. It may be that Christians can enable Jews to rediscover that element of their tradition. Jews can also discover through the dialogue that Christianity is not monolithic. There are diverse expressions and theologies. Perhaps, as some Jewish scholars have argued (Maimonides and Franz Rosenzweig, for example) Jews can see Christianity as a legitimate path for bringing Gentiles to God. Christianity should not be embraced solely as a form of the Noahide Covenant but actually a faith tradition that moves beyond it.

The following comments that I wish to make are related to a personal experience of the loss of a close friend and dialogue-partner, David Hill to whom this book is dedicated. The events surrounding his death provide a practical example of just how far solidarity between Jews and Christians can go. For me and others in the local Council of Christians and Jews, his death embodied a practical way of bringing Jews and Christians together. It was his wish that his closest friends and family sit with him during the difficult days and nights before his death. Religious differences were not relevant. Jews and Christians, because they were his friends, shared some of the painful and yet special moments of his dying. After his death, the funeral reflected David's ability to bring about the extraordinary—for his funeral was a Catholic Requiem Mass in an Anglican parish church with the eulogy given by the leader of the Jewish community, Frank Gent. It was a remarkable achievement given the difficulty which many Jews have in going into a church let alone attending a Mass. It is a vision of what may be possible. Not that Jews should become Christian or participate in a Christian service, but that they should be present at one and show solidarity with their Christian dialogue-partners is remarkable. For me, it highlights the fact that issues of friendship and humanity can transcend religious differences.

The direction of the future relationship will surely move beyond getting to know one another, learning the basic tenets of the other's tradition, and challenging particular theological perspectives. Those elements are indeed important and must continue; however as the relationship strengthens there can be a profound solidarity and understanding that allows space for differences and yet endorses the insights into the nature of Ultimate Reality found in the faith experience of 'the other'. Judaism and Christianity can be enriched by a shared human experience and yet not blur the boundaries to provide a 'religious soup'.

We as Jews and Christians are on a spiritual journey. We can use the insights of our respective traditions to enhance that journey. It is the common task of both faiths to build the kingdom of God. It may be that no faith-community can do so alone. As we approach the third millennium it is perhaps time to acknowledge that Christianity and Judaism are distinct and separate faiths—yes; but also interdependent communities.

CONCLUSION

Jews and Christians have much to be thankful for. We have travelled a long way together in rebuilding our relationship and repairing the damage of the past. It has not been without its costs on either side. The progress is significant and deserves serious reflection. Our work is cut out for the future—not least in encouraging those in our communities who have yet to participate in the dialogue. It is time to take our insights from the dialogue back into our respective communities. I hope that those who have not encountered 'the other' will take time to read this book and find its sources a valuable introduction. The central message comes in the words of the famous first century Rabbi, Hillel: If not now, when?

BIBLIOGRAPHY

BOOKS AND JOURNALS

Allswang, Benzion. *The Final Resolution: Combating Anti-Jewish Hostility* (Feldheim, 1989).

Ateek, Naim. *Justice and Only Justice* (Orbis, 1989).

Athans, Mary Christine. 'Antisemitism or Anti-Judaism?' in Michael Shermis and Arthur E. Zannoni (eds) *Introduction to Jewish–Christian Relations* (Paulist Press, 1991).

Baum, Gregory. 'Rethinking the Church's Mission after Auschwitz' in Eva Fleischner (ed.) *Auschwitz: Beginning of a New Era?* (Ktav Publishing House, 1977).

Bayfield, Tony. 'Mission—A Jewish Perspective' in *Theology* (May/June 1993).

Bayfield, Tony and Braybrooke, Marcus (ed.). *Dialogue With a Difference* (SCM Press, 1992).

Beck, Norman. *Mature Christianity: The Recognition and Repudiation of the Anti-Jewish Polemic of the New Testament* (Associated University Presses, 1985).

Berenbaum, Michael. *After Tragedy and Triumph* (Cambridge University Press, 1990).

Berger, David and Wyschogrod, Michael. *Jews and Jewish Christianity* (Ktav, 1978).

Berkovits, Eliezer. *Faith After the Holocaust* (Ktav, 1973).

Bivin, David and Blizzard, Roy. *Understanding the Difficult Words of Jesus: New Insights from a Hebraic Perspective* (Center for Judaic–Christian Studies, Dayton, 1983).

Borchsenius, Poul. *Two Ways to God: Judaism and Christianity* (Vallentine Mitchell, 1968).

Bosch, David. *Transforming Mission: Paradigm Shifts in Theology of Mission* (Orbis, 1991).

Braybrooke, Marcus (ed.). *Stepping Stones to a Global Ethic* (SCM Press, 1992).

Braybrooke, Marcus. *Christian–Jewish Relations: A New Look* (Publication of The Council of Christians and Jews, 1992).

Braybrooke, Marcus. *Children of One God: A History of the Council of Christians and Jews* (SCM Press, 1991).

Braybrooke, Marcus. 'The Resurrection in Christian-Jewish Dialogue', in *Common Ground* no. 1, (1991).

Braybrooke, Marcus. *Time to Meet: Towards a Deeper Understanding Between Jews and Christians* (SCM Press, 1990).

Breslauer, Daniel S. 'Salvation: A Jewish View' in Leon Klenicki and Geoffrey Wigoder (eds) *A Dictionary of the Jewish–Christian Dialogue* (Paulist Press, 1984).

Buber, Martin. *I and Thou*, translated by Ronald G. Smith (T&T Clark, 1987).

Buber, Martin. *Two Types of Faith* (Macmillan, 1951).

Büchmann, Christina and Spiegel, Celina. *Out of the Garden: Women Writers on the Bible* (Harper Collins, 1994).

Budd, Rt. Revd Christopher. *'Pastoral Letter for 1st Sunday of Advent 1994 About our Links With the Jewish People'*, 10 November 1994.

Burrell, David and Landau, Yehezkel (eds). *Voices From Jerusalem: Jews and Christians Reflect on the Holy Land* (Paulist Press, 1992).

Carey, George. 'Tiny Shoes' in *Common Ground* no. 1, (1991).

Charlesworth, James (ed.). *The Messiah: Developments in Earliest Judaism and Christianity* (Fortress, 1992).

Charlesworth, James (ed.). *Jews and Christians: Exploring the Past, Present and Future* (Crossroad, 1990).

Charlesworth, James. *Jesus Within Judaism* (SPCK, 1988).

Christ, Carol and Plaskow, Judith (eds). *Womenspirit Rising: A Feminist Reader in Religion* (Harper Collins, 1979).

Clorfene, Chaim and Rogalsky, Yakov. *The Path of the Righteous Gentile* (Targum Press, 1987).

Cohen, Arthur (ed.). *Arguments and Doctrines: A Reader of Jewish Thinking in the Aftermath of the Holocaust* (Harper and Row, 1970).

Cohen, Martin and Croner, Helga (eds). *Christian Mission—Jewish Mission* (Paulist Press, 1982).

Cohen, Martin. 'The Mission of Israel After Auschwitz' in Helga Croner and Leon Klenicki (eds) *Issues in the Jewish–Christian Dialogue: Jewish Perspectives on Covenant, Mission, and Witness* (Paulist Press, 1979).

Cohen, Naomi (eds). *Essential Papers on Jewish–Christian Relations in the United States* (New York University Press, 1990).

Cohn-Sherbok, Dan. *The Crucified Jew* (Harper Collins, 1992).

Cohn-Sherbok, Dan. *Issues in Contemporary Judaism* (Macmillan, 1991).

Cohn-Sherbok, Dan. *Holocaust Theology* (Lamp Press, 1989).

Cohn-Sherbok, Dan. *On Earth as it is in Heaven: Jews, Christians, and Liberation Theology* (Orbis, 1987).

Croner, Helga and Klenicki, Leon (eds). *Issues in the Jewish–Christian Dialogue: Jewish Perspectives on Covenant, Mission, and Witness* (Paulist Press, 1979).

Davies, W. *The Territorial Dimension of Judaism* (University of California Press, 1982).

Daz-Mías, Paloma. *Sephardim: The Jews From Spain* (University of Chicago Press, 1992).

Ditmanson, Harold. 'Judaism and Christianity: A Theology of Co- Existence' in Richard W. Rousseau (ed.) *Christianity and Judaism: The Deepening Dialogue* (Ridge Row Press, 1983).

Ditmanson, Harold (ed.). *Stepping Stones to Further Jewish–Lutheran Relationships* (Augsburg, 1990).

Dubois, Marcel. 'Israel and Christian Self-Understanding' in D. Burrell and Y. Landau (eds) *Voices From Jerusalem* (Paulist Press, 1992).

Dunn, James. *The Partings of the Ways Between Christianity and Judaism and their Significance for the Character of Christianity* (SCM Press, 1991).

Dunn, James. *Christology in the Making* (SCM Press, 1989).

Ecclestone, Alan. *The Night Sky of the Lord* (Darton, Longman and Todd, 1980).

Eckardt, Alice and Eckardt, Roy, A. *Long Night's Journey Into Day: A Revised Retrospective on the Holocaust* (Pergamon Press, 1988).

Eckhardt, Alice, and Eckhardt, Roy, A. *Encounter With Israel: A Challenge to Conscience* (Association, 1970).

Ellis, Marc, *Toward a Jewish Theology of Liberation* (SCM Press, 1988).

Eron, Lewis John. 'The Problem of a Jew Talking to a Christian about Jesus' in Leonard Swidler, Lewis John Eron, Gerard Sloyan, and Lester Dean (eds) *Bursting the Bonds: Jewish–Christian Dialogue on Jesus and Paul* (Orbis, 1990).

Evans, Craig and Hagner, Donald. *Anti-Semitism and Early Christianity* (Fortress, 1993).

Fackenheim, Emil. *To Mend the World: Foundations of Future Jewish Thought* (Schocken, 1982).

BIBLIOGRAPHY

Fackenheim, Emil. *The Jewish Return into History* (Schocken Books, 1978).

Falk, Harvey. *Jesus the Pharisee: A New Look at the Jewishness of Jesus* (Paulist Press, 1985).

Falk, Randall. 'Understanding Our Relationship to Jesus: A Jewish Outlook', in Walter Harrelson and Randall M. Falk, *Jews and Christians: A Troubled Family* (Abingdon Press, 1990).

Federici, Tommaso. 'The Mission and Witness of the Church', in *Fifteen Years of Catholic–Jewish Dialogue 1970–1985: Selected Papers* (Libreria Editrice Vaticana, 1988).

Fiorenza, Elisabeth Schüssler. *Jesus: Miriam's Child, Sophia's Prophet. Critical Issues in Feminist Christology* (SCM Press, 1995).

Fischer, Kathleen. *Women at the Well* (SPCK, 1989).

Fisher, Eugene. *Faith Without Prejudice* (Crossroad, 1993).

Fisher, Eugene (ed.). *Interwoven Destinies: Jews and Christians Through the Ages* (Paulist Press, 1993).

Flannery, Edward. *The Anguish of the Jews* (Paulist Press, 1985).

Fornberg, Tod. *Jewish–Christian Dialogue and Biblical Exegesis* (Uppsala University Press, 1988).

Friedlander, Albert (ed.). *Out of the Whirlwind* (Schocken, 1976).

Gager, John. *The Origins of Anti-Semitism* (Oxford University Press, 1983).

Gordan, Haim and Gordan, Rivca (eds). *Israel/Palestine: The Quest for Dialogue* (Orbis, 1991).

Gorsky, Jonathon. 'A Jewish Response to the Decade of Evangelism' in *The Way*, vol 34, no 4 (October 1994).

Greenberg, Blu. 'Mission, Witness, and Proselytism' in *Evangelicals and Jews in an Age of Pluralism* (University Press of America, 1990).

Greenberg, Blu. *On Women and Judaism: A View From Tradition* (Jewish Publication Society of America, 1981).

Greenberg, Moshe. 'Theological Reflections—Land, People and the State', in *Immanuel* 22/23 (1989).

Greenspan, Frederick (ed.). *Scripture in the Jewish and Christian Traditions: Authority, Interpretation, Relevance* (Abingdon, 1982).

Grossman, Susan and Haut, Rivka. *Daughters of the King: Women and the Synagogue* (The Jewish Publication Society, 1992).

Grounds, Vernon C. 'The Problem of Proselytization' in *Evangelicals and Jews in an Age of Pluralism* (University Press of America, 1990).

Harries, Richard. 'Theodicy Will not Go Away' in Tony Bayfield and Marcus Braybrooke (eds) *Dialogue With a Difference* (SCM Press, 1992).

Harrington, Daniel J. 'The Teaching of Jesus in His Context' in Eugene Fisher (ed.) *Interwoven Destinies* (Paulist Press, 1993).

Haynes, Stephen. *Prospects for Post-Holocaust Theology* (Scholars Press, 1991).

Hellwig, Monika. 'Bible Interpretation: Has Anything Changed?' in Lawrence Boadt, Helga Croner, and Leon Klenicki (eds) *Biblical Studies: Meeting Ground of Jews and Christians* (Paulist Press, 1980).

Heschel, Abraham Joshua, *Israel: An Echo of Eternity* (Farrar, Straus and Giroux, 1967).

Heschel, Susannah (ed.). *On Being A Jewish Feminist: A Reader* (Schocken, 1983).

Heschel, Susannah. 'The Denigration of Judaism as a Form of Christian Mission' in Clark Williamson (ed.) *A Mutual Witness: Toward Critical Solidarity Between Jews and Christians* (Chalice Press, 1992).

Hick, John and Knitter, Paul (eds). *The Myth of Christian Uniqueness* (SCM Press, 1987).

Hill, David. *An Annotated Description and Personal Experience of the CCJ Young Adults Israel Study Tour 18–29 July 1993*, unpublished work.

Hillman, Eugene. *Many Paths* (Orbis, 1989).

Hilton, Rabbi M. and Marshall, Gordian. *The Gospels and Rabbinic Judaism* (SCM Press, 1988).

Hoffman, Lawrence (ed.), *The Land of Israel: Jewish Perspectives* (Notre Dame Press, 1986).

Hood, John. *Aquinas and the Jews* (University of Pennsylvania Press, 1995).

Immanuel 26/27: Orthodox Christians and Jews on Continuity and Renewal—The Third Academic Meeting between Orthodoxy and Judaism (including a history and bibliography of dialogue between Orthodox Christians and Jews) (Jerusalem: Ecumenical Fraternity, 1994).

Immanuel 24/25: The New Testament and Christian–Jewish Dialogue—Studies in Honor of David Flusser (Jerusalem: Ecumenical Fraternity, 1990).

Immanuel 28/29: Thirty Years of Jewish–Christian Dialogue in Israel (Jerusalem: Ecumenical Fraternity, in preparation).

Jacob, Walter. *Christianity Through Jewish Eyes* (Hebrew Union College Press, 1974).

James, Graham. 'Bridging the Gulf' in *Manna* no 41 (Autumn 1993).

John Paul II. *Crossing the Threshold of Hope* (Jonathan Cape, 1994).

Jones, Gareth Lloyd. *Hard Sayings: Difficult New Testament Texts for Jewish–Christian Dialogue* (Publication of The Council of Christians and Jews, 1993).

Kellenbach, von, Katharina. 'Jewish–Christian Dialogue on Feminism and Religion', *Christian–Jewish Relations*, vol. 19, no. 2 (1986).

Keshishian, Aram. *Orthodox Perspectives on Mission* (Regnum Lynx, 1992).

King, Ursula. *Women and Spirituality* (Macmillan, 1989).

Klein, Charlotte. *Anti-Judaism in Christian Theology* (SPCK, 1978).

Klenicki, Leon and Neuhaus, Richard. *Believing Today: Jew and Christian in Conversation* (Eerdmans, 1989).

Knight, Henry. 'Meeting Jacob at the Jabbok: Wrestling with a Text—A Midrash on Genesis 32:22–32', in *Journal of Ecumenical Studies*, 29:3–4 (Summer–Fall 1992).

Kravitz, Leonard. 'A Jewish Reading of the New Testament' in Lawrence Boadt, Helga Croner, and Leon Klenichi (eds). *Biblical Studies: Meeting Ground of Jews and Christians* (Paulist Press, 1980).

Küng, Hans. *Global Responsibility: In Search of a New Ethic* (SCM Press, 1991).

Küng, Hans. 'Christianity and Judaism' in James Charlesworth (ed.). *Jesus' Jewishness* (Crossroad, 1991).

Kushner, Harold. *To Life: A Celebration of Jewish Being and Thinking* (Little, Brown and Company, 1993).

Lapide, Pinchas and Küng, Hans. *Brother or Lord?* (Fount Books,1977).

Lapide, Pinchas and Luz, Ulrich. *Jesus in Two Perspectives: A Jewish–Christian Dialog* (Augsburg, 1985).

Lee, Bernard. *The Galilean Jewishness of Jesus* (Paulist Press, 1988).

Littell, Franklin. *The Crucifixion of the Jews* (Mercer University Press, 1986).

Lodahl, Michael. *Shekhinah/Spirit: Divine Presence in Jewish and Christian Religion* (Paulist Press, 1992).

Lowe, Malcolm (ed.). *Orthodox Christians and Jews on Continuity and Renewal* (*Immanuel 26/27*, 1994).

Lubarsky, Sandra. *Tolerance and Transformation* (Hebrew Union College Press, 1990).

Lyden, John. 'Atonement in Judaism and Christianity' in the *Journal of Ecumenical Studies*, vol. 29, no. 1 (1992).

Maccoby, Hyam. *Jewish Views of Jesus* (Centre for Inter-Faith Dialogue, Middlesex University, 1995).

Maclennan, Robert. *Early Christian Texts on Jews and Judaism* (Atlanta, 1990).

Maduro, Otto (ed.). *Judaism, Christianity, and Liberation: An Agenda for Dialogue* (Orbis, 1991).

Magonet, Jonathan. *A Rabbi Reads the Psalms* (SCM Press, 1994).

Magonet, Jonathan. *A Rabbi's Bible* (SCM Press, 1991).

Magonet, Jonathon. 'How A Rabbi Reads the Bible' in the *Catholic Gazette*, vol 68, no 4, (1977).

Markham, Ian. *Plurality and Christian Ethics* (Cambridge University Press, 1994).

McCauley, Deborah. '*Nostra Aetate* and the New Jewish–Christian Feminist Dialogue' in Roger Brooks (ed) *Unanswered Questions* (University of Notre Dame Press, 1988).

McCauley, Deborah and Daum, Annette. 'Jewish–Christian Feminist Dialogue: A Wholistic Vision', in *Union Seminary Quarterly Review*, vol. 38 (1983).

McDade, John. 'The Epistle of James for Jews and Christians', in *SIDIC*, vol. XXVII, no.1 (1994).

McGarry, Michael. 'The Holocaust' in Michael Shermis and Arthur Zannoni (eds). *Introduction to Jewish–Christian Relations* (Paulist Press, 1991).

McGarry, Michael. 'Interreligious Dialogue, Mission, and the Case of the Jews', in Paul Mojzes and Leonard Swidler (eds). *Christian Mission and Interreligious Dialogue* (Edwin Mellen Press, 1990).

Mojzes, Paul and Swidler, Leonard (eds). *Christian Mission and Interreligious Dialogue* (Edwin Mellen Press, 1990).

Moltmann, Jürgen. 'Christology and the Jewish–Christian Dialogue', in Val A. McInnes (ed.). *New Visions: Historical and Theological Perspectives on the Jewish–Christian Dialogue* (Crossroad, 1993).

Moran, Gabriel. *Uniqueness: Problem or Paradox in Jewish and Christian Traditions* (Orbis, 1992).

Motte, Mary and Lang, Joseph (eds). *Mission in Dialogue* (Orbis, 1982).

Neusner, Jacob. *Telling Lies: The Urgency and Basis for Judeo–Christian Dialogue* (Westminster/John Knox Press, 1993).

Neusner, Jacob. *What is Midrash?* (Fortress, 1987).

Novak, David. *Jewish–Christian Dialogue: A Jewish Justification* (Oxford University Press, 1989).

Novak, David. *The Image of the Non-Jew in Judaism* (Edwin Mellen Press, 1983).

Oberman, Heiko. *The Roots of Antisemitism in the Age of Renaissance and Reformation* (Fortress, 1984).

Oesrerreicher, John. *The New Encounter Between Christians and Jews* (Philosophical Library, 1986).

O'Neill, Maura. *Women Speaking, Women Listening* (Orbis, 1990).

Papademetriou, George. *Essays on Orthodox Christian–Jewish Relations* (Wyndham Press, 1990).

Parkes, James. *End of an Exile: Israel, the Jews and the Gentile World* (Micah Publications, 1982).

Parkes, James. *The Conflict of the Church and Synagogue* (Atheneum, 1969).

Parkes, James. *Prelude to Dialogue* (Vallentine Mitchell, 1969).

Parkes, James. *The Foundations of Judaism and Christianity* (Vallentine Mitchell, 1960).

Parkes, James. *Judaism and Christianity* (The Camelot Press, 1948).

Pawlikowski, John. *Christ in the Light of the Jewish–Christian Dialogue* (Paulist Press, 1982).

Peck, Abraham (ed.). *Jews and Christians After the Holocaust* (Fortress, 1982).

Peli, Pinhas. 'Hear O Israel: Witness to the One God' in *SIDIC*, vol XVI, no. 2 (1983).

Petuchowski, Jakob. 'A Rabbi Looks at the Lord's Prayer', in Val McInnes (ed.). *New Visions: Historical and Theological Perspectives on the Jewish–Christian Dialogue* (Crossroad, 1993).

Plaskow, Judith. 'Feminist Anti-Judaism and the Christian God', in *Journal of Feminist Studies in Religion*, Vol. 7, no. 2 (Fall 1991).

Plaskow, Judith. *Standing Again at Sinai* (Harper Collins, 1990).

Plaskow, Judith and Christ, Carol. *Weaving the Visions: New Patterns in Feminist Spirituality* (Harper Collins, 1989).

Polish, Daniel. 'Jewish attitudes to Mission and Conversion' in Martin Cohen and Helga Croner (eds) *Christian Mission—Jewish Mission* (Paulist Press, 1982).

Rahner, Karl and Lapide, Pinchas. *Encountering Jesus—Encountering Judaism: A Dialogue* (Crossroad, 1987).

Rausch, David. *Communities in Conflict: Evangelicals and Jews* (Trinity Press, 1991).

Rausch, David. *A Legacy of Hatred: Why Christians Must Not Forget the Holocaust* (Moody, 1984).

Rivkin, Ellis. *What Crucified Jesus?* (SCM Press 1984).

Romain, Jonathan. *Faith and Practice* (Reform Synagogues of Great Britain, 1991).

Rose, Aubrey. 'Jesus, the Nazarene—a Jewish View', *Common Ground*, no. 1 (1990).

Rosen, David. 'Letter From Jerusalem' in *Common Ground*, no. 1 (1994).

Rosenberg, Stuart, *The Christian Problem: A Jewish View* (Hippocrene Books, 1986).

Rosenzweig, Franz. *The Star of Redemption* (Holt, Rinehart and Winston, 1970).

Rottenberg, Isaac. *The Turbulent Triangle: Christians, Jews and Israel* (Red Mountain Associates, 1989).

Rousmaniere, John. *A Bridge To Dialogue: The Story of Jewish–Christian Relations* (Paulist Press, 1991).

Rubenstein, Richard. *After Auschwitz* (Johns Hopkins University Press,1992 edition).

Rudin, James. *Israel for Christians* (Fortress, 1983).

Ruether, Rosemary Radford. 'Feminism and Jewish–Christian Dialogue', in John Hick (ed.). *The Myth of Christian Uniqueness* (SCM, 1987).

Ruether, Rosemary Radford. *To Change the World* (SCM Press, 1981).

Ruether, Rosemary Radford. *Faith and Fratricide: The Theological Roots of Anti-Semitism* (Seabury Press, 1974).

Ruether, Rosemary Radford. *Religion and Sexism: Images of Women in the Jewish and Christian Traditions* (Simon and Schuster, 1974).

Sacks, Jonathan. *Faith in the Future* (Darton, Longman and Todd, 1995).

Sacks, Jonathan. *Crisis and Covenant* (Manchester University Press, 1992).

Sacks, Jonathan. *Tradition in an Untraditional Age* (Vallentine Mitchell, 1990).

Sanders, E P. *Jesus and Judaism*, (SCM Press 1985).

Saperstein, Marc. *Moments of Crisis in Jewish–Christian Relations* (SCM Press, 1989).

Schneiders, Sandra. 'Christian Tradition on Women', in *SIDIC*, vol. IX, no. 3 (1976).

Schoneveld, Jacobus. 'Christians in Conflict and Dialogue with Jews', *Common Ground*, no. 2 (1994).

Segal, Alan. *Rebecca's Children: Judaism and Christianity in the Roman World* (Harvard University Press, 1986).

Sered, Susan Starr. 'Two Women's Shrines in Bethlehem', in *Journal of Feminist Studies in Religion*, vol. 2, no. 2 (Fall 1986).

Shepherd, Naomi. *A Price Below Rubies: Jewish Women as Rebels and Radicals* (Weidenfeld and Nicolson, 1993).

Sheridan, Sybil (ed.). *Hear Our Voice: Women Rabbis Tell Their Stories* (SCM Press, 1994).

Sherwin, Byron. 'Who do you say that I am? (Mark 8 v.29): A New Jewish View of Jesus' in *Journal of Ecumenical Studies*, 31:3–4, (Summer–Fall 1994).

Simpson, William. *Jews and Christians Today* (Epworth Press, 1940).

Sölle, Dorothee. 'God's Pain and Our Pain' in Otto Maduro (ed.) *Judaism, Christianity and Liberation* (Orbis, 1991).

Solomon, Norman. *Judaism and World Religion* (Macmillan, 1991).

Solomon, Norman. 'Themes in Christian–Jewish Relations' in Rabbi Leon Klenicki (ed.). *Toward A Theological Encounter: Jewish Understandings of Christianity* (Paulist Press, 1991).

Sullivan, Francis. *Salvation Outside the Church?* (Geoffrey Chapman, 1992).

Swidler, Leonard (ed.). *Toward a Universal Theology of Religion* (Orbis, 1987).

Thoma, Clemens and Wyschogrod, Michael. *Parable and Story in Judaism and Christianity* (Paulist Press, 1989).

Thoma, Clemens and Wyschogrod, Michael. *Understanding Scripture: Explorations of Jewish and Christian Traditions of Interpretation* (Paulist Press, 1987).

Trachtenberg, Joshua. *The Devil and the Jews: The Medieval Conception of the Jew and its Relation to Modern Anti-Semitism* (The Jewish Publication Society of America, 1961).

Ucko, Hans. *Common Roots, New Horizons* (World Council of Churches Publication, 1994).

Umansky, Ellen and Ashton, Dianne (eds). *Four Centuries of Jewish Women's Spirituality: A Sourcebook* (Beacon, 1992)

Van Buren, Paul. *A Theology of the Jewish–Christian Reality: Part 3* (Harper and Row, 1988).

Wiesel, Elie. 'Why I am Afraid', in James Charlesworth (ed.) *Overcoming Fear Between Jews and Christians* (Crossroad, 1993).

Wiesel, Elie. *Night* (Farrar, Straus and Giroux, 1960).

Wigoder, Geoffrey. 'Israel–Vatican Agreement Signals an End to "theological distortion" by Catholic Church', *Jewish Chronicle* (December 31, 1993).

Wigoder, Geoffrey. *Jewish–Christian Relations Since the Second World War* (Manchester University Press, 1988).

Wilken, Robert. *John Chrysostom and the Jews* (University of California Press, 1983).

Willebrands, Johannes Cardinal. *Church and the Jewish People* (Paulist Press, 1992).

Williamson, Clark. *Is there a Mission to Jews?* in Clark Williamson (ed.), *A Mutual Witness: Toward Critical Solidarity between Jews and Christians* (Chalice Press, 1992).

Williamson, Clark (ed.). *A Mutual Witness: Toward Critical Solirdarity between Jews and Christians* (Chalice Press, 1992).

Williamson, Clark and Allen, Ronald. *Interpreting Difficult Texts: Anti-Judaism and Christian Preaching* (SCM Press, 1989).

Wilson, Marvin. *Our Father Abraham* (Eerdmans, 1989).

Wistrich, Robert. *Anti-Semitism: The Longest Hatred* (Thames Methuen, 1991).

Yerushalmi, Yosef Hayim. 'The History of Christian Theology and the Demonization of the Jews' in Eva Fleischner (ed.) *Auschwitz: Beginning of a New Era?* (Ktav, 1977).

Young, Brad. *Jesus and His Jewish Parables: Rediscovering the Roots of Jesus' Teaching* (Paulist Press, 1989).

Zannoni, Arthur (ed.). *Jews and Christians Speak of Jesus* (Fortress, 1994).

BIBLIOGRAPHY OF CHURCH PUBLICATIONS/DOCUMENTS

'Ecumenical Considerations on the Jewish–Christian Dialogue, Geneva, 1982' in *The Theology of the Churches and the Jewish People* (World Council of Churches Publication, 1988).

'Jews, Christians, and Muslims: The Way of Dialogue' from The Lambeth Conference (1988).

'World Council of Churches Consultation on the Church and the Jewish People: Report', Sigtuna, Sweden (1988).

'Notes on the Correct Way to Present the Jews and Judaism in Preaching and Catechesis in the Roman Catholic Church' (1985).

'Guidelines and Suggestions for Implementing the Conciliar Declaration Nostra Aetate' (1974).

'Declaration on the Relationship of the Church to Non-Christian Religions', *Nostra Aetate*, no.4 (October 28, 1965).

BIBLIOGRAPHY OF LECTURES AND PAPERS

Dubois, Yves. 'Recent Developments in the Liturgical Life of the Orthodox Church', 1995, unpublished paper.

Fry, Helen. 'Towards A Christian Theology of Judaism', paper delivered to the Second Annual Postgraduate Conference on Religious Pluralism, Dept of Theology and Religious Studies, University of Bristol, England (1 March 1994).

Jakobovits, Immanuel. *'Where was Man at Auschwitz?'*, an address delivered at the meeting between President Lech Walesa of Poland and Heads of Delegations at Wawel Castle, Cracow (26 January 1995).

John Paul II. An address to the Jewish community in the Great Synagogue of Rome, 13 April 1986.

Sheridan, Sybil. *'Are We Prisoners of our History?'* a lecture for Jewish—Christian—Muslim Conference, Bendorf, Germany (March 1995).

'Unity and Mission in the Context of the Middle East', a paper delivered to the Plenary Commission on Faith and Order: World Council of Churches, Budapest, Hungary (1989).

COPYRIGHT ACKNOWLEDGEMENTS

The editor and the publisher would like to thank the following for permission to use copyright material from their publications:

Augsburg Fortress Publishers for selections from *Stepping-Stones to Further Jewish–Lutheran Relationships*, edited by Harold Ditmanson, copyright © 1990 Augsburg Fortress, reprinted by permission; *Jesus in Two Perspectives* by Pinchas Lapide and Ulrich Luz, translated by Lawrence W. Denef, copyright © 1985 Augsburg Publishing House. Used by permission of Augsburg Fortress.

Baker Book House Company for selections from *Evangelical and Jews in an Age of Pluralism* edited by Mark Tanenbaum, Marvin Wilson and A. Rudin, copyright © 1984 Baker Book House Company.

Tony Bayfield for selections from 'Mission—A Jewish Perspective' in *Theology*, May/June 1993, copyright © 1993 Tony Bayfield.

Georges Borchardt, Inc. for selections from *The Jewish Return into History* by Emil Fackenheim, copyright © 1978 Emil Fackenheim.

Rt. Revd Christopher Budd for selections from the *Pastoral Letter for the First Sunday of Advent 1994, Our links with the Jewish People,* copyright © 1994 Bishop Christopher Budd.

The Catholic Truth Society for selections from the official Catholic documents *Nostra Aetate* (1965), *Guidelines* (1974), and *Notes* (1985).

The Central Board of Finance of the Church of England for selections from *The Truth Shall Make You Free*, published by Church House Publishing on behalf of the Anglican Consultative Council. Copyright © 1988 Secretary General of the Anglican Consultative Council.

Chalice Press for selections from 'The Denigration of Judaism as a Form of Christian Mission' by Susannah Heschel; and 'Is there a Mission to Jews' by Clark Williamson, in *A Mutual Witness: Toward Critical Solidarity Between Jews and Christians* edited by Clark Williamson, copyright © Chalice Press 1992. Reprinted by permission of Chalice Press.

312

LIST OF AUTHORS AND
SOURCES QUOTED

AUTHORS

Ateek, Naim. *Justice and Only Justice* (Orbis, 1989). Chapter 5.

Athans, Mary Christine. 'Antisemitism or Anti-Judaism?' in Michael Shermis and Arthur E. Zannoni (eds) *Introduction to Jewish—Christian Relations* (Paulist Press, 1991). Chapter 2.

Baum, Gregory. 'Rethinking the Church's Mission after Auschwitz' in Eva Fleischner (ed) *Auschwitz: Beginning of a New Era?* (Ktav Publishing House, 1977). Chapter 4.

Bayfield, Tony. "Mission—A Jewish Perspective" in *Theology* (May/June 1993). Chapter 4.

Berger, David and Wyschogrod, Michael. *Jews and Jewish Christianity* (Ktav, 1978). Chapter 8.

Berkovits, Eliezer. *Faith After the Holocaust* (Ktav, 1973). Chapter 3.

Braybrooke, Marcus. *Christian—Jewish Relations: A New Look* (Publication of The Council of Christians and Jews, 1992). Chapter 2.

Braybrooke, Marcus. 'The Resurrection in Christian—Jewish Dialogue', in *Common Ground* no. 1, (1991). Chapter 3.

Braybrooke, Marcus. *Time to Meet: Towards a Deeper Understanding Between Jews and Christians* (SCM Press, 1990). Chapter 4.

Breslauer, S. Daniel. 'Salvation: A Jewish View' in Leon Klenicki and Geoffrey Wigoder (eds) *A Dictionary of the Jewish—Christian Dialogue* (Paulist Press, 1984). Chapter 8.

Budd, Rt. Revd.Christopher. *'Pastoral Letter for 1st Sunday of Advent 1994 About our Links With the Jewish People'*, 10 November 1994. Chapter 6.

Carey, George. 'Tiny Shoes' in *Common Ground* no. 1, (1991). Chapter 3.

Clorfene, Chaim and Rogalsky, Yakov. *The Path of the Righteous Gentile* (Targum Press, 1987). Chapter 8.

Cohen, Martin. 'The Mission of Israel After Auschwitz' in Helga Croner and Leon Klenicki (eds) *Issues in the Jewish—Christian Dialogue: Jewish Perspectives on Covenant, Mission, and Witness* (Paulist Press, 1979). Chapter 4.

Cohn-Sherbok, Dan. *Issues in Contemporary Judaism* (Macmillan, 1991). Chapter 3.

Cohn-Sherbok, Dan. *On Earth as it is in Heaven: Jews, Christians, and Liberation Theology* (Orbis, 1987). Chapter 10.

Ditmanson, Harold (ed). *Stepping Stones to Further Jewish—Lutheran Relationship* (Augsburg, 1990). Chapter 8.

Dubois, Marcel. 'Israel and Christian Self-Understanding' in D. Burrell and Y. Landau (eds) *Voices From Jerusalem* (Paulist Press, 1992). Chapter 5.

Eron, Lewis John. 'The Problem of a Jew Talking to a Christian about Jesus' in Leonard Swidler, Lewis John Eron, Gerard Sloyan, and Lester Dean (eds) *Bursting the Bonds: Jewish—Christian Dialogue on Jesus and Paul* (Orbis, 1990). Chapter 6.

Fackenheim, Emil. *The Jewish Return into History* (Schocken Books, 1978). Chapter 3.

Falk, Randall. 'Understanding Our Relationship to Jesus: A Jewish Outlook', in Walter Harrelson and Randall M Falk, *Jews and Christians: A Troubled Family* (Abingdon Press, 1990). Chapter 6.

Federici, Tommaso. 'The Mission and Witness of the Church', in *Fifteen Years of Catholic—Jewish Dialogue 1970–1985: Selected Papers* (Libreria Editrice Vaticana, 1988). Chapter 4

Fisher, Eugene. *Faith Without Prejudice* (Crossroad, 1993). Chapter 7.

Gorsky, Jonathon. 'A Jewish Response to the Decade of Evangelism' in *The Way*, vol 34, no 4 (October 1994). Chapter 4.

Greenberg, Blu. 'Mission, Witness, and Proselytism' in *Evangelicals and Jews in an Age of Pluralism* (University Press of America, 1990). Chapter 4.

Greenberg, Blu. *On Women and Judaism: A View From Tradition* (Jewish Publication Society of America, 1981). Chapter 9.

Greenberg, Moshe. 'Theological Reflections—Land, People and the State', in *Immanuel* 22/23 (1989). Chapter 5.

Grounds, Vernon C. 'The Problem of Proselytization' in *Evangelicals and Jews in an Age of Pluralism* (University Press of America, 1990). Chapter 4.

Harries, Richard. 'Theodicy Will not Go Away' in Tony Bayfield and Marcus Braybrooke (eds) *Dialogue With a Difference* (SCM Press, 1992). Chapter 3.

Harrington, Daniel J. 'The Teaching of Jesus in His Context' in Eugene Fisher (ed) *Interwoven Destinies* (Paulist Press, 1993). Chapter 6.

Hellwig, Monika. 'Bible Interpretation: Has Anything Changed?' in Lawrence Boadt, Helga Croner, and Leon Klenicki (eds) *Biblical Studies: Meeting Ground of Jews and Christians* (Paulist Press, 1980). Chapter 7.

Heschel, Susannah. 'The Denigration of Judaism as a Form of Christian Mission' in Clark Williamson (ed) *A Mutual Witness: Toward Critical Solidarity Between Jews and Christians* (Chalice Press, 1992). Chapter 4.

Hill, David. *An Annotated Description and Personal Experience of the CCJ Young Adults Israel Study Tour 18-29 July 1993*, unpublished work. Chapters 3, 5.

Hilton, Rabbi M, and Marshall, Gordian. *The Gospels and Rabbinic Judaism* (SCM Press, 1988). Chapter 7.

James, Graham. 'Bridging the Gulf' in the journal *Manna* no 41 (Autumn 1993). Chapter 10.

Jones, Gareth Lloyd. *Hard Sayings: Difficult New Testament Texts for Jewish—Christian Dialogue* (Publication of The Council of Christians and Jews, 1993). Chapter 7.

Kellenbach, von, Katharina. 'Jewish—Christian Dialogue on Feminism and Religion', *Christian—Jewish Relations*, vol. 19, no. 2 (1986). Chapter 9.

Knight, Henry. 'Meeting Jacob at the Jabbok: Wrestling with a Text—A Midrash on Genesis 32:22–32', in *Journal of Ecumenical Studies*, 29:3–4 (Summer-Fall 1992). Chapter 7.

Kravitz, Leonard. 'A Jewish Reading of the New Testament' in Lawrence Boadt, Helga Croner, and Leon Klenichi (eds). *Biblical Studies: Meeting Ground of Jews and Christians* (Paulist Press, 1980). Chapter 7.

Küng, Hans. 'Christianity and Judaism' in James Charlesworth (ed). *Jesus' Jewishness* (Crossroad Publishing, 1991). Chapter 6.

Kushner, Harold. *To Life: A Celebration of Jewish Being and Thinking* (Little, Brown and Company, 1993). Chapter 5.

Lapide, Pinchas and Luz, Ulrich. *Jesus in Two Perspectives: A Jewish—Christian Dialog* (Augsburg, 1985). Chapter 6.

Littell, Franklin. *The Crucifixion of the Jews* (Mercer University Press, 1986). Chapter 2.

Lyden, John. 'Atonement in Judaism and Christianity' in the Journal of Ecumenical Studies, vol. 29, no. 1 (1992). Chapter 8.

Maccoby, Hyam. *Jewish Views of Jesus* (Centre for Inter-Faith Dialogue, Middlesex University, 1995). Chapter 6.

Magonet, Jonathon. 'How A Rabbi Reads the Bible' in the *Catholic Gazette*, vol 68, no 4, (1977). Chapter 7.

Markham, Ian. 'Theological Problems and Israel', commissioned for the Reader. Chapter 5.

McCauley, Deborah. '*Nostra Aetate* and the New Jewish—Christian Feminist Dialogue' in Roger Brooks (ed) *Unanswered Questions* (University of Notre Dame Press, 1988). Chapter 9.

McCauley, Deborah and Daum, Annette. 'Jewish—Christian Feminist Dialogue: A Wholistic Vision', in *Union Seminary Quarterly Review*, vol. 38 (1983). Chapter 9.

McDade, John. 'The Epistle of James for Jews and Christians', in *SIDIC*, vol. XXVII, no.1 (1994). Chapter 7.

McGarry, Michael. 'The Holocaust' in Michael Shermis and Arthur Zannoni (eds). *Introduction to Jewish—Christian Relations* (Paulist Press, 1991). Chapter 3.

McGarry, Michael. 'Interreligious Dialogue, Mission, and the Case of the Jews', in Paul Mojzes and Leonard Swidler (eds). *Christian Mission and Interreligious Dialogue* (Edwin Mellen Press, 1990). Chapter 4.

Moltmann, Jürgen. 'Christology and the Jewish—Christian Dialogue', in Val A McInnes (ed). *New Visions: Historical and Theological Perspectives on the Jewish—Christian Dialogue* (Crossroad, 1993). Chapter 6.

Novak, David. 'A Jewish Theological Understanding of Christianity in Our Time', in *Toward A Theological Encounter: Jewish Understandings of Christianity*, edited by Rabbi Leon Klenicki (Paulist Press, 1991). Chapter 10.

Papademetriou, George. *Essays on Orthodox Christian—Jewish Relations* (Wyndham Press, 1990). Chapter 5.

Parkes, James. *Judaism and Christianity* (The Camelot Press, 1948). Chapter 4.

Pawlikowski, John. *Christ in the Light of the Jewish—Christian Dialogue* (Paulist Press, 1982). Chapter 8.

Peli, Pinhas. "Hear O Israel: Witness to the One God" in *SIDIC*, vol XVI, no. 2 (1983). Chapter 4.

Petuchowski, Jakob. 'A Rabbi Looks at the Lord's Prayer', in Val McInnes (ed). *New Visions: Historical and Theological Perspectives on the Jewish—Christian Dialogue* (Crossroad, 1993). Chapter 7.

Plaskow, Judith. 'Feminist Anti-Judaism and the Christian God', in *Journal of Feminist Studies in Religion*, Vol. 7, no. 2 (Fall 1991). Chapter 9.

Polish, Daniel. 'Jewish attitudes to Mission and Conversion' in Martin Cohen and Helga Croner (eds) *Christian Mission—Jewish Mission* (Paulist Press, 1982). Chapter 4.

Rahner, Karl and Lapide, Pinchas. *Encountering Jesus—Encountering Judaism: A Dialogue* (Crossroad, 1987). Chapter 8.

Rausch, David. *Communities in Conflict: Evangelicals and Jews* (Trinity Press, 1991). Chapter 4.

Romain, Jonathan. *Faith and Practice* (Reform Synagogues of Great Britain, 1991). Chapter 5.

Rose, Aubrey. 'Jesus, the Nazarene – a Jewish View', *Common Ground*, no. 1 (1990). Chapter 6.

Rosen, David. 'Letter From Jerusalem' in *Common Ground*, no. 1 (1994). Chapter 5.

Rosenberg, Stuart. *The Christian Problem: A Jewish View* (Hippocrene Books, 1986). Chapter 6.

Rosenzweig, Franz. *The Star of Redemption* (Holt, Rinehart and Winston, 1970). Chapter 8.

Rubenstein, Richard. *After Auschwitz* (John Hopkins University Press, 1992 edition). Chapter 3.

Ruether, Rosemary Radford. 'Feminism and Jewish—Christian Dialogue', in John Hick (ed). *The Myth of Christian Uniqueness* (SCM, 1987). Chapter 9.

Ruether, Rosemary Radford. *To Change the World* (SCM Press, 1981). Chapter 2.

Sacks, Jonathan. *Crisis and Covenant* (Manchester University Press, 1992). Chapter 3.

Sacks, Jonathan. *Tradition in an Untraditional Age* (Vallentine Mitchell, 1990). Chapter 10.

Schneiders, Sandra. 'Christian Tradition on Women', in *SIDIC*, vol. IX, no. 3 (1976). Chapter 9.

Schoneveld, Jacobus. 'Christians in Conflict and Dialogue with Jews', *Common Ground*, no. 2 (1994). Chapter 6.

Sered, Susan Starr. 'Two Women's Shrines in Bethlehem', in *Journal of Feminist Studies in Religion*, vol. 2, no. 2 (Fall 1986). Chapter 9.

Sherwin, Byron. 'Who do you say that I am? (Mark 8 v.29): A New Jewish View of Jesus' in *Journal of Ecumenical Studies*, 31:3–4, (Summer-Fall 1994). Chapter 6.

Sölle, Dorothee. 'God's Pain and Our Pain' in Otto Maduro (ed) *Judaism, Christianity and Liberation* (Orbis, 1991). Chapter 3.

Solomon, Norman. 'Three International Inter-Faith Conferences', in *Ends and Odds*, no 51, July 1993. Chapter 10.

Solomon, Norman. *Judaism and World Religion* (Macmillan, 1991). Chapter 3.

Solomon, Norman. 'Themes in Christian—Jewish Relations' in Rabbi Leon Klenicki (ed). *Toward A Theological Encounter: Jewish Understandings of Christianity* (Paulist Press, 1991). Chapter 2.

Ucko, Hans. *Common Roots, New Horizons* (World Council of Churches Publication, 1994). Chapter 8.

Wiesel, Elie. 'Why I am Afraid', in James Charlesworth (ed) *Overcoming Fear Between Jews and Christians* (Crossroad, 1993). Chapter 3.

Wigoder, Geoffrey. "Israel–Vatican Agreement Signals an End to 'theological distortion' by Catholic Church", *Jewish Chronicle* (December 31, 1993). Chapter 5.

Willebrands, Johannes Cardinal. Church and the Jewish People (Paulist Press, 1992). Chapter 8.

Williamson, Clark. 'Is there a Mission to Jews?' in Clark Williamson (ed), *A Mutual Witness: Toward Critical Solidarity between Jews and Christians* (Chalice Press, 1992). Chapter 10.

Wilson, Marvin. *Our Father Abraham* (Eerdmans, 1989). Chapter 6.

Yerushalmi, Yosef Hayim. 'The History of Christian Theology and the Demonization of the Jews' in Eva Fleischner (ed) *Auschwitz: Beginning of a New Era?* (Ktav, 1977). Chapter 2.

CHURCH PUBLICATIONS AND DOCUMENTS QUOTED

'Ecumenical Considerations on the Jewish—Christian Dialogue, Geneva, 1982' in *The Theology of the Churches and the Jewish People* (World Council of Churches Publication, 1988). Chapters 2 & 5.

Jews, Christians, and Muslims: The Way of Dialogue' from The Lambeth Conference (1988). Chapters 2 & 4.

'World Council of Churches Consultation on the Church and the Jewish People: Report', Sigtuna, Sweden (1988). Chapter 4.

'Notes on the Correct Way to Present the Jews and Judaism in Preaching and Catechesis in the Roman Catholic Church' (1985). Chapter 6.

'Guidelines and Suggestions for Implementing the Conciliar Declaration Nostra Aetate' (1974). Chapters 4 & 6.

'Declaration on the Relationship of the Church to Non-Christian Religions', *Nostra Aetate*, no.4 (October 28, 1965). Chapters 2, 4 & 8.

LECTURES AND PAPERS QUOTED

Dubois, Yves. 'Recent Developments in the Liturgical Life of the Orthodox Church', 1995, unpublished paper. Chapter 2.

Fry, Helen. 'Towards A Christian Theology of Judaism', paper delivered to the Second Annual Postgraduate Conference on Religious Pluralism, Dept of Theology and Religious Studies, University of Bristol, England (1st March 1994). Chapter 2.

Jakobovits, Immanuel. *'Where was Man at Auschwitz?'*, an address delivered at the meeting between President Lech Walesa of Poland and Heads of Delegations at Wawel Castle, Cracow (26 January 1995). Chapter 3.

John Paul II. An address to the Jewish community in the Great Synagogue of Rome, 13 April 1986. Chapter 4.

Sheridan, Sybil. *'Are We Prisoners of our History?'* a lecture for Jewish—Christian—Muslim Conference, Bendorf, Germany (March 1995). Chapter 9.

'Unity and Mission in the Context of the Middle East', a paper delivered to the Plenary Commission on Faith and Order: World Council of Churches, Budapest, Hungary (1989). Chapter 4.

Index